Early Modern Literature in History

General Editors: **Cedric C. Brown**, Professor of English and Dean of the Faculty of Arts and Humanities, University of Reading; **Andrew Hadfield**, Professor of English, University of Sussex, Brighton

Advisory Board: **Donna Hamilton**, University of Maryland; **Jean Howard**, University of Columbia; **John Kerrigan**, University of Cambridge; **Richard McCoy**, CUNY; **Sharon Achinstein**, University of Oxford

Within the period 1520–1740 this series discusses many kinds of writing, both within and outside the established canon. The volumes may employ different theoretical perspectives, but they share an historical awareness and an interest in seeing their texts in lively negotiation with their own and successive cultures.

Titles include:

Andrea Brady
ENGLISH FUNERARY ELEGY IN THE SEVENTEENTH CENTURY
Laws in Mourning

Mark Thornton Burnett
CONSTRUCTING 'MONSTERS' IN SHAKESPEAREAN DRAMA AND EARLY MODERN CULTURE

Dermot Cavanagh
LANGUAGE AND POLITICS IN THE SIXTEENTH-CENTURY HISTORY PLAY

Patrick Cheney
MARLOWE'S REPUBLICAN AUTHORSHIP
Lucan, Liberty, and the Sublime

Danielle Clarke and Elizabeth Clarke (*editors*)
'THIS DOUBLE VOICE'
Gendered Writing in Early Modern England

David Coleman
DRAMA AND THE SACRAMENTS IN SIXTEENTH-CENTURY ENGLAND
Indelible Characters

Katharine A. Craik
READING SENSATIONS IN EARLY MODERN ENGLAND

James Daybell (*editor*)
EARLY MODERN WOMEN'S LETTER-WRITING, 1450–1700

Matthew Dimmock and Andrew Hadfield (*editors*)
THE RELIGIONS OF THE BOOK
Christian Perceptions, 1400–1660

Tobias Döring
PERFORMANCES OF MOURNING IN SHAKESPEAREAN THEATRE AND EARLY MODERN CULTURE

Sarah M. Dunnigan
EROS AND POETRY AT THE COURTS OF MARY QUEEN OF SCOTS AND JAMES VI

Mary Floyd-Wilson and Garrett A Sullivan Jr (*editors*)
ENVIRONMENT AND EMBODIMENT IN EARLY MODERN ENGLAND

Teresa Grant and Barbara Ravelhofer
ENGLISH HISTORICAL DRAMA, 1500–1660
Forms Outside the Canon

Andrew Hadfield
SHAKESPEARE, SPENSER AND THE MATTER OF BRITAIN

William M. Hamlin
TRAGEDY AND SCEPTICISM IN SHAKESPEARE'S ENGLAND

Elizabeth Heale
AUTOBIOGRAPHY AND AUTHORSHIP IN RENAISSANCE VERSE
Chronicles of the Self

Constance Jordan and Karen Cunningham *(editors)*
THE LAW IN SHAKESPEARE

Claire Jowitt *(editor)*
PIRATES? THE POLITICS OF PLUNDER, 1550–1650

Gregory Kneidel
RETHINKING THE TURN TO RELIGION IN EARLY
MODERN ENGLISH LITERATURE

Edel Lamb
PERFORMING CHILDHOOD IN THE EARLY MODERN THEATRE
The Children's Playing Companies (1599–1613)

Jean-Christopher Mayer
SHAKESPEARE'S HYBRID FAITH
History, Religion and the Stage

Scott L. Newstock
QUOTING DEATH IN EARLY MODERN ENGLAND
The Poetics of Epitaphs Beyond the Tomb

Jennifer Richards *(editor)*
EARLY MODERN CIVIL DISCOURSES

Marion Wynne-Davies
WOMEN WRITERS AND FAMILIAL DISCOURSE
IN THE ENGLISH RENAISSANCE
Relative Values

The series Early Modern Literature in History is published in association
with the Renaissance Texts Research Centre at the University of Reading.

Early Modern Literature in History
Series Standing Order ISBN 0–333–71472–5
(outside North America only)

You can receive future titles in this series as they are published by placing a standing order. Please contact your bookseller or, in case of difficulty, write to us at the address below with your name and address, the title of the series and the ISBN quoted above.

Customer Services Department, Macmillan Distribution Ltd, Houndmills, Basingstoke, Hampshire RG21 6XS, England

Marlowe's Republican Authorship

Lucan, Liberty, and the Sublime

Patrick Cheney

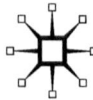

© Patrick Cheney 2009

All rights reserved. No reproduction, copy or transmission of this publication may be made without written permission.

No portion of this publication may be reproduced, copied or transmitted save with written permission or in accordance with the provisions of the Copyright, Designs and Patents Act 1988, or under the terms of any licence permitting limited copying issued by the Copyright Licensing Agency, Saffron House, 6-10 Kirby Street, London EC1N 8TS.

Any person who does any unauthorized act in relation to this publication may be liable to criminal prosecution and civil claims for damages.

The author has asserted his right to be identified as the author of this work in accordance with the Copyright, Designs and Patents Act 1988.

First published 2009 by
PALGRAVE MACMILLAN

Palgrave Macmillan in the UK is an imprint of Macmillan Publishers Limited, registered in England, company number 785998, of Houndmills, Basingstoke, Hampshire RG21 6XS.

Palgrave Macmillan in the US is a division of St Martin's Press LLC, 175 Fifth Avenue, New York, NY 10010.

Palgrave Macmillan is the global academic imprint of the above companies and has companies and representatives throughout the world.

Palgrave® and Macmillan® are registered trademarks in the United States, the United Kingdom, Europe and other countries.

ISBN-13: 978–1–4039–3341–6 hardback
ISBN-10: 1–4039–3341–3 hardback

This book is printed on paper suitable for recycling and made from fully managed and sustained forest sources. Logging, pulping and manufacturing processes are expected to conform to the environmental regulations of the country of origin.

A catalogue record for this book is available from the British Library.

Library of Congress Cataloging-in-Publication Data

Cheney, Patrick Gerard, 1949–
   Marlowe's republican authorship : Lucan, liberty,
and the sublime / Patrick Cheney.
     p. cm.—(Early modern literature in history)
   Includes index.
   ISBN-13: 978–1–4039–3341–6
   ISBN-10: 1–4039–3341–3
   1. Marlowe, Christopher, 1564–1593 – Criticism and interpretation.
2. Marlowe, Christopher, 1564–1593 – Political and social views.
3. Republicanism in literature. 4. Republicanism – England – History – 16th century. 5. Liberty in literature. I. Title.

PR2677.P6C47 2009
822'.3—dc22   2008030134

10 9 8 7 6 5 4 3 2 1
18 17 16 15 14 13 12 11 10 09

Printed and bound in Great Britain by
CPI Antony Rowe, Chippenham and Eastbourne

*For Laura Lunger Knoppers and Garrett A. Sullivan, Jr.,
beloved colleagues in the Renaissance Program at Penn State*

His pen was sharp pointed lyke a poinyard...His sight pearst like lightning into the entrails of all abuses. ...He was no timorous servile flatterer of the commonwealth wherein he lived. ...Princes hee spard not, that in the least point transgrest. His lyfe he contemned in comparison of the libertie of speech.

Thomas Nashe, *The Unfortunate Traveler* (1594), tribute to Marlowe (in McKerrow 2: 264–5)

Contents

List of Abbreviations	viii
Acknowledgements	ix
Note on Texts and References	xii

	Introduction: Was Marlowe a Republican?	1
1	Republican Representation: Marlowe, the Age of Elizabeth, and *Lucan's First Book*	24
2	Authorship, Freedom, and Rapture in Marlowe's Ovidian Poems	50
3	'Defend His Freedom 'Gainst a Monarchy': Empire and Liberty in *Dido, Queen of Carthage* and *Tamburlaine, Parts One* and *Two*	78
4	Machevill's Republican Monarchy: Civil War in *The Jew of Malta, The Massacre at Paris*, and *Edward II*	121
5	'Make man to live eternally': The Skeptical Sublime in *Doctor Faustus*	165
	Afterword: The Afterlife of Marlowe's Republican Authorship – Nashe to Milton	188

Notes	193
Works Cited	227
Index	243

Abbreviations

DF	*Doctor Faustus*
Dido	*Dido, Queen of Carthage*
E2	*Edward II*
HL	*Hero and Leander*
JM	*The Jew of Malta*
LFB	*Lucan's First Book*
MacLure CH	Millar MacLure, ed., *Christopher Marlowe: The Critical Heritage, 1588–1896* (London: Routledge and Kegan Paul, 1979)
MacLure Poems	Millar MacLure, ed., *The Poems: Christopher Marlowe* (London: Methuen, 1968)
MCP	Patrick Cheney, *Marlowe's Counterfeit Profession: Ovid, Spenser, Counter-Nationhood* (Toronto: University of Toronto Press, 1997)
MP	*The Massacre at Paris*
OE	*Ovid's Elegies*
OED	*Oxford English Dictionary*
Ph	*Pharsalia*
PL	*Paradise Lost*
Pr	Prologue
'PS'	'The Passionate Shepherd to His Love'
SD	Stage Direction
1 Tamb	*Tamburlaine, Part One*
2 Tamb	*Tamburlaine, Part Two*

Acknowledgements

This book has grown out of a long interest in grappling with the enigma of Marlowe's historic authorship. In particular, it grows out of my work in *Marlowe's Counterfeit Profession: Ovid, Spenser, Counter-Nationhood*, published by Toronto in 1997, which, as its title indicates, attempts to classify Marlowe as an 'Ovidian' author, one who writes a canon of poems and plays to 'counter' the national poetry of England's Virgil, Edmund Spenser. The present book aims to complement the first by classifying Marlowe as 'Lucanian', an author who works within a late-sixteenth-century milieu of literary and political thought that recent scholarship terms 'republican'.

For reasons that I hope will become clear, readers should not expect an exhaustive study of topics identified in the book title, or of individual works by Marlowe. I consider Marlowe's *Republican Authorship: Lucan, Liberty, and the Sublime* a preliminary study, no more. When I began the project, I could not find any criticism on the connection between Marlowe and republicanism, and since then, not much has changed. In the previous book, I had looked into Lucan and liberty, and I have not tried to duplicate what I have said there, although some overlaps remain. The sublime has long been a word of use in Marlowe criticism, but we still lack a detailed study. Finally, like the other terms in my title, 'authorship' has produced its own sub-industry of scholarship and criticism, although my own most recent attempts to sift through the topic appear in two books about Marlowe's rival, Shakespeare. By combining the topics I do in a single book, I may take a risk, but I offer this consolation: I've written the book I wanted to write, in the time I had to write it. Readers can expect the pace to change a bit in chapters 3 and 4, where I condense discussion of six Marlowe plays in two chapters, longer than the rest. For these chapters, I advise periodic rest, especially between sections on individual plays.

My work on literary republicanism has been inspired by two books in particular: David Norbrook's *Writing the English Republic: Poetry, Rhetoric, and Politics, 1627–1660*, published by Cambridge in 1999; and Andrew Hadfield's *Shakespeare and Republicanism*, also published by Cambridge, in 2005. Professor Norbrook has generously answered questions via email and in conversation, and deserves credit for writing a magisterial study that serves as a fount and beacon to many, including to me. Professor Hadfield has been kind enough to include my book in his series on Early Modern Literature and History, and, as a close friend over many years, he has also functioned as a formal advisor during the entire project, offering scrupulous suggestions for revision toward the end.

In the process of completing the book, I have benefited by presenting several papers that now form part of it, and I am grateful to the following for their courtesy: the Marlowe Society of America, especially its President, Robert A. Logan, for allowing me to present the first two hearings on the topic, one at the Fourth International Conference on Marlowe, July 2003, at Cambridge University, and the other at the Modern Language Association (MLA) Convention in San Diego, December 2003; the International Spenser Society, and its President at the time, Katherine Eggert, meeting also in San Diego, December 2003; Nigel Smith and Denis Feeney, organizers of the International Lucan Conference at Princeton University, October 2003; and the Milton Society of America, especially Christophe Tournu, organizer of the eighth International Milton Symposium in Grenoble, France, June 2005. Most recently, I would like to thank Philip Hardie and Henry Day for inviting me to present a paper at their symposium on 'The Classical Sublime' at Trinity College, Cambridge, March 2008. At this remarkable gathering of classicists, I also benefited from the papers of, and personal conversations with, William Fitzgerald, Richard Hunter, Andrew Laird, Charles Martindale, James Porter, Alesandro Schiesaro, and Michael Silk. At this conference as well, I had the pleasure of meeting Philip Shaw, author of the New Critical Idiom volume on *The Sublime*, a book that has been a constant source of help in the late stages of composition.

An essay based on my Grenoble paper, 'Milton, Marlowe, and Lucan: The English Authorship of Republican Liberty', will appear in *Milton Studies*, Vol. 49, pp. 1–19 published by Pittsburgh University Press. I summarize this essay in the Afterword, but record here my gratitude to Al Labriola for his help with this part of the project. I am also grateful to Zachary Lesser and Benedict Robinson for including the pilot essay for the book, ' "Defend his freedom 'gainst a monarchy": Marlowe's Republican Authorship', in their collection honoring Anne Lake Prescott, *Textual Conversations in the Renaissance: Ethics, Authors, Technologies* (Aldershot, Hampshire: Ashgate Press, 2006), pp. 27–44. Many thanks to both Ashgate and Pittsburgh for permitting me to reprint in different form some of the material from their pages.

At Penn State, I would like to thank an intrepid band of undergraduate interns – Matt Daily, Matt Dyjak, Keith Donnell, Joanna Gulden, and Eric Brune – as well as my graduate Research Assistants for the project: Lesley Owens and LeAnne Kline. The amount of work these young scholars did was amazing, and I'm grateful for their diligence and achievement, including toward the end when the 'two Matts' did such a great job of checking quotations and citations, and Lesley heroically compiled the index. I've also benefited from the work of several graduate students who have taken my seminars over the past few years, especially 'Elizabethan Republican Authorship: Spenser, Marlowe, and Shakespaere': Tim Arner, Katharine

Cleland, James Goodwin, Giuseppina Iacono, Julius Lobo, Steele Nowlin, and Dustin Stegner.

At Penn State, I would also like to thank my current English Department Head, Robin Schulze, and my past Department Head, Robert Caserio, for their heart-warming support, financial and collegial; and, as always, the Head of Comparative Literature over many years, Caroline D. Eckhardt. Robert R. Edwards continues to serve as my mentor and close friend, and throughout the project offered judicious professional advice.

Both in the United States and in the United Kingdom, I have benefited from conversation with the following colleagues: Susanna Braund; Lukas Erne; Ewan Fernie; Elizabeth Fowler; Laurie Maguire; Curtis Perry; Mike Schoenfeldt; Bart van Es; and John Watkins. In addition to Andrew Hadfield, three colleagues have read the entire typescript, offering expert guidance for revision, and I am grateful to them for the time they spent and the care they took: Laura Knoppers; Charles Martindale; and Philip Hardie. What grace! Henry Day taught me how to think about Lucan and the sublime, kindly reading the introduction and chapter 1, and offering many suggestions for emendation.

At Palgrave, I would like to thank Paula Kennedy, Senior Commissioning Editor for Literature/Theatre & Performance; Steven Hall, her Editorial Assistant; and Cedric Brown, co-editor of the book series with Andrew Hadfield. The Press produced an anonymous 'clearance report', for which I am grateful: the series of supporting remarks and useful suggestions came at just the right time.

At home, personal thanks go to Debora, Evan, and Kelton for their continued love and support.

Finally, let me thank the two dedicatees of this book. Laura Knoppers has been my colleague at Penn State for twenty years; a valued friend, she has talked with me about our shared work in the profession on countless occasions, exchanged work with me, and created a model of professional responsibility and achievement. Garrett Sullivan has been my colleague for fifteen years, as well as my running partner for most of them, and for all of them my compatriot in the taste of good ale, American and British, including most recently at Otto's Brew Pub in State College. I value my friendship with these two fine early modern scholars immensely, and am pleased to dedicate *Marlowe's Republican Authorship* to them.

Note on Texts and References

Quotations from Marlowe's plays come from *Christopher Marlowe: The Complete Plays*, ed. Mark Thornton Burnett, Everyman Library (London: Dent; Rutland, VT: Tuttle, 1999), while quotations from Marlowe's poems come from *The Collected Poems of Christopher Marlowe*, ed. Patrick Cheney and Brian J. Striar (New York: Oxford University Press, 2006), unless otherwise noted. All statistics coming from Marlowe's poems and plays derive from *A Concordance to the Plays, Poems, and Translations of Christopher Marlowe*, ed. Robert J. Fehrenbach, Lea Ann Boone, and Mario A. Di Cesare (Ithaca: Cornell University Press, 1982).

All quotations of Lucan in English translation come from *Civil War*, trans. Susan H. Braund, Oxford World's Classics (Oxford: Oxford University Press, 1992), except for Book 1, where translations will come from Marlowe, unless otherwise noted. Latin quotations come from *Lucan: 'The Civil War'*, trans. J.D. Duff, Loeb Classical Library, 2 vols. (Cambridge, MA: Harvard University Press; London: Heinemann, 1928).

All quotations from Longinus come from *On Sublimity, Classical Literary Criticism*, ed. D.A. Russell and Michael Winterbottom, Oxford World's Classics (Oxford: Oxford University Press, 1972), pp. 143–87.

Quotations from Spenser's poetry come from *The Poetical Works of Edmund Spenser*, ed. J.C. Smith and Ernest de Sélincourt, 3 vols. (Oxford: Clarendon, 1909–10).

All quotations from Shakespeare's poems and plays come from *The Riverside Shakespeare*, ed. G. Blakemore Evans (Boston: Houghton, 1997).

Quotations from Milton's works come from *John Milton: Complete Poems and Major Prose*, ed. Merritt Y. Hughes (Indianapolis: Bobbs-Merill, 1957).

Quotations from Ovid come from *Ovid in Six Volumes*, Loeb Classical Library, trans. Frank Justis Miller, 2nd ed., rev. G.P. Goold, 6 vols. (Cambridge, MA: Harvard University Press; London: Heinemann, 1977–89), with the exception of the *Amores*, where I use Marlowe's translation (*Ovid's Elegies*), unless otherwise noted. The numbering of the *Amores* elegies in the Loeb volume differs from that in Marlowe's translation, because the Loeb prints 3.5 on Ovid's dream vision, which Marlowe does not translate, since it did not appear in the edition he was using. Thus those poems in *Ovid's Elegies* after 3.4 differ in numbering from the Loeb volume. Similarly, the line numbering in the Cheney and Striar edition of *Ovid's Elegies*, which begins with the four-line prologue to the work, differs from that in the Loeb, which begins with 1.1.

Note on Texts and References xiii

Unless otherwise noted, quotations and translations from other classical authors – including Virgil – come from the Loeb Classical Library. As the Works Cited list at the end of the book reveals, major exceptions include Homer's *Iliad* and *Odyssey*, which come from the translations of Richmond Lattimore; Plato's dialogues, from the edition of Edith Hamilton and Huntington Cairns; Aristotle's works, from the edition of Richard McKeon; and the Bible, from the facsimile of the Geneva edition of 1560 published by the University of Wisconsin Press. (Works merely cited in passing but not quoted in the text do not appear separately in the Works Cited list.)

Throughout, I modernize the archaic i–j and u–v of Renaissance texts, as well as other obsolete typographical conventions such as the italicizing of names and places.

For citation, I rely on the 'works cited' format from *The MLA Style Manual* (1985); this format depends on a system of abbreviation in the text and the notes, and thus it includes full citations only in the list of Works Cited at the end. In particular, I use the following citation format to refer to a given primary work's book number, section or chapter number, and page number, such as Longinus' *On Sublimity*: 1.4: 144 (or sometimes, minus the section or chapter number: 10: 105). For *Vindiciae*, the citation 3: 89 means that the quotation comes from Question 3, page 89, in the Garnett edition. For secondary works of more than one volume, such as Quentin Skinner's *The Foundations of Modern Political Thought*, I use the following format to refer to volume and page number: 2: 205.

Introduction: Was Marlowe a Republican?

In this book, I aim to open up the topic of 'Marlowe's republican authorship'. My title phrase indicates a concern to sort out the relation in the Marlowe canon between two important topics of current scholarship: republicanism as an early modern political program; and authorship as an early modern literary practice. My general argument will be that during the late sixteenth century Marlowe is the pioneer author in the literary writing of English republicanism.[1]

Typically, Marlowe gets erased from our main critical narrative about the advent of modern English authorship. For instance, in an authoritative essay from *The Cambridge Companion to English Literature 1500–1600*, titled 'Authorship and the Material Conditions of Writing', Wendy Wall locates the advent of modern notions of authorship in Spenser and then in Jonson: 'When Spenser and Jonson used the book format to generate the author's laureate status, ... they produced ... modern and familiar images of literary authority – classically authorized writers who serve as the origin and arbiter of a literary monument that exceeds its place in everyday cultural transactions' (86).[2]

The concept of the 'laureate' poet, as originally formulated by Richard Helgerson, now defines the achievement of early modern authorship: Spenser is Renaissance England's 'first laureate poet', because he uses the nascent medium of print to present himself as a national author in the context of eternity, while Jonson succeeds Spenser in the laureate enterprise, to be followed by Milton.[3]

Marlowe has been relegated from the received narrative of modern English 'authorship' largely because leading post-structuralist critics have replaced 'Marlowe' with a 'Marlowe effect'.[4] Indebted to Michel Foucault's concept of the 'author function' and Roland Barthes' 'death of the author', a number of leading Marlovians have de-centered Marlowe as an individuated author of literary works, and have come to emphasize the ways in which his works were (and are) 'socially constructed', the product of a complex cultural collaboration between authors, scribes, printers, actors, businessmen, and other social agents.[5] A collaborative model of authorship seems appropriate to Marlowe, we are told, because the texts we have of his works tend to be notoriously unstable, with the case of *Doctor Faustus* especially infamous – its 1604 A-text and its 1616 B-text long an editorial nightmare.[6] As Wall herself concludes, 'changing texts of *Faustus* might be said to be "authorized" by him as "Marlowe's" even though they were not modified literally by him, for they cohere around a theatrical style associated with his name' ('Dramatic Authorship' 5).

Recently, however, other important critics have been forming a backlash to this post-structuralist model. Acknowledging the textual problems, they attend to what has been so striking about Marlowe since 1588, when Robert Greene identifies Marlowe with his stage character Tamburlaine.[7] As Stephen Greenblatt puts the case 400 years later, with considerable subtlety, 'In his turbulent life and, more important, in his writing, Marlowe is deeply implicated in his heroes, though he is far more intelligent and self-aware than any of them'.[8] We might say, then, that it is precisely Marlowe's signature as an early modern professional that implicates him so deeply in his stage heroes, turning each into a palimpsest of Marlovian authorship itself.[9] As a result of this palimpsest, we may attend less to Marlowe the man as he appears in his works and more to a Marlovian fiction or representation of authorship.[10]

We may also extend Marlowe's self-reflexive intratextuality of authorship from his plays to his poems. The most famous example derives from his much-discussed maneuver of transplanting the personal voice from 'The Passionate Shepherd to His Love' – 'Come live with me, and be my love' – to his stage drama: 'Come, gentle Ganymede, and play with me', says Jupiter to open *Dido, Queen of Carthage* (1.1.1) – and indeed Marlowe's dramatic career.[11] As the example of *Dido* indicates, Marlowe's poems and plays are intricately bound up with each other, and to get at his authorship more fully, we need to consider the two forms together, including their interpenetration.

The relative balance of poems and plays in Marlowe's career – seven tragedies and five poems – allows us to identify this author as the pioneer figure in Elizabethan England of a particular type of authorship: he is a poet-playwright.[12] Significantly, the two most famous models of the poet-playwright turn out to be the classical authors whom Marlowe translates: Ovid and Lucan. Ovid is the author not simply of such elegies as the *Amores* and the counter-Virgilian epic, the *Metamorphoses*, but also of the tragedy *Medea*, extant in two lines. Ovid refers to this play elsewhere in his poetry; it becomes famed in antiquity as the measure of his true genius; and eventually Jonson presents the character 'Ovid' in *Poetaster* referring to it.[13] Like his counter-Virgilian master, Ovid, Lucan becomes known in the Renaissance as the author of both epic (the *Pharsalia*) and tragedy (not extant). As Francis

Meres recalls in his 1598 *Palladis Tamia*, Lucan 'made famous and eloquent' the 'Latine tongue' not only by 'mournefully depaint[ing] … the civil wars of Pompey and Caesar' but also by writing 'two excellent tragedies, one called *Medea*, the other *De incendio Troiae cum Priami calamitate*' (rpt. G.G. Smith, ed. 315, 316, 319). Modeled on Ovid and Lucan, Marlowe's career-combination of poems and plays remains fragmented, but enough of his canon exists to demarcate this particular contribution as a milestone in English literature.

Equally to the point here, the rather large industry of scholarship about the rise of English republicanism in the early modern period neglects Marlowe's pioneering role. We shall look into this topic in more detail in Chapter 1, but a few highlights are in order here. In 1995, Markku Peltonen followed up on the work of Quentin Skinner, Patrick Collinson, and others by including the opening two chapters of *Classical Humanism and Republicanism in English Political Thought 1570–1640* as a counter to the received wisdom, which reads: 'before the Civil War there were no discernible signs of republicanism'. As an alternative, Peltonen argues that, 'far from being absent, classical republicanism (as a constitutional stance) had a limited but undoubted impact on English political thought in the late sixteenth and early seventeenth centuries' (11–12).[14] While briefly discussing Sir Thomas More, Sir Philip Sidney, and Edmund Spenser, Peltonen concentrates on prose treatises, such as those by John Barston and Thomas Beacon, but nonetheless he demonstrates that sixteenth-century English writers took up the topic of classical republicanism in a substantive way. Since Peltonen's goal is to identify republican 'political thought' within Elizabethan culture – rather than, say, its literary representation – it is understandable that he never mentions Marlowe; but his argument becomes valuable here for its rich contextualizing of republican thought during Marlowe's lifetime.

In contrast, David Norbrook's 1999 *Writing the English Republic: Poetry, Rhetoric, and Politics, 1627–1660* does focus on republican literary authorship. Even though he concentrates on the seventeenth century, Norbrook recalls in passing that Marlowe was the translator of Book 1 of Lucan's *Pharsalia* (41).[15] When discussing the pre-Stuart era, however, Norbrook cites Shakespeare and Jonson, Marlowe's two great legitimate heirs, but not Marlowe himself: 'Elizabethan writers … encouraged a degree of openness to alternative forms of political order. Shakespeare and Jonson vividly realized past republican cultures for a popular audience' (12). Like Peltonen, then, Norbrook is instrumental here, especially for theorizing the political activism of literary republicanism as a form of writing, and for foregrounding Lucan's role in this early modern project.[16]

The one literary critic who has moved the conversation firmly back to the Elizabethan era, Andrew Hadfield, locates republican leanings in both

Shakespeare and Spenser during the 1590s, but until quite recently he has had little to say about Marlowe.[17] In his 2005 *Shakespeare and Republicanism*, however, Hadfield includes a short discussion of Marlowe (58–65) in his helpful review of 'Literature and Republicanism in the Age of Shakespeare' (54–95). Referring to the *Tamburlaine* plays, *The Massacre at Paris*, *Edward II*, and *Lucan's First Book*, Hadfield shows that 'Marlowe's works ... are relentlessly hostile not just to kings, but to the conception of hereditary kingship, and political power preserved in the hands of the few': 'one of his key targets was the restrictive lack of social mobility and access to political institutions and offices characteristic of republican critiques of absolutist government and prevalent in England in the 1580s and 1590s' (65).[18]

Marlowe's relative absence in criticism on early modern republicanism is not difficult to account for. Most work on republicanism comes from either early modern political historians (like Peltonen) or seventeenth-century English literary historians (like Norbrook). Moreover, the field of republican political thought is itself relatively new, having emerged primarily in the 1970s, and it has entered early modern literary circles only during the past decade or so.[19] Work specifically on the Elizabethan era remains in short supply, and work on literary authors like Marlowe shorter still.

As I shall argue here, Marlowe deserves to be placed at the forefront of any conversation about the writing of English republicanism during the early modern era. In the remainder of this Introduction, I will first say a word about terminology and methodology; next, introduce three primary pieces of evidence in support of my argument, announced in the book's subtitle, 'Lucan, Liberty, and the Sublime'; then, forecast the structure of the book, introducing a taxonomy of secondary evidence; and finally, address the question of significance.

Terminology and methodology

At the top of the term list is the word *republican* itself. I shall not argue that Marlowe is a 'republican' the way Milton is; we do not have enough evidence to say so. As we will see in Chapter 1, during the monarchy of Queen Elizabeth I, Marlowe was accused of a lot of things, but never (to my knowledge) of being a republican.[20] I suggest rather that Marlowe's works unmistakably participate in a cultural conversation, at once political and literary, that recent scholars describe as republican, and further, that Marlowe performs an inaugural role in this conversation.

Scholars make clear that republicanism is vastly intricate as a topic in its own right. According to the *Oxford English Dictionary*, the word does not even exist in Marlowe's lifetime; the first recorded use of the term appears in 1691, meaning 'Belonging to the commonwealth or community' (Def. A.1). Similarly, the term 'republican' does not emerge until 1697, meaning 'One who believes in, supports, or prefers a republican form of government'

(Def. B.2). Thus, as Norbrook observes, during the sixteenth and even the seventeenth century, '"Republicanism" ... was not a fixed entity. Nor, for that matter, was "royalism"' (18), and he demonstrates how these two oppositional concepts intertwine during the period, sometimes amicably. In particular, he distinguishes between republicanism as a 'language' and as a 'program' (5–6). He disagrees with J.A. Pocock, who, in his 1975 *Machiavellian Moment*, argues that before 1649 'English republicanism was "a language, not a programme"' (5). Alternatively, Norbrook shows, 'republican language was a more powerful presence than has been recognized' (6), even though the presence Norbrook emphasizes emerges well after Marlowe's death (his title dates are '1627–1660'). In distinguishing between republicanism as an idea 'actively imagined' and as a 'political practice' (12), Norbrook suggests that for Tudor 'humanists' like More and Sidney, 'who lived under a well-established monarchy, republicanism was indeed a matter of imagination', not the political practice it became for mid-seventeenth-century republicans like Henry Marten. According to Norbrook, then, 'Historians of political thought have remarked on the absence of explicit republican theory in England before the 1650s; they have paid less attention to the many situations in which republican political practice was actively imagined' (12).[21]

Norbrook's formulations allow us to discern a historical evolution to republicanism and to place Marlowe within it. Marlowe belongs to a phase of English republicanism that we might call *imaginative* and *linguistic*; this phase is *pre-programmatic, pre-practical*. In such a phase, which is influenced by humanism and its recollection of classical thought, writers from More and Sidney to Shakespeare and Jonson conduct political debate 'obliquely through the dramatization and publication of the classics' (13). Primarily, Norbrook means Arthur Gorges and Thomas May, who in 1614 and 1627 (respectively) print complete translations of Lucan's *Pharsalia*.[22]

Finally, we can follow Norbrook and others in defining republicanism as 'a state which was not headed by a king and in which the hereditary principle did not prevail in whole or in part in determining the headship' (17).[23] To put it more affirmatively, republicanism takes form as 'the spirit of free and open speech amongst equals' as instituted by political or constitutional program (12) – what Norbrook calls a 'politics of open speech and dialogue' (20). When it comes to defining republicanism succinctly, however, perhaps no one can compete with Lucan himself: 'libera regum' – free of kings (6.301; see Norbrook 29).

Using Norbrook's terms, let us see where we are: *obliquely imagined republican language*. This is hardly a solid ground for scholarship. The ground begins to tremble once we place Marlowe on it. His meteoric life and career were truncated at the age of 29; insoluble problems plague the two sets of evidence to which we have access: the archive of Marlowe's life and his 13 extant works.[24] Yet it is precisely on this trembling ground that we might hear a challenge to our current critical methodology about the authorship of English republicanism in the early modern period.

In Marlowe's works, I suggest, the author conducts political debate about republicanism obliquely: he actively imagines republican political practice; and he creates a formal English republican language, without putting it into a program. In both his poems and his plays, he inscribes a significant register of republican representation, both for the late-Elizabethan era and for the first half of the seventeenth century, as the English nation moves toward the nightmare of a Lucanian Civil War.[25]

For the most part, then, we will find it difficult to discern a republican form of government in Marlowe's works. In the instances where we may, we hardly discover a republican polemic along Miltonic lines. What we discern rather plainly is what I term *republican representation*: the author's representational foregrounding of his own republican frame of art. According to Hadfield, republicanism was not just 'a language and a belief system' or even a 'political programme': it was also 'a collection of *topoi* or ... "places", examples or triggers that signalled and stood for a larger argument or set of beliefs': 'Republicanism was a fund of stories and potent images' (*Republicanism* 13). Hadfield terms this phenomenon 'literary republicanism' (80), and that shall be our focus here.

While acknowledging that republicanism at this time was 'inchoate and unformed', we may follow Hadfield in 'pay[ing] more attention to the importance of this diverse collection of powerful, miscellaneous scraps of literature, history and culture' (*Republicanism* 13). Usefully, Hadfield reminds us that 'Advocates of republican thought and ideas' in the 1590s could not 'risk' being 'explicit' in their writings; 'rather, they had to rely on suggestive hints, references and lavish praise of foreign and historical nations, rarely on outright and sustained expression' (51).[26] The danger, of course, is that nearly anything can be classified as republicanism. The danger is real, and I shall do my best to circumvent it.

By speaking of 'republican representation', I mean both the *literary representation* or mimesis of republican thought in literature, and *political representation through the process of government* (see Worden, 'Republicanism, Regicide and Republic' 318). Since scholars have had considerable difficulty in identifying Marlowe's political allegiances, I concentrate on the way that the political matrix of his works foregrounds a specifically literary representation. We may not have access to Marlowe's politics, but perhaps we may come to terms with what I am calling his republican authorship.[27]

Primary evidence: Lucan, liberty, and the sublime

The first piece of evidence for speaking about Marlowe's republican authorship – indeed the primary rationale for the book – comes from his translation of Book 1 of Lucan's *Pharsalia*. *Lucan's First Book* is not simply an academic exercise but a historic achievement in its own right – and has been understood as such. Marlowe is the first Englishman to translate the classical author whom Norbrook calls 'the central poet of the republican imagination' from antiquity through the seventeenth century (24).[28] While some classicists resist labeling Lucan a 'republican', they agree that he writes from within the bowels of the Neronian empire to mourn the loss of the Roman Republic.[29] As such, Lucan's distinction in the history of republican writing is acutely paradoxical, and he himself appears apprised of the paradox: caught thrillingly inside the prison of Empire, he howls at the loss of the Republic. Similarly, I suggest, Marlowe formally writes republicanism in his historic translation yet lacks access to a republican government. In navigating such complex literary territory, phrases such as 'republican imagination' and 'republican poem', however dissatisfying they seem, may turn out to be as historically accurate as we are likely to get.

We do not know what Marlowe's plans were for *Lucan's First Book*: whether he intended to complete the translation of the extant ten books, to let Book 1 stand on its own, or even to publish it. Nor do we know when he made the translation; it was not published until 1600, seven years after his death.[30] Most likely, Marlowe made the translation during 1592–3, when the theatres closed due to plague, at about the same time that he wrote *Hero and Leander*.[31] The late dating of *Lucan's First Book* helps explain why it shows up in the Stationers' Register on 28 September 1593, back-to-back with *Hero and Leander*. The strange yoking of these two works suggests that late in his life Marlowe was entering an 'epic' phase to his career. Such a phase complements his earlier elegiac or lyric phase, represented by *Ovid's Elegies* and 'The Passionate Shepherd', as well as his subsequent tragic phase, represented by his seven extant plays.[32]

Lucan's First Book is historic for other reasons. Charles Martindale calls it 'arguably one of the most underrated masterpieces of Elizabethan literature', and C.S. Lewis judges it of 'very great merit' – so much so that he was convinced Marlowe couldn't have written it.[33] Marlowe's authorship is no longer in dispute. Indeed, his masterpiece is thought to be significant to the development of English literature. In the words of O.B. Hardison, Jr., *Lucan's First Book* is 'the only sustained sixteenth-century heroic poem in blank verse after Surrey['s translation of the *Aeneid*]' (265). J.B. Steane puts the significance this way: 'In this poem blank verse has already, virtually before Shakespeare, become the Shakespearean instrument' (276–7). And Millar MacLure goes even further: Marlowe's '*Lucan* remains the chief monument in undramatic unrhymed English pentameters between Surrey and Milton' (ed., *Poems* xxxvi).

Despite the historic achievement of Marlowe's 'heroic poem', Renaissance critics continue to ignore it. We possess only a few article-length studies and one note.[34] While tending to focus on the quality of Marlowe's line-by-line translation, the little criticism that exists tends to emphasize both the temperamental and the biographical kinship between two authors who did not survive their twenties: these free-spirited young men became enmeshed in the violence of an imperial engine, and both authors appear to have died, quite amazingly, at work on the same poem.[35] However true Marlowe remains to Lucan in his translation, critics agree that he makes the *Pharsalia* his own.[36]

We might pause to wonder about the near blackout on Marlowe's pioneering authorship of English republicanism. It is not simply Norbrook and Hadfield who have little to say; it is Gorges and May as well.[37] Why did Marlowe get erased from this important historical conversation? One answer is that from Lucan to Milton, Marlowe alone writes republicanism without being patriotic. The English writers discussed by Norbrook, Hadfield, and others take up republican thought to express loyalty to England. With Marlowe, we have a rather different case. Who would call him a patriot?[38]

To look in on this problem, we can do no better than turn to Blair Worden's gauge for determining the existence of 'republicanism': whether an author 'aim[s]' to 'undermine' rather than 'fortify' the 'English monarchy' ('Republicanism, Regicide and Republic' 312). Worden's gauge, which criticizes 'literary representations' (311) and is based on a principle of patriotic activism, cannot measure Marlowe's republican authorship but in fact helps explain why it became erased: 'What we seek in vain is evidence that imaginative literature reflected or fostered a desire for republican rule' (309). *Desire for republican rule*: this methodological standard aims to exclude not simply the 'imaginative' discourse emphasized by Norbrook and Hadfield but, more importantly, the unpatriotic imaginative discourse that appears in the works of Marlowe.

We have here, then, a genuine contradiction, and I for one am pleased to take it to heart: Marlowe is arguably the first English author to *trouble* the writing of republicanism. Perhaps, then, like everything associated with this author, he wrote an afflicted republicanism, not of the pure color. For his imagination, we might say, republican values were not so much the grand solution as a deep structural problem.

Yet it is Norbrook who most helps us understand what Marlowe scholars neglect: 'The first book of the *Pharsalia* was in fact much cited by two of the leading seventeenth-century theorists of republicanism, James Harrington and Algernon Sidney' (36–7). Whatever Marlowe's intentions might have been, we can classify his translation of Lucan's first book as in some sense a republican document: it is arguably the first great literary representation of republicanism in the English Renaissance. In other words, Book 1 of the *Pharsalia* was not just any book; it is not even the best book; but during the English Renaissance it was the arch-republican book, a Lucanian republican epic in brief.

Marlowe's translation is a Lucanian republican epic in brief; he is the arch-abbreviated republican author.[39]

Typologically, Book 1 stands on its own two feet because it ends with the Bacchic Roman matron's frenzied prophecy of Pompey's severed head, which rolls in Book 8: 'This headless trunk that lies on Nilus' sand/I know'.[40] In a 1598 continuation of *Hero and Leander*, Henry Petowe appropriates this Lucanian image to portray the truncated Ovidian authorship of Marlowe himself: 'This history, of *Hero and Leander*, penned by that admired poet Marlowe, but not finished (being prevented by sudden death) and the same ... resting like a head separated from the body' (rpt. Cheney and Striar, eds. 268–9). Petowe's graphic image helps us see the congruence between two narrative poems that otherwise seem so different, but more importantly it compels us to re-define Marlowe's authorship: not simply Ovidian, it is simultaneously Lucanian.

Rather than being a curious anomaly, then, *Lucan's First Book* forms a keystone to Marlowe's canon of poems and plays. Back in 1956, William Blissett suggested that the 'heroic figures of Marlowe's plays are ... blood brothers to [Lucan's] Caesar', noting Tamburlaine (*1 Tamb* 3.3.152), Machevill (*JM* Pr.19), Gaveston (*E2* 1.1.173), and the Guise (*MP* 2.98, 19.66, 19.85), all of whom cite as their model of conduct Lucan's Caesar, the giant who destroys the Republic to invent the Empire.[41] To this list, we can add Mephistopheles, who detects Faustus' innate Caesarism (A-text 3.1.45–6). Blissett also sees Marlowe's Lucanian characterology as 'supplemented by allusions to details in Lucan', the 'most important' being 'the general pervasion of the Lucanic point of view' (565), but also Marlowe's 'wealth of geographical and ethnological detail', his 'rationalism' or contempt for orthodox supernaturalism, and finally even his mighty line (566). Blissett's short discussion deserves to be augmented, and that shall be a primary goal here.

By building Lucan's Caesar into his plays, Marlowe hints at the deep Lucanism structuring his plots.[42] As we shall see, Lucan's story about the military battle between Republic and Empire most obviously informs Marlowe's fictions about the tragedy of civil war (*The Massacre at Paris*, *Edward II*, to an extent *The Jew of Malta*), but also his tragedies about international war (*Dido*, *1* and *2 Tamburlaine*). Lucanian militarism, not simply Ovidian amor, forms the groundwork of Marlowe's dramatic fiction.[43] Like Marlowe's plays, his poems turn out to be imbued with Lucanism, especially 'The Passionate Shepherd' and *Hero and Leander*, but also, somewhat remarkably, *Ovid's Elegies*, the Latin original of which, the *Amores*, is penned years before Lucan himself is born. In both poems and plays, Marlowe tends to tell a narrative that is Lucanian in shape: it is about the defeat of liberty.

Thus, Marlowe's fictions of liberty constitute a second primary piece of evidence for speaking about his republican authorship. According to Quentin Skinner, 'liberty' is the 'central value' of republican political thought (*Foundations* 1: 41). Thus freedom is located at the heart of modern critical work on republicanism.[44] In his 1978 two-volume work, *The Foundations of Modern Political Thought*, Skinner structures volume 1 (on 'The Renaissance') around 'The ideal of liberty' (title to chpt. 1), to foreground his central paradigm: 'The term "liberty" ... came to connote both political independence and republican self-government' (1: 7; see 1: 12, 41, 53, 77–8, 139, 157–8), by which he means 'liberty in the sense of being free from external interference as well as in the sense of being free to take an active part in the running of the commonwealth' (1: 77). Consequently, Skinner tracks the history of what he calls 'the relationship between freedom and power' (1: 80), with each phase dilating on its own idiosyncratic version of this relationship, from classical Rome to sixteenth-century Florence to seventeenth-century England: from Cicero to Machiavelli to Milton. Calling liberty 'this precious jewel', Skinner repeatedly shows how writers through the ages argue that 'the preservation of liberty depends above all on ensuring that the citizens and their government remain one and the same' (1: 148), in open combat against tyranny, which operates by its own (imperial) value: slavery.

According to Skinner, early modern 'theorists of Republican liberty tend to think of *virtù* as that quality which enables a free people to maintain their freedom and enhance the greatness of their commonwealth' (1: 177). Hence, throughout this period writers defend liberty through 'one of the special merits of a Republican form of government': 'it enables men of the highest *virtù* to pursue the goals of honour, glory and fame in the service of their community' (1: 180). The details of Skinner's history are too complex to enumerate here (we shall return to them in Chapter 1), but this brief sketch alerts us to some key terms nestling around the republican idea of liberty in the early modern period.

Lucan critics also identify liberty as the central value of the *Pharsalia*. According to W.R. Johnson, Lucan composes his epic as 'an eternal contest between freedom and slavery ... freedom versus Caesar': for Lucan, 'freedom is incompatible with empire', and 'this underground thought ... haunts the poem' (*Monsters* 30, 88). Lucan's most famous formulation, which Johnson echoes, occurs in Book 7, when Pompey leaves the climactic battle of Pharsalus in defeat, an event so momentous it prompts the poet to intervene, complaining that Romans 'will be inspired / no longer ... by Pompey's name .../... but by that pair of rivals always with us –/Liberty and Caesar' (693–6). As this utterance indicates, most of Lucan's remarks about liberty take the form of mourning, often tinged with grim irony, as evidenced by this from Book 9 about citizens watching Caesar's theatricalized grief over the assassination of Pompey: 'they hide their groans and veil their hearts/ with happy brow, and cheerfully – O happy liberty! – they dare/to gaze upon the bloody crime though Caesar grieves' (1106–8). Lucan can scarcely stop talking about liberty, but since no such thing exists – neither in Caesar's

Rome nor in Nero's – Lucan can only register its negation. As Cotta puts it to Metellus in Book 3, 'The freedom of a people coerced by tyranny/perishes by freedom; its semblance you will preserve/if willingly you do whatever ordered' (145–6). In the domain of liberty, Lucan supremely dares to write about what he cannot find.

Similarly, English Renaissance critics spent the past century emphasizing Marlowe's commitment to liberty, without acknowledging its republican origins. For instance, Stephen Greenblatt historicizes 'radical freedom' as the Marlovian gold standard, yet never mentions the word republicanism, while Jonathan Dollimore formally sets the pace that holds today: *Tamburlaine* is a 'transgressive text: it liberates from its Christian and ethical framework the humanist conception of man as essentially free, dynamic, and aspiring; more consciously, this conception of man is not only liberated from a Christian framework but re-established in open defiance of it'.[45] Most recent criticism operates within the template of Marlowe's freedom-seeking heterodoxy, and thus can be seen to support the research of the present book.[46]

In his poems and plays, Marlowe uses the word 'liberty' and its cognates 16 times, and he uses cognates of 'freedom' an additional 46, bringing the total to 62. Not all of these uses speak to republican *libertas*, but a sufficient number do, making the concept central to the Marlovian imagination. As the monarchist Ceneus puts it rather critically in *1 Tamburlaine*, Tamburlaine 'with shepherds and a little spoil/Durst, in disdain of wrong and tyranny,/ Defend his freedom 'gainst a monarchy' (2.1.54–6; see Chapter 3, including note 42).

Centering as they do on political liberty, Marlowe's poems and plays warrant being classified in some sense as 'republican' documents. Greenblatt and his heirs emphasize Marlowe's theatrical originality in putting at center stage a series of aliens, outsiders, and exiles – an African queen, a Scythian shepherd, a German scholar, a Maltese Jew, even an English homoerotic king who lacks clear political organization – without recognizing such figuration as forming a strong republican ethos. Dido might speak for all of Marlowe's figures when she says, 'I am not free. O would I were!' (3.4.5). To this *dramatis personae*, we can add, from Marlowe's poems, an Ovidian lover, a passionate shepherd, a pair of star-crossed lovers, and of course those egregious Gemini at the core of Lucan's Roman civil war, Caesar and Pompey. Accordingly, the famed Marlovian narrative, in both poems and plays, tells how a freedom-seeking individual is oppressed, always to annihilation, by those in power, whether represented by a corrupt government, by the angry gods, or by both.

Yet Marlowe's recurrent fiction about the tragic defeat of liberty constitutes only a nominal story. There's a *second* story, superimposed onto the first (also like a palimpsest), and its effect is to give Marlowe's works their feel of exhilaration: this is a Lucanian fiction not about a tragic character but about the author himself. Such a fiction, typically overlooked in Marlowe criticism, presents the author *writing* freedom through an exalted discourse known since antiquity as the sublime. Throughout his poems and plays, Marlowe foregrounds arguably the apex of his achievement, which he derives in large part from Lucan: out of the imperial narrative of defeated liberty, he invents a poetics of the sublime.

The sublime constitutes a third and final piece of primary evidence for speaking about Marlowe's republican authorship. Even more than the history of liberty, the history of the sublime is dizzyingly complex, and we shall track it both here and in Chapter 1. Our first theorist of the sublime is the author known as Dionysius Longinus, who wrote a treatise in Greek, *On Sublimity* (*Peri Hypsous*), most likely in the first century AD – perhaps, that is, about the very time Lucan was writing the *Pharsalia*. The origins to Longinus' theorizing of the sublime lie in classical rhetorical theory about the three styles, in which the high or grandiloquent style most powerfully affects the audience's passions (Cicero, *De oratore* 21.69; Quintilian, *Institutio* 12.10.58), but also in Plato's poetic theory of divine inspiration (e.g., *Phaedrus*).[47] Longinus introduces his divine poetics of the sublime as the key antidote to the rhetorical art of logical persuasion. According to *The Oxford Classical Dictionary* (from which this material comes), the word 'sublime', derived from the Latin *sublimitas*, means 'that quality of genius in great literary works which irresistibly delights, inspires, and overwhelms the reader' (1450).

Here is Longinus' own definition:

> Sublimity is a kind of eminence or excellence of discourse. It is the source of the distinction of the very greatest poets and prose writers and the means by which they have given eternal life to their own fame. For grandeur produces ecstasy rather than persuasion in the hearer; and the combination of wonder and astonishment always proves superior to the merely persuasive and pleasant. (Longinus, *On Sublimity* 1.3–4, trans. Russell and Winterbottom 143)

Most of the later philosophers mesmerized by the sublime – the distinguished list includes Burke, Kant, Coleridge, Derrida, Lyotard, Lacan, Žižek – define the concept primarily as a form of *experience*. Thus, in our most recent and authoritative study of the sublime, Philip Shaw, even though discussing Longinus (12–32), emphasizes 'the postmodern sublime' (3): 'the definition of the sublime is not restricted to value judgements; it also describes a state of mind. ... In broad terms, whenever experience slips out of conventional understanding, whenever the power of an object or event is such that words fail and points of comparison disappear, *then* we resort to the feeling of the sublime. ... Sublimity, then, refers to the moment when the ability to apprehend, to know, and to express a thought or sensation is defeated. Yet through this very defeat, the mind gets a feeling for that which lies beyond thought and language' (1–3; his emphasis).

Such a model of sublimity is so complex it requires a book to articulate it, and usefully Shaw charts its history as it develops from Longinus to Žižek. To place Marlowe within this history, we need to recall its key phases, which will also allow us to discover important terms, topics, and problems.[48]

The first phase to a history of the sublime, represented by Longinus in antiquity, is *linguistic*: here the sublime is understood as a discursive tool of rhetoric, most powerfully exemplified in literary works like Homer's *Iliad* and Sophocles' *Oedipus Rex*, and it aims to arouse strong emotion in the reader about the terrifying powers of the divine (we shall return to this phase presently). The second phase, represented by Thomas Burnet's 1684–9 *Sacred Theory of the Earth*, is *naturalist*: here the sublime is understood to be located in objects from the natural world, such as majestic mountains or the swirling ocean, and signals 'the biblical apocalypse', a 'darker meditation ... on the nature of the self and relations with the external world' (Shaw 5). The third phase, represented by Edmund Burke's 1556 *Philosophical Enquiry* – which 'has had a massive and lasting impact on discussion of the sublime' (Shaw 48) – introduces an *empiricist* understanding: the sublime becomes primarily a psychological and secular phenomenon of the mind as it fixes on the terrible in nature to produce an exalted emotional state of alienating pleasure (Shaw 53–4). The fourth phase, represented by Immanuel Kant's 1789 *Observations on the Feeling of the Beautiful and Sublime*, is *rationalist*: the sublime becomes a cognitive site of consciousness that demonstrates 'the ascendancy of the rational over the real', so that 'the mind of man ... is greater than anything ... in nature' (Shaw 6). The fifth and current phase, represented by such 'poststructuralist theorists' as Paul de Man, Jacques Derrida, Jean-François Lyotard, and S. Žižek, remains skeptical of the Kantian sublime even while operating within it: whether understood as linguistic, naturalist, empiricist, or rationalist, the sublime is fundamentally 'paradoxical, unfulfilled, or self-baffling', even though a theorist like Žižek can discover in it a 'spiritual' value that powerfully combats the deflating modern commitment to the 'material' (Shaw 8).

At stake in each phase are a series of questions, which each theorist tends to answer individually, and all of which bear on Marlowe's representation of the sublime:

1. What is *the origin* of the sublime: is it the natural world and its objects, the human mind, emotions, and senses, or language and words?
2. What *form* does the origin of the sublime take: can the origin be anything grand, elevated, and beautiful, or only the terrible?
3. What *effect* does the sublime produce: is it psychological, emotional, linguistic, or literary? And is the effect liberating or debilitating, the source of pleasure or of pain?

4. Is the sublime *gendered*: is it fundamentally masculine or feminine?
5. What is the *metaphysics* of the sublime: is it divine or secular, Christian or pagan?

As we shall see, a final question emerges, which we need to highlight here, in part because Longinus ends *On Sublimity* with it, even though it tends to receive subordinate importance in Shaw's study:

6. Does the sublime have a *political* goal: does it operate in service of royalism or republicanism, absolutism or democracy?

While a full history of the sublime, with its key terms, topics, and problems, continues to preoccupy theorists of the sublime, we need to recall that only the first or Longinian phase is historically pertinent to Marlowe. Moreover, readers will notice that the above history of the sublime jumps from the first century AD to the late seventeenth century – right over the Christian Middle Ages and the European Renaissance. In fact, for this era the history of the sublime remains to be written.[49] In the absence of detailed research on the sublime particularly in Elizabethan England, I take the cue of Longinus to approach the Marlovian sublime as fundamentally a mode of 'discourse' – a form of language, the *expression* of 'experience' – and further, to emphasize the linguistic form of the sublime as *literary*, exemplified by 'the very greatest poets'.

To my knowledge, theorists of the sublime neglect Longinus' most valuable contribution to a literary theory of the sublime, including for Marlowe and Lucan: Longinus presents the expression of the sublime within a work of literature as a site of what I call intertextual authorship. Famously, he begins by using a simile to show how the sublime eschews harmony to participate in violence: 'Sublimity ... produced at the right moment, tears everything up like a whirlwind' (1.4: 144). Thus, while the sublime can take countless forms, the one that Longinus privileges – and the one that becomes important to both Lucan and Marlowe – occurs in the special 'interval between earth and heaven': 'the whole universe' is 'overthrown and broken up', and the boundaries between the human and the divine disappear, illustrated powerfully in the *Iliad*: 'Homer ... has done his best to make men of the Trojan war gods, and the gods men' (9.5–7: 150–1).

Yet Longinus does not simply define the sublime as an elevated form of literary discourse mapping the cataclysmic interstice between the human and the divine. He turns the sublime into a form of literary authorship in three fundamental ways. First, he marks out the sublime as a discourse in which 'the poet is accustomed to enter into the greatness of his heroes' (9.10: 152). He quotes Euripides' Orestes, when the young man spies the Furies: 'O! O! She'll kill me. Where shall I escape?' (*Orestes* 255–7; cited Russell and Winterbottom, ed. 238). According to Longinus, 'The poet himself saw the Erinyes, and has as good as made his audience see what he imagined' (15.2: 159). Longinus makes this authorial principle even clearer later in a section his modern editors title 'Lapses into Direct Speech' (27.1–4: 170–1):

> Sometimes a writer, in the course of a narrative in the third person, makes a sudden change and speaks in the person of his character. This kind of thing is an outburst of emotion.
>
> Hector shouted aloud to the Trojans
> To rush for the ships, and leave the spoils of the dead.
> 'If I see anyone away from the ships of his own accord,
> I will have him killed on the spot.'
>
> Here the poet has given the narrative to himself, as appropriate to him, and then suddenly and without warning has put the abrupt threat in the mouth of the angry prince. ... [T]he change of construction is so sudden that it has outstripped its creator. (Longinus, *On Sublimity* 27.1, trans. Russell and Winterbottom 170)

This first feature of sublime authorship identifies the literary expression of a character's experience: he stands on the violent threshold between the human and the divine, expressing the very moment in the work when the author speaks to the reader in his or her own voice.

Second, Longinus defines the sublime as a principle of literary authorship in a section his modern editors title 'Imitation of Earlier Writers as a Means to Sublimity' (13.2–14.3: 158–9). Here he records that he borrows the idea from 'Plato', who, 'if we will read him with attention, illustrates yet another road to sublimity': 'This is the way of imitation and emulation of great writers of the past' (14.2: 158). According to Longinus, the best way to write the sublime is to read it; after reading it, the writer imitates what he has read. Such a textual origin means that any expression of the sublime is intertextual. The *intertextual sublime*, I suggest, becomes a formal Longinian principle of authorship.[50]

Third, by exposing the rib of its own intertextual authorship, the Longinian sublime reveals not simply a literary origin for its invention but a literary end: what Longinus calls 'posthumous fame' (14.3: 159), which applies to everyone involved in the process: the original (imitated) writer, the writer himself (or herself), and the reader. For Longinus, in other words, the sublime is finally a mode of immortality, a route to the eternal. When he opens his treatise by saying that writers depend on the sublime to give 'eternal life to their own fame' (already quoted), he suggests a telos that is important to sort out: during the process of composition, the writer enters the eternal; in turn, the reader, in reading the sublime, experiences an eternizing power; and finally, through the reader's experience, the writer becomes famous.[51]

Longinus finds a model for the eternizing intertextual sublime in the ancient story of 'the Pythia at Delphi' (14.2: 158):

> She is in contact with the tripod near the cleft in the ground which (so they say) exhales a divine vapour, and she is thereupon made pregnant by the supernatural power and forthwith prophesies as one inspired. Similarly, the genius of the ancients acts as a kind of oracular cavern, and effluences flow from it into the minds of their imitators. (Longinus, *On Sublimity* 14.2, trans. Russell and Winterbottom 158)

Here Longinus interprets the ancient story of the priestess at Delphi in her relationship with Apollo as an allegory of the author's eternizing experience of the intertextual sublime. The work of an earlier writer functions as a womblike 'oracular cavern' of invention, from which mystically sacred 'effluences' flow into the 'mind' of the imitating author, impregnating him with 'supernatural power', the power of the sublime.[52]

This Longinian allegory of the sublime has a striking erotic (and even homoerotic) dimension, one that genders the sublime. The allegory presents the author of the sublime as a female who becomes impregnated by the masculine source of the imitated text (evidently, even when that text is Sappho's [10.1–2: 154]). There is thus an intriguing principle of cross-dressing that underlies the literary form of the sublime, and hence a form of theatricality.[53]

At the end of his treatise, Longinus takes up a topic that he touches on earlier (17.1–2: 164): the political character of the sublime (44.1–12: 185–7). Specifically, he records the comments of his friend Terentianus on the political cause of literary decline during their era. According to Terentianus, literature has declined because of the loss of political liberty:

> 'Are we to believe', he went on, 'the common explanation that democracy nurtures greatness, and great writers flourished with democracy and died with it? Freedom, the argument goes, nourishes and encourages the thoughts of the great, as well as exciting their enthusiasm for rivalry with one another and their ambition for the prize. In addition the availability of political reward sharpens and polishes up orators' talents by giving them exercise; they shine forth free in a free world'. (Longinus, *On Sublimity* 44.2–3, trans. Russell and Winterbottom 185–6)

According to Longinus' friend, a democratic government practicing the principle of freedom is a natural home of the sublime author, in part because a democracy allows for open literary competition, which motivates excellence. In contrast to those living in the past, Terentianus goes on to say, 'We of the present day ... seem to have learned in infancy to live under justified slavery, ... never allowed to taste that fair and fecund spring of literature, freedom' (44.3: 186). In this astonishing statement, the Longinian text pauses to identify political freedom as the generative fountainhead of 'literature' – especially a literature of the sublime.

In contrast to Terentianus, however, Longinus himself chooses to locate the cause of literary decline not in the political loss of democratic freedom but in the moral depravity of human desire: 'I wonder whether what destroys great minds is not the peace of the world, but the unlimited war which lays hold on our desires, and all the passions which beset and ravage our modern life' (44.6: 186). In this way, the Longinian text raises a fundamental question: does a free government promote the sublime or not?[54] In 1652, John Hall argues that it does. During Oliver Cromwell's republican rule, Hall published the first English translation of Longinus, writes Norbrook, 'in an explicitly republican spirit', translating the word 'democracy' as both 'Democracie' and 'Republic': Longinus may not 'directly endorse' the republican character of the sublime, Norbrook adds, 'but he has earlier declared that "*Wealth, Honour, Repute, Empire*, and all those other things that to the *outward* appearance seem most *majestick*" are inimical to the sublime' (Hall's translation; qtd. Norbrook 138).[55]

While Longinus was theorizing the sublime somewhere out in the Empire, Lucan was writing the sublime deep within the bowels of the Empire. Yet only recently have critics begun to connect Lucan with the sublime. In 1999, for instance, Norbrook identifies the 'sublime' as a key signature of Lucan's anti-monarchical poetics, seeing it in opposition to Virgil's 'imperial monumentality' (32), and adding that in the seventeenth century Thomas Hobbes objected to 'Lucan's aiming at sublimity', which Hobbes 'identified with soaring fancifully above due limits' (137). In 2005, Charles Martindale observes that 'Lucan could easily be seen as a poet of the Longinian sublime' (*Latin Poetry* 235), but he does not amplify. As recent as 2008, Henry Day becomes the first to study the Lucanian sublime as a topic in its own right; his goal is to 'examine how Lucan's *Bellum Civile* ... represent[s] the paradoxical dynamic of sublime experience'.[56] According to Day, 'The sublime experience ... is that experience which transcends or exceeds our everyday categories of comprehension', which operates through 'the dialectic of loss and recuperation', the 'paradoxical experience of rupture and wholeness' (MS 1). As we shall see in Chapter 1, Day emphasizes what he calls 'the historical sublime': 'the way in which experience of the past can be sublime', through 'breaking away from the present' (MS 1)

Hopefully, readers will grasp the relevance of the Lucanian (and Longinian) sublime to Marlowe. As with liberty, critics during the past hundred years connect Marlowe with the sublime, usually to describe his style, voice, and mighty line. The first to use the word 'sublime' is evidently Thomas Campbell in 1819, who says that Marlowe 'had powers of no ordinary class, and even ventured a few steps into the pathless sublime', adding (as if with Longinus in mind), 'his pathos is dreary, and the terrors of his Muse remind us more of Minerva's gorgon than of her countenance' (rpt. MacLure, ed., *CH* 13). In 1820, William Hazlitt criticized Faustus for being 'a personification of the pride of will and eagerness of curiosity, sublimed beyond the reach of fear and remorse' (rpt. MacLure, ed., *CH* 78), but in 1888 Edward Dowden praised the inventive 'energy' of Barabas: 'Even his love of money has something in it of sublime, it is so huge a desire' (rpt. MacLure, ed., *CH* 109). In 1885, an anonymous reviewer wrote of Marlowe's 'learning': 'it is most often dignified, sometimes impressive and even splendid; now and then, indeed, it is fairly sublime' (rpt. MacLure, ed., *CH* 148). In 1888, the proceedings of the Clifton Shakespere Society are more direct: 'There are passages in ... which Marlowe rises to sublime poetic pitch', citing Edward II's abdication scene (rpt. MacLure, ed., *CH* 168).

Among early commentators, however, it is Algernon Charles Swinburne who rhapsodizes most eloquently, highlighting Marlowe's historic penning of the sublime in a 1908 essay on 'The Age of Shakespeare':

> The first great English poet was the father of English tragedy and the creator of English blank verse. ... [N]o poet is great as a poet whom no one could ever pretend to recognise as sublime. Sublimity is the test of imagination as distinguished from invention or from fancy: and the first English poet whose powers can be called sublime was Christopher Marlowe. (Swinburne, rpt. MacLure, ed., *CH* 177–8)

Swinburne was a Whig republican, and he does two things simultaneously here: he presents Marlowe as a poet-playwright, and he locates the sublime as the central achievement of this Elizabethan writer's dual model of English authorship.[57]

In subsequent remarks, Swinburne amplifies on what he means when he says that sublimity is the test of imagination, the literary faculty of highest creation because it frees the author, his work, and presumably the reader from mere 'invention or from fancy':

> The majestic and exquisite excellence of various lines and passages in Marlowe's first play [*Tamburlaine*] must be admitted to relieve, if it cannot be allowed to redeem, the stormy monotony of Titanic truculence which blusters like a simoon through the noisy course of its ten fierce acts. With many and heavy faults, there is something of genuine greatness in 'Tamburlaine the Great'; and for two grave reasons it must always be remembered with distinction and mentioned with honour. It is the first poem ever written in English blank verse ...; and it contains one of the noblest passages, perhaps indeed the noblest in the literature of the

world, ever written by one of the greatest masters of poetry in loving praise of the glorious delights and sublime submission to the everlasting limits of his art. (Swinburne, 'The Age of Shakespeare', rpt. MacLure, ed., *CH* 178)

Swinburne gleans in the *Tamburlaine* plays not simply great poetry but poetry of a distinctive and original sort: *noble, majestic, exquisite*, but also *sublime*: poetry that praises both the 'glorious delights' and the 'sublime submission' to 'the everlasting limits of ... art'. In this paradoxical formulation, Swinburne articulates his own version of Marlowe's seminal achievement: the Elizabethan author uses sublime poetry to pluck freedom out of a politics of defeat.

Evidently, what captivates Swinburne is the exaltation that emerges from within the prison-house of Marlowe's art. The Swinburnian phrase, 'everlasting limits', seems to suggest that Marlowe's art is sublime because it merges the eternal with the finite: Marlowe's art is innovative because it locates the 'everlasting' within a 'limit'.[58] Not simply the eternal, and not simply the finite, but the presence of the eternal within the finite, the free within the bound. Thus, Swinburne admires Marlowe for an unprecedented 'delight' in and a 'submission' to what we might call the *eternal-finite*, a principle not strictly of transcendence but more precisely of transcendent immanence, locating the transcendent within the immanent.[59]

Although Swinburne discusses each of Marlowe's other plays and major poems, his judgment of *Lucan's First Book* is especially pertinent here, not least because it is the first detailed comment on record:[60]

> His translation of the first book of Lucan alternately rises above the original and falls short of it; often inferior to the Latin in point and weight of expressive rhetoric, now and then brightened by a clearer note of poetry and lifted into a higher mood of verse. Its terseness, vigour, and purity of style would in any case have been praiseworthy, but are nothing less than admirable, if not wonderful, when we consider how close the translator has on the whole ... kept himself to the most rigid limit of literal representation. (Swinburne, 'The Age of Shakespeare', rpt. MacLure, ed., *CH* 183)

Swinburne admires the feat of the translation, but his terms link *Lucan's First Book* with the sublime: 'rises above ... lifted into a higher mood of verse ... terseness, vigour, and purity of style ... admirable, if not wonderful'. In this way, Swinburne qualifies as the first theorist of Marlowe's Lucanian sublime.

Perhaps in large part because of Swinburne, modern critics use the 'sublime' to characterize Marlowe's art – so much so that it is hard to pick up a piece of twentieth- or twenty-first-century criticism that does not include the word 'sublime' in it. In the 1950s, for instance, Harry Levin makes famous Marlowe's 'preoccupation' with the central Lucanian metaphor of the sublime as pinpointed by Hobbes, 'unfettered soaring' (*Overreacher* 134; see 123, 148), along with its two central classical myths: Icarus, who uses wings invented by his father, Daedalus, to fly too close to the sun and tragically falls; and Phaethon, who borrows the chariot of his father, Apollo, and loses control on his flight across the heavens. 'In each instance', Levin says, 'it is a question of flying too high' (112).[61]

In 1986, Kimberly Benston produced the only Marlowe essay on the sublime, titled 'Beauty's Just Applause: Dramatic Form and the Tamburlanian Sublime'. Influenced by Harold Bloom (himself a student of the sublime [Shaw 23, 131]), Benston argues that 'Tamburlaine is a transcendentally solipsistic *poet* of the Sublime' (207; his emphasis):

> [The play itself] conflates verbal and physical power in the structure of rhetorical conflict which theorists from Longinus to Thomas Weiskel have termed the sublime. ... Marlowe's revisionary insight [is] ... to isolate the sublime crisis of violence and language for a dramatic examination of unprecedented vigor and complexity in English literature. ... At its most intense, the hero's linguistic assertion is also a defense against death and the primacy of Creation evoking the sublime's defining effort to appropriate the authority of origins. (Benston, 'The Tamburlanian Sublime' 208–9)

For the first formal time, a critic links Marlowe with the Longinian sublime, locating Marlowe's historic accomplishment in a language at once violent and exalted.[62] We might take issue, however, with the conclusion that Benston draws: 'This is the last time, in Marlowe – indeed, in the English canon – that we are to hear such sublime rhetoric as more than compensation for tragic loss ... [H]e had begun to revalue his most audacious proclamation of imaginative freedom in terms of the innate limitations and external oppositions imagination seeks to overcome' (227).

Although there is a certain truth to this conclusion – and it has been stated often enough, especially in criticism on *Edward II* – I shall show that Marlowe may come to fetter the freedom of the sublime, but he retains the artistic pattern Benston well articulates, a pattern that best accounts for Marlowe's remarkable legacy: from *Dido* through *Faustus*, he asserts an eternizing poetics of the sublime as a phoenix arising from the ashes of defeat.[63]

Marlowe's poetics of the sublime lends to his tragic canon a certain comedic voice, introducing the audience to an alternative art-form that breaks free from the constraints of tyranny, human or divine. Marlowe is the first canonical author in English to foreground the poet-playwright as the imagined leader of a free art. Rather than locating liberty in the magistrate, the people, or the individual citizen, to form what Skinner calls a *'political* theory of revolution' (*Foundations* 2: 338; his emphasis), Marlowe follows Lucan (and before him Ovid) in locating liberty in the sublime verse of the author himself. Lucan, liberty, and the sublime, I shall aim to show in this book, become the trinal crown of Marlowe's republican authorship.

Structure of the book

To further examine Marlowe's republican authorship, I divide the book into five chapters, each locating Lucan, liberty, and the sublime within particular Marlowe works. The first two chapters focus on the poems, and the final three chapters focus on the plays. Chapter 1 introduces three pieces of secondary evidence for Marlowe's republican authorship: the biographical, which looks at the archive of Marlowe's life for his knowledge of and interest in republican thought; the contextual, which examines republicanism within Elizabethan culture; and the analytical, which investigates the presence of republican authorship in Marlowe's works, with the opening chapter focusing on *Lucan's First Book* itself. Then the remaining chapters extend the analytical evidence to the other major poems and the plays. Chapter 2 considers Marlowe's Ovidian poems, concentrating on the idea of rapture in *Ovid's Elegies*, 'The Passionate Shepherd to His Love', and *Hero and Leander*. Chapter 3 examines Marlowe's three 'imperialist' plays in terms of the Machiavellian paradigm of 'empire and liberty': *Dido, Queen of Carthage* and *Tamburlaine, Parts One* and *Two*. Chapter 4 studies Marlowe's three Machiavellian 'plays of policy' about civil or international war, each with reference to a particular historical context: *The Jew of Malta*, with reference to the republican paradigm of liberty and wealth within what was known as the *Respublica Hebraeorum*; *The Massacre at Paris*, with reference to the civil war in France between Catholic monarchists and republican Huguenots; and *Edward II*, with reference to the civil war in England between absolutist monarchy and aristocratic republic, especially as expressed through the 1590s movement known as Tacitism. Chapter 5 concludes the formal study of the Marlowe canon by attending to what I term 'the skeptical sublime' in *Doctor Faustus*, a tragedy that acquires world-class stature in part because it fuses 'the dominant problem of modern philosophy', skepticism, with 'the preeminent modern aesthetic category', sublimity (Sedley 153). In an Afterword, I look briefly into the afterlife of Marlowe's republican authorship, highlighting two figures in particular: Nashe, in *The Unfortunate Traveler* passage excerpted for the epigraph to this book; and Milton, in *Paradise Lost*, who equates Satan, 'the Author of all ill'

(2.381), with what Gabriel Harvey splendidly called 'no Religion, but precise Marlowisme'.[64]

Significance

Marlowe's republican authorship might be significant initially because it helps us to historicize Marlowe as an early modern individual more accurately than other models currently available. During the past four hundred years, commentators have turned up an impressive list of original Marlovian achievements: the first to translate Lucan (and Ovid's *Amores*); the first to make blank verse the standard on the stage; the first to put Machiavelli in the theatre; and so forth.[65] Yet Marlowe is also the first important Elizabethan author to write literary republicanism in English. Marlowe's republican authorship, we have seen, is strange and unique; it shows not a patriotic political program but an afflicted imaginative expression, at once obsessed with and tormented by the republican fantasy of freedom, and thus inextricably bound by its binary opposite, the servitude of empire. By recalling Marlowe's pioneering role, we may refine the scholarly project of reconstructing his originary place in English literary history.

Additionally, Marlowe's republican authorship might be significant for helping to fill in an important phase in a much larger historical narrative, linking republican thought in classical Rome with that in mid-seventeenth-century England. According to Skinner, we can see the origins of the English Civil War in classical views of civil liberty: 'By the time Charles I confronted his Parliament in 1640, ... these observations by the Roman historians about "free states" and the attendant dangers of enslavement had all been turned into works of English political thought' ('Classical Liberty' 2: 13). Yet we can go further, taking the cues of Collinson, Peltonen, and others, to sketch out the Elizabethan crucible of mid-seventeenth-century republicanism, especially the 1590s fascination with alternate forms of government and a willingness to criticize the Queen's monarchy, represented in the opposed circles surrounding the earl of Essex and Sir Walter Raleigh, within which authors such as Sidney, Spenser, Shakespeare, and Jonson moved.[66] Recent criticism has produced substantive studies of these four Elizabethan authors, but, surprisingly, for the most notorious dissident among them, we lack any study whatsoever.[67] The current book aims to supply the gap. As we shall see in more detail, the Elizabethan phase of the 1590s catches classical liberty and English republicanism in its representational phase rather than in a constitutional one. The Elizabethan representation of republicanism plays a crucial transitional role between 'classical liberty' and 'the English Civil War'.

Was Marlowe a republican? We may not have sufficient evidence to say so, but by *troubling* this author of the republican imagination, and by discovering Lucan, liberty, and the sublime within his poems and plays, we may witness Marlowe performing a vital role in the advent of modern English authorship.[68]

1
Republican Representation: Marlowe, the Age of Elizabeth, and *Lucan's First Book*

> The world now a dayes, is set all upon liberty.
> Richard Bancroft, *A Survey* (1593, page 7)

Because the Introduction to this book has concentrated on the primary evidence for Marlowe's republican authorship – 'Lucan, liberty, and the sublime' – this opening chapter looks into the secondary evidence, dividing it into three types: biographical; contextual; and analytical. The biographical evidence comes from the available archive on Marlowe's life, and helps us understand his connection to early modern republican thought. Conversely, the contextual evidence emerges from the age of Elizabeth itself, and the light its republican thought sheds on Marlowe's poems and plays. The analytical evidence arises initially from within one of Marlowe's poems, *Lucan's First Book*, and what this work can tell us about his republican authorship. Altogether, the chapter argues that Marlowe's life, culture, and texts help to advance the case for seeing his republican authorship as a historic achievement in early modern England. (Chapters 2–5 will then extend the analytical evidence to the rest of the Marlowe canon.)

Biographical evidence

The biographical archive includes some tantalizing information linking Marlowe with early modern republican thought.[1] The first piece of information is the republican basis of the grammar school education that Marlowe would have received at the King's School, Canterbury. Underlying this education is the humanist edict of Thomas Cranmer, Archbishop of Canterbury, who, when the school was founded, went against the practice of the time to determine that sons of poor fathers were worthy to attend grammar school when the sons of rich fathers proved inept (Riggs, 'Marlowe's Life' 26–7). This edict led to an egalitarian flood, in which poor boys across England had access to the same classical and Christian education as the rich. The curriculum that Marlowe would have studied at the King's School was based on classical Rome, and several of the featured authors play a central role in the story of early modern republicanism, especially Cicero, Virgil, and Ovid (Kuriyama 23–5). While neither Virgil nor Ovid was a 'republican', each became part of the republican conversation in early modern England: Virgil, for his official championing of the Augustan empire and his unofficial sympathy for the premier victim of empire, the Carthaginian queen, Dido (see Chapter 3); Ovid, for his resistance to the Augustan regime and his bold championing of *libertas* over civic duty to the empire (Chapter 2).[2] In contrast, Cicero was a staunch republican, the author not simply of *The Republic* (much of it lost until modern times) but of one of the founding texts of early modern republicanism, *De officiis* (*On Obligations*). Moreover, one of the two entry-level texts introducing students to Roman culture was William Lyly's *Short Introduction to Grammar*, which, writes David Riggs, was 'based ... on Roman usage from the classical period. It prepared Marlowe and his schoolfellows to think like Ovid and Cicero rather than St. Thomas Aquinas': 'Marlowe belonged to the first generation that received this classical education on a widespread basis' (*World* 37).

Like Riggs, Park Honan believes that such reading trained Marlowe to resist Elizabethan orthodoxy. Classical authors, including Horace, Seneca, and Lucan, 'gave Marlowe leave to compare ideas freshly, to question the Canterbury society he knew, to find great allies in old and modern Italy, and to interrogate the value of any truth he heard. ... What he came to dislike were works which denied an audience the right to think' (52, 63). In particular, Honan observes, the fate of Lucan, who 'had lost his life for the crime of offending the politically powerful', provided a cautionary tale (68).

Not just the classics but early modern continental writers like Erasmus also exerted an influence on Marlowe: 'The mocking, intense spirit of Erasmus, playing over Scripture as well as the classics, set a keynote for much that Marlowe would have heard or thought in the sixth form' (Honan 60). From Erasmus' influential theory of the educational curriculum, Marlowe could have learned an argument against hereditary succession as the basis of sound government: good leaders are not born but made (Skinner, *Foundations* 1: 241–3). At the King's School, then, Marlowe's reading likely planted a seed that would fertilize his imagination in plays and poems alike: republican liberty.

When Marlowe subsequently benefited from a Matthew Parker scholarship to attend Corpus Christi College, Cambridge, he had further opportunity to refine his classical and continental education in the republican value of liberty. He would have continued reading a host of writers important to the early modern republican imagination: Aristotle, Cicero, Ovid, Seneca, and especially Lucan. According to Skinner, the Elizabethan age was 'exactly ... the first time' when the major authors of classical civil liberty 'became available in English': Nicholas Grimalde's translation of Cicero's *De officiis* appeared in 1556, with a dual language version in 1558; Henry Savile's translation of Tacitus' *Histories* and *Agricola* appeared in 1591; Richard Greneway's translation of Tacitus' *Annals* and *Germanica* came out in 1599; and Philemon Holland's translation of Livy's *History of Rome* emerged in 1600; while Thomas Heywood's translation of Sallust's *Bellum Catilinae* and *Bellum Iugurthinum* appeared in 1608 (although Alexander Barclay had translated the former c. 1520), and Cicero's key text, Aristotle's *Politics*, was translated in 1598 from Louis Le Roy's French translation.[3] To the list supplied by Skinner, we need to add Polybius, whose *Rise of the Roman Empire* was 'one of the canonical works of European politics', cited, for instance, by the French Huguenot François Hotman 'as a key plank in his attack on the tyranny of the French monarchy', and partially translated into English by Christopher Warton in 1568 (Hadfield, *Republicanism* 26).[4] To a budding scholar like Marlowe, editions of these works in Latin and other European languages were also available. Indeed, it would be surprising if the translator of Ovid and Lucan, and the paraphraser of Virgil and Musaeus, did not benefit from these texts, especially those most neglected in criticism on Marlowe: Livy, Sallust, and Tacitus.[5]

Among recent biographers, Riggs especially attends to Marlowe's classical education at Cambridge. He reveals that Marlowe had access to the classical republican texts of Aristotle, Cicero, Livy, and Polybius mentioned above. Although further research needs to be done, classical republicanism was a durable part of the curriculum that Marlowe would have studied.[6] Furthermore, Riggs makes it clear that Marlowe's education in the classics trained him to oppose the official Christian education that Queen Elizabeth, William Cecil, the Chancellor at Cambridge, and its leading educator, John Whitgift, attempted to instill in young scholars. To these officials' commitment to class hierarchy, Marlowe learned class conflict (*World* 78), even receiving unofficial license to 'aspire beyond the ... appointed place in society' (71). Marlowe's training in the rhetorical art of dialectic provided him specifically 'with a prolonged education in skepticism', including through Cicero, who 'opened the way for a sceptical critique of modern faiths' (83) – a topic we shall take up formally in Chapter 5. As Riggs concludes, 'If the King's School taught Marlowe to speak like a Roman, Cambridge showed him to think like one' (84). Although Riggs concentrates on logic, ethics, and philosophy, giving short shrift to politics, he demonstrates that 'the ancient prototypes of modern unbelief' were accessible to Marlowe at Cambridge (89). Riggs even goes so far as to say that Marlowe's university education was more grounded in the classics than the 'medieval' education that the future republican John Milton would receive at the same institution in the seventeenth century (86). In the early modern history of Cambridge, then, Marlowe's time there was unique for its focus on republican political thought.

While classical republicans remain understudied in Marlowe criticism, a good deal of work has been done on the most infamous Continental conduit for sixteenth-century republican thought: Machiavelli.[7] We shall discuss this topic in Chapters 3 and 4, but for now we may recall that during the late 1570s and 80s Machiavelli was being read all around Cambridge, and not simply *The Prince*, but also *The Discourses on Livy*, 'the most important discussion of republican government since the classical period' (Bondanella and Bondanella, eds. xvi). According to Honan, both of Machiavelli's treatises 'had excited the colleges at Cambridge' (257). As Gabriel Harvey wrote to Spenser in 1579, 'You cannot step into a scholar's study...but (ten to one) you shall likely find open either Bodin's *De Republica* or LeRoy's Exposition upon Aristotle's *Politics* or some other like French or Italian politique discourses. And I warrant you some good fellows amongst us begin now to be pretty well acquainted with a certain parlous book called, as I remember me, *Il Principe* di Nicolo Machiavelli' (rpt. Honan 75).[8] We have already mentioned Le Roy's translation of Aristotle's *Politics*, but Harvey also mentions Bodin, another key player on the sixteenth-century republican stage.[9]

As we shall see, editors of Marlowe's works document that Marlowe was likely reading both *The Prince* and the *Discourses*, especially when composing *The Jew of Malta*. Although we may be used to thinking of Machiavelli as the notorious protector of monarchy, such thinking is misleading. As scholars such as Skinner insist, there are not two Machiavellis, one monarchical and the other republican. There is a single Machiavelli: he wrote both treatises; and he did so out of a firm faith in republican political government, even if the defeat of the Florentine Republic compelled him to serve the Medicis, and thus abandon a political discourse organized around 'liberty' for one organized around 'security' (Skinner, *Foundations* 1: 153–68: 156).[10] Marlowe is well known to be the first English dramatist to put 'Machevill' on the stage, but we have yet to consider the republican ramifications of his doing so.

According to Honan, the office of Sir Francis Walsingham, Elizabeth's Master Secretary, 'introduced Marlowe to a Machiavellian system which somehow worked: at least it trapped hostile interlopers (priests included) and scotched conspiracies' (128). Recent research has attended to Marlowe's work as a Walsingham spy, but we might also consider what such work means for Marlowe's republican authorship. For instance, according to Skinner, Machiavelli and his republican contemporaries argued that to 'uphold...the value of liberty' a republic had to foster 'a sense of civic pride and patriotism on the part of the people' (Skinner, *Foundations* 1: 175). As Skinner adds, 'Machiavelli makes his basic meaning clear as early as the Preface to the first Discourse, in which he observes that the men who possess the highest virtù are those "who have gone to the trouble of serving their country"' (1: 176). As we intimated in the Introduction, however, Marlowe's life as a government spy likely compromised his commitment to the republican value of patriotism. Thus, writes Charles Nicholl, 'The typical Elizabethan spy' is one who has 'motivations ... boiled down to greed or fear, or a mix of the two, with the question of patriotism coming a poor third. ... These agents constantly played both ends against the middle, and fed information to both sides [Protestantism and Catholicism]. In a sense they did not even know which side they were really working for. The spy kept a foot in both camps, and was ready to jump either way. His commitment to Mr Secretary, to Protestantism, to Queen and Country would be cast off in a moment' (*Reckoning* 108, 113). We might, then, come to see Marlowe as Europe's first government spy who puts the leading republican theorist on the stage and translates the central poet of the republican imagination. Perhaps it is this strange biographical profile that has kept Marlowe, for so long, below the republican radar.

Probably, we will look in vain in Marlowe for what Hadfield terms 'a key republican concept', one that 'absorbed Shakespeare's imagination': the attempt 'to make ... citizens behave virtuously' (*Republicanism* 215; see 212–16). Cognates of the words 'citizen', 'virtue', and 'nobility' recur in the Marlowe canon: 'citizen', 9 times; 'virtue', 27 times; and 'nobility', 74. But the poems and plays hardly display 'a theory of citizenship, public virtue and true nobility based essentially on the classical humanist and republican traditions ... fully endorsed throughout the period' (Peltonen, *Republicanism* 12). Marlowe takes up this very project, and studies it, as he does in Tamburlaine's soliloquy in *Part One*: 'virtue solely is the sum of glory,/And fashions men with true nobility' (5.1.189–90). But rather than endorsing the project, he complicates it, opens it up to scrutiny. In the end, he writes republicanism in a completely idiosyncratic way.

Perhaps we are so used to thinking of Marlowe as struggling amidst the English Reformation, with its deadly opposition of Protestant and Catholic, that we sometimes forget the political form that the Reformation took.[11] Not just in Italy but all around Europe the conflict emerged between a Catholic monarchy and a Protestant republic, and the biographical archive finds Marlowe implicated in at least three national disputes: in France; in the Netherlands; and in Scotland.

First, the French connection. Because of a meeting of the Privy Council in 1587, during which Marlowe 'was determined to have gone beyond the seas to Reames and there to remaine' (rpt. Kuriyama 202), we believe that he was serving as a government agent in France while still at Cambridge. We know that Marlowe took an acute interest in the French Wars of Religion, because he wrote a play about its climactic event: the 1572 Bartholomew Day's Massacre. The Catholic slaughter of Huguenots in Paris and elsewhere derived from the political opposition between monarchical and republican thought – a topic to which Skinner devotes the final two chapters of his two-volume *Foundations of Modern Political Thought*, when 'the first full-scale revolution within a modern European state' led the Huguenots to their fatal 'defence of religious liberty' (2: 241, 244). As Skinner observes, 'The summer of 1572 saw the final collapse of Huguenot hopes, when Catherine [de Medici] suddenly abandoned any further attempts at conciliation and sanctioned the mass-murder of the Huguenot leadership in the massacre of St Bartholomew' (2: 242). At one point, Skinner even refers to Marlowe's *The Massacre at Paris* (2: 307), discussing at length the leading Huguenot republican, Hotman, whom Marlovians know as one of the major 'sources' for his tragic play (Thomas and Tydeman, eds. 261–73).

Second is Marlowe's Dutch connection, which turns out to be linked to the French, for the 'immediate threat in the summer of 1572 arose out of [Admiral] Coligny's demands for a campaign in support of the developing – and partly Calvinist – opposition to the rule of the Spanish in the Netherlands' (Skinner, *Foundations* 2: 242). As historians of republicanism point out, the Netherlands were not just any country besieged by imperial Spain; unlike Huguenot France, they were an actual European republic.[12] In theory as in practice, England was in the Netherlands to help the Dutch retain their Protestant republican freedom against the imperial Catholic aggression of Philip II. Marlowe refers to this conflict more than once in his plays, usually with reference to the 'Prince of Parma' (*DF* 1.1.95; *MP* 21.87). Yet Marlowe also *visited* the Netherlands, and was arrested there in 1592 by Sir Robert Sidney, Governor of Flushing, on a charge of counterfeiting (rpt. Kuriyama 209–10). Whether Marlowe was serving as a government agent or not (Kuriyama 107–12), we can determine that he returned to England with first-hand experience of having lived in a working European republic.

Third is Marlowe's Scottish connection. In the spring of 1593, after his death in Deptford, Kyd wrote to the Lord Keeper, Sir John Puckering, that Marlowe 'wold perswade with men of quallitie to goe ynto the k of Scotts whether I heare Royden is gon and where if he had livd he told me when I sawe him last he meant to be' (rpt. MacLure, *CH* 36). In 1593, what did it mean to go unto the king of Scots? On the surface, it might mean only that Marlowe was interested in turning away from Queen Elizabeth to invest leadership in her likely successor, King James VI of Scotland.[13] Yet is there more to the story? We cannot say for certain, but Scotland, like the Netherlands and France, had a strong republican tradition. According to Skinner, during the 1550s Scotland became the first European country to institute Huguenot Calvinist resistance theory – what he calls 'a fully populist as well as a completely secularised theory of the right to resist'. The deposition of Mary Queen of Scots in 1567 formally enacted this right, which then precipitated 'an extensive discussion of whether the people could properly be said to have the right to repudiate a legitimate prince' (Skinner, *Foundations* 2: 339). The key Scottish political theorist was George Buchanan, who wrote *The Right of the Kingdom of Scotland* (1579) in support of resistance theory. Buchanan's most famous pupil was James himself, even though the sovereign would later break with the tutor when the latter mounted a campaign to depose his mother (Hadfield, *Republicanism* 35–40). According to Andrew Hadfield, 'Buchanan was widely read in England', including by the Sidney circle, 'who were especially interested in Protestant resistance theory' (38).

To my knowledge, scholars have never linked Marlowe with Buchanan, but well they might, since Buchanan is notable for a 'highly individualist and even anarchic view of the right of political resistance': 'since each individual must be pictured as agreeing to the formation of the commonwealth for his own greater security and benefit, it follows that the right to kill or remove a tyrant must be lodged at all times "not only with the whole body of the people" (*universo populo*) but "even with every individual citizen" (*singulis etiam*)' (Skinner, *Foundations* 2: 343–4). If Marlowe were interested in going to the king of Scots, then perhaps he hoped for a less oppressive government than the one he was currently serving, or perhaps he was interested in Scottish resistance theory.

Marlowe's connection to Scotland, the Netherlands, and France may have a cohesion neglected by recent biographers. According to Jonathan Scott, during the 'late 1630s and early 40s' Milton made a 'series of entries' in his *Commonplace Book* 'in support of the contention that "subjects are at liberty to ward off by force a force advanced against them contrary to the law, even by magistrates' " (*Commonwealth Principles* 113–14). The entries help explain what in Marlowe's life might otherwise seem haphazard – his going across the sea to Rheims, his counterfeiting of the Queen's image in the Netherlands, and his plan to go unto the king of Scots: for Milton cites, as historical precedent for his resistance theory, François Hotman's *Francogallia*, 'The Estates General of Holland [in] tak[ing] away Philip's power', and 'The Scottish Nobles' in driving 'Mary...from the kingdom' (*Commonwealth Principles* 114). France, the Netherlands, and Scotland: these are not just any countries in Europe but the very homes of republican resistance theory (see *Commonwealth Principles* 109–30).

Kyd does not accuse Marlowe of being a republican, but he does charge him with 'mutinous sedition toward the state' (rpt. MacLure, ed. *CH* 35). According to Kyd (and others like the informer Richard Baines), Marlowe's primary crime was that of being an 'Atheist' (33). Nonetheless, Kyd is careful to cast his accusation in terms of his own 'revered meaning to the state', which opposes Marlowe's 'irreligious' one (33). Baines supplies more detail about Marlowe's irreligious Elizabethan politics, charging Marlowe with calling St Paul 'a timerous fellow in bidding men to be subject to magistrates against his Conscience', with believing that he 'has as good Right to Coine as the Queen of England', and thus with coining 'ffrench Crownes pistoletes and English shillinges' (rpt. MacLure, ed. *CH* 37). This report of Marlowe's counterfeiting of the Queen's image retains a rather dark vestige of Marlowe's anti-monarchical thought – one that is inextricably bound to monarchy. Yet it is Riggs who helps us see that at least one of 'Marlowe's articles of atheism' in the Baines note has a formal republican provenance: Marlowe 'grasped the Machiavellian idea, also available from Polybius or Livy, that ancient priests and rulers invented supernatural powers to keep their subjects in awe', citing Kyd's letter on 'things esteemed to be done by divine power' (*World* 326).

Although Kyd, Baines, Thomas Beard, and others indict Marlowe for the dangerous liberation of his 'Epicurisme and Atheisme' (MacLure, ed. *CH* 46), several contemporaries praise Marlowe's heroic commitment to liberty. As we have seen, in his 1594 novel, *The Unfortunate Traveler*, Thomas Nashe offers our first formal republican tribute to the dead man: 'His life he contemned in comparison of the liberty of speech' (McKerrow 2: 265). The remark is important, because it suggests that Marlowe located his premier value not in his life within a monarchy but rather in the republican liberty of his language. Similarly, George Chapman in his 1598 continuation of *Hero and Leander* praises 'th'eternall Clime/Of [Marlowe's]...free soule' (rpt. MacLure, ed. *CH* 45) – a remark that re-locates republican liberty from speech in society to the author's inner spirit.

Marlowe's death on 30 May 1593 at the age of 29, perhaps through government assassination ordered by the monarch herself (Riggs, 'Killing', *World*), sadly impedes any chance we might have to uncover the actual politics of his republican representation. Nonetheless, everything we have said suggests that had he lived, Marlowe would have written republicanism in order to trouble it. Some may continue to see Marlowe as 'Plato's first kind of madman, whose fury arises not from divinity, but from alcohol, lechery, or mental disturbance' (Hulse 100), but recently Debora Shuger helps us grasp the difficulty this young man had gotten himself into: 'Many oppositional writers of the period...seem to have been rather unbalanced and violent personalities' (*Censorship* 152). Usefully, Shuger attributes this writerly condition to 'the absence of a Tudor-Stuart public sphere' (151). While it may be true, as she argues, that in England before Milton's 1644 *Areopagitica* 'no one wanted a free press' (4), it is also true that in the 1580s and early 1590s a sublime madman, Christopher Marlowe, violently used his 'free soule' to defend the 'liberty of speech', even with his life.

Contextual evidence: 'the monarchical republic of Queen Elizabeth I'

Whether we recognize a Habermasian 'public sphere' or not, the age of Elizabeth unquestionably experienced an unparalleled surge of republican energy during the 1590s, forcing the government, writes John Guy, to toughen its policies: 'Whereas in the 1560s and 1570s the doctrine of "mixed polity" was the prevailing orthodoxy in political discourse, by the 1590s careerists were advancing the thesis that Elizabeth possessed an "imperial" sovereignty, that she alone enacted the laws, and that she herself was above the law by the prerogatives of her *Imperium*' (12).[14]

By 'mixed polity', Guy means a classical model of government, derived from Aristotle's *Politics*, advocated most influentially in Polybius' *Rise of the Roman Empire*, developed in Cicero's *Republic*, and brought up to date by Machiavelli in both *The Prince* and the *Discourses*, in which the most effective form of rule combines the three traditional types of government: monarchy (government by the one), aristocracy (government by the few), and democracy (government by the many). During the Elizabethan era, the key spokesman for a mixed polity was Sir Thomas Smith, whose *De Republica Anglorum* was published in 1583, but which became available to a wide reading audience in such influential works as Holinshed's 1577 *Chronicles of England, Scotland and Ireland* (Hadfield, *Republicanism* 20).[15] In chapter 6 of Book 1, Smith observes, 'so seldome or never shall you finde any common wealthe or governement which is absolutely and sincerely made of the one above named, but always mixed with an other' (52). According to Smith, 'A common wealth is called a society or common doing of a multitude of free men collected together and united by common accord and covenauntes among themselves, for the conservation of themselves aswell in peace as in warre' (1.10: 57). As Smith develops his argument, he emphasizes the importance of 'the people' in the government of the commonwealth: 'according to the nature of the people, so the commonwealth is to it fit and proper' (1.15: 62). Specifically, the people are accorded a formal voice in English government through Parliament's House of Commons, which balances the House of the Lords (1.18: 68). To conclude Book 1, Smith summarizes the way in which the 'Monarch', the 'Baronie', and what he calls the 'yeomanrie' all participate in the rule of English government (77).

Smith's treatise did not circulate in a vacuum. As Patrick Collinson argues in one of the most important essays on early modern English history, titled 'The Monarchical Republic of Queen Elizabeth I', 'Elizabethan England was a republic which happened to be a monarchy: or vice versa' (119). Remembering the town of Swallowfield in 1596, and analyzing the debates in the 1572 Parliament on Mary Queen of Scots and the 1584 Bond of Association requiring allegiance to Elizabeth, Collinson discovers a paradoxical environment in which a monarchy operates through republican principles. Swallowfield was 'in effect, a self-governing republic' (111); the Mary Stuart debate revealed that 'the monarch is taken to be not an indelible and sacred anointing but a public and localized office' (122); and the Bond of Association, which ostensibly 'defended the life of the Queen', constituted 'a quasi-republican statement' that relied on the 'body politic' to enforce punishment against Elizabeth's enemies (125). Follow-up research by Markku Peltonen, David Norbrook, Hadfield, and others helps us see just how 'republican' the monarchy of Elizabeth was.[16]

The phrasing here aims to be precise: the government of Queen Elizabeth was not republican but monarchical, yet it allowed for the dissemination of republican acts, such as the three that Collinson discusses, but also the printing of treatises such as Smith's. There were countless others, from such 1576 works as Richard Robinson's translation of Francesco Patrizi's *A Moral Method*, John Bartson's *A Safeguard of Societie*, and Thomas Rogers *A Philosophical Treatise*, to John Foord's 1582 *Synopsis Politica* and Richard Beacon's 1594 *Solon his Follie*.[17] Perhaps the most important treatise is *Vindiciae, Contra Tyrannos*, a Huguenot treatise published in 1579 and written by one 'Stephanus Junius Brutus, the Celt' (title page), but now thought to be written by Philippe du Plessis Mornay (perhaps in conjunction with Hubert Languet, mentor to Philip Sidney), and translated in part into English in 1588 as *A Short Apologie for Christian Souldiours* (Hadfield, *Republicanism* 33). *Vindiciae* divides into four 'questions', each centering on whether the people have power over the prince or the prince over the people, and all responding from the Huguenot position of godly faith against 'the false and pestiferous doctrines of Niccolo Machiavelli' (8). This vigorous indictment against the century's leading republican theorist, in one of the most influential republican tracts, indicates the strange complexity of republicanism at this time.[18]

Brutus presents himself as a modern-day Lucius Junius Brutus, who helped overthrow the Tarquin kings after the rape of Lucrece. In particular, Brutus presents the 'Machiavellians' as the 'slaves of tyrants' (10) – evidently, those who have not read the *Discourses*. The core idea that emerges, iterated over and over, is that 'subjects are not obliged to obey kings, if they order anything against the law of God' (1: 33). Brutus is careful to deny power to individual subjects over kings, lending power rather to 'all together as a whole' (2: 47). In a section titled 'Kings are Made by the People', he asserts that 'God institutes kings, gives kingdoms to them, and elects them', adding that 'the people constitutes kings, confers kingdoms, and approves the election by its vote' (3: 68). In this, Brutus rejects hereditary succession, since 'absolutely no-one is born a king' (71): 'the whole people is more powerful than the king' (74). Throughout, Brutus singles out Julius Caesar as the icon of the tyrant who operates by 'private likes and dislikes' (81) rather than the 'public good' (157). What Caesar robs the commonwealth of is 'the liberty of the people' (91). According to Brutus, then, 'men are free by nature, impatient of servitude' (92), and they instinctively remain eager to ensure that 'right should be done to all equitably' (94).

Popular treatises like *Vindiciae* and *De Republica Anglorum* alert us to the tip of a republican iceberg within Elizabethan culture. In keeping with this metaphor, Blair Worden observes that even during the seventeenth century 'ideas of English republicans are not easy to classify' ('English Republicanism' 443). He goes on to identify 'three main stages' in 'the emergence' of the republican tradition in England, the first one being '1649–60' (443). Worden does offer this caveat: 'Republican ideas might be missing from the political treatises of the generation before the Civil War, but they were often explored in imaginative literature: in Sir Philip Sidney's *Arcadia* and the verse of his friend Fulke Greville...; and in plays by Shakespeare, Jonson, and their contemporaries' (445).[19] Worden is mistaken about pre-Civil War treatises, as more recent work on *Vindiciae* and *De Republica Anglorum* testifies, but he opens the door to 'Republican ideas' in the plays (and poems) of Christopher Marlowe.

In chapter 2 of *Shakespeare and Republicanism*, titled 'Literature and Republicanism in the Age of Shakespeare', Hadfield discusses a wide range of Elizabethan authors who penned republican stories in their poems and plays: not simply Marlowe himself (58–65) but a number of authors who wrote plays formally about classical Rome: Lodge, who wrote *The Wounds of Civil War* (c. 1586; pub. 1594), about Marius and Sulla (66–73); the anonymous *Caesar's Revenge* (c. early 1590s; pub. 1607), about Caesar and Pompey (73–6); the anonymous *Tragedie of Claudius Tiberius Nero, Romes Greatest Tyrant*, Lucan's emperor (pub. 1607) (76–9); and Chapman, who wrote *Caesar and Pompey* (c. 1605, rev. 1612–13) (76–80).[20] Throughout, Hadfield demonstrates the way in which Marlowe and his colleagues put republican fictions on both page and stage: 'republicanism had set the political agenda in Shakespeare's England' (95).

One work Hadfield and other republican critics curiously neglect, however, is rather close to home: Kyd's 1594 play *Cornelia*, a translation of the French tragedian Robert Garnier, whose *Cornélie* appeared in 1574. According to Lukas Erne, whose work on the play remains our only recent commentary (*Beyond* 203–16), Kyd did not intend his tragedy for performance but wrote it as a closet drama (203). Erne identifies Lucan's *Pharsalia* as Kyd's 'most important source' (206), and calls the translation 'an original play' (209). Consequently, Kyd produces what might qualify as England's first formal Lucanian tragedy: 'Following Lucan, Garnier and Kyd are less inclined to side with Caesar, and paint a very different picture of his aspirations' than 'many' would have done at this time, when patriots were seeing 'Caesar as an heroic figure, effecting a providential shift from the Republic to the

Empire' (208). As Erne's account allows us to see, Kyd and Marlowe were likely working on dramatic and poetic versions of Lucan's counter-Virgilian epic at about the same time: 'Interestingly, Kyd and Marlowe, one-time companions and co-founders of modern English tragedy, both translate a work dealing with the Roman Civil War.... While Lucan and Marlowe focus on the political horror of Civil War, Garnier and Kyd look at the events from the personal perspective of Cornelia (208), the wife of Pompey'.

As we shall see, however, Garnier and Kyd are in fact embroidering a neglected feature of the *Pharsalia*: Lucan's stunning commitment to the integrity of Pompey's beloved spouse. Calling *Cornelia* a 'tragedy of grief' foregrounding the Republican wife as a 'spectator' unable to affect 'political events', reduced to mourning and endurance (213), Erne allows us to grasp Kyd's achievement: Cornelia is an Elizabethan icon lamenting the Fall of the Republic, a decisive literary mourning over the 'providential' propaganda of Elizabethan culture.

Cornelia is also a tragedy obsessed with 'liberty' and 'freedom' – words that recur with cognates, respectively, 17 and 13 times, a total of 30. Cicero himself opens the play, announcing that, now that Caesar has defeated Pompey, 'we live despoild and robd by one/Of th' ancient freedom wherein we were borne' (1.1.120–1), to which Cornelia responds, 'Then let me die, my libertie to save;/For tis a death to lyve a Tyrants slave' (2.1.324–5). Those last concepts – slavery and tyranny – dominate the discourse, and are the center of Cicero's *De officiis* and thus the republican tradition stemming from this treatise.[21] As the Chorus of ladies puts it, referring to Lucius Junius Brutus, 'let another Brutus rise,/Bravely to fight in Romes defence,/To free our Towne from tyrannie' (2.1.406–8). Indeed, Kyd relies repeatedly on formal republican language, as evidenced by the Chorus opening Act 3:

> Now we have lost our conquered libertie,
> Our Common-wealth, our Empyre, and our honors,
> Under thys cruell Tarquins tyrannie.
> (Kyd, *Cornelia* 3.1.30–2)

In Act 4, Cassius tries to convince Brutus to 'save' Rome's 'libertie' by assassinating Caesar and his 'hatedst Monarchie' (4.1.6–7). As the Chorus reinforces, 'free the truth from tyrannie,.../T'enlarge his countries liberty' (195–7).

The play, however, ends rather surprisingly, with Cornelia declaring, 'being free borne, I shall not die a slave' (5.1.320). Rather than committing suicide like Brutus and Cassius, she ends with stoic resolution – designed (no doubt) to show that she leads a life consistent with Christian faith: 'Cornelia must live (though life she hateth)/To make your Tombes, and mourne upon your hearses,/Where (languishing) my fumous, faithful teares/May trickling bathe your generous sweet cynders' (5.1.456–9). By presenting Cornelia's resolve to live, Kyd crystallizes his heroine as the feminine voice of republican mourning over the loss of liberty.[22]

The case of *Cornelia* invites us to ask, more specifically: How we are to know republican thought when we see it? To help us respond, Hadfield offers a useful inventory of six 'characteristics of republicanism' (73):

- 'concern for the establishment and maintenance of a civic culture';
- 'hatred of tyrannical rule';
- 'suspicion of hereditary succession';
- 'belief that the ruler is really a servant of the people';
- 'interest in political assassination'; and
- 'an awareness of the key features of the history of the Roman republic and a desire to show that they have widespread significance and application'.

(Hadfield, *Republicanism* 73)

Readers might recognize here how prominently Marlowe's poems and plays exhibit all six characteristics. For instance, we see a concern for the establishment and maintenance of a civic culture in such works as *The Jew of Malta*, *Edward II*, and *Lucan's First Book*; a hatred of tyrannical rule in the *Tamburlaine* plays, *The Massacre at Paris*, *Edward II*, and *Lucan*; suspicion of hereditary succession in the *Tamburaline* plays, *Edward II*, and *Lucan*; belief that the ruler is really a servant of the people, in these same works; an interest in political assassination, in these works plus *The Massacre at Paris*; and finally, an awareness of the key features of the history of the Roman republic and a desire to show that they have widespread significance, in all of these works plus *Ovid's Elegies*. We shall follow the presence of these republican characteristics in the chapters that follow.

To the characteristics Hadfield introduces, we can add a specific Marlovian discourse of republicanism. In the introduction, we surveyed the key term, 'liberty', and here we may recall other republican words circulating around it. Although Marlowe never uses the word 'republic', he does use the term 'commonwealth' in *Edward II*, evoking the sixteenth-century debate between monarchy and an aristocratic form of republicanism.[23] As Edward's royalist brother, Kent, puts it, 'O, miserable is that commonweal, where lords/Keep courts and kings are locked in prison!' (5.3.63–4). Accordingly, Marlowe twice refers to the republican ideal of the 'common good' (*JM* 1.2.101, *MP* 2.40), while 22 times he uses the word 'common' to refer to the 'commons', as in *1 Tamburlaine*'s reference to the 'commons of this mighty monarchy' (1.1.138). 'Consent' is another important word of republican thought, because it depends on freedom (Skinner, *Foundations* 2: 161–6, 329–31), and appropriately Marlowe uses it thirteen times, three with reference to consent in government, as this from *Doctor Faustus* on 'papal government': 'Without election and a true consent' (B-text 3.1.108). 'Rights' has become an important topic of early modern republican thought, and Marlowe uses the term 27 times with reference to law, some of them in a very interesting way, as another phrase from *Faustus* communicates: 'right of law' (B-text 3.1.125). The Marlowe canon is obsessed with the violation of rights, and not surprisingly the concept of tyranny recurs, a total of 35 times. As Agydes tells Techelles of Tamburlaine, 'Go wander free from fear of tyrant's rage' (*1 Tamb* 3.2.102). Thus the role of the counselor figures prominently – it is another cardinal feature of republican values – with cognates of the word 'counsel' occurring 27 times. In *Edward II*, for instance, Canterbury admonishes the king, 'Be patient, my lord,/And see what we your counsellors have done' (1.4.43–4).

Peltonen helps us augment the republican vocabulary when he observes that 'three central characteristics of classical republicanism' are 'meritocracy', 'mixed constitution', and 'elect[ion]' (*Republicanism* 308–9). While the phrase 'mixed constitution' never shows up in Marlowe, its representation recurs, including three times in the *Tamburlaine* plays (see Chapter 3). The other two words do show up. The term 'election' and its cognates occurs eight times, and almost always with republican resonance, including a striking phrase from *Edward II*: 'elected king' (5.1.78; see Chapter 4). Similarly, 'merit' and its cognates occurs ten times, with the *Tamburlaine* plays especially important, since they stage a republican meritocracy. Indeed, Tamburlaine's utterances come right out of the early modern republican handbook; as he tells Theridimas, echoing 'The Passionate Shepherd', 'If you will willingly remain with me/You shall have honours as your merits be –/Or else you shall be forced with slavery' (*1 Tamb* 1.2.253–5).

Finally, we need not belabor Marlowe's use of the word 'policy', which recurs 16 times, 13 in *The Jew of Malta* alone. According to Hadfield, the 'term denotes the language of reason of state, outlined in Machiavelli's writings, but also in such figures as Botero, Justus Lipsius, and Guicciardini, and most crucially here perhaps, Tacitus' (*Republicanism* 163). For the word 'policy', as for most words in the inventory above, Marlowe brings in his own perspective, often *darkening* what appears in others as exemplary.

One term, however, which has largely escaped the net of criticism on sixteenth-century republicanism is crucial to Marlowe's republican authorship: the sublime. As we have seen in the Introduction, Marlowe invents a historic discourse of the sublime as a form of literary freedom, in response to the political oppression of the 1580s and 90s, as highlighted by Guy and others. The question we might now ask is: Where was Marlowe coming from? from whence did he invent the sublime? The question is especially complex, since he himself never uses the word or any of its cognates, and since Longinus, the first theorist of the sublime, does not become a critical figure until the seventeenth century. How, then, can we speak about the Marlovian sublime historically? While it is true that critics do not connect Marlowe with the sublime until the nineteenth century, sufficient evidence of the Longinian sublime exists in the sixteenth.[24]

As Bernard Weinberg has shown, the first known edition of Longinus was published in 1554 by Robortello (146); the first Latin translation, in 1566, by Domenico Pizzimenti (147); and the first English edition, in 1636, a combined Greek and Latin text, by Gerard Langbaine (151). As we have already seen, the first English translation, by John Hall, appears in 1652. Of the 11 medieval manuscripts on which these editions were based, 'the tenth-century Paris MS 2036... is the eldest and incontestably the best', even though 'the Paris codex bears a number of grievous wounds, missing leaves at seven points in the manuscript totaling more than a thousand lines' (Macksey).

Longinus may have become widely known in England only in the seventeenth century, but he was known in the sixteenth (Vickers, ed. 25–6, 31) – and once more rather close to home. George Chapman, in his 1614 dedicatory epistle to Robert Carr, earl of Somerset, prefacing his translation of *The Whole Works of Homer*, pauses to criticize Longinus for praising the *Iliad* at the expense of the *Odyssey*:

> Much wondered at therefore, is the censure of Dionysius Longinus (a man otherwise affirmed grave, and of elegant judgement), comparing Homer in his *Iliads* to the sun rising, in his *Odysses* to his descent or setting, or to the ocean robbed of his aesture [turbulence, boiling], many tributary floods and rivers of excellent ornament withheld from their observance.... But this proser Dionysius, and the rest of these grave and reputatively learned (that dare undertake for their gravities the headstrong censure of all things, and challenge the understanding of these toys in their childhoods, when even these childish vanities retain deep and most necessary learning enough in them to make them children in their ages, and teach them while they live) are not in these absolutely divine infusions allowed either voice or relish. (Chapman, *Whole Works of Homer*; rpt. Vickers, ed. 522–3)

The English translator of the *Odyssey* naturally takes issue with Longinus, but he also praises him as a man of 'grave, and of elegant judgement'. More to the point, we need not assume that Chapman waited till 1614 to read Longinus. In short, the poet-scholar who in 1598 continued Marlowe's *Hero and Leander* reveals that he had read Longinus and that he was willing to challenge him in print.

The sixteenth-century recovery of Longinus coincides with the increasing use of the word 'sublime' in Elizabethan discourse, even though we cannot determine a specific Longinian influence. The *OED* records as its only example before the late seventeenth century a passage from the 1586 *English Secretary*, when Angel Day discusses the traditional three styles of rhetoric: the '*Humile*' or low style; the '*Mediocre*' or middle style; and the '*Sublime*' or high style. The sublime style, Day says, is 'the highest and stateliest maner, and loftiest deliverance of any thing that maie bee, expressing the heroicall and mightie actions of Kinges, Princes, and other honourable personages, the stile whereof is said to be tragicall swelling in choice, and those the most haughtiest termes, commended, described, amplified and preferred also by Orators, which manie excellent figures and places of Rhetorique' (Day, *English Secretary* 10). Day does not identify which 'Orators' he has in mind, but it is not unreasonable to speculate that he is thinking of Longinus, for everything he says is consistent with *On Sublimity*: from his linguistic definition of the sublime, to the word's meaning as high, stately, and heroical, to its 'tragicall' character, and even to its link with the politics of monarchs and 'other honourable personages'.[25]

Everything Day says is also consistent with what we know about 'Marlowe's mighty line' – or what Jonson elsewhere calls its 'scenicall strutting and furious vociferation' (rpt. MacLure, ed. *CH* 50), and what more recently Russ McDonald terms the line's 'irrepressible energy, thrilling sonorities, and dazzling verbal pictures' (56). As McDonald reminds us, 'Critics as different as Jonson and Swinburne have recognized that the sound of the verse is one of its defining characteristics: commanding without being bombastic, it partakes of the affective power of artifice without seeming stiff or excessively rhetorical' (56–7).

The *OED* notwithstanding, Day is hardly the first in sixteenth-century England to call the high style 'sublime'. In 1542, for instance, Thomas Elyot tracks the meaning of the word in his *Bibliotheca Eliotae Eliotis librarie*:

> *Sublime*, on hygh.
> *Sublimis, me*, hygh, that which is aboue us.
> *Sublimitas*, heyght.
> *Sublimiter*, hyghly, on heyght.
> *Sublimo, mare*, to sette on hygh.
> (Elyot, *Bibliotheca Eliotae Eliotis librarie*,
> sig. 6.1.ii)

Then, in the 1570 *Scholmaster*, Roger Ascham uses the word when discussing the three styles, finding '*Ciceroes* Orations' handling in an 'excellent' manner the '*sublime*' style (58). Accordingly, in 'To the Gentlemen Readers, health', prefacing the 1589 *Menaphon*, Robert Greene reports that he writes in the sublime style: 'If Gentlemen you finde my stile either *magis humile* in some place, or more sublime in another, if you finde darke Ænigmaes or strange conceipts as if Sphinx on the one side, and Roscius on the other were playing the wagges; thinke the metaphors are well ment' (3). Such comments indicate that the grand style discussed by Shuger includes more than just 'sacred rhetoric' – that it could find a presence within imaginative literature associated with the Elizabethan theatre and the print-house.[26]

Perhaps one of the most intriguing uses of the word 'sublime', however, comes from the poetry of King James, probably written during the 1580s:

> O thou that mightlie does toone
> My warbling holie Harpe,
> And does sublime my Poëmes als
> That I thereon do carpe,
> And marying so my heauenly verse
> Unto the Harpes accords,
> Inspires my sacred Muse to sing
> Unto the Lord of Lords.
> (King James, 'The Translators Invocation', *Poems* 12)

Here James uses the word 'sublime' to describe his own 'Poems', composed in a Christian register. Written within the tradition of the Christian grand style, the sovereign's verse nonetheless differs from the works emphasized by Shuger, for James speaks of his divinely inspired Christian poetry as 'sublime'. Perhaps, then, we may add this *attraction* as a rationale for Marlowe's (supposed) trip to see the king of Scots.

Yet among Marlowe's contemporaries, the writer who uses the term most often is Fulke Greville, when also describing the height of Christian experience (*Caelica*, Sonnet 56; *An Inquisition upon Fame and Honour* 29; *A Treatise of Religion* 215, 312; *A Treatise on Monarchy* 848). In *A Treatise on Monarchy* (c. 1610), he locates the 'sublime' within a political context, associated initially with tyranny:

> Make not mens Conscience, Wealth, and Liberty,
> Servile without book to unbounded Will,
> *Procrustus* like he racks Humanity,
> That in pow'rs own mould casts their good will,
> And slaves men must be by the sway of time,
> Where Tyranny continnes thus sublime.
> (Greville, *A Treatise on Monarchy* 1718–23)

Evidently, for Greville, tyranny is sublime in the Longinian sense that political oppression is *terrible*. Later, however, Greville associates the sublime with the Republic of Rome:

> For instance of which strange inconstancy,
> Take *Rome*, that sublime Senators estate;
> Did she not first the Sons iniquity
> Plague in the aged guiltless Fathers fate?

And then her Monarch into Consuls throw,
Under which yet *Rome* did an Empress grow?
(Greville, *A Treatise on Monarchy* 3527–32)

In remembering the history of the Roman nation, Greville imagines the Senate as sublime, presumably because it did awe-inspiring work as the legal habitation of heightened eloquence.

Yet for Marlowe perhaps the most astonishing use of the word 'sublime' in the sixteenth century comes from the man who gave his name to the scholarship that sent Marlowe to Cambridge. In 'To the Reader' prefacing his *The Whole Psalter Translated into English Metre* (c. 1567), Matthew Parker writes,

Accent in place: your voyce as needth,
    note number, poynte, and time:
Both lyfe and grace: good reading breedth,
    flat verse it reysth sublime.
(Parker, 'To the Reader', *Whole Psalter* 13–16,
Sig. A. ii)

Here the Archbishop of Canterbury instructs the godly person in the art of singing, in the process referring to 'verse' as 'sublime'. Such a usage is notable for its intersecting of English Renaissance sacred rhetoric with the sublime art of poetry.[27]

Important to Marlowe as well is the link between the sublime as a style and the genre of tragedy, intimated by Day. Above all, Marlowe was known to his contemporaries as a tragedian. In 1598, Francis Meres called him 'our tragicall poet', and reported that appropriately 'his Epicurisme and Atheisme had a tragicall death' (rpt. MacLure, ed. *CH* 46). About the same time, the Cambridge authors of the *Parnassus* plays observed that 'Marlowe was happy in his buskind muse' (rpt. MacLure, ed. *CH* 46), voicing a paradox that speaks to Marlowe's sublime achievement in the genre. According to Raymond Williams, 'Important tragedy seems to occur, neither in periods of real stability, nor in periods of open and decisive conflict. Its most common historical setting is the period preceding the substantial breakdown and transformation of an important culture'. Elizabethan tragedy, with Marlowe its pioneer, emerges in its own period on the brink of breakdown, in a clash between monarchism and republicanism.[28]

The link between tragedy and the sublime is longstanding. Longinus himself makes the link, not simply when he says that 'Sublimity...tears everything up like a whirlwind' (1.4: 144), or even when he foregrounds his favorite sublimist, Homer in the *Iliad*, but also when he exemplifies the sublime through the Greek tragedians (e.g., 15.1: 159; 15.5: 160; 3.2: 145). Not surprisingly, modern theorists link tragedy with the sublime, from Nietzsche (rpt. Drakakis and Liebler, eds. 56) through Benjamin (rpt. Drakakis and Liebler, eds. 112), including Susanne Langer (rpt. Drakakis and Liebler, eds. 333). As Nietzsche famously puts it in *The Birth of Tragedy*, in pure Longinian fashion, 'the spirit of the sublime ... subjugates terror by means of art' (rpt. Drakakis and Liebler, eds. 56).

While it is well known that Marlowe develops his heightened tragic discourse out of a heterodox temperament skeptical about Elizabethan orthodoxy, we might recognize that he invents what I am going to call the skeptical sublime out of a profound disaffection not simply with Christian faith but simultaneously with monarchical government (see Chapter 5). Marlowe's achievement is precisely to keep his 'buskind happy' within the discourse of skeptical sublimity.

We cannot tell if Marlowe knew Longinus, but recently David Sedley helps us see that it may not matter. Relying on recent scholarship that characterizes the early modern period as 'an age of the marvelous' (9), and foregrounding the sublime in the late sixteenth-century French essayist Montaigne, Sedley observes: 'Awareness of the availability of *On the Sublime* long before its vogue ... suggests that interest in Longinus did not cause interest in sublimity so much as the other way around: it was the search for something more than admiration [*admiratio*] that led to the rediscovery of Longinus' (10).

The Marlovian sublime looks uncannily like the Longinian sublime in many of its 'tragic' contours, but one of the arguments of this book takes us on a different route: Marlowe could have learned the sublime from one of the classical poets he so historically translates.[29]

Analytical evidence: *Lucan's First Book*

Accordingly, we can find our first analytical evidence of Marlowe's republican authorship within the text of *Lucan's First Book* itself. To see the extent to which this is so, let us first review the reception of Lucan during the Renaissance.[30] The most authoritative reception history comes from Gerald M. MacLean's 1990 study of 'The Debate over Lucan's *Pharsalia*'. As MacLean allows us to see, the debate proceeds in two primary phases. The first, which runs from Boccaccio, Scaliger, and Caselvetro to Carlo Signio, Ronsard, and Tasso, is *aesthetic*, and debates whether Lucan was a poet or a historian (27–31): 'the *Pharsalia* became a touchstone in the debate over poetry and history among Renaissance literary theorists who were concerned more ... with its ambiguous generic status than its republican critique of arbitrary power' (27). The second phase, which emerges largely in seventeenth-century England, is *political*, and debates whether Lucan was a royalist or a republican (31–44), with the scale tipping toward the latter: 'in seventeenth-century Britain discussion of the *Pharsalia* was explicitly bound up with political discourse, in particular with critiques of arbitrary or tyrannical power' (37). Important moments in this second phase are the translations by Arthur Gorges in 1614 and Thomas May in 1627 (34–41). MacLean privileges Gorges, in part to foreground a prefatory sonnet by 'W.R.', most likely Sir Walter Ralegh, Gorges' cousin and friend:

> Had Lucan hid the truth to please the time,
> He had beene too unworthy of thy Penne:
> Who never sought, noe ever car'd to clime
> By flattery, or seeking worthlesse men.
> (W.R., sonnet prefacing Gorges' translation
> of Lucan; rpt. MacLean 38)

As MacLean observes, Ralegh 'praises those poets who challenge absolutist claims to control over the truth rather than give in to the temptations of self-advancement through flattering members of the ruling classes' (38).

MacLean's two-phase history jumps from sixteenth-century Europe to seventeenth-century England, and never mentions Marlowe's translation, nor any other Elizabethan Lucanian. He does follow Frederick Ahl in noting that 'those historical moments when critics have debated Lucan's text typically correspond...with moments of specific political upheaval' (34). Thus, we might identify the time when England's first translation of Lucan was made as an earlier moment of such upheaval. Important to the present argument, MacLean shows that 'the debate over Lucan's *Pharsalia*' was over the aesthetics of political representation itself:[31] 'This elaborate and highly nuanced debate over the formal and aesthetic components of representation constitutes a struggle for control over the means of producing "history".... And the critical debate over Lucan's antimonarchist *Pharsalia* was precisely that, a struggle for control over the status and meaning of historical poetry' (44).

Let us take MacLean's cue, and locate a precipitating moment of this debate in Marlowe's translation of Lucan. *Lucan's First Book* inaugurates the struggle for control over the status and meaning of historical poetry. In Marlowe's translation, as in the texts MacLean discusses, 'aesthetics typically replaces and disguises politics by elevating poetry beyond the political conditions of its production and reception.... Yet this hedging seldom hides the knowledge that poets, like Lucan, who write on historical themes are engaged in a fundamentally political activity' (34).[32]

In 694 masterful lines, Book 1 of the *Pharsalia* introduces the reader to Lucan's strange republican authorship: the seven-line prologue, with its central topic, civil war, and its central principle, civic self-slaughter; the superbly ambiguous invocation to Nero as the divine inspiration for the poem; the poet's principal goal, to narrate the causes of the Roman civil war, with its key analysis of human and divine dissolution built into the nature of things (cosmic, civic, physiological); the poet's disarming claim that he will accomplish this goal through an impartial poetic method that refuses to judge the principals (the republican hero Pompey, and the imperial hero, Julius Caesar, along with the third key figure, the republican stoic Cato); and the precipitating event of civil war, Caesar's crossing of the Rubicon, with its immediate consequence, his entry into Rome. We also meet a few supporting actors, such as Caesar's 'fee'd' man, the 'sometime tribune' Curio (271–2); Laelius, 'the chief centurion' (338); and the augurer Arruns, who masterfully reads the entrails of a slaughtered bull to prophesy dissolution for the Republic. Lucan's display of violent masculinity, however, concludes with his portrait of the Bacchic Roman matron, who delivers a riveting prophecy of Pompey's beheading in Book 8.

Above all, Lucan's poem presents Marlowe not as a staunch republican but as an impassioned narrator of the originary story about the death of the Roman Republic.[33] It is Marlowe's Lucanian analysis of the causes of this death, the self-reflexive poetic methodology he deploys to narrate it, the language of republicanism he invents to describe it, the Roman ideal of liberty he foregrounds, and finally his portrait of that titanic impediment to republican liberty, Caesar, that turn out to be so crucial for Marlowe's poems and plays.

The prologue to *Lucan's First Book* introduces Marlowe's republican authorship through a self-reflexive critique of both Virgil's *Aeneid* and the Elizabethan epic written by 'the Virgil of England' – as Marlowe's friend, Thomas Nashe, called Edmund Spenser in 1592 (McKerrow, ed. 1: 299). In other words, from the outset Marlowe presents his poem in formal opposition to the monarchical epic privileged by the governments of both Augustan Rome and Elizabethan England:

Wars worse than civil on Thessalian plains,
And outrage strangling law, and people strong
We sing, whose conquering swords their own breasts launched,
Armies allied, the kingdom's league uprooted,
Th' affrighted world's force bent on public spoil,
Trumpets and drums like deadly threat'ning other,
Eagles alike displayed, darts answering darts.[34]
                                    (*Lucan's First Book* 1–7)

Marlowe follows Lucan in focusing on Rome's illegal self-slaughter as the central principle of civil war. Yet long ago Harry Levin noticed that Marlowe went 'out of his way to insert the phrase, "conquering swords", into the invocation as a kind of signature', and that he 'replaced *signis* a few lines later with "trumpets, and drums"' (10). Levin is referring to the Prologue to *1 Tamburlaine*: 'you shall hear the Scythian Tamburlaine/Threat'ning the world with high astounding terms/And scourging kingdoms with his conquering sword' (4–7).[35] In this way, Marlowe remains faithful to Lucan's original but stamps it with his own voice. This voice, we may add, is formally that of an Elizabethan poet-playwright.

In the invocation to Nero following, Marlowe masterfully renders Lucan's ambiguity when identifying the emperor as the inspiration for the nightmare that is his poem:

> Thou, Caesar, at this instant art my god:
> Thee if I invoke, I shall not need
> To crave Apollo's aid or Bacchus' help,
> Thy power inspires the Muse that sings this war.
>
> (*Lucan's First Book* 63–6)

Marlowe's language, like Lucan's, outwardly praises Nero as the 'god' who 'inspires' the poet to write the poem, while inwardly critiquing that origin. Caesar is Lucan's god but only 'at this instant' – a bold intimation not simply of the occasional nature of the inspiration but of Nero's fragile mortality. The conditional 'if' looks especially self-protective: grammatically speaking, Lucan does not 'invoke' the emperor but considers the possibility of doing so, only to eschew help from either Apollo or Bacchus: evidently, Nero is so self-sufficient that he appears above the gods of poetry and tragedy. Finally, the Neronian 'power' that 'inspires the Muse' to 'sing' of civil 'war' displaces responsibility from the male poet to a female 'Muse', while slyly implicating 'Caesar' as the cause of the intestine broil.[36]

Since we possess so few statements by Marlowe in the first person, we might consider what the personal 'I' means here. According to Stephen Orgel, 'to the Elizabethans, this classic study of the horrors of civil war had a special relevance.... Lucan's concerns were the substance of modern history.... [I]n such circumstances Lucan should have been regarded more as a model for the treatment of recent events' (ed. 253). Perhaps, then, by using the personal 'I', Marlowe invokes the imperial deity of his own nation; if so, his ambiguous phrasing presents his own monarch as an inspiration to civil war.[37]

Not surprisingly, Marlowe goes on to present himself as the Lucanian poet of first causes:

> The causes first I purpose to unfold
> Of these garboils, whence springs a long discourse,
> And what made madding people shake off peace.
>
> (*Lucan's First Book* 67–9)

The sentiment is grimly republican, as the poet blames all Romans, irrespective of class, of being 'madding people' who join together only to 'shake off peace'. Yet quickly the poet appears to protect himself, locating the first cause to lie above the civic 'garboils'; here, Marlowe produces his most disturbingly eloquent expression in *Lucan's First Book*:

> Rome was so great it could not bear itself.
> So when this world's compounded union breaks,
> Time ends, and to old Chaos all things turn,
> Confused stars shall meet, celestial fire
> Fleet on the floods, the earth shoulder the sea,
> Affording it no shore, and Phoebe's wain
> Chase Phoebus, and enraged affect his place,
> And strive to shine by day, and full of strife
> Dissolve the engines of the broken world.
> All great things crush themselves. ...
> O Rome, thyself art cause of all these evils.
>
> (*Lucan's First Book* 72–84)

After such a detailed description of cosmic dissolution, that last line, an indictment of 'Rome' as 'the cause of all these evils', appears all the more audacious. Clearly, the verse is working hard both to criticize the politically powerful and to protect itself, fusing a civic cause to a cosmic one.[38] Marlowe's text critiques more than a long-dead Roman emperor.

The above passage is justly famous, and marks Lucan out as our great poet of dissolution.[39] The Fates, the universe, Rome: all operate by the principle of catastrophic implosion: the 'world' is organized for self-destruction. Yet in saying that 'All great things crush themselves', Marlowe engages in his most notable accomplishment; he invents a poetry of *sublime* dissolution. Lucan's apocalyptic vision of the organized universe metamorphosing into a black hole produces some of Elizabethan England's most stunning verse. The vision of nothingness is haunting in its own right, but perhaps all the more so because amid all the colliding stars the poet confidently stays within the bounds of the blank-verse line.

The Lucanian poet's sublimely dissolving vision helps explain why the only formal expression of liberty could be so negative, reserved darkly for the 'people': 'Again, this people could not brook calm peace,/Them freedom without war might not suffice' (172–3). This is Lucan at his best, offering the reader a piercing contradiction that both indicts and thrills; in this lexicon, human beings are splendidly wired for self-butchery. Evidently, what we cannot tolerate is the ideal that drives Western political thought, from Cicero to Machiavelli to Skinner: the bliss of freedom through peace. For humankind, the republican ideology of 'freedom without war' is worthless; to put it as sharply as the poem allows, 'freedom' can exist only within the 'state of war'.

This helps explain, not simply why a vision of the dissolving engines of the world excites the poet, but why Caesar – rather than the republicans, Pompey and Cato – commands total obedience of the gods:

> Pompey could bide no equal,
> Nor Caesar no superior: which of both
> Had justest cause unlawful 'tis to judge.
> Each side had great partakers: Caesar's cause
> The gods abetted, Cato liked the other.
> *(Lucan's First Book* 125–9)

If Magnus betrays the Republic and its liberating principle of equality, through innate intolerance of the other, what hope could the 'cause' have? For his part, Caesar is a supreme tyrant; he cannot tolerate a 'superior'. Cato might 'like' the Republican cause, but the gods 'abet' his arch-enemy, for Caesar alone embodies the sublime Jove-like power of the lightning rod, the strength to enact singularity, the most magnificent republic of all: a Caesarian republic of one.[40]

In the only analysis of the sublime in Lucan's epic, Henry Day emphasizes 'Casear as sublime superman' (section title, MS 3), showing that Caesar 'and his action are repeatedly imaged in terms of the natural sublime', as in lines 152–8, where 'Lightning, thunderbolts and sudden flashes of light have a well-established pedigree as objects of the natural sublime' – not simply Edmund Burke in the eighteenth century but Longinus in the first, who located the sublime in 'the whirlwind' that 'tears everything up' (1.4: 144). Here is Marlowe's translation, describing Caesar's special penchant for challenging 'fortune' and the 'gods' with his 'proud desire', happy only when 'blood and ruin made him way' (149–51):

> So thunder which the wind tears from the clouds,
> With crack of riven air and hideous sound
> Filling the world, leaps out and throws forth fire,
> Affrights poor fearful men, and blasts their eyes
> With overthwarting flames, and raging shoots
> Alongst the air, and, nought resisting it,
> Falls, and returns, and shivers where it lights.
> *(Lucan's First Book* 152–8)

According to Day, the 'length of this simile, its density of detail and its prominent position in the poem's opening book set up the lightning storm as Caesar's natural corollary and, like a musical theme, the motif recurs throughout the poem' (MS 4). Marlowe's translation of these lines is especially graphic; the first line is a virtual paraphrase of the famous description of the Longinian whirlwind. Yet Marlowe also captures the frightening effect of Caesar's lightning on 'poor fearful men', whose 'eyes' become 'blasted' by the light, unable to 'resist'.

In this regard, continues Day, Caesar's crossing of the Rubicon 'becomes, like civil war itself, a paradigm of sublimity' (MS 5): 'Now Caesar overpassed the snowy Alps;/His mind was troubled, and he aimed at war,/...coming to the ford of Rubicon' (185-7). Like the lightning, writes Day, 'Mountains...have frequently been reckoned a source of sublimity', with the Alps not needing to wait for the eighteenth century to become 'the classic instance of a sublime landscape' (MS 5). We might add that Marlowe translates Lucan's key verb 'superaverat' as 'overpassed'; as Day says, 'One word is all it takes for [Caesar]...to surmount the Alps, to rise above (*super*) their sublime height' (MS 5). Thus, Day allows us to see that Caesar's overpassing of the Alps and his crossing of the Rubicon become the quintessential actions of the Lucanian sublime.

The poet also locates the sublime in the spectacular supernatural effect of Caesar's precipitating action, as all hell breaks loose, around Rome and above it:

> Great store of strange and unknown stars were seen
> Wandering about the north, and rings of fire
> Fly in the air, and dreadful bearded stars,
> And comets that presage the fall of kingdoms;
> ...
> Lightning in silence stole forth without clouds,
> And from the northern climate snatching fire
> Blasted the Capitol.
> (*Lucan's First Book* 524-33)

The poet's striking image of the Caesarian lightning, blasting the seat of Rome's republican government, magnificently politicizes Marlowe's Lucanian sublime: this overpassing tyrant pierces the heart of liberty itself.

Yet not all the praise is Caesar's. *Lucan's First Book* ends in a grim space largely free of Caesar, as if the poet were clearing the stage for himself, cross-dressed theatrically, in the guise of the Bacchic Roman matron, running frenzied through the streets of Rome, able to articulate horror only through a prophetic address to the god of poetry, the details of which are so sublime we may quote them in full:

> 'Whither turn I now? thou lead'st me toward th' east,
> Where Nile augmenteth the Pelusian sea;
> This headless trunk that lies on Nilus' sand
> I know. Now throughout the air I fly

To doubtful Syrtes and dry Afric, where
A fury leads the Emathian bands; from thence
To the pine-bearing hills, hence to the mounts
Pyrene, and so back to Rome again.
See, impious war defiles the Senate-house,
New factions rise; now through the world again
I go; O Phoebus, show me Neptune's shore,
And other regions, I have seen Philippi'.
This said, being tired with fury she sunk down.
      (*Lucan's First Book* 682–94)

Classicists observe that Lucan uses the maddened Roman matron to insert his own voice into the poem.[41] While the matron 'disclos[es]...Phoebus' fury' about civil war across the known world, climaxing in the gripping vision of the decapitated corpse that she cannot identify, the poet here at the close uses a raving matron to project the nature of his own weird epic, with its climactic event, the beheading of Pompey in Egypt (Book 8).

The poet's identification with the matron also participates in the sublime, for her spiritual progress during an aerial voyage anticipates the flight of the bodiless soul of Pompey after his beheading. Inspired by Phoebus, the matron imagines herself out of control, 'borne aloft', on a sublime flight from Greece to Egypt to Africa to Rome. She has seen Philippi, but also the landscape of Lucan's own poem. In her 'fury', she marks off the Lucanian republican author as free only in a Bacchic state of intoxication, 'As Maenas full of wine on Pindus raves' (674), able to 'fly' only once the republic is lost. The Lucanian sublime, like the Marlovian (and perhaps the Longinian), differs radically from the version celebrated by John Hall and others in the seventeenth century, in which a republic allows the individual to experience an exalted spiritual freedom. For Longinus and for Lucan, as here for Marlowe, the sublime is always *poetic*, not simply political, always violent and disruptive: about the loss of freedom. In translating *Lucan's first Book*, Marlowe discovers the liberating center of his historically sublime republican authorship.

2
Authorship, Freedom, and Rapture in Marlowe's Ovidian Poems

> Verse is immortal, and shall ne'er decay.
> To verse let kings give place, and kingly shows,
> And banks o'er which gold-bearing Tagus flows.
> (*Ovid's Elegies* 1.15.32–4)

In addition to *Lucan's First Book*, Marlowe wrote four other freestanding poems that bear importantly on his republican authorship. These poems span the entirety of his career, from the mid-1580s up to the time of his death, and they traverse a variety of poetic forms.[1] *Ovid's Elegies*, which scholars date to Marlowe's years at Cambridge, around 1585, is a historic translation of the *Amores*, the very first into any European vernacular, and the inaugural volume of 48 elegies in Ovid's Roman literary career.[2] 'The Passionate Shepherd to His Love', which scholars date around 1587–8, is a pastoral lyric indebted to the classical and Renaissance genre of the invitation poem, with primary roots in Theocritus, Virgil, Ovid, and Spenser. *Hero and Leander*, which most scholars date to 1592–3, when the theatres close due to plague, is an Ovidian epyllion or minor epic written in English, tracing to the fifth century AD Greek poet Musaeus and to Ovid's elegiac poem the *Heroides*, epistles 18 and 19. Finally, in a category apart, a little-known 11-line Latin epitaph on Sir Roger Manwood, preserved only in manuscript, postdates the Elizabethan jurist's death on 14 December 1592, and likely traces to the months before Marlowe's own death on 30 May 1593. As diverse as these scattered rhymes are, they cohere in their Ovidian character, and they allow us in this chapter to explore the ways Marlowe's Ovidian poems complement – and interpenetrate – his Lucanian translation of the *Pharsalia*.

As we shall see, *Ovid's Elegies*, 'The Passionate Shepherd', and *Hero and Leander* all rely on the politics of Marlowe's Ovidian poetics to critique the monarchy of Queen Elizabeth I, and do so by relying on a republican ethos.[3]

Analysis of these *poetic* works helps revise the twentieth-century classification of 'Marlowe, Christopher, The Dramatist' (British Library catalogue heading), to view this pioneering author as Renaissance England's first major poet-playwright.

Rarely do critics view Marlowe's poems as a body of work in its own right, and when they do they tend to emphasize the poems' classicism, or their radical eroticism, or both.[4] Yet, as Heather James recently demonstrates, during the English Renaissance the Ovid on whom Marlowe's classical eroticism depends was also deeply politicized.[5] Attending to a single Marlovian genre, James concludes that 'Ovidian elegy approaches its political commitments' not directly but as 'a *mode of engagement*: it takes up the expressive liberties of classical republicanism, which had been compromised if not wholly lost for the purposes of open political debate, and finds room for them in "the pastoral fields of Ovidian lyricism", in Harry Levin's delicious phrase' ('Erotic Elegy' 126; qting. H. Levin, *Overreacher* 32; her emphasis).

Yet during the English Renaissance it was also common to link Ovid with Lucan as dissident writers, and to see both as celebrating free speech.[6] As Stephen Gosson puts it in his 1579 *School of Abuse*, 'Augustus...banished Ovid: And Nero...charged Lucan, to put up his pipes, to stay his penne, and write no more' (qtd. James, 'Erotic Elegy' 116). In the words of Thomas Lodge, published the same year in his *Defence of Poetry*: 'I like not of a wicked nero that wyll expel Lucan, yet admit I of a zealous gouernour that wil seke to take away the abuse of poetry. I like not of an angrye Augustus which wyll banishe Ouid for enuy. I loue a wise Senator, which in wisedome wyll correct him, and with aduise burne his follyes: vnhappy were we, yf like poore Scaurus we shoulde find Tiberius that wyll put us to death for a tragedy making; but most blessed were we, if we might find a judge that seuerely would amende the abuses of Tragedies' (76). Not simply was Ovid banished by Augustus, and Lucan charged to commit suicide by Nero, but both authors were poet-playwrights who combined an array of poetic genres, especially epic, with tragedy (see Introduction); and both used their corpus to combat the tyranny of the Roman empire. While classicists remain reticent in classifying Ovid as a republican author, they agree that his works join Lucan's poem in offering a profound attack on imperial power.[7] In Elizabethan England, Ovid's counter-monarchical poetics joins Lucan's republican-based poetics in supplying a rich storehouse of political disaffection.

Yet what especially makes Marlowe's Ovidian poems historic is not strictly their politics but their representation of what we might term their *freedom of poetic rapture*. As we shall see, freedom and its cognates are important terms in Marlowe's poems, and what brings freedom to the poet (sometimes to his subject) is his sublime entrance into the erotic state of rapture. The representation of liberating rapture becomes Marlowe's greatest poetic legacy – not (simply) the formal inventions of the blank verse line and the heroic couplet (Brown, 'Marlowe's Poems' 106–7).[8]

Not long after Ovid, Longinus *theorized* rapture and called it the *sublime*. In particular, Longinus singles out Sappho as the poet who exemplifies the sublime 'skill in selecting the outstanding details and making a unity of them', for the Greek poetess depicts 'the feelings involved in the madness of being in love' (10.1: 154), as revealed in her most famous lyric:

> To me he seems a peer of the gods, the man who sits
> facing you and hears your sweet voice
>   and lovely laughter; it flutters my heart in my breast. When
> I see you only for a moment, I cannot speak;
>   my tongue is broken, a subtle fire runs under my skin; my
> eyes cannot see, my ears hum;
>   cold sweat pours off me; shivering grips me all over; I am
> paler than grass; I seem near to dying;
> but all must be endured. ...
>   (Sappho; rpt. Longinus, *On Sublimity* 10.2, ed.
>   Russell and Winterbottom 154)

For Longinus, Sappho's lyric is sublime because it so exquisitely expresses her own 'feelings' amid her maddened state of eroticism, producing the artistic condition of transcendence. As Longinus wonders, 'Do you not admire the way in which she brings everything together – mind and body, hearing and tongue, eyes and skin? She seems to have lost them all, and to be looking for them, as though they were external to her. She is cold and hot, mad and sane, frightened and near death, all by turns. The result is that we see in her not a single emotion, but a complex of emotions' (10.3: 154). Later, Longinus reports that 'emotion is ... [an] essential ... part of sublimity' (29.2: 172), and he defines the sublime emotion as 'ecstasy ... wonder and astonishment' (1.4: 143).[9] However, as the center of Longinus' Sapphic Sublime, the emotional condition of rapture creates a 'risk', for it 'aim[s] at the heights', 'incur[ring] danger' (33.2: 175), and 'rang[ing] ... beyond the boundaries' (35.3: 178): 'sublimity raises us towards the spiritual greatness of god' (36.1: 178). Such sublime flight is worth the risk, however, since 'everyone is at liberty to enjoy what he takes pleasure in' (36.4: 179).[10]

It is Longinus' Sapphic version of the sublime that helps us theorize the heart of Marlowe's Ovidian poems, to discover a remarkable blueprint for Marlowe's Ovidian sublime: an intoxicating poetry that is high flying, rapturous, always dangerous, and committed to suffering, yet paradoxically liberating because it is godlike.[11] In *Ovid's Elegies* 2.18, which foregrounds what I elsewhere call the Ovidian *cursus* of elegy, tragedy, and epic (*MCP* 38–9), the poet refers to 'Sappho' – twice, and with reference to her historical identity as both poet and lover: first, as she who 'loved the Aonian harp'

(26); and then as she whose 'vowed harp lays at Phoebus' feet' (34). As Roma Gill explains the latter reference, the poet 'gives a partial table of contents of...the *Heroides*', in which Epistle 15 is 'addressed by the poet Sappho...to Phaon, the youth whose coldness caused her to commit suicide' (*Works*, ed. 1: 238). Not simply, therefore, can we say that Marlowe knew of Sappho as a poet willing to die for love, but we can trace his knowledge of the sublime Sappho to the very poet and poem that he himself translates.

Ovid's Elegies

Marlowe's translation of the *Amores* follows the Ovidian original in telling a captivating story about the young author who first tries to pursue a literary career in the high genres of epic and tragedy, but then is ambushed by the god of love elegy, Cupid, who capriciously causes the poet's infatuation with Corinna.[12] Five elegies foreground Ovid's attempt to open his literary career: those beginning the three books show him turning away from the imperial genres of epic and tragedy to write love elegy, while 2.18 puts all three genres into a single oscillating pattern, designed to counter the progressive Virgilian model of pastoral, georgic, and epic. Elegy 1.15, from which the epigraph to this chapter comes, presents the poet claiming the immortalizing power of fame over social and political envy, while Elegy 3.14 concludes the collection with the poet's announcement of his turn from elegy to tragedy. Other elegies, such as 3.8 on the death of the poet Tibullus, carry the conversation about authorship further, often with additional claims to poetic fame, as this from Elegy 1.10: 'In verse to praise kind wenches 'tis my part,/And whom I like eternize by mine art..../The fame that verse gives doth for ever last' (59–62). Such programmatic elegies are important because they deter us from viewing *Ovid's Elegies* as simply an erotic work.[13] The five elegies foregrounding the role of the poet identify *Ovid's Elegies* as a poem fundamentally about authorship, with *amor* its animating spirit.

For the most part, the other elegies exhibit Ovid shamefully caught in the throes of erotic desire, principally in relationship with Corinna, but sometimes her maid, and sometimes any girl at all. In Elegy 2.4, for instance, the poet presents himself as a real democrat when it comes to women: '*Quod amet muliers, cuinscunque formae sint*' (elegy heading: 'He loves every kind of woman'):

No one face likes me best, all faces move,
A hundred reasons make me ever love.
If any eye me with a modest look,
I burn, and by that blushful glance am took.
            (*Ovid's Elegies* 2.4.9–12)

Elegy 2.10 is more selective but depends on a witty republican ethos: 'For now I love two women equally' (4).[14]

Yet Ovid's democracy of desire focuses on a kingdom of one woman in particular, and recurrently he presents his erotic relationship with Corinna in terms of male dominance and female submission. The most famous elegy is 1.5, Corinna's noontime visit to Ovid's bedroom, which Marlowe translates with considerable zest:

> I snatched her gown; being thin, the harm was small,
> Yet strived she to be covered therewithal,
> And striving thus as one that would be cast,
> Betrayed herself, and yielded at the last.
> ...
> I clinged her naked body, down she fell.
> Judge you the rest: being tired she bade me kiss;
> Jove send me more such afternoons as this.
> (*Ovid's Elegies* 1.5.13–16, 24–6)

The poet gets rough with Corinna, and in the collection's opening two poems he explains why: he is himself subject to a 'tyrant' (1.8.70). In the fiction, the tyrant turns out to be a boy, Cupid, who in the first elegy uses his 'power' to 'change' Ovid's verse 'line' from the epic dactylic hexameter to the elegiac distich (1.1.9) in order to enlarge his 'kingdom' (1.1.17). Then, in the second elegy Cupid enslaves the poet as a histrionic victim in a formal Roman 'triumph', forcing him to march 'captive-like', 'manacled and bound', in 'worship' of 'a king' (1.2.28–33).[15]

Yet to conclude this particular 'show' (1.2.39), Ovid slyly introduces the prospect of a second (and interrelated) tyrant:

> Forbear to hurt thyself in spoiling me.
> Behold thy kinsman's Caesar's conquering bands,
> Who guards the conquered with his conquering hands.
> (*Ovid's Elegies* 1.2.50–2)

The poet warns Cupid not to hurt him because the god's own 'kinsman', Augustus Caesar (descended from Aeneas, Cupid's step-brother), stands by as the poet's 'guard'. Ostensibly, the poet praises the emperor, for both his divine genealogy and his loving protection of a subject. But simultaneously he employs the overpowering polyptoton of 'conquering ... conquered ... conquering' to emphasize Caesar's imperial subjection of Rome's great elegiac author.

This particular representation of politicized eros forms part of a larger strategy in the collection as a whole. On the surface, the poet presents himself simply as a sexy young man about town, yet he situates his erotic acts and free expressions within Rome's imperial culture. In the background, on the other hand, is the Roman institution of slavery, which runs like an undercurrent through *Ovid's Elegies*: 'A free-born wench no right 'tis up to lock,/So use we women of strange nations' stock' (3.4.33–4). In Elegy 1.8, when Ovid overhears Corinna being instructed by the witch Dipsas in how to deceive men, he confronts her with: 'The vain name of inferior slaves despise' (64). In Elegy 1.15, Marlowe translates Ovid's 'servus' as 'bondmen' (17), unlike Ben Jonson, who translates the word as 'slaves'.[16] In Elegies 2.7 and 2.8, we meet Corinna's slave-girl Cypassis, and in the latter poem the poet threatens to blackmail the maid if she does not sleep with him. The key to Corinna's bedroom also lies in the hand of a slave, called by Ovid 'Ianitor', and translated by Marlowe as 'porter' (1.6.1), while later the poet addresses two elegies to the eunuch Bagous (2.2, 2.3). In the first, the poet admonishes the slave to free Corinna from his watch, in return for his freedom: 'Stol'n liberty she may by thee obtain,/Which giving her, she may give thee again' (2.2.15–16). The verse remains witty, urbane, and sexy, but the poet presents himself as an author operating within a Roman political dynamic, in which wives are bound to their husbands, and slaves to their masters: 'Do this and soon thou shalt thy freedom reap' (40).[17]

At least three additional elegies depict the poet in relationship with the emperor himself. In one of the most risky utterances, he makes more explicit Augustus' erotic origin:

> Had Venus spoiled her belly's Trojan fruit,
> The earth of Caesars had been destitute.
> (*Ovid's Elegies* 2.14.17–18)

A similar, though more incidental moment appears in Elegy 3.7, when the poet objects to a rival for Corinna's love, offsetting Roman culture's penchant for building 'temples brave' to 'Bacchus, Alcides, and now Caesar' (51–2) with his own authoritative craftsmanship and identity: 'I, the pure priest of Phoebus and the Muses' (23). Then, in Elegy 3.11 the poet makes his final direct reference to Augustus:

> 'Tis doubtful whether verse avail or harm,
> Against my good they were an envious charm.
> When Thebes, when Troy, when Caesar should be writ,
> Alone Corinna moves my wanton wit.
> (*Ovid's Elegies* 3.11.13–16)

Referring back to Elegies 1.1 and 2.1, which have announced the poet's abandonment of epic, the imperial genre of the Caesars, here he boldly recenters his source of authority, from Augustus to Corinna.

Yet in Elegy 1.15 the most powerful anti-Caesarian moment does not mention the Emperor directly:

> Verse is immortal, and shall ne'er decay.
> To verse let kings give place, and kingly shows,
> And banks o'er which gold-bearing Tagus flows.
> (*Ovid's Elegies* 1.15.32–4)

This is not simply the conclusion to the poem's opening book but a rich and vigorous assertion of the poet's power over the empire of Augustus. The poet declares that he is more powerful than 'kings', for he alone commands immortality: his 'verse' is free of 'decay', lasting forever, unlike the emperor's political acts, which are mere 'show', and thus destined to disappear. Yet the Ovidian poet does not rest content with simple comparison; he boldly commands 'kings' to 'give place', just as the earthen banks of the gold-filled Tagus River should give place to poetry.

This last image expresses what Longinus means by the sublime. As we saw in Chapter 1, the sublime emerges in the pure flow of empowered water, as one of Longinus' quotations from Homer's *Iliad* about the sea god Poseidon reveals:

> The high hills and the forest trembled,
> and the peaks and the city of Troy and Achaean ships
> under the immortal feet of Poseidon as he went his way.
> He drove over the waves, the sea-monsters gamboled around him,
> coming up everywhere out of the deep; they recognized their king.
> The sea parted in joy; and the horses flew onward.
> (Homer, *Iliad*; rpt. Longinus, *On Sublimity* 9.8, ed. Russell and Winterbottom 151–2)

Here, Longinus says, the sublime 'represent[s] divinity as genuinely unsoiled and great and pure' (9.8: 151). Indeed, Longinus frequently locates the sublime in liquidity. At one point, he even uses the flow of water to describe the grand style of the Platonic sublime: 'Plato...combines the "soundless flow" of his smooth style with grandeur' (13.1: 157).

Just previously, in a textually mangled passage, we find a fragment about what Longinus calls 'the intense, Demosthenic kind of sublimity', which proceeds 'in indignant exaggeration, in violent emotion' (12.5: 157). The fragment begins with an image similar to the Ovidian poet's line about the gold-filled Tagus overflowing its banks: '... spreads out richly in many directions into an open sea of grandeur' (12.3: 157). That Longinus considers rivers a precise rhetorical figure for the sublime becomes even clearer later: 'It is a natural inclination that leads us to admire not the little streams, however pellucid and however useful, but the Nile, the Danube, the Rhine, and above all the Ocean' (35.4: 178).[18] In the Ovidian passage that serves as this chapter's epigraph, the poet distinctly politicizes the river trope, using it to figure the powerful way that the truth of the Ovidian poet's immortalizing verse surpasses a king's theatrical show.[19]

Accordingly, the poet ends his collection with an elegy that boldly presents the Ovidian author of amor with both a counter-Virgilian career and a counter-Augustan politics. Elegy 3.14 is important to Ovid's literary career because it concludes with his claim to poetic immortality right when he makes his turn from love elegy to tragedy:

> Horned Bacchus greater fury doth distil,
> A greater ground with great horse is to till.
> Weak Elegies, delightful Muse, farewell;
> A work that after my death here shall dwell.
> (*Ovid's Elegies* 3.14.17–20)

Ovid's Elegies is fundamentally about the young poet's successful inauguration of a counter-Virgilian career structured on the genres that Ovid in fact goes on to pen: elegy (e.g., *Ars amatoria*), tragedy (*Medea*), and epic (*Metamorphoses*).

Yet it is the opening to Elegy 3.14 that mentions Virgil directly, and in the process most powerfully veils the Ovidian poet's counter-Augustan politics:

> Tender Love's mother, a new poet get;
> This last end to my Elegies is set,
> Which I, Peligny's foster-child, have framed
> (Nor am I by such wanton toys defamed),
> Heir of an ancient house, if help that can,
> Not only by war's rage made gentleman.
> In Virgil Mantua joys, in Catull Verone,
> Of me Peligny's nation boasts alone,
> Whom liberty to honest arms compelled,
> When careful Rome in doubt their prowess held.
> (*Ovid's Elegies* 3.14.1–10)

In turning from Venus to Peligny, Ovid asserts his identity not as a Roman citizen but as a member of the Paelignian tribe. In lines 9–10, he refers to 'the war in 90 BCE between Rome and other Italian communities in which Paeligini distinguished themselves' (Cheney and Striar, eds. 135). In other words, here at the close of the collection Ovid detaches his birthright from the Augustan 'nation' – the history of Rome and its empire – and relocates nationhood in his own place of birth: he is 'Peligny's foster-child', the most famous citizen of 'Peligny's nation'. (And so he is.)

Moreover, the word 'liberty' in line 9 reveals that the poet relocates the central value of the Roman Republic, *libertas*, not in Rome, but in 'wat'ry Sulmo's walls' (11) – in the true civic fountain of poetic inspiration, not the seat of national government. Here at the end, in other words, we learn what has been at stake from the outset. Recurrently, *Ovid's Elegies* uses the words 'liberty' and 'freedom' and their cognates – two times and nine times, respectively, bringing the total to eleven. Sometimes, freedom seems purely incidental, as in Ovid's complaint to Cupid in Elegy 2.9: 'Horse freed from service range abroad the woods' (22). Whether incidental or not, in the larger fiction, horses, eunuchs, maids, wives, and even male poets are subject to bondage; they cry out for freedom, promise it, or on occasion claim it: 'Now have I freed myself, and fled the chain', the poet says (3.10.3).

In the *Amores*, Marlowe may not have found what Ovid dares to say in the *Tristia*, once Augustus has relegated him to Tomis in the Black Sea, in antiquity's supreme moment of anti-monarchial dissidence: 'my mind is nevertheless my comrade and my joy; over this Caesar could have no right' (3.7.47–8: 'ingenio tamen ipse meo comitorque fruorque:/Caesar in hoc potuit iuris habere nihil'). Nonetheless, in the *Amores* Marlowe could have found a critical narrative about the Ovidian poet pursuing his literary career in opposition to the great poet of empire, flaunting his sexual escapades with his all-powerful mistress (and other girls like Cypassis), and periodically challenging the authority of the emperor himself. We might say, then, that Marlowe inaugurates his literary career by translating Elizabethan England's most infamous tabooed poem about the poet's rapturous claim to a liberating victory over 'kingly shows'.[20]

Within its original English context, one of the kingly shows involved the propaganda and pageantry of Elizabeth as the Virgin Queen.[21] Marlowe's text remains discreet, but a number of particular translations evoke his female monarch. Conspicuous among them are references to the mythological figure of Diana, who 'painted stands/All naked holding in her wave-moist hands' (1.14.33–4). Later, he calls her 'Coat-tucked Diana', whose 'legs' are 'painted' (3.2.31), or, alternatively, Cynthia, the moon goddess, who appears in an even more dangerous-sounding topical verse: 'The moon sleeps with Endymion every day' (1.13.43). At Elegy 2.12, Marlowe dares to insert the word 'queen' when referring to Helen of Troy as the cause of international warfare: 'Nor is my war's cause new; but for a queen/Europe and Asia in firm peace had been' (17–18: 'Nec belli est nova causa mei. nisi rapta fuisset/Tyndaris, Europae pax Asiaeque foret'). Not surprisingly, Marlowe takes full advantage of Ovid's alternate name for Queen Dido of Carthage, 'Elissae', which during the sixteenth century functions as an alternate name for Queen Elizabeth, especially in Spenser: 'Aeneas to Elisa answer gives' (*OE* 2.18.31).[22] In this context, one of Marlowe's most striking anachronisms is his use of the word 'nun', which recurs three times (1.10.50, 3.6.21, 3.12.27), the second of which reads, 'Pure rose she, like a nun to sacrifice'. Without question, Marlowe's portrait of Corinna, with her 'lusty thigh' (1.5.22), shameless adultery, and illegal abortion (2.13–14), wages a dissident campaign not simply against the Petrarchan beloved but also against the cult of the virgin queen.[23]

That Marlowe's poem threatened to succeed in this project becomes clear posthumously. For in 1599 the Bishops of the Church of England issued a ban against seditious works, including *Ovid's Elegies* and its companion in the early editions, Sir John Davies' *Epigrams*. Like Marlowe's translation, Davies' collection displays the poet as a man about town, as he, his friends, his rivals, and his beloveds operate freely within a Roman culture shot through with the imagery of Elizabethan England.[24] In this regard, *Ovid's Elegies*, like Ovid himself, suffered at the hands of empire, in part because his poem records a radical authorship in accord with republican values.

'The Passionate Shepherd to His Love'

Modern annotation on *Ovid's Elegies* rarely records an origin for the sublime discourse of 'The Passionate Shepherd' in Elegy 1.3:

> Come live with me, and be my love,
> And we will all the pleasures prove.
> ...
> If these delights thy mind may move,
> Then live with me, and be my love.
>   ('The Passionate Shepherd to His
>   Love' 1–2, 23–4)

> I love but one, and her I love change never,
> If men have faith, I'll live with thee for ever.
> The years that fatal destiny shall give
> I'll live with thee, and die, ere thou shalt grieve.[25]
>   (*Ovid's Elegies* 1.3.15–18)

In this elegy, Ovid tries to convince Corinna to come live with him and be his love. The verbal repetition pairs the two poems in the early or lyric phase of Marlowe's literary career, and it identifies a neglected 'Ovidian' origin to what I wish to identify as the root-text of Marlowe's republican sublime.[26] In particular, this proposed Ovidian source-text includes the conditional nature of the Marlovian invitation ('If men have faith'), but more importantly it supplies the centralizing telos of the passionate shepherd's philosophy: the eternal ('for ever').[27] At the same time, the Ovidian source-text anticipates the two companion poems to Marlowe's pastoral lyric published in *England's Helicon* (1600): Sir Walter Ralegh's 'The Nymph's Reply', with its reminder of eternity's binary opposite, 'Time' (5;

cf. Marlowe's 'fatal destiny'), and its tragic consequences, death and mourning (9–12; cf. Marlowe's 'die, ere thou shalt grieve'); and the anonymous 'Another of the Same Nature, Made Since', the first to introduce the concept of eternity explicitly:

> The seat for your disport shall be
> Over some river, in a tree,
> Where silver sands and pebbles sing
> Eternal ditties with the spring.
> ('Another of the Same Nature' 9–12;
>   rpt. Cheney and Striar, eds. 161).

Like the Ovidian source-text, both response-poems render fertile the eternizing seed hibernating in Marlowe's original.

To the Ovidian origin of 'The Passionate Shepherd' in *Ovid's Elegies*, we may add a potential Lucanian one. In Book 9 of the *Pharsalia*, Pompey's son Gnaeus learns of his father's assassination, and breaks into an excited complaint, inviting his generals, 'come with me', by relying on the rhetoric of promise prominent in Marlowe's lyric:

> Generals, come with me (nowhere in civil warfare
> has there been so great a prize) to bury the unburied shade,
> to sate Magnus with the blood of the eunuch tyrant.
> Shall I not engulf in sluggish Mareotis the rotting flesh of Pella,
> Alexander's body from its sanctuary uncovered?
> Shall not Amasis, torn out from the pyramid tombs,
> and the other kings go floating down the rushing Nile for me?
> Let all their tombs pay penalty for your unburied, Magnus.
> Isis, power in the eyes of the world, from her tomb I shall evict
> And Osiris clothed in linen I shall scatter through the crowd
> and I shall burn the head by placing gods beneath it. The land will pay
> this penalty to me: I shall leave the fields devoid of cultivators,
> nor will there be anyone to benefit from rising Nile; you will be sold lord
> of Egypt, father, when I have driven out the gods and peoples.
>   (Lucan, *Civil War* 9.150–64; trans. Braund)

In 'high astounding terms' reminiscent of Tamburlaine (*1 Tamb* Pr.5), Gnaeus deploys the hyperbole for which both Lucan and Marlowe are famous (Steane 257). In his state of 'rag[e]' and 'indignant love' (9.147), young Pompey calls on his generals to seek revenge against his father's assassins, imagining a victory that resounds with (exaggerated) triumph: he will 'engulf' the 'rotting flesh' of pharaohs like 'Alexander' in Lake Mareotis; he will tear out the corpse of the pharaoh Amasis from his 'pyramid tomb' and set it sailing down the Nile with 'other kings'; he will 'evict' the Egyptian goddess Isis from her 'tomb' and 'scatter' the sacred linen-clad body of Osiris 'through the crowd', burning Pompey's 'head by placing gods beneath it'; and he will massacre the 'cultivators' of the Egyptian 'fields' – indeed, 'anyone' benefiting from the 'rising Nile'. In the end, when he is done with Egypt, he will 'drive...out the gods and peoples'.

In this fantasy of a son's revenge for the death of a father, Marlowe may have found a new voice of sublimity that he would re-sound throughout England. The Lucanian sublime adds to the Ovidian origin a series of vectors: to amor, that of politics; to men and women living together in love, men joined together in battle-revenge; and to the prospect of erotic eternity, political oblivion. Lucan's passage is also notable for its attention to the land, the material, the ritualistic, as the son imagines a series of unsettling rifts to what a culture holds dear in order to console himself for loss. Yet what young Pompey finally voices is not the fulfillment of this fantasy but its utter impotence: 'He had spoken and was fiercely hurrying the fleet towards the waves;/ but Cato praised and curbed the young man's wrath' (165–6). Then, without ado, the scene cuts to Cornelia, Pompey's widow. Yet it may well be that in the youth's impotence Marlowe found the seed of his own artistic strength.

Lucanian revenge, militarism, and genocide seem a far cry from 'the pastoral fields of Ovidian lyricism', but Marlowe recurrently transposes the soft discourse of 'The Passionate Shepherd' to the harsh fields of battle, as we shall see when we turn to the plays in Chapters 3 and 4.[28] As Longinus allows us to discern, Marlowe's dramatic repetition of the sublime discourse of 'The Passionate Shepherd' allows the author to present his own voice in the anonymous medium of the theatre: 'Sometimes a writer, in the course of a narrative in the third person, makes a sudden change and speaks in the person of his character. This kind of thing is an outburst of emotion' (27.1: 170). By making the sublime outburst of emotion on the stage recognizable as the voice of Christopher Marlowe, the author does not merely overgo Longinus; he overgoes Lucan, who is notorious (where Virgil is not) for inserting his own voice into his epic (Hardie 106–7).

One reason we might take the Lucanian origin of the Marlovian sublime to heart is that subsequent imitators frequently situate 'The Passionate Shepherd' within a republican discourse of civil war, including during the English Civil War itself. In the 1611 *Alchemist*, Ben Jonson, called by T.S. Eliot 'the legitimate heir of Marlowe', presents the Marlovian sublime from 'The Passionate Shepherd' in political service to the republican state, when Doll Common questions Sir Epicure Mammon on his use of the philosopher's stone.[29] Deceived by Face and Subtle into thinking Doll the Fairy Queen, Mammon moves into the Marlovian sublime to persuade her to come and be his love:

> come forth
> And taste the air of palaces; eat, drink

> The toils of emp'rics, and their boasted practice –
> Tincture of pearl and coral, gold and amber;
> ...
> When the jewels
> Of twenty states adorn thee and the light
> Strikes out the stars, that, when thy name is mentioned,
> Queens may look pale, and, we but showing our love,
> Nero's Poppea may be lost in story!
> Thus will we have it.
> (Jonson, *The Alchemist* 4.1.134–46)

Perhaps it is Mammon's hapless monarchical reference to the mistress of Lucan's emperor, along with his use of such imperial terms as 'Queens', that cues Doll's (amusing) resistance:

> I could well consent, sir.
> But in a monarchy how will this be?
> The prince will soon take notice, and both seize
> You and your stone, it being a wealth unfit
> For any private subject.
> (Jonson, *The Alchemist* 4.1.146–50)

To which Mammon slyly replies, 'If he knew it' (151). When Doll persists in her (performed) fear that Mammon's philosophically sublime stone will prove intolerable in a 'monarchy' governed by a 'prince', Mammon agrees, but only to discover his escape route in the political formality of the republican sublime:

> 'Tis no idle fear!
> We'll therefore go with all, my girl, and live
> In a free state, where we will eat our mullets
> Soused in high-country wines, sup pheasants' eggs,
> And have our cockles boiled in silver shells,
> Our shrimps to swim again, as when they lived.
> (Jonson, *The Alchemist* 4.1.153–8)

According to Quentin Skinner, 'free state' was a technical term for a republican government: 'Within the classical republican tradition, the discussion of political liberty was generally embedded in an analysis of what it means to speak of living in a "free state"': 'Like a free person, a free state is one that is able to act according to its own will, in pursuit of its own chosen ends' ('Political Liberty' 301). Skinner adds that this definition derives from Livy, Sallust, and above all Cicero, but that Machiavelli is their 'greatest heir' and thus the bridge to James Harrington and John Milton during the English Civil War (300). Skinner also identifies 'two principal benefits' to the free state: 'civic greatness and wealth' and 'personal liberty', the latter of which he defines as meaning that 'each citizen remains free from any elements of constraint (especially those which arise from personal dependence and servitude) and in consequence remains free to pursue his own chosen ends' (301–2). The key to the free state is the individual who possess Cicero's '*virtus*' and Machiavelli's '*virtú*' or what 'English republicans translated as civic virtue or public-spiritedness' (303).

According to Harry Levin, Jonson viewed the late Elizabethan 'shift' from a 'popular monarchy ... fostering democratic notions' to 'more or less absolute pretensions' in terms of 'the historic contrast between the Roman Republic and the Roman Empire' ('Ben Jonson' 46). Sir Epicure Mammon's grand vision of sailing off with his beauteous Fairy Queen to the 'free state', to 'live' the glorious life of appetitive hedonism, explodes the republican ideals of '*virtú*' and 'liberty' that Skinner describes. As the royalist artist of King James I, Jonson dissents, turning the republican fantasy into a grand materialist deception.[30]

None of this is especially new, but what might be is Jonson's reading of the republican 'free state' into Marlowe's sublime discourse from 'The Passionate Shepherd'. From Jonson's vantage point, the Marlovian free state lends liberty to eating well and drinking deep – to the 'Epicurean' fantasy of sensual pleasure. The Marlovian republic is all appetite; yet it is not pure appetite. For Jonson politicizes what the Marlovian Mammon proposes. His partner in the proposal, the Fairy Queen Doll Common, is a splendid representation. Certainly a whore of the republic – 'your republic', she says (1.1.110) – Doll is also the republic as a whore, a stage-worthy figure for the central metaphor of English government, that of the house or body politic (Smith, *De Republica Anglorum* 1.11: 58–9). As Doll herself puts it, 'begun out of equality, .../All things in common' (134–5).[31]

Yet Mammon's lurid (self-deceived) republican vision has a further dimension. Not simply does Jonson showcase the sublime quality of Sir Epicure's Longinian discourse, but the poet-playwright makes the word 'sublime' one of Mammon's favorite terms. In a play titled *The Alchemist*, we should expect that the sublime refers to the chemical process of 'sublimation', meaning 'vaporization and distillation to purify a substance' (Kernan, ed., *Alchemist* 238). Indeed, this is what Subtle means when he tells the ungrateful Face, '[I have] Sublimed thee, exalted thee, and fixed thee/I'the third region, called our state of grace' (1.1.68–9). Later, Mammon will tell his companion Pertinax Surly about the alchemist's art of gold: 'dragon's teeth' serve as 'mercury sublimate', and other materials become 'sublimed so often till they are fixed' (2.1.96–100). Yet in imagining his sublime 'dream' of 'turn[ing] the age to gold' (1.4.29), Mammon repeatedly moves into the Marlovian register, often betraying his royal lust:

> For I do mean
> To have a list of wives and concubines
> Equal with Solomon, who had the stone
> Alike with me, and I will make me a back
> With the elixir that shall be as tough
> As Hercules, to encounter fifty a night.
> ...
> ...Where I spy
> A wealthy citizen or rich lawyer
> Have a sublimed pure wife, unto that fellow
> I'll send a thousand pound to be my cuckold.
> (Jonson, *The Alchemist* 2.2.34–56)

Later, Mammon comes close to imitating Longinus in seeing the sublime as a form of poetic (even Ovidian) discourse, when he auto-erotically addresses himself: 'Now, Epicure,/Heighten thyself. Talk to her all in gold/Rain her as many showers as Jove did drops/Unto his Danaë' (4.1.24–7). Since in this play alchemical sublimation turns out to be a cheat, Jonson identifies the true sublime as theatrical language itself. And indeed, Sir Epicure is one of this author's greatest inventions. 'I have cast mine eye/Upon thy form', Mammon tells Doll, 'and I will rear this beauty/Above all styles' (4.1.116–18).[32] In sum, Jonson goes on record as being perhaps our first sustained reader of Marlowe's republican authorship, with its liberating discourse of the sublime.[33]

During the English Civil War, both royalist and republican poets imitate 'The Passionate Shepherd'. In the royalist camp, Robert Herrick offers one of the most famous of all imitations. In 'To Phillis to love, and live with him', the cavalier poet divests the Marlovian sublime of politics, but, writes Ann Baynes Coiro, within the carefully constructed 1648 *Hesperides* volume the *carpe diem* poems offset 'the late poems on the civil war', and thus advertise the idea that the 'island paradise [of the volume title] exists in time' (9):

> Live, live with me, and thou shalt see
> The pleasures I'll prepare for thee:
> What sweets the Country can afford
> Shall bless thy bed, and bless thy board.
>   (Herrick, 'To Phillis to love, and live
>   with him' 1–4)

The capitalized word 'Country' nominally means *countryside*, but it retains a vestige of nationhood, a meaning that emerges more clearly halfway through the poem, when the poet promises Phillis that she shall be 'The

Queen of Roses for that year' (32). The May Day festivities here and elsewhere, Leah Marcus shows, put into play 'the politics of mirth', in which 'festival "liberty"' works through 'both normative and revisionary impulses' to 'undermine and reinforce' the monarchical status quo: 'More often than we have recognized, the appeal to "public mirth" in the Stuart period was an appeal to royal authority' (*Politics of Mirth* 7–8). In her chapter on Herrick, titled 'Churchman among the Maypoles', Marcus emphasizes what she calls this poet's '"economics of festival" by which traditional customs do not merely "keep up" institutions in a political sense but also insure basic subsistence and well-being' (143): 'a magical practice is revived, assimilated to the economics of festival, and surrounded with a diffuse aura of religiosity' (148). At the end of the poem, Herrick slips in the key term, promising Phillis that he will 'make' for herself 'free mirth' (49) – a phrase that appropriates political liberty for the sanctified purpose of pastoral pleasure.[34]

In the republican camp, J. Paulin turns the 'free mirth' of 'The Passionate Shepherd' to the formal cause of the English republic. In an undated manuscript collection of miscellaneous poems, dating to the 1640s (MS Harvey 6918, folio 92; Orgel, ed. 260), Paulin's 32-line 'Love's Contentment' embeds the Marlovian discourse of erotic invitation within the turmoil of the Civil War: 'We fear no enemy's invasion' (21). Paulin's most significant change to the Marlovian original is to equate the 'state' of the two lovers' erotic relationship (4) with the freedom of the republican state:

> Come, my Clarinda, we'll consume
> Our joys no more at this low rate;
> More glorious titles let's assume
> And love according to our state.
> ...
> For if Contentment wears a crown
> Which never tyrant could assail,
> How many monarchs put we down
> In our Utopian commonweal?
> (Paulin, 'Love's Contentment'; rpt.
>   Cheney and Striar, eds. 165)

The poet imagines the lovers as opponents to a tyrannical monarch able to form their own commonwealth, a free 'state' devoid of imperial bondage, even deploying Sir Epicure Mammon's Ovidian metaphor:

> As princes rain down golden showers
> On those in whom they take delight,
> So in this happier court of ours,
> Each is the other's favourite.
> (Paulin, 'Love's Contentment'; rpt.
>   Cheney and Striar, eds. 165)

Accordingly, Paulin removes two cardinal virtues of republicanism, counsel and rhetorical persuasion, to the erotic sphere:

> We fear no enemy's invasion,
> Our counsel's wise and politic;
> With timely force, if not persuasion,
> We cool the homebred schismatic.
> (Paulin, 'Love's Contentment'; rpt.
> Cheney and Striar, eds. 166)

Stephen Orgel glosses 'homebred schismatic' this way: 'In Caroline England on the verge of civil war, this had a variety of applications, ranging from political schismatics who refused Charles his ship money to Scottish Presbyterians who resisted the imposition of the new prayer book. Since Charles' "timely force" was, on the whole, singularly ineffective, the following two lines have an ironic force that it is difficult to believe was unintentional' (ed. 261). Paulin then concludes the poem by giving his sublime republican voice a Shakespearean inflection:

> That when, our souls together fled,
> One urn shall our mixed dust enshrine,
> In golden letters may be read,
> Here lie Content's late King and Queen.[35]
> (Paulin, 'Love's Contentment'; rpt.
> Cheney and Striar, eds. 166)

Since Paulin joins Jonson in re-voicing 'The Passionate Shepherd' in terms of the republican 'free state', both poets appear to have found republican meaning in Marlowe's original poem. Unlike Paulin or Jonson, however, Marlowe himself is reticent in using overt political terms, but he does people his pastoral landscape with the common sort: 'The shepherd swains shall dance and sing,/For thy delight each May-morning' (21–2). Yet the passionate shepherd's promise of gifts to his beloved invites us to recall the social and political environment within which shepherds live: the world Paulin calls 'the court' (11) and thus the government of Queen Elizabeth. Like Paulin, Marlowe does not imagine a pastoral world devoid of 'kings and queens' but rather one in which the material wealth of 'monarchs' ends up in the hands of the common man (and woman).

Without question, however, the most important appropriation of 'The Passionate Shepherd' during the Civil War era comes where we might expect it: from Milton. For instance, *L'Allegro* and *Il Penseroso* each concludes with a couplet that re-writes the famed opening and ending to Marlowe's lovely pastoral lyric:

> These delights if thou canst give,
> Mirth, with thee I mean to live.
> (Milton, *L'Allegro* 151–2)

> These pleasures Melancholy give,
> And I with thee will choose to live.
> (Milton, *Il Penseroso* 175–6)

Even though critics have long recognized Milton's Marlovian borrowings, commentary remains sparse and rudimentary. For instance, in his widely-used edition of Milton's works, Merritt Y. Hughes supplies no Marlowe gloss at all.[36] Yet Milton's structural reliance on Marlovian lyric in these early poems alerts us to something important: early in his poetic career, Milton appears to have been attracted to the Marlovian sublime.[37]

Milton's engagement with Marlowe in *L'Allegro* begins formally in line 33, in the address to Mirth:

> Come, and trip it as ye go
> On the light fantastic toe,
> And in thy right hand lead with thee,
> The Mountain Nymph, sweet Liberty;
> And if I give thee honor due,
> Mirth, admit me of thy crew
> To live with her, and live with thee,
> In unreproved pleasures free.[38]
> (Milton, *L'Allegro* 33–40)

In this inventive intertextual narrative of English authorship, Milton directs Lady Mirth to join her right hand to 'sweet Liberty', imagined not as an urban dweller in the civic state but as simply 'The Mountain Nymph'. Moreover, Milton exquisitely deploys the Marlovian conditional from 'The Passionate Shepherd': if Milton honors Mirth and she admits him to their woodland dance, then he will 'live' with both figures in 'unreproved pleasures free'. Unmistakably, Milton's diction and syntax render Marlowe's sublime fantasy. Yet the thought that emerges differs radically.

Whereas Marlowe writes an erotic seduction poem, in which the shepherd woos the pastoral nymph for the purpose of sexual union, Milton produces a displaced version about poetic consciousness itself: a poet communes with the feminine spirits of his imaginative world. The allegorical figure of 'Mirth' replaces Marlowe's golden girl in a rhetorical set-piece designed to advertise the inner poetic authority of the young author. Most importantly here, Milton assigns to the Marlovian sublime the key terms 'Liberty' and 'free', indicating perhaps his own reading of Marlowe and his pastoral lyric. Critics might disagree about whether Milton's reading identifies the young Elizabethan radical as a figure of republican liberty.[39] Yet it is striking that in a poem referring formally to Marlowe's two most potent heirs – 'Jonson' with his 'learned Sock' and 'sweetest Shakespeare, fancy's child' (132–3) – the young Milton should erase the name of the free-spirited author who frames his poetic conversation.[40]

Altogether, the companion poems display Milton's knowledge especially of Marlowe's pastoral lyric and his Ovidian epyllion. *L'Allegro* and *Il Penseroso* derive their sublime fantasy of authorial freedom in part from Marlowe's lyric and narrative poetry. Indeed, the companion poems invaluably show the young Milton already aware of Marlowe as a sublime figure of artistic freedom, and they display an innate attraction to him – a topic we shall see come to fruition in *Paradise Lost* (Afterword).

In stanza 1 of 'The Passionate Shepherd', Marlowe's shepherd offers 'all the pleasures' of the natural world, but his geography includes the landscape of the sublime: 'valleys, groves, hills, and fields,/Woods, or steepy mountain' (1–4).[41] In stanza 2, Marlowe specifies the pleasures of the pastoral world through tropes of sublime inspiration: 'shepherds' feed their 'flocks' by 'shallow rivers', and 'melodious birds' sing 'madrigals' to the tumble of waterfalls (5–8). Stanza 3 then marks a shift from the gifts of nature to those of art – in particular, erotic attire 'made' by the shepherd for his beloved: 'beds of roses', sweet-smelling 'posies', a floral 'cap', and a 'kirtle' (9–11). Finally, stanzas 4 and 5 continue the inventory of the shepherd-made gifts: gown, slippers, belt – all costly, all erotic, all sublime.

Anticipating Herrick, Marlowe works within the 'politics of mirth' from the May Day tradition.[42] Through his pastoral voice, Marlowe catches the springtime splendor of youth withdrawing into the physical, the material, the concrete – so sublime that the poet frees himself, and his audience, from the danger of time, allowing them magically to disappear into the ecstasy of the eternal present. In 'The Passionate Shepherd to His Love', the Ovidian author invents a new sublime discourse of freedom that originates in a Lucanian longing for republican rapture. Marlowe's lovely pastoral lyric formulates a republican principle of authorship in the technical sense that what it liberates is not just anyone's politics but rather everyone's pen. In 'The Passionate Shepherd', sublime liberation succeeds by virtue of the many authors who became inspired to come live with Marlowe and be his love, from Mammon to Milton.

Hero and Leander

Unlike most of Marlowe's plays, his great Ovidian epyllion does not directly re-voice the discourse from 'The Passionate Shepherd'. Nonetheless, it continues the authorial project of freedom and rapture that we have traced in the pastoral lyric and in *Ovid's Elegies*. While critics continue to view the epyllion through the lens of Elizabethan Ovidianism, we might wish to take the cue provided by the Stationers' Register, which just a few months after Marlowe's death places *Hero and Leander* back to back with *Lucan's First Book*. By taking this cue, we may adjust criticism in two ways (both of which complement recent Ovidian scholarship).[43] First, we may come to view *Hero and Leander* as joining *Lucan's First Book* in forming an epic or proto-epic phase of Marlowe's career, extending his work from lyric and tragedy.[44] Second, more important here, we may become attuned to the Lucanism written into Marlowe's Ovidian epyllion. By adjusting criticism in both ways, we may see *Hero and Leander* as an integral part of Marlowe's republican authorship.

In the *Pharsalia*, Lucan represents the landscape of Hero and Leander no fewer than four times. In the first, toward the end of Book 2, Caesar traps the republican hero Pompey at Brundisium by 'barricad[ing]…/the waves and wide ocean with barriers and with rocks hurled down' (661–2), prompting Lucan to remember the bridge that Xerxes, king of Persia, built over the Hellespont in 486–65BC:

> Rumour sings that such were the roads constructed over water
> by the arrogant Persian when with his bridges bold
> he brought together Europe and Asia, Sestos and Abydos,
> and marched across the strait of rapid Hellespont.
> (Lucan, *Civil War* 2.672–5; trans. Braund)

In this self-reflexive passage about the fame of poetry, Lucan demarcates the political significance of Marlowe's erotic landscape: Sestos and Abydos are the ports of 'Europe and Asia', and the 'Hellespont' is the watery locale where east and west meet. Centuries later, George Chapman, in his 1616 translation of Musaeus' *Hero and Leander*, a source-text for Marlowe's poem (see Braden) and a follow-up to Chapman's continuation of Marlowe's poem, recalls the political significance of this landscape: 'Abydus and Sestus were two ancient towns; one in Europe, another in Asia; East and West, opposites' (Chapman, ed. Shepherd 2: 94).

Lucan's second reference to the Hellespont is more incidental, occurring near the opening of Book 4, when he pauses to mythologize the climate surrounding his action: 'warm…Titan brought back by the spring-time carrier/of fallen Helle, looking back towards the constellations' (56–7). According to Susan H. Braund, 'the Ram (Aries)…carried Helle and Phrixus on his back over the sea; Helle fell off and her name was given to the sea, the Hellespont (sea of Helle). Lucan means when the sun had entered Aries, in March' (ed. 258–9). Such mythologizing of the landscape complements Lucan's earlier politicizing of it.

In the third reference, near the opening of Book 6, Lucan depicts Caesar building a rampart to trap Pompey during the battle at Dyrrachium:

> Yet all that toil was wasted.
> All those hands could have joined Sestos to Abydos
> and ejected Phrixus' sea by heaping in the soil;
> or could have broken off Ephyra from the wide realms
> of Pelops, sparing ships long Malea's curve;
> or could have altered for the better any place on earth,
> though Nature said no.
> (Lucan, *Civil War* 6.54–60; trans. Braund)

Mixing myth with history, Lucan means that Caesar has employed enough troops at Dyrrachium to have done the impossible: in bridging the Hellespont, he has 'joined' Hero's city to Leander's, except that 'Nature said no', preventing the success of such an engineering feat. Marlowe may glance at this incident during the Neptune episode, when Leander swims the Hellespont to visit Hero:

> Where having spied her tower, long stared he on't,
> And prayed the narrow toiling Hellespont
> To part in twain, that he might come and go,
> But still the rising billows answered 'No'.
> (*Hero and Leander* 633–6 [2.149–52])

Marlowe's marine topography here is identical to Lucan's, and in both passages the natural world of the ocean says 'no' to human ambition and effort.[45]

Finally, toward the end of Book 9, Lucan mentions Hero and Leander themselves, and their introduction turns out to be pivotal to the narrative. For Caesar leaves 'the slaughter of Emathia' (950), site of the climactic defeat of Pompey at Pharsalus, and sails through the Hellespont on his way to 'burnt-out Troy' (964):

> Following his traces scattered uselessly
> on land, with rumour as his guide, he goes towards the waves
> and coasts along the Thracian straits, water swum
> in love, and Hero's towers on the melancholy shore
> where Helle, daughter of Nephele, conferred upon the sea its name.
> Nowhere does a smaller wave of water separate
> Asia from Europe.
> (Lucan, *Civil War* 9.952–8; trans. Braund)

Lucan probably knew epistles 18 and 19 of Ovid's *Heroides*, and thus he would have associated Hero and Leander with the voice of Ovidian complaint. If so, we can witness here not merely the meeting of Europe and Asia but of Ovid and Lucan, amor and empire. But this is not all, for Caesar's subsequent visit to Troy evokes the epics of both Virgil and Homer, creating a panoramic intertextual canvas of Greek and Roman authors. In particular, by presenting Caesar leaving Pharsalus and sailing through the Hellespont, 'scene of Hero and Leander's fatal love' (Burrow 181), Lucan identifies the anti-hero of empire as the impediment not just of the Roman Republic but of companionate love. Effectively, the *Pharsalia* Lucanizes Ovid, reading amor politically in terms of the universal combat between empire and republic, ambition and freedom.[46]

Within this Lucanian context, we may re-view the four-line prologue to Marlowe's *Hero and Leander*:

> On Hellespont, guilty of true love's blood,
> In view and opposite two cities stood,
> Sea-borderers, disjoined by Neptune's might:
> The one Abydos, the other Sestos hight.
>   (*Hero and Leander* 1–4)

Not simply does Marlowe's story of the two lovers form a career-diptych with Lucan's story of civil war between male warriors, but both minor epics take place in the same tragic locale. In both poems, the Hellespont becomes the landscape of tragic epic conflict, military and sexual, civic and erotic, public and private. The young lovers are doomed to tragic separation ('disjoined'), but so are their 'two cities' ('opposite').

Hero and Leander intersects with the *Pharsalia* in other ways. For instance, Marlowe's much-discussed architectural description of Venus' Church (135–57) finds its blueprint in Lucan's description of Cleopatra's palace in Book 10:

> The place itself was equal to a temple which an age
> more corrupt would hardly build; the paneled ceilings
> showed her riches, thick gold concealed the beams.
> The house shone, not encrusted with veneers of marble
> on the surface; in its own right, not useless, stood the agate
> and the purple stone; in all the palace onyx
> in abundance was trodden on; ebony of Meroë does not veil
> the door-posts huge but stands in place of ordinary timber,
> the support, not the adornment, of the house. The halls are clothed
> by ivory, and Indian tortoise-shells, stained by hand,
> are inlaid in the doors, their spots embellished with abundant emeralds.
> Jewels glitter on the couches and the furnishings are tawny with jasper.
>   (Lucan, *Civil War* 10.111–22; trans. Braund)

The description carries on for another 20 lines, while detail about the occupants' 'luxury, made mad by empty ostentation' (156–7) continues for another 30. In the passage quoted above, Lucan compares the secular lovehouse of this Egyptian Venus to a 'temple', as does Marlowe (133). Both erotic architectures are splendidly built, and share two precious stones: Lucan's 'jasper' and 'agate' show up in Marlowe's description: 'The walls were of discoloured jasper stone,/Wherein was Proteus carved, and o'erhead/A lively vine of green sea agate spread' (136–8). Moreover, both sites of erotic indulgence are paved with stone: Cleopatra's with onyx; Venus' with jasper.[47] Both houses have multiple floors, and both specialize in the fruit of Bacchus: in Marlowe, 'by one hand, light-headed Bacchus hung,/And with the other, wine from grapes outwrung' (139–40); in Lucan, 'huge jeweled cups/received the wine, but not of Mareotic grape,/but noble, fierce Falernian which Meroë/had aged in not many years, compelling it to foam' (160–3).

The central occupant of the royal Egyptian palace may even have supplied a model for the ornate opening description of Hero (5–36), with her 'Buskins of shells all silvered .../And branched with blushing coral to the knee,/Where sparrows perched, of hollow pearl and gold' (31-3):

> on her neck and in her hair
> Cleopatra wears a fortune and she strains beneath her finery.
> Her white breasts shine through the Sidonian thread
> which, tightly made by Seres' comb, the Nile's needle
> loosens, opening up the strands by stretching out the cloth.
> (Lucan, *Civil War* 10.139–43; trans. Braund)

For a poet celebrated for homosocial militarism, few poets in the West – perhaps not even Ovid himself – can compete with Lucan when it comes to photography of the feminine. A case in point is that deft single-line description of Cleopatra, when she slyly greets Caesar in a see-through gown, breasts gleaming with (Marlovian) invitation.[48]

Lucan's stirring depiction of Caesar's inflamed desire for Cleopatra – 'O what madness, blind/and frantic with ostentation – to reveal one's treasures/to a man waging civil war, to inflame the mind/of a guest bearing weapons' (146–9) – reminds us that Lucan follows Ovid in portraying companionate marriage memorably.[49] In the *Pharsalia*, Lucan presents marriage as a republican experience. For instance, while Cato's marriage to Marcia offers a model of austere service to the state (e.g., 2.326–91), and Pompey's earlier marriage to Julia (daughter of Caesar) presents a haunting model of political alliance (*LFB* 111–17; *Ph* 3.8–350), the marriage of Pompey and Cornelia gives the poem its most enduring portrait of the tragedy of companionate marriage.

In Book 5, Lucan's representation of Pompey in bed with Cornelia is among the most endearing moments of the poem. Here the poet who is renowned for the macabre violence of desert snakes (Book 9) discovers quiet calm in the marriage bed, where husband and wife are literally wrapped up in each other: 'Wife, dearer to me than life', the doomed Republican great tells his partner for life (739: 'Non nunc vita mihi dulcior,...coniunx'). Lucan even pauses to record a marital cause to the great man's doom: 'Love made even you, Magnus, hesitant/and afraid of battle; the only thing you wished not to expose/to the blow of Fortune which was waiting for the world and Roman destiny/was your wife' (728–31). True to her husband's republican politics, Cornelia articulates a principle of equality in marriage that out-Ovids Ovid: 'Do you believe my safety is different/from yours? Have we not long depended on one and the same chance?' (768–9).

In Book 8, Lucan presents Cornelia as the icon of the great republican woman, beloved by the people of Lesbos, who offer her sanctuary from the tyranny of Caesar: 'with such deep love her purity had bound/some to her, her goodness others and the modesty of her virtuous face,/because in spirit she was humble' (155–7). And in a remarkable anticipation of Milton's Adam in *Paradise Lost*, who chooses Eve over God to pay the tragic price, Pompey chooses Cornelia over Rome: 'My companion and the pledge that I deposited/I have regained; before, I was certain which shores I desired;/now Fortune will provide a harbour' (190–2: 'Comitem pignusque recepi/ Depositum; tum certus erasm, quae liora vellem,/Nunc portum fortuna dabit'). Accordingly, after her husband's death, the republican wife fulfills her vow to convey orders to their eldest son, Sextus, so as to continue civil war against Caesar's empire (84–116). No wonder Marlowe's roommate, Thomas Kyd, translated Robert Garnier's *Cornélie*!

When viewed within this Lucanian context, Marlowe's young lovers are notable for creating an erotic republic, based on equality, and freed from the tyranny of the public sphere:

> He asked, she gave, and nothing was denied;
> Both to each other quickly were affied.
> Look how their hands, so were their hearts united,
> And what he did she willing requited.
> (Sweet are the kisses, the embracements sweet,
> When like desires and affections meet,
> For from the earth to heaven is Cupid raised,
> Where fancy is in equal balance peised.)
>   (*Hero and Leander* 509–16)

Marlowe's portrait of young love forms a stirring counterpart to Lucan's portrait of old love; with the old, the young share the tragic freedom of 'embracements sweet'.[50]

As we saw in Chapter 1, rhetoric is an essential value of republican thought. In *Hero and Leander*, Marlowe re-situates republican rhetoric from its public forum of government to a private conversation between equal citizens, as Leander delivers a long oration on the value of marriage over virginity to persuade Hero to love him (199–328): 'Virginity, albeit some highly prize it,/ Compared with marriage, had you tried them both,/Differs as much as wine and water doth' (262–4).

Yet embedded within the 'rhetoric' (338) of 'the bold sharp sophister' (197) is an inset Lucanian fantasy of the sublime, on the compelling topic of lost virginity:

> this fair gem, sweet in the loss alone,
> When you fleet hence, can be bequeathed to none.
> Or if it could, down from th' enameled sky
> All heaven would come to claim this legacy,
> And with intestine broils the world destroy,
> And quite confound nature's sweet harmony.
> (*Hero and Leander* 247–52)

Here, Ovid and Lucan meet, and destroy the Virgilian world between them. In this passage, Marlowe penetrates to the eternizing core of the male's fantasy about female virginity. The word 'sweet' at the center of the first line evokes the animating force of the Longinian sublime – feeling, emotion, the inward condition of pleasure, the mind sensing the body's bliss: to experience the high value of sweetness, the female must lose her virginity. Yet once she loses it, she finds herself trapped inside another paradox, for no longer can she bequeath the value she has just surrendered: she loses her 'legacy', her inheritance, her right to a future. But 'if' she could bottle such sweetness, the gods themselves would come to claim the legacy, making her immortal. Such exquisite transcendence produces a bang so big it destroys the cosmos.

In this inset fantasy, hinted at by the Lucanian image of 'intestine broils' (cf. 'civil broils' at *LFB* 14), Marlowe *Ovidianizes* Lucan, echoing the famed description of universal dissolution discussed in the last chapter: 'and full of strife/Dissolve the engines of the broken world./All great things crush themselves' (79–81). The passage in *Hero and Leander* constitutes a formal version of the sublime, in which, as Longinus says, the harmony of 'the whole universe' is 'overthrown and broken up' (9.6: 151).

Finally, both *Hero* and *Lucan* end with the same graphic image: a female sinks down under masculine oppression. As we have seen, Lucan's first book ends with a Bacchic Roman matron delivering a prophecy about the death of the republic: '"I have seen Philippi". This said, being tired with fury she sunk down' (693–4). Similarly, at the close of *Hero and Leander*, Marlowe presents Hesperus, the evening star, expelling 'ugly Night,/Till she, o'ercome with anguish, shame, and rage,/Danged down to hell her loathsome carriage' (816–18).

While Marlowe's 818-line Ovidian epyllion is most notable for its sublime portraiture of young love, it occasionally gestures to the wider world of politics: in Leander's 'brow' fit 'to banquet royally' (86); in the reference to 'great princes' (129); in the Mercury digression, where the country maid is 'proud', 'for lofty Pride that dwells/In towered courts is oft in shepherds' cells' (393–4) or here even in the etiology of poverty-stricken scholarship where 'few great lords in virtuous deeds...joy' (479); and later in reference to the imperial authority of Hero's virginity: 'Ne'er king more sought to keep his diadem,/Than Hero this inestimable gem' (561–2). Accordingly, critics read Hero as an Elizabeth figure (Berry 138), and specific evocations of the queen emerge: in the royalizing reference to the Endymion myth, where the Cynthian moon is 'crowned with blazing light and majesty' (110); in what looks like a topical reference to 'some [who] have wronged Diana's name' (284); in the rather dangerous reference to 'virginity' as the 'gentle queen of love's sole enemy' (317–8); and in the reference to 'chaste Diana when Actaeon spied her' (745). For, as critics emphasize, *Hero and Leander* mounts a stunning 'critique' of the queen's cult of virginity (Brown, *Redefining* 131). In the process, though, Marlowe's epyllion mounts a radical critique of monarchy. As an alternative to this form of government, the poem proffers two things simultaneously: a tragic depiction of free and equal sex that ends tragically in female shame and male voyeurism; and a rapturous experience of liberation for generations of readers.[51] As in 'The Passionate Shepherd' and *Ovid's Elegies*, in the political valence of *Hero and Leander* the young lovers momentarily occupy a space beyond monarchy, a 'free state' of sexual 'liberty' – Marlowe's most enduring contribution to English literature:

> So ran the people forth to gaze upon her,
> And all that viewed her were enamoured on her.
>   (*Hero and Leander* 117–8)

The republic of the primeval poet

Underlying Marlowe's Lucanian move of identifying the Ovidian author as the sublime leader of the commonwealth is the tradition of the 'primeval poet'. In 1981, Clarke Hulse called Marlowe a 'primeval poet', and identified *Hero and Leander* as the inaugural poem of an Elizabethan 'genre of primeval poetry'. This genre traces to Musaeus, who, for the Renaissance, formed part of a group of primeval poets, including Orpheus and Amphion. Marlowe, I suggest, might have been drawn to the primeval poets as a republican community because of the tradition that poets preceded monarchs in the evolution of civilization.

Countless classical writers refer to the myth, in one version or another, from Plato (*Protagoras* 322a–b) and Isocrates (*Nocodes or the Cyrians* 5.9) to Horace (*Ars poetica* 391–407) and Cicero (*De inventione* 1.2.2–1.2.3, 1.8.32–4), but Lucretius is most explicit in setting up the Renaissance version I shall emphasize:

> Already men lived fenced in with strong towers, and the earth was divided up and distributed for cultivation. Then the deep sea was blooming with sail-flying ships, men had already allies and friends under formal treaty, when poets began to commemorate doughty deeds in verse; nor had letters been invented long before. For this reason our age cannot look back upon what happened before, unless in any respect reasoning shows the way. Ships and agriculture, fortifications and laws, arms, roads, clothing and all else of this kind, all life's prizes, its luxuries also from first to last, poetry and pictures, artfully wrought polished statues, all these as men progressed gradually step by step were taught by practice and the experiments of the active mind. (*De rerum natura* 1. 440–55; trans. Rouse)

Here Lucretius imagines an early phase of civilization, when poets use their art to commemorate the 'doughty deeds' of 'allies and friends under formal treaty'. Renaissance versions appear in Elyot's *The Governor* (rpt. Gilbert, ed. 237), in Sir Philip Sidney's *Defence of Poetry* (rpt. Gilbert, ed. 410, 430, 441–2, 457), and William Webbe's *Of English Poetry* (rpt. Gilbert, ed. 232–4).

It is George Puttenham's 1589 *Arte of English Poesie*, however, that formulates the most lucid political model of poets as the predecessors of kings in a primeval commonwealth:

> The profession and use of Poesie is most ancient from the beginning, ... before, any civil society was among men. For it is written that Poesie was th'original cause and occasion of their first assemblies. ... Whereupon it is fayned that Amphion and Orpheus, two Poets of the first ages, one of them, to wit Amphion, built up cities. ... [T]hey were the first lawmakers to the people, and the first polititiens, devising all expedient meanes for th'establishment of Common wealth, to hold and containe the people in order and duety by force and vertue of good and wholesome lawes, made for the preservation of the publique peace and tranquillitie. (Puttenham, *Arte of English Poesie*, in Smith, ed. 2: 6–8)

Here Puttenham presents the primeval poets as the originary leaders of the republic or 'Common wealth', before the institution of kings and monarchies, as the myth of Amphion clarifies.

It is the free and rapturous sublimity of the primeval republican poet that Michael Drayton famously portrays in 1627:

> Marlow bathed in the Thespian springs,
> Had in him those brave translunary things,

> That the first Poets had, his raptures were,
> All Ayre, and fire, which made his verses cleere,
> For that fine madness still he did retaine,
> Which rightly should possess a Poets braine.
> (Drayton; rpt. MacLure, ed., *CH* 47)

Whether Marlowe knew Longinus or not, Drayton is only one contemporary who invents his own language for the sublime art that Swinburne will later make famous (see Chapter 1): *liquid, translunary, elemental, originary, rapture, clear*. Years before, George Chapman finds Marlowe in this same eternizing liquid; yet, when describing the process of authorship that allows the completion of *Hero and Leander*, Chapman attaches to the rapture of the Marlovian sublime the concept of republican freedom:

> now (as swift as Time
> Doth follow Motion) find th' eternal clime
> Of his free soul, whose living subject stood
> Up to the chin in the Pierian flood,
> And drunk to me half this Musaean story,
> Inscribing it to deathless memory.
> (Chapman, *Hero and Leander* 3.187–92)

3
'Defend His Freedom 'Gainst a Monarchy': Empire and Liberty in *Dido, Queen of Carthage* and *Tamburlaine, Parts One* and *Two*

In a recent essay titled 'Empire and Liberty: A Republican Dilemma', David Armitage reconstructs an early modern political paradox that we might bring to bear on the three plays about empire early in Marlowe's dramatic career: *Dido, Queen of Carthage* (1585–6) and *Tamburlaine, Parts One* and *Two* (1587–8). In this paradox, a republican government needs to balance its primary value, liberty, with the glory and greatness of imperial dominion. According to Armitage, Machiavelli becomes the early modern spokesman for this paradox, which derives from the Roman historian Sallust (30), and which then is inherited by 'British republicans' from the sixteenth through the eighteenth centuries (35–46), including Richard Beacon in 1594, James Harrington in 1656, Algernon Sidney in 1663–4, and David Hume in 1752:

> This Sallustian and Machiavellian tradition encouraged the belief that the greatness of the republic derived originally from its liberty. However, Sallust's continuation of his narrative showed that the consequences of pursuing such *grandezza* would lead inevitably to the loss of that liberty both for the republic and for its citizens. ... The virtuous and the courageous became greedy, ambitious and impious, the character of the republic was changed, and the government itself became cruel and intolerable.
> (Armitage, 'Empire and Liberty' 30–1)

In Armitage's continuation of the story, Machiavelli sees that '*Imperio* and *liberta* would, at last, be incompatible' (33). Yet the drive to solve 'Machiavelli's dilemma' (36) is precisely what organizes republican theory thereafter. An important solution emerges in Henry Bolinbroke's *The Idea of a Patriot King* (1738), which features 'a monarch committed above all to the public good, who would hence be that republican oxymoron, a patriot king' (42).

As Armitage goes on to reveal, from antiquity through to the early modern period and beyond, republican political thinkers carried on a vigorous conversation about the relationship between empire and freedom. They framed the question whether a nation could bridge the gap between two such seemingly incompatible concepts, and discovered a solution in the notion of a republican sovereign, a king who justly serves the interests of the people and the state, not simply his private desires.[1] In *Bellum Catiliniae*, Sallust locates the narrative of the dilemma in Lucius Sulla, who first turned the Roman Republic into a dictatorship (Handford, trans. 151), preparing the way for Julius Caesar to end the Republic once and for all: 'After Sulla had used armed force to make himself dictator, and after a good beginning turned out a bad ruler, there was universal robbery and pillage' (182). In his 'Preface', Sallust tells how originally in Rome the 'monarchy...had served to safeguard liberty', but that subsequently this 'constitutional government...degenerated into an oppressive despotism', leading to the birth of the Republic through the election of two consuls: 'It was in this period that individuals were first able to distinguish themselves and display their talents to greater advantage.... Indeed, it almost passes belief what rapid progress was made by the whole state when once it had gained its liberty' (179). Sadly, however, liberty led Rome 'in her quest for empire', which in turn bred the twin vices of 'Avarice' and 'Ambition': 'Rome changed: her government, once so just and admirable, became harsh and unendurable' (181–2).[2]

Machiavelli rehearses Sallust's narrative in his *Discourses* but goes beyond it, arguing that empire is necessary to the state wishing to pursue liberty, and recommending, in Armitage's formulation, that '*grandezza* was a greater good than [republican] stability' (32).[3] In arguably the central set-speech on republican liberty in the *Discourses*, Machiavelli defends Rome's original 'affection for a free way of life...because experience demonstrates that cities have never enlarged their dominion or increased their wealth unless they have lived in liberty. It...is...wondrous to consider how much greatness Rome achieved after it freed itself of its kings'. As Machiavelli goes on to suggest, 'The reason is easy to understand, because it is not the private good but the common good that makes cities great. And without any doubt, this common good is pursued only in a republic.... The opposite occurs when there is a prince' (2.2: 156–7). Like Sallust, however, Machiavelli traces the arc of Rome's fall back into despotism, locating two 'cause[s]' to the fall of 'the Roman republic' and its 'free way of life': 'one was the struggles that arose over the agrarian laws; the other was the prolongation of military commands' (3.24: 315). And like Sallust as well, Machiavelli locates the causes of the fall in the despotic individualism especially of Sulla and later of Julius Caesar (3.24: 316). In this way, the great early modern theorist of republican liberty became the era's most infamous theorist of empire: 'a city which lives in freedom has two goals, the first is to acquire territory, the other is to keep itself free' (1.29: 85; see 1.33: 99; 2.4: 163–7; 2.19: 206).[4]

As the mid-1590s example of Beacon illustrates, Elizabethans carried on this Machiavellian conversation well before the English Civil War (or the Enlightenment). According to Armitage, 'The Machiavellian typology of republics for expansion and those for stability first appeared as a tool to analyse English policy in 1594 when Richard Beacon, the disaffected former Queen's Attorney for the Irish county of Munster, published his Machiavellian "Politique Discourse" on the state of Ireland, *Solon his Follie*' (35). Beacon's major idea was that England should combine expansion with liberty (35–6). Although his treatise was published the year after Marlowe's death, it reveals nonetheless that during the early 1590s Elizabethans were intent, as Armitage puts it, to 'reconcil[e] ... liberty and empire' (36), and thus to imagine 'an empire for liberty' (43).[5]

While Armitage joins Quentin Skinner, Markku Peltonen, and others in telling the narrative of Roman 'Empire and Liberty' as central to the early modern English imagination, these historians do not recall that one poet in particular had framed an epic narrative precisely on this 'dilemma'. As we have seen, Lucan organizes the *Pharsalia* around the dynamic of 'Liberty and Caesar' (7.96). In translating Lucan's first book, Marlowe Englishes the Lucanian version of the Sallustian and Machiavellian narrative for Elizabethan culture – a kind of imaginative analogue to Beacon's treatise.

In this chapter, then, I propose to situate Marlowe's first three tragedies within the historical conversation about freedom and empire. By doing so, I argue broadly, we may come to terms with the political tension at the center of all three plays, and thus prepare ourselves to determine their specific contribution to the larger republican conversation. That contribution, we shall see, is at once historic and strange. Historic because *Dido* and the *Tamburlaine* plays are arguably Elizabethan England's first sustained theatrical representations of the republican dilemma between empire and freedom; strange because, rather than simply following Sallust, Machiavelli, Beacon, and the rest, to posit the ideal link between the two concepts and then to mourn their incompatibility, Marlowe invents a weird theatrical representation that does two things simultaneously. First, he constructs a plot that appears to savage the ideal form of the paradigm; and second, from this, he salvages what interests him to start with: not so much an ideal political state featuring the freedom of a patriot king, but a tragic literary authorship that locates freedom in poetic utterance itself – what we have called, with respect to the poems, the freedom of sublime rapture (Chapter 2). As in the poems, in the early plays we can discern this authorial project in the strange dramatic discourse yoking freedom and empire; in the presence of the most famous literary work structured on this collision, Lucan's *Pharsalia*; and finally, in Marlowe's supreme invention, the Lucanian discourse of the republican sublime, especially as derived from 'The Passionate Shepherd to His Love'.

As the phrase quoted in the title to this chapter intimates, the *Tamburlaine* plays script Marlowe's unusual republican authorship formally, relying on technical republican terms and concepts, to present the protagonist as a republican freedom-fighter who wants to be a king. *Dido*, however, represents an earlier, less technical phase, featuring a queen who simply wishes to be free from the tragic engine of empire: 'I am not free. O would I were' (3.4.5), she says wistfully, referring to her love for Aeneas, the Roman hero of empire.[6] Not simply, then, do *Dido* and the *Tamburlaine* plays represent different phases of Marlowe's republican authorship, but they represent different subject-positions within it. Dido emerges as Marlowe's icon of the female victim of empire, along with its corollary, lost liberty, while Tamburlaine becomes an icon of the violent success required to yoke liberty to empire.

Not surprisingly, then, the words 'freedom' and 'empire' recur throughout all three plays, and do so in greater abundance here than elsewhere in the Marlowe canon. While the word 'empire' and its cognates occur nine times in Marlowe's poems and plays, 'empery' 8 more, and 'imperial' 22, bringing the total to 39, a full 25 of these occur in *Dido* and the *Tamburlaine* plays.[7] Similarly, as we have seen in the Introduction, Marlowe uses the word 'liberty' and its cognates 16 times in his canon, and he uses cognates of 'freedom' an additional 46, bringing the total to 62, yet 22 occur in *Dido* and the *Tamburlaine* plays, while of these *1* and *2 Tamburlaine* register 19.

Since Stephen Greenblatt's groundbreaking 1980 chapter in *Renaissance Self-Fashioning*, 'Marlowe and the Will to Absolute Play', critics have viewed the political operation of Marlowe's plays within the context of European and English colonization and imperialism, to emphasize the plays' subversive power within Elizabethan culture.[8] More recently, Emily Bartels has devoted a full book to the topic of 'Imperialism, Alienation, and Marlowe' – the subtitle to her 1993 *Spectacles of Strangeness*. In particular, Bartels situates Marlowe's recurrent staging of an alien other against the backdrop of 'England's nascent imperialism' (3), arguing that 'Marlowe's plays, in bringing alien types to center stage, subversively resist that exploitation and expose the demonization of an other as a strategy for self-authorization and self-empowerment' (xv). Without saying so, Bartels intimates that the texts of Marlowe pluck liberty out of empire – for the benefit of the author perhaps, and sometimes for his characters, but primarily for the audience, who end up in a state of 'sympathy' (20). Thus, Bartels refers in passing to Marlowe's 'liberating agenda' (26). Without question, however, she emphasizes 'Marlovian drama's liminal position between the inside and the outside', which 'finally makes its subversive vision so disturbing, convincing, and compelling' (26). Like Armitage and the political theorists, however, Bartels never mentions Lucan, nor the sublime, and thus she neglects the light that *Lucan's First Book* might shed on Marlowe's sublime project. That shall be the general goal of this chapter, as we attend to what Bartels calls Marlowe's three '"imperialist" plays', all 'deal[ing] with non-European subjects and imperial domination' (23).

Dido, Queen of Carthage

Recent critics agree that Marlowe in his first tragedy puts the *Aeneid* on the London stage to 'critique' the 'imperialism' of Virgilian epic and Elizabethan colonialism and its narratives (Bartels 37, 29).[9] Critics also agree that Marlowe selects Ovid as the chief agent of the critique – principally Ovid in the *Heroides*. In Letters 7 and 8, Ovid counters the Virgilian story of Dido and Aeneas from Books 1–4 of the *Aeneid* by allowing the heroine who is silenced after her suicide (*Aeneid* 6.450–76) both a voice and a form of immortality (Bartels 34–44). Finally, critics agree that Marlowe fuses Ovidian amor to Senecan fatalism to critique the providentialist design of the *Aeneid* and of Elizabethan ideology, especially as popularized by Spenser through *The Shepheardes Calender* (1579) and *The Faerie Queene* (1590), a Virgilian pastoral and epic that cohere in their encomium to 'fayre Eliza, Queene of shepheardes all' (*Aprill* 34). That Marlowe re-voices Virgilian epic for the purpose of Elizabethan (and Spenserian) critique becomes especially clear in Act 4, scene 2, when the abject king of Gaetulia, Iarbas, delivers a pastoral complaint in a Spenserian register:

> Hear, hear, O hear Iarbas' plaining prayers,
> Whose hideous echoes make the welkin howl,
> And all the woods 'Eliza' to resound![10]
> (*Dido, Queen of Carthage* 4.2.8–10)

To the broad and intricate intertextuality of the play emphasized by critics, we need to add Lucan, to see how central this dissident Roman poet is to Marlowe's lyric poetics of the sublime from 'The Passionate Shepherd', and thus to discern a specific republican dynamic in his tragedy. Although Virgil, Ovid, Seneca, and Spenser are *Dido*'s most visible intertexts, Lucan warrants a place, and it is this author whom we shall emphasize here.

Yet not before acknowledging the difficulty this play presents. For, as with most Marlowe texts, with *Dido* we confront uncertainty about the date of composition, about authorship, about textual stability, and about original performance. For the most part, however, scholars believe that Marlowe first wrote *Dido* around 1585–6; that he served as the play's sole author, with Thomas Nashe (whose name appears in smaller print than Marlowe's on the title page to the first text extant, 1594) serving as editor; that Marlowe appears to have revised the original play in the early 1590s; and that he did so for the Children of Her Majesty's Chapel, with Elizabeth herself perhaps in attendance.[11] This performance history foregrounds a distinct monarchical frame for a play about a 'Queen', played by actors from 'Her Majesty's Chapel', in what Jackson Cope calls 'Marlowe's best piece of total theater' (63).

Dido is also unusual in Marlowe's dramatic career because it contains no direct reference to the anti-hero of Lucan's counter-Virgilian epic, Julius Caesar. Unlike Tamburlaine, Machevill in *The Jew of Malta*, the Guise in *The Massacre at Paris*, Gaveston in *Edward II*, or Mephistopheles in *Doctor Faustus*, no one ever speaks of 'Caesar riding in the Roman street' (*E2* 1.1.172) – perhaps simply to maintain historical verisimilitude. In fact, Dido is akin to Caesar's great opponent, Pompey, who in Lucan is the victim of Caesar's empire – in large part because he remains attached to his spouse (see Chapter 2).

Perhaps, then, Dido's resounding complaints of sorrow and misfortune owe in part to Cornelia's complaints in the *Pharsalia*:

> Hardly in her weakness could she bear a grief
> so great, and her senses left her stunned breast.
> At last her voice was able to express her mournful protests:
>   'No complaint is left to me about the gods, about the destiny
> of marriage, Magnus: our love is not broken by death
> or by the final torch of hideous pyre, but I lose my husband,
> divorced in a fate frequent and too common.
> ...
> Though I refuse to be a slave to hardships but with ready death
> follow you down to the shades'.
>   (Lucan, *Civil War* 5.759–74; trans. Braund)

As the originary poet of civil war, Lucan is not often remembered as a poet who sympathizes with oppressed women; in this, however, he is the most immediate heir to Ovid – a republican-longing heir.[12]

In the *Pharsalia*, Cornelia may be the chief figure of feminine complaint, but she is not the only one. We have seen the Bacchic Roman matron collapse in oppression at the end of Lucan's first book, but Pompey's first wife, Julia, the daughter of Caesar, also makes a cameo appearance in Marlowe's translation, at once menacing and poignant: 'for Julia,/Snatched hence by cruel fates with ominous howls,/Bare down to hell her son, the pledge of peace,/And all bands of that death-presaging alliance' (111–14).[13] Yet as a feminine victim of empire, few can compete with Phemonoe, the priestess of Apollo at Delphi, ravished by her beloved 'Paean':

>   at last Paean
> mastered her Cirrhaean breast and never more completely
> invaded his priestess' frame, drove out her former mind,

and told the mortal part to leave her breast to him
entirely. Mad, she runs wild through the cave with frenzied neck.
(Lucan, *Civil War* 5.165–9; trans. Braund)

Madness, sexual ravishment, the loss of feminine innocence and chastity: this is the hallmark of the Dido story, in Ovid and Virgil as in Marlowe, and it does not seem unreasonable to imagine Lucan's unsettling feminine tragedy haunting Marlowe's Carthaginian queen.

Nor does it seem unreasonable that Marlowe might have begun his translation of Lucan while still at Cambridge, and that he then worked on it later, especially in 1592–3, when the theatres closed due to plague. If so, Marlowe could have been working on *Dido* and *Lucan* at about the same time, first in Cambridge and later in London. Modern scholarship provides supporting evidence. In her edition of *Dido*, for instance, Roma Gill glosses Act 5, scene 1, lines 156–9 not only with *Aeneid* 4.365–7 but also with *Lucan's First Book* 327–30 (ed., *Works* 1: 289), in which Lucan indicts Pompey for licking warm blood from Sulla's cool sword:

A brood of barbarous tigers, having lapped
The blood of many a herd, whilst with their dams
They kenneled in Hircania, evermore
Will rage and prey.
(*Lucan's First Book* 327–30)

Similarly, Dido indicts Aeneas for his own betrayal:

Thy mother was no goddess, perjured man,
Nor Dardanus the author of thy stock;
But thou art sprung from Scythian Caucasus,
And tigers of Hyrcania gave thee suck.
Ah, foolish Dido, to forbear this long!
Wast thou not wracked upon this Libyan shore.
(*Dido, Queen of Carthage* 5.1.156–61)

Dido's reference to 'Scythian' looks forward to Tamburlaine, but *Lucan's First Book* also refers to these barbarians three times (19–20, 368–9, 441–2), the second of which Dido may echo: 'Well, lead us then to Syrtes' desert shore,/Or Scythia, or hot Libya's thirsty sands'. If correct, the echo forms a kind of imperial palimpsest, in which Marlowe writes the Virgilian landscape through with the landscape of Lucan, compelling us to read Malrowe's tragedy of Dido in terms of the fall of the Roman Republic.

L.C. Martin helps confirm this speculation when he finds Dido echoing Lucan as she reacts to Aeneas's departure from Carthage (ed. 287):

> Only Aeneas' frown
> Is that which terrifies poor Dido's heart.
> Not bloody spears, appearing in the air,
> Presage the downfall of my empery,
> Nor blazing comets threatens Dido's death:
> It is Aeneas' frown that ends my days.
> (*Dido, Queen of Carthage* 4.4.115–20)

As we have seen, during the most sublime part of his translation, Marlowe describes the cosmic reaction to Caesar's invasion of the Republic in terms of prodigious dissolution:

> Great store of strange and unknown stars were seen
> Wandering about the north, and rings of fire
> Fly in the air, and dreadful bearded stars,
> And comets that presage the fall of kingdoms;
> The flattering sky glittered in often flames,
> And sundry fiery meteors blazed in heaven,
> Now spear-like.
> (*Lucan's First Book* 524–30)

Dido recalls Lucan's 'speak-like' meteors presaging the 'downfall' of her 'empery', even though she sidesteps his astral determinism to emphasize Ovidian erotic subjectivity.[14]

Marlowe's discourse of liberty also firms up the presence of Lucan in *Dido*. The queen's longing to be 'free' noted earlier emerges during the famous storm scene (3.4), when Dido inquires how Aeneas has found her secret cave: 'By chance, sweet Queen, as Mars and Venus met' (3). It is this reference to Vulcan's netting of his adulterous wife and lover that prompts Dido's discourse of freedom:

> Why, that was in a net, where we are loose;
> And yet I am not free. O would I were.
> (*Dido, Queen of Carthage* 3.4.4–5)

Dido means 'free' in her desire to love openly the man she meets during the divinely planned storm. Earlier, Dido makes a similar statement, when showing Aeneas the gallery of 'pictures' of 'kings' who have courted her, all of whom she has rejected: 'I am free from all;/And yet, God knows, entangled unto one' (3.1.151–3).

Dido's wistful fantasies of erotic freedom speak to the larger action of the play, which emphasizes the imperial engine of fate binding her to destruction. The human agent of destruction is the very man she loves, whom Achates identifies as the instrument of Trojan freedom: 'Brave Prince of Troy, thou only art our god,/That by thy virtues free'st us from annoy' (1.1.152–3). No wonder Dido will come to think of Aeneas as Caesarism incarnate: 'Speaks not Aeneas like a conqueror?' (4.4.93). In Marlowe's hands, the divinely appointed Virgilian hero of empire metamorphoses from a figure of political freedom into a despot of the heart.

While the Lucanian language of freedom sounds intermittently in *Dido*, Marlowe's discourse of the sublime becomes his play's most resonant feature. In fact, much of the language taps into the sublime, especially as voiced in 'The Passionate Shepherd', as both the first line and the last make clear, spoken respectively by Jupiter and Dido's sister, Anna:

> Come, gentle Ganymede, and play with me.
> (*Dido, Queen of Carthage* 1.1.1)

> Now, sweet Iarbas, stay; I come to thee!
> (*Dido, Queen of Carthage* 5.1.328)

In between these two lines, Marlowe inserts five substantive scenes of the sublime, one in each Act, thereby buttressing the frame structurally: (a) Jupiter's seduction of Ganymede (1.1.1–49); (b) Venus' seduction of Ascanius with help from Cupid (2.1.305–31); (c) Dido's wooing of Aeneas (3.1.81–33, 170); (d) the old Nurse's seduction of Cupid in disguise as Ascanius (4.5.1–16); and (e) Dido's hallucinating vision of Aeneas and subsequent curse on his legacy.[15] This strategy of self-quotation suggests that *Dido* is an imperial play about the invention of Marlovian tragedy itself, the dramatic authoring of sublime freedom in the theatre.[16]

In gauging the function of the sublime, we might recall the recent review of criticism on *Dido* by Sara Munson Deats, who distinguishes between, on the one hand, a 'romantic' reading, mounted by 'pro-passion advocates', who 'stress the tragic elements of the play, embracing the victimized queen and censuring Aeneas as a callous deserter'; and, on the other, a 'moralistic, pro-duty reading' that 'emphasizes the comic elements of the play, adducing alterations in the sources that deface the tragic stature of Dido and thus the romantic ethos she represents' ('*Dido*' 197–8). While Deats encourages us to remain 'receptive to both the play's heroic verse and its comic interludes' if we wish to 'achieve the fullest appreciation of this interrogative drama' (199), alternatively we might attempt to reconcile what Deats calls 'the sublimity of the play's tragic mood' with its 'deflat[ion] of Dido as a tragic hero' (198).[17] Whether a character's deployment of the sublime appears exuberant (as often with Dido) or ludicrous (as with the old Nurse), Marlowe's discourse manages to sound in a consistently elevated register. Thus, it may not be sufficient to say that different viewers or readers will react differently, depending on their inclinations for or against the romantic ethos: Marlowe's sublime is what we remember about this play. Whether it is Dido or the Nurse, Anna or Jupiter, the language of 'The Passionate Shepherd' floats free, giving the play its historic achievement. The Marlovian sublime may be subject to internal critique, but the heightened discourse becomes the tragedy's most lasting legacy.[18]

In the first scene of the sublime, Jupiter's opening dialogue with Ganymede, Marlowe boldly uses 'The Passionate Shepherd' to voice a heterodox metaphysics, at once amusing and troubling. Innovatively, Marlowe divides the Passionate Shepherd's voice between the god and his cupbearer. While Jupiter opens, 'Come, gentle Ganymede, and play with me', the boy introduces the Marlovian conditional: 'Grace my immortal beauty with this boon,/And I will spend my time in thy bright arms' (21–2). The two then share the sublime between them. Hence, Jupiter vows to 'Control proud fate, and cut the thread of time' (29):

> Vulcan shall dance to make thee laughing sport,
> And my nine daughters sing when thou art sad;
> From Juno's bird I'll pluck her spotted pride,
> To make thee fans wherewith to cool thy face;
> And Venus' swans shall shed their silver down,
> To sweeten out the slumbers of thy bed;
> Hermes no more shall show the world his wings,
> If that thy fancy in his feathers dwell,
> But, as this one, I'll tear them all from him,
> Do thou but say, 'their colour pleaseath me'.
> (*Dido, Queen of Carthage* 1.1.32–41)

Jupiter's promises transpose the Passionate Shepherd's material gifts for the Nymph to the metaphysical domain. Instead of pastoral entertainments, beautiful flowers, and aristocratic clothes, he offers divine entertainment, accoutrements, and sublimity: the mock dance of Vulcan; the Muses' song; a fan from the feather of Juno's peacock; a bed of down from Venus' swans; and the transcendent wings of Hermes. In other words, Jupiter offers a sublime life of leisure and joy, free of labor and turmoil – a life (as it were) in the clouds, detached from the trauma of politics and war. To an extent, Longinus would be pleased, not simply with the recurrent transcendent images of flight – the divine wings of Juno's peacock, Venus' swans, and Hermes' feet – but also with the images of annihilation: the *plucking* of Juno's peacock, and especially the violent *tearing* of Hermes' wings.[19] To transact the promise of divine pleasure, Jupiter would engage in imperial theft, taking from the lesser gods the very values they prize: 'Why, are not all the gods at thy command,/And heaven and earth the bounds of thy delight?' (30–1). In Jupiter's Marlovian hands, the sublime is joyfully mocked by the drive for monarchical conquest and tyranny, the sacrifice of the community for the sexual desire of the self and other.

Ganymede consents, yet he requests gifts of a more down-to-earth variety, followed slyly by his own conditions, to which the great god agrees:

> *Ganymede.* I would have a jewel for mine ear,
>   And a fine brooch to put in my hat,
>   And then I'll hug with you a hundred times.
> *Jupiter.* And shalt have, Ganymede, if thou wilt be my love.
>   (*Dido, Queen of Carthage* 1.1.46–9)

Here 'boy eternal' engages in a rather modest fantasy, requesting only two precious stones to make him look better – an ear ring and a hat brooch – in the consent to pederastic 'play'. Equally slyly, Jupiter consents to supply the gifts if only Ganymede will be his love.[20]

The opening dialogue, interrupted appropriately by Venus, may be both playful and blasphemous, yet beneath the banter lies an Ovidian and Lucanian metaphysical philosophy of some seriousness: (homo)erotic desire is the divinity that shapes our ends, rough-hew them how we will. Through the sublime discourse of 'The Passionate Shepherd', Marlowe deftly equates 'Fate' with sex; immortality ('cut the thread of Time') with a masculine eros free of the feminine.

In *Dido*, the sublime is a heavily ornate language, at once material and mythological, in which Marlowe's mighty blank verse line powerfully renders the precious concretion of valuable objects fused with an etherealizing classical divinity. The effect is to identify the material with the divine, to locate the eternal within the temporal, and finally to equate sublimity with sexuality. Marlowe encapsulates this idea twice in Act 4, the first exuberantly when Dido anticipates Faustus by saying of Aeneas, 'in his looks I see eternity,/And he'll make me immortal with a kiss' (4.4.122–3; cf. *DF* A-text 5.1.91); and the second, parodically, when the Old Nurse says to Cupid disguised as Ascanius, 'If there be any heaven on earth, 'tis love' (4.5.27).[21] Such heightened language, whether performed as comical or tragical, is offset from everyday speech, ensuring that a trip to the Marlovian place of the stage means an entry into his thrilling theatre.

In the second scene of the sublime, Venus's seduction of her grandson Ascanius (with help from her son Cupid) wittily transposes the divinity of the homoerotic sublime between adulterating pederasts to the incestuous sphere of heterosexual desire between mother and child. Like heaven's first family, this one is sublimely dysfunctional:[22]

> *Venus.* Fair child, stay thou with Dido's waiting maid;
>   I'll give thee sugar-almonds, sweet conserves,

> A silver girdle, and a golden purse,
> And this young prince shall be thy playfellow.
> *Ascanius.* Are you Queen Dido's son?
> *Cupid.* Ay, and my mother gave me this fine bow.
> *Ascanius.* Shall I have such a quiver and a bow?
> *Venus.* Such bow, such quiver, and such golden shafts,
> Will Dido give to sweet Ascanius.
> For Dido's sake I take thee in my arms
> And stick these spangled feathers in thy hat;
> Eat comfits in mine arms, and I will sing.
> (*Dido, Queen of Carthage* 2.1.304–15)

As the audience learns, the discourse of invitation is openly duplicitous, for Venus and Cupid carry out their plan to steal Ascanius from his father and put Cupid in the boy's place. Venus does so by promising the prince rare gifts: sweet condiments, fine clothes, royal companionship. Cupid proves even more convincing by producing the 'fine bow' that his mother has given him. When Ascanius bites, Venus moves into the sublime, making promises of material wealth akin to those made earlier by Jupiter to Ganymede: feathers in his hat, sweet snacks during an embrace with a lovely female, and her own maternal song. Unlike Jupiter, however, Venus transposes her sublime from heaven to earth; crossing the border between divinity and mortality, she obscures the boundary between divinely ordained fate and imperial politics.

For the only time in his canon, Marlowe presents the effect of the sublime on its audience as the sweet condition of slumber, and quite naturally Ascanius' peaceful sleep whets the goddess' appetite for heightened discourse:

> Amongst green brakes, I'll lay Ascanius,
> And strew him with sweet-smelling violets,
> Blushing roses, purple hyacinth;
> These milk-white doves shall be his centronels,
> Who, if that any seek to do him hurt,
> Will quickly fly to Cytherea's fist.
> (*Dido, Queen of Carthage* 2.1.317–22)

This speech differs from her first in that Venus does not aim to seduce anyone – except perhaps the audience. That is, the discourse functions theatrically, as a description of an action that never occurs except in our imagination. As Venus lays the boy in a flower-strewn paradise and plants her doves as guardians over his slumber, we momentarily escape the politics of empire to experience the freedom of natural beauty, luxurious leisure, and transcendent peace. As Venus herself puts it, 'Sleep, my sweet nephew, in these cooling shades,/Free from the murmur of these running streams,/ The cry of beasts, the rattling of the winds' (2.1. 334–6). For all the serenity of this version of the sublime, however, Venus mouths something alarming in the Marlowe canon. Recurrently, this author's tragic voicing of the sublime forecloses union, leaving the speaker (whether deity or human) detached from the object of desire. Such detachment may be subject to psychoanalysis (of the author himself), but it is also joyfully at home in a medium designed to operate primarily through 'verbal spectacles'.[23]

In the third scene, Dido's wooing of Aeneas in Act 3, scene 1, we gain purchase on the literary stakes of Marlowe's sublime authorship. To create the showpiece of the play, he re-locates the sublime discourse fully in the human sphere and its domain of heterosexual lovemaking. Once Cupid-Ascanius wounds Dido with desire for Aeneas, she voices the sublime discourse of the gods, who control not just her destiny but her body, as she rhapsodizes first in soliloquy:

> I'll make me bracelets of his golden hair;
> His glistering eyes shall be my looking-glass,
> His lips an altar, where I'll offer up
> As many kisses as the sea hath sands;
> Instead of music I will hear him speak.
> His looks shall be my only library;
> And thou, Aeneas, Dido's treasury,
> In whose fair bosom I will lock more wealth
> Than twenty thousand Indias can afford.
>   (*Dido, Queen of Carthage* 3.1.84–92)

Here the sublime depicts the female in the throes of desire. No doubt, Marlowe uses the heightened discourse to express the hurried passion of the heart – an erotic mode of subjectivity – but in this dialogue of self and soul he also reveals the social and material form that Dido's fantasy takes. In a blazon, Dido imagines the way she will use Aeneas' body: his hair will function as her bracelet; his eyes, her mirror; his lips, an altar for sacrificing herself for sex; his tongue, her music; his face, her library. Except for the altar, her images are all domestic, evoking, variously, a person in church at prayer, a lady in her bedroom during her *toilette*, and a scholar in his library with books and music. For Dido, Aeneas assumes the object-position of bracelet, mirror, altar, music, and book – wealthy, beautiful, sacred, harmonious, learned. Aeneas' body becomes 'Dido's treasury'; her supreme value, a small chest of infinite riches, which only she can lock inside his 'fair bosom'.

Yet this is not all. For Dido attempts to *author* Aeneas, and to do so in counter-imperial terms. The word 'author' is rare in the Marlowe canon, occurring only three times, yet two of them come from *Dido* (the third comes from *2 Tamb* 2.4.56). Amidst the queen's sublime speech, Aeneas enters with his men, prompting her to use the sublime as a topos for a heterodox exuberance expressive of female immodesty: 'O, here he comes! Love, love, give Dido leave/To be more modest than her thoughts admit,/ Lest I be made a wonder to the world' (93–5). (And so she is.) Aeneas enters precisely to request the imperial riggings (104) that will allow him to set sail for Rome ('sails', 'oars', 'stern', 'anchor', 'masts' [105–9]), 'Which piteous wants if Dido will supply,/We will account her author of our lives' (110–11). According to Mark Thornton Burnett, 'What the play charts is Dido's attempt to reconstitute Aeneas according to her own priorities. For Dido, Aeneas represents the blank page upon which she writes. Such are Dido's reconstructive instincts that she is drawn to inventory Aeneas' physical attributes with all the representational ability of the Elizabethan sonneteer' (ed. xxiv).[24] While Dido's blazon is akin to the sonneteers' technique, Marlowe also re-routes his own technique of the sublime from 'The Passionate Shepherd'. Thus, Marlowe uses the sublime as a *creative* device of literary authorship. Such a device, as Burnett remarks earlier, has a gender dynamic to it, since Dido has 'a debilitating effect on [Aeneas'] masculinity' (ed. xxiii).[25] Marlowe's inscription of authorship in this scene compels us to discern a further palimpsest, revealing beneath the text of the fiction another text about the work of the author.[26] In Marlowe's hands, the sublime becomes a 'transvestite' signature (Brown, *Redefining* 155) of his own self-quotational authorship.

Taking Aeneas' cue of authorship, Dido communicates her immodestly sublime desire to him, imitating 'The Passionate Shepherd' more directly:

> Aeneas, I'll repair thy Trojan ships,
> Conditionally that thou wilt stay with me,
> ...;
> I'll give thee tackling made of rivelled gold,
> Wound on the barks of odoriferous trees;
> Oars of massy ivory, full of holes,
> Through which the water shall delight to play.
> ...
> The sails of folded lawn, where shall be wrought
> The wars of Troy, but not Troy's overthrow;
> For ballace, empty Dido's treasury.
>   (*Dido, Queen of Carthage* 3.1.112–25)

On the surface, Dido outlines a reclamation plan for his sea-wracked ships, but she manages to shoot her practicality through with sublime submission to Aeneas' sexual penetration of her rich 'ballace'. Remarkably, she presents her offer to repair his ships in terms of her own captivating body. There is a rhetoric here, an art of persuasion, and we may call it sublime, as Dido promises to supply the missing ship-parts 'Conditionally' to Aeneas' men if only he will stay with her and be her love. Yet there is also a self-conscious intertextual authorship here: Dido's promise to supply sails made of lawn, painted with the 'wars of Troy, but not Troy's overthrow', is an imaginative rewriting of the frescoes of Troy that Virgil's Aeneas finds in Dido's temple of Juno in Book 1 of the *Aeneid*.

Dido's discourse of sublime authorship becomes more explicit in the second half of her speech, when she addresses Aeneas' second-in-command: 'Achates, thou shalt be so meanly clad/As sea-born nymphs shall swarm about thy ships,/And wanton mermaids court thee with sweet songs,/So that Aeneas may but stay with me' (3.1.327–32). Here Dido reveals her histrionic obsession with dressing poorly clothed men in fine costumes (2.1.79–80), an obsession gleefully at one with theatre. For instance, toward the end of the play, after Aeneas announces his plan to depart, she finds ways to ridicule him, first denying that 'Dardanus [is] the author of [his] stock' (5.1.157), and then recalling their past: 'And cam'st to Dido like a fisher swain?/Repaired not I thy ships, made thee a king' (5.1.162–3). The word 'made' speaks to Dido's recurrent attempt to 'make' Aeneas, but it also highlights Marlowe's attempt to turn the Virgilian story of empire into a sublime fantasy of authorship: a male author cross-dresses his dramatic voice in the histrionic speech of a female, who in turn seeks to 'author' the arch-male hero of empire in 'effeminate' terms.[27]

Perhaps because Marlowe makes this fiction of cross-dressing authorship so dominant he can mock it in his fourth scene of the sublime, when the old Nurse tries to seduce Cupid doubling as Ascanius:

Nurse. My lord Ascanius, ye must go with me.
Cupid. Whither must I go? I'll stay with my mother.
Nurse. No, thou shalt go with me unto my house.
   I have an orchard that hath store of plums,
   Brown almonds, services, ripe figs, and dates,
   Dewberries, apples, yellow oranges;
   A garden where are bee-hives full of honey,
   ...
   Where thou shalt see the red-gilled fishes leap,
   White swans, and many lovely water-fowls.
   Now speak, Ascanius, will ye go or no?
Cupid. Come, come, I'll go.
   ...
       will you carry me?
Nurse. Ay, so you'll dwell with me and call me mother.
Cupid. So you'll love me, I care not if I do.
                    (*Dido, Queen of Carthage* 4.5.1–17).

More successfully than elsewhere, Marlowe creates dramatic dialogue out of the monologic 'Passionate Shepherd', but the dynamic of self-quotation here is even more complex than before. An elderly female, played by a boy actor, deploys the masculine voice of lyric invitation before a god in disguise as a boy (also played by a boy actor), and together the two contribute to the author's own self-quotation. In other words, the dialogue crosses a number of boundaries: between age and youth, male and female, divine and mortal, lyric and theatre. Yet the details of the invitation become ludicrous when the old woman offers a god mortal food and a landscape of natural beauty filled with animals. As critics have long recognized, Marlowe's self-parody unfolds a political significance, burlesquing his elderly queen's penchant for courting young favorites, such as Sir Walter Ralegh.[28] We might go so far as to say that Marlowe can burlesque his queen because he burlesques himself.[29]

In the final scene of the sublime, when Dido contends with the trauma of her lover's departure at the end of the play, Marlowe turns the Carthaginian queen's romance fantasy of feminine authorship into tragedy:

> I'll frame me wings of wax like Icarus,
> And o'er his ships will soar unto the sun,
> That they may melt and I fall in his arms;
> ...
> O Anna, fetch Arion's harp,
> That I may tice a dolphin to the shore
> And ride upon his back unto my love!
> Look, sister, look, lovely Aeneas' ships!
> See, see, the billows heave him up to heaven.
>   (*Dido, Queen of Carthage* 5.1.243–52)

This may well be the earliest version of Marlowe's Faustian sublime (see Chapter 5). Here, Marlowe does not simply eroticize the sublime; through Icarus and Arion, he *poeticizes* it, rendering the spiritual state literary.

Icarus and Arion are both poet-figures. As Marlowe reveals, Arion is a harpist, using his music to tame animals; like Orpheus, he is a figure for the civilizing power of the poet. Specifically, Dido calls on Anna to 'fetch Arion's harp' so that she can 'tice' a dolphin into taking her to Aeneas in his ship – appropriating the civilizing art for erotic ends. For his part, Icarus has become a figure for the Marlovian 'overreacher', the individual who aspires beyond human capacity to pay the price. Linked with Arion, Icarus specifically becomes an authorial figure, and thus an author of sublimity, 'soar[ing] unto the sun'.[30] Both mythological figures represent elemental action, a power over the sea or the air, as Dido imagines a masculine vehicle catapulting her into the 'arms' of her lover: the surge toward the sublime climaxes in a displaced form of orgasm, as Dido's key verb, 'melt', intimates. If the rhapsodic female lapses into sublime mythological discourse to imagine sexual union, the author gestures to a literary authorship of the sublime state:[31]

> Now too would the sea's vast mass have *risen to the stars*
> had the ruler of the gods not subdued the waves with clouds.
> That night was not a night of heaven.
> ...
> *The sails touch the clouds.*
> ...
> As this he said, the tenth wave – remarkable to tell –
> *lifts him with his flimsy boat,* and did not cast him
> down again from the sea's high heap but carried him on.
> (Lucan, *Civil War* 5.625–7, 642, 672–4;
> trans. Braund; emphasis added)

Like Caesar in his tempest-tossed boat, Aeneas in Dido's imagination rises toward the heaven – a reminder perhaps of the imperial end toward which Virgil's Dido is sacrificed.

In her suicide speech, with Aeneas out of reach, Dido participates in her final form of sublime authorship:

> Now, Dido, with these relics burn thyself,
> And make Aeneas famous through the world
> For perjury and slaughter of a queen.
> ...
> These letters, lines, and perjured papers all
> Shall burn to cinders in this precious flame.
> And now, ye gods that guide the starry frame
> And order all things at your high dispose,
> Grant, though the traitors land in Italy,
> They may be still tormented with unrest,
> And from mine ashes let a conqueror rise,
> That may revenge this treason to a queen.
> (*Dido, Queen of Carthage* 5.1.292–307)

A lot is going on here. As Burnett observes, Dido threatens to turn Aeneas into 'an unseaworthy relic collection', for when her project to 'transmogrify' Aeneas fails, she 'transfers her attentions away from men and on to herself, emerging as a representative of parthenogenetic female power': 'Like the phoenix, to which she obliquely refers (V.i.306), she will create herself anew to wreak vengeance upon her enemies. By the same token, she "authors" Aeneas once more by carving out for him an unflattering place in posterity'. In the end, that is, Dido 'reinvent[s] her past to secure the major part in her own mythology' (ed. xxiv–xxv). For Dido, the sublime is a dead end, because it turns the beloved into an artifact, leaving her alone on the threshold of annihilation, simply to author her own legacy, as the self-reflexive discourse of 'letters, lines, and perjured papers' suggests.

What has escaped attention is the republican ring to Dido's concluding prophecy of the phoenix-like 'rise' out of her own 'ashes': it is about the 'conqueror' Hannibal (5.1.306; see Burnett, ed. 571). As 'one of the greatest generals in history' (*Oxford Classical Dictionary* 666), and thus in Roman history, Hannibal (247 BC–183/2 BC) becomes part of all histories of Rome coming out of antiquity, primarily as the arch-Carthaginian enemy of Rome, eventually defeated by the great republican hero, Scipio Africanus.[32] Accordingly, Hannibal figures prominently in the republican histories discussed in Chapter 1, from Polybius to Cicero, Livy, and Tacitus to Machiavelli. He is especially prominent in Polybius' *Rise of the Roman Empire* (ed. 178–277), which pauses to describe 'The Character of Hannibal': 'It is impossible to withhold our admiration for Hannibal's leadership, his courage and his ability in the field. For sixteen years he waged ceaseless war against the Romans in Italy, and throughout that time he never released his army from service in the field, but, like a good pilot, kept those great numbers under his control and free from disaffection either towards himself or one another. ... [T]he skill of their commander was such that he could impose the authority of a single voice and a single will even upon men of such totally diverse origins' (11.19: 427–8; see also 'The Character of Hannibal' at 9: 22–6: 399–403).

As the arch-enemy of Republican Rome, Hannibal only appears to be the enemy of republican values. He is the charismatic leader of the common soldier but also a figure of admiration from Polybius through to Machiavelli.[33] According to Quentin Skinner, the Carthaginian general is one of Machiavelli's 'favourite heroes of antiquity', because Hannibal's ' "outstanding virtù" and fame' consists in his ' "impiety, faithlessness and cruelty" to an extreme degree' (Skinner, *Foundations* 1: 185). As Skinner explains this conundrum, Hannibal can never be as great as Scipio (1: 93) but he joins Scipio in 'shak[ing] off the demands of Christian virtue, wholeheartedly embracing the very different morality which his situation dictates' (1: 134–5). Not surprisingly, Hannibal gets written into literary works supporting 'Republican values', such as Silius Italicus' *Punic Wars*. When Silius narrates the battle between Hannibal and Scipio at Zama, for instance, he makes the two heroes, writes Philip Hardie, 'interchangeable' (25). Hardie gets to the heart of the matter when he observes that 'Hannibal is a hero in the mould of Lucan's Caesar, but this thunderbolt of demonic energy also turns out to be a vehicle' for the author himself: 'In Hannibal's oath at the shrine of Dido, which is also the poem's promise to remain faithful to the *Aeneid* in exchange for the release of the model's creative powers, we may also read the man Silius' cultivation of the shade of Virgil in the hope of his own poetic birth (or rebirth)' (164–5). In other words, this pro-Virgilian author equates himself with the reputed enemy of his own nation.[34]

At the end of *Dido*, when the queen prophesies the 'revenge' of Hannibal against Rome, Marlowe re-routes republican discourse, using the anti-imperial general to critique not simply the imperial Virgil but also imperial England (with its myth of Roman origin) and finally Elizabethan England's Virgilian epicist, Spenser. Then, when the play concludes just as it began, with a clear echo of 'The Passionate Shepherd', Marlowe does not simply bookend his play with the sublime; formally, he reinvents tragedy as a literary genre about the author's own republican authorship: 'Now, sweet Iarbus, stay; I come to thee' (5.1.328).[35]

1 Tamburlaine

Even further than *Dido*, the two *Tamburlaine* plays formalize the conflict between empire and liberty within Marlowe's sublime republican authorship.[36] Not simply do *1* and *2 Tamburlaine* discover fresh ways to get the Lucanian sublime and its discourse of freedom from 'The Passionate Shepherd' onto the stage, but they do so by introducing a formal republican language for the first time in the Marlowe canon. As we have seen, the terms of empire and of liberty abound, but they are buttressed by such important early modern republican words as 'merit', 'equal', 'consent', and 'right', as well as by their opposites: 'slavery', 'birth', 'power', 'tyranny', and 'theft'.[37]

At the heart of the two plays, the conflict between liberty and empire speaks to the larger European 'dilemma' made prominent by such political theorists as Machiavelli and Beacon, with origins in Aristotle's *Politics* and its development in Aquinas' *Summa Theologica*. Central to the dilemma, writes Skinner, is the 'theory of popular sovereignty', which resulted from a debate about whether ' "the ruler" should be the whole body of the people' or 'a single and unified "human legislator" '. Ideally, republicans argue, a single human legislator would embody the people of the republic (*Foundations* 1: 53, 61). Such a debate dominated fifteenth-century Italy but 'enter[ed] the sixteenth century in the writings of Almain and Mair, passing from there into the age of the Reformation and beyond' (1: 65). As such, the 'theory of popular sovereignty was destined to play a major role in shaping the most radical version of early modern constitutionalism', including in England (1: 65).

The *Tamburlaine* plays, I propose, respond to the republican theory of popular sovereignty, discovering an icon in the 'Scythian Shepherd' who becomes a 'Mighty Monarch' (title page, 1590), and thereby they explode the Tudor myth of hereditary monarchy, the divine right of kings.[38] As we have intimated, however, the plays are not patriotic republican treatises – and thus, perhaps, not of much professional interest to intellectual historians like Skinner – but rather, unique dramatic representations that *trouble* the republican political agenda, and do so with Marlowe's signature, especially his weird Lucanism and his own brand of sublimity. The result is a powerfully original literary voice that ends up taking London by storm.[39]

The quoted phrase appearing in the title to this chapter comes from *1 Tamburlaine*, and shows Ceneus, a lord who works for Mycetes, King of Persia, as criticizing Tamburlaine for being a staunch republican:

> He that with shepherds and a little spoil
> Durst, in disdain of wrong and tyranny,
> Defend his [freedom] 'gainst a monarchy,
> What will he do supported by a king,
> Leading a troop of gentlemen and lords,
> And stuffed with treasure for his highest thoughts.[40]
> (*1 Tamburlaine* 2.1.54–9)

The phrasing here is politically precise: Ceneus presents Tamburlaine as a republican freedom-fighter. As a shepherd, Tamburlaine disdains political tyranny, and sets out to defend his freedom, and that of his friends, against the wrong of monarchical government. Ceneas, a loyal supporter of monarchy, finds in Tamburlaine's populist republicanism a chink that he thinks the Persians can exploit: by nature, the common man is attracted to his superiors – kings, gentlemen, and lords – and especially to their wealth. In this way, Ceneus reduces the republican shepherd's 'highest thoughts' to sheer greed. Yet it is precisely the link between the imperial discourse of the sublime and the republican discourse of liberty that this play performs.

Recurrently, the play presents Tamburlaine as a figure of liberty. As he himself tells his future wife, Zenocrate, 'I love to live at liberty' (1.2.26). Tamburlaine even voices his commitment to the arch-republican value in terms of appetite: 'Then let us freely banquet and carouse' (4.4.5). Not surprisingly, what the shepherd finds intolerable is slavery: '[I] must maintain my life exempt of servitude' (1.2.31). Indeed, the word 'free' occurs three times in this play; 'freedom', twice; 'freely', once; and 'liberty' (or 'liberties'), seven times, bringing the total to thirteen. Marlowe's archly masculine hero takes freedom so seriously that he opens it into a space we might not expect; at the end of the play, he identifies his beloved as the political agent of freedom, saying of Zenocrate to the Soldan, 'Thy princely daughter here shall set thee free – /She that hath calmed the fury of my sword' (5.1.436–7). Earlier, Zenocrate anticipates this role when she blesses her future husband with a prayer, 'And may my love, the King of Persia,/Return with victory, and free from wound!' (3.3.132–3). Sometimes Marlowe's discourse of liberty works more inadvertently; midway through the play, for instance, Tamburlaine tells the Turkish Basso that he and his friends will 'first subdue the Turk', Bajazeth, 'and then enlarge/Those Christian captives which you keep as slaves' (3.3.46–7) – the word 'enlarge' meaning 'free'.[41]

A less well-known value of republican political thought emerges in another recurrent word in *1 Tamburlaine*: the plural 'friends', which occurs 11 times.[42] According to Tacitus in his *Histories*, the republican hero Helvidius Priscus says, 'Good friends are the most effective instruments of good government' (4.7: 175). Marlowe's use of the word 'friends' speaks to the strong communal edge of Tamburlaine's identity and regime; he begins with two close friends, Techelles and Usumcasane, and he soon acquires a third, Theridimas. Together, these four men overrule a number of single monarchs around the East: Mycetes (Act 1), Cosroe (Act 2), Bajazeth (Acts 3–4), and the Soldan and his prospective son in law, the King of Arabia (Act 5). As this inventory suggests, Marlowe structures his play on the opposition between a sturdy republican coalition and a sliding set of monarchs. As Tamburlaine voices his ethos of friendship: 'These are my friends, in whom I more rejoice/Than doth the King of Persia in his crown' (1.2.240–1). Friendship opposes kingship, and in so doing helps define Tamburlaine's republican rule.[43]

At times, Tamburlaine's republican discourse of friends is startlingly precise. As he tells Theridamus, Techelles, and Usumcasane,

> Both we will reign as consuls of the earth,
> And mighty kings shall be our senators.
> Jove sometime masked in a shepherd's weed,
> And by those steps that he hath scaled the heavens
> May we become immortal like the gods.
> Join with me now in this my mean estate –
> ...
> And when my name and honour shall be spread
> As far as Boreas claps his brazen wings
> Or fair Bootes sends his cheerful light,
> Then shalt thou be competitor with me
> And sit with Tamburlaine in all his majesty.
> (*1 Tamburlaine* 1.2.196–208)

The word 'consuls' identifies the leading office of the Roman republican government, as Livy describes it near the beginning of his *Rise of Rome*: 'The monarchy at Rome from her foundation to her liberation lasted two hundred and forty-four years. Two consuls were then elected.... They were Lucius Iunius Brutus and Lucius Tarquinius Collatinus.... One might ... say that the birth of liberty was owing more to the annual nature of the consuls' tenure than to any lessening of the power the kings had possessed' (1.60–2.1: 70–1).[44]

In Marlowe's first line above, Tamburlaine tells his friends that they will reign as the consuls of a republican government. In the second, he measures the way in which his new republican rule will change the state government of the East: by having 'kings' function as 'senators'. This is the very role that Tamburlaine's three friends go on to play; he makes them all kings, but they continue to serve as senators who counsel him: 'Why, say, Theridamas, wilt thou be a king? ... /What says my other friends? Will you be kings? ... /And would not all our soldiers soon consent/If we should aim at such a dignity' (2.5.65–79). Thus, in the speech indented above Tamburlaine invites his three friends to reign with him equally – as his 'competitor'. Yet central to his republican discourse is the notion of the sublime, as represented by his heightened imagery of scaling the heavens (with Jove as precedent) and of Boreas clapping his wings (a Longinian metaphor for sublime thunder and lightning): Tamburlaine uses the notion of republican consulship to attain the divine state of immortality – a pastoral fantasy if ever there was one.

As all of these representations intimate, however, Marlowe's play does not allow pure republican government to reign unalloyed. If initially he presents his hero as a republican freedom-fighter who opposes slavery and monarchy, locating government in a group of 'friends' operating as 'consuls', subsequently Tamburlaine's imperialist desire dominates the action: this freedom-fighter is obsessed with becoming a king. As he asks his friends rhetorically, 'Is it not passing brave to be a king,/"And ride in triumph through Persepolis"' (2.5.53–4). Most likely, it is Tamburlaine's obsession with kingship that readers remember most. Thus, he makes his monarchical goal no secret: 'I shall be the Monarch of the East' (1.2.184; see 1.1.43). Later, after defeating Mycetes and then his brother Cosroe, Tamburlaine places the crown on his head: 'will I wear it in despite of them/As great commander of this eastern world,/If you but say that Tamburlaine shall reign' (2.7.61–3). As the condition of the last line indicates, and as the line following insists, Tamburlaine's imperial rule exists through republican vote:

All. Long live Tamburlaine, and reign in Asia!
Tamburlaine. So, now it is more surer on my head
Than if the gods had held a parliament
And all pronounced me King of Persia.
                    (*1 Tamburlaine* 2.7.64–7)

Switching from Roman to English law, Tamburlaine compares the vote of his consuls and soldiers to 'a parliament', and identifies himself as an elected king. The switch is not as unusual as it might at first seem. According to Thomas Smith in *De Republica Anglorum*, 'the barony or degree of Lordes doeth answere to the degree of Senators of Rome' (1.17: 66). Indeed, Smith goes on to compare the English Parliament to the government of ancient Rome: 'When the Romanes did write *senatus populusque Romanus*, they seemed to make but two orders, that is of the Senate and of the people of Rome...: so when we in England do say the Lordes and the commons' (1.18: 68), wherein 'the consent of the Parliament is taken to be everie mans consent' (2.1: 79). For Smith, 'Parliament' is the 'most high and absolute power of the realme of Englande', and distinguishes his nation from others such as France (2.1: 78). Repeatedly, Tamburlaine performs his function as a king with reference to the common man, as when he tells the three ill-fated contributory kings of Bajazeth, 'every common soldier of my camp/Shall smile to see thy miserable state' (3.3.85–6).

While Marlowe may be staging the early modern theory of popular sovereignty, his Elizabethan audience would have recognized Tamburlaine's political organization as a 'mixed' form of government, as discussed influentially by Smith: 'Now although the governments of common wealthes be thus divided into three' (monarchy, aristocracy, democracy), 'yet you must not take that ye shall finde any common wealth of governement simple, pure and absolute in its sort and kind' but 'always mixed' (1.6: 52). In Tamburlaine's popular sovereignty, he is an elected king, while his three 'friends' serve as 'consuls' or 'senators' and his soldiers as the common people. In this eastern 'parliament', all have the right to 'consent'. Toward the end of the play, Tamburlaine firms up his standing as a republican hero when presenting the crowns of Argier, Fez, and Morocco to Theridamus, Techelles, and Usumcasane, his own (more happily fated) 'contributory kings' (4.4.122–3).

While Marlowe appears to be working within the early modern discourse on government available to him, something seems peculiar, at times perverse. The Persian King Cosroe first expresses confusion about the play's political representation: 'The strangest men that ever Nature made!/I know not how to take their tyrannies' (2.7.40–1).[45] The perplexity intensifies as the play progresses, for Tamburlaine repeatedly announces that his republican kingship is ordained: 'fates and oracles of heaven have sworn/To royalize the deeds of Tamburlaine/And make them blest that share in his attempts' (2.3.7–9). In other words, Marlowe's new Elizabethan icon appears to display a contradiction: the divine right of a republican king. In all its grim violence, it is hard to tell whether this is the mixed government of Queen Elizabeth's monarchical republic or its photographic negative.[46]

As Cosroe indicates, Tamburlaine may express his commitment to liberty, but his enemies accuse him of tyranny. After becoming emperor, he is called a 'tyrant' no fewer than five times (3.2.102, 4.2.7, 4.4.22, 4.4.109, 5.1.405), the first being perhaps the most haunting, when Tamburlaine invites Zenocrates' protector, Agydus, to commit suicide: 'Go wander free from fear of tyrant's rage' (3.2.102). Tamburlaine has overheard Agydus attempting to persuade Zenocrate to avoid giving in to the shepherd's advances, which enacts slavery, and he promises that her father will 'Redeem' her 'from this deadly servitude' (3.2.34).

There is, in other words, a second phase to the narrative, which competes with the first: if in the initial part of the play Tamburlaine emerges as a republican hero of liberty, by the middle he becomes the republican enemy to liberty. This second phase initially becomes prominent when Tamburlaine turns the Turkish king Bajazeth and his wife Zabina into 'slaves' (4.4.27), with the infamous 'cage' as the theatrical prop (4.2.SD), inside of which husband and wife find themselves bound for display in a Roman 'triumph' (4.2.86). Just before their husband-and-wife suicide, Zabina accuses Tamburlaine of 'infamous, monstrous slaveries', 'oppression', and 'obscure infernal servitude' (5.1.241, 251, 254) – provoked by Tamburlaine himself, who taunts her husband, 'And now, my footstool, if I lose the field,/You hope of liberty and restitution' (5.1.209–10).

To his credit, Marlowe both writes republicanism and slips through its cracks. On the one hand, Philippe du Plessis Mornay, author of the French republican resistance treatise *Vindiciae, Contra Tyrannos*, would hardly approve of Tamburlaine: 'Will it be lawful for...Spartacus the gladiator – for, I say, any private individual – to call the slaves to freedom...? Most definitely not. The commonwealth is not entrusted to individuals or private persons', for the 'sword is not conceded to individuals either by God or by the people' (168–9). (So much for Tamburlaine's 'conquering swords'.) Yet on the other hand, Tamburlaine does not qualify for Mornay's title of 'tyrant' either, as described in the chapter on 'Who Tyrants Are' (140–8): 'Now you cannot define those who are called tyrants by practice as easily as those who are truly kings, because desire commands the former and reason the latter....A tyrant crops the tallest ears in the cornfield; he oppresses the leading men of the commonwealth with deceit, fraud, and false accusations. He often fabricates conspiracies initiated against himself, in order the more swiftly to remove these men from its midst, as Tiberius, Maximinus, and others did. Finally, he does not even spare his relatives and brothers....A king protects each man in his rank, cherishes the leading men as friends of the kingdom, and is no less anxious to consider them than he is himself' (3: 143–4). By nearly every criterion, Tamburlaine fails the test of the tyrant: he may work by 'desire', but he also possesses 'reason'; the tallest ears in the cornfield are midgets compared to him; he never fabricates a conspiracy, or operates by deceit; and, quite remarkably, like a good 'king', he protects men in their rank, cherishes the leading men as 'friends', and considers them as much as he does himself.[47]

Yet even more notable is the republican conundrum represented in Tamburlaine's vicious siege of Damascus, a city that Marlowe presents as a republic, as the stage direction to the final Act reveals: '[Enter] the Governor of Damascus, with three or four citizens, and four Virgins with branches of laurel in their hands'. Like the Island of Malta (Chapter 4), Damascus is not run by a king but by a 'Governor', who operates in dialogue with 'citizens', including virginal young women. Accordingly, the Governor voices a republican ethos, straight out of Livy, Tacitus, or Machiavelli:

> Well, lovely virgins, think our country's care
> Our love of honour, loath to be enthralled
> To foreign powers and rough imperious yokes,
> Would not with too much cowardice or fear,
> Before all hope of rescue were denied,
> Submit yourselves and us to servitude.
> Therefore, in that your safeties and our own,
> Your honours, liberties, and lives, were weighed
> In equal care and balance with our own,
> Endure as we the malice of our stars,
> The wrath of Tamburlaine and power of wars.
> (*1 Tamburlaine* 5.1.34–44)

Yet this is not Machiavelli but Marlowe, who goes on to ironize republicanism when the Governor sacrifices the virgins to protect the city. Thus, even at its best, the discourse of equality and liberty falls hollow: 'Farewell, sweet virgins, on whose safe return/Depends our city, liberty, and lives' (5.1.62–3). Farewell indeed. When the virgins repeat Tamburlaine's discourse back to him – 'liberties,...loves, or lives' (95) – he orders them to be 'put...to the sword' (134).[48] Through this two-phase plot, Marlowe appears to stage the cynical perverseness of Machiavelli's dictum in the *Discourses*: 'it is impossible for a republic to succeed in standing still while enjoying its liberty within its narrow borders, because if the republic does not trouble others, others will trouble it' (2.19: 206). Yet Marlowe manages to out-Machiavelli Machiavelli.[49]

Critics have long found Machiavelli lurking in *1 Tamburlaine*, but never in quite these terms.[50] If Marlowe could have found in the *Discourses* the Sallustian dilemma of liberty and empire, he could also have found the human subject who enacts the dilemma, what Machiavelli terms the 'single man' of 'exceptional ability':

> this must be taken as a general rule: that never or rarely does it happen that a republic or kingdom is organized well from the beginning or is completely reformed apart from its old institutions, unless it is organized by one man alone; or rather, it is necessary for a single man to be the one who gives it shape, and from whose mind any such organization derives. Thus, the prudent founder of a republic, one who has this courageous desire to serve not his own interests but the common good, and not his own heirs but rather everyone in their native land, must strive to assume sole authority. (Machiavelli, *Discourses* 1.9: 45)

Repeatedly, Machiavelli turns to the competition between 'Ability or Fortune' (2.1 chapter title), concluding that even though Roman history 'mixe[s]' 'good fortune...with exceptional ability', in the end 'exceptional skill' is 'more effective' than 'fortune' in 'acquiring...empire' in the defense of 'liberty' (2.1: 154–5).[51]

One even wonders whether Marlowe might have seized on Machiavelli's chapter titled 'Strong Republics and Excellent Men Retain in Every Kind of Fortune the Same Spirit and Dignity' (3.31: 327–31). Machiavelli opens with Camillus, another of his heroes, as a Tamburlaine-like '*exemplum*, a model of the Roman citizen-farmer-soldier ideal' who became an elected 'Dictator' in 390 BC (Joyce, trans. 293).

> Among the other magnificent things that our historian [Livy] has Camillus say and do, to show how an excellent man must be made, he puts these words into his mouth: 'My resolution has never gained anything from dictatorship, any more than it lost anything in exile'. His words show that great men always remain the same in every kind of fortune, and if it varies,...they themselves never change but always keep a firm resolve, joined in such a manner to their way of life that anyone can easily recognize that fortune has no power over them. (Machiavelli, *Discourses* 3.31: 327–8)

We know that Marlowe knew about Camillus because he mentions him twice, first in his translation of Ovid's *Amores* (*OE* 3.2.12), then in his translation of Lucan's first book (170–1). While Marlowe might have read further about Camillus in Livy, Machiavelli, and others, it is to Lucan and his grim imperial conqueror that we need to turn, precisely because Marlowe himself licenses us to do so.

In Act 3, scene 3, Tamburlaine selects Lucan's Caesar as his own *exemplum*:

> My camp is like to Julius Caesar's host,
> That never fought but had the victory;
> Nor in Pharsalia was there such hot war
> As these my followers willingly would have.
> Legions of spirits fleeting in the air
> Direct our bullets and our weapons' points
> And make your strokes to wound the senselss air;
> And when she sees our bloody colours spread,
> Then Victory begins to take her flight.
> (*1 Tamburlaine* 3.3.152–60)

We can read this speech as an authorial signature, because 'Marlowe's spelling ["Pharsalia" rather than "Pharsalus"] recalls the title of Lucan's poem on the war, the first book of which he translated' (Romany and Lindsey, eds. 591). Not simply William Blissett but recent editors such as J.S. Cunningham and David Fuller follow the early lead of Una Ellis-Fermor (see her edition, pages 131, 138, and 161) in detecting the influence of Lucan's poem, and of Marlowe's own translation, on the play. As Cunningham puts it here, 'The glance towards Lucan strengthens the inference that Marlowe's knowledge of the *Pharsalia* contributed to the tonalities of violence in *Tamburlaine*' (ed. 170; see Fuller, ed. 200).

Remarkably, no one has studied the presence of Lucan in *1 Tamburlaine*, despite considerable evidence linking the two works. In his edition, Cunningham cites five other passages from *Lucan's First Book* as subtexts for *1 Tamburlaine*, bringing the total to six: the distinct word 'resolved' at 1.2: 101 (*LFB* 221: ed. 128); the mistakenly named river 'Araris' at 2.1.63 (*LFB* 434–5: ed. 139), which, because such a river does not exist, shows Marlowe to be glancing at his own translation; 'bullets like Jove's dreadful thunderbolts' at 2.3.19 (*LFB* 529–30: ed. 143); 'glut' at 3.3.164 (*LFB* 39: ed. 171); and 'noisome' at 5.1.256 (*LFB* 650: ed. 205). In his more recent edition, Fuller repeats the gloss only on 'Araris' (ed. 181), but he adds two others, the last of which comes from outside *Lucan's First Book*: 'tilt...lightning' at 3.2.79–81 (*LFB* 152: 196); and 'Thessalian drugs' at 5.1.133 (*Ph* 6: ed. 217). Together, then, Cunningham and Fuller turn up eight glosses from Lucan in *1 Tamburlaine* alone, with several of them important to the present discussion. Altogether, they encourage us to see the *Pharsalia* as an important intertext for Marlowe's play.

In his reference to 'Pharsalia', Marlowe presents Tamburlaine voicing a Lucanian origin, as the mighty monarch compares his own 'camp' to the 'host' of 'Caesar' and his own battle against Bajazeth to Caesar's battle against Pompey at Pharsalus. If Jamie Masters is correct about 'the conflict at the heart of Lucan's relation to the epic genre' – that the poet identifies with both Caesar's 'ambition' and Pompey's 'remorse' – we might be struck by Blissett's argument that Tamburlaine, like Marlowe's overreacher in general, identifies only with Caesarian ambition.[52] Yet the speech shows Tamburlaine identifying a republican authority – the will of his followers – as the key to his military triumph. Thus we need to distinguish between Tamburlaine and Caesar. If Lucan's despot is an absolutist tyrant, Marlowe's hero is a republican tyrant.[53] As the Messenger informs the Soldan:

> Did your greatness see
> The frowning looks of fiery Tamburlaine,
> That with his terror and imperious eyes
> Commands the hearts of his associates,
> It might amaze your royal majesty.
> (*1 Tamburlaine* 4.1.12–16)

In these terms, Tamburlaine's paradox is that he uses his eye of imperialism to form a republican army organized around the 'hearts of his associates'. No wonder the 'royal majesty' of the Soldan is amazed. Yet Tamburlaine also ends up exhibiting an unexpected resemblance to Lucan's Pompey, whose republican drive is always controlled internally from an absolutist command center (*LFB* 125–6). Collinson speaks of 'an anti-monarchical virus which was part of the legacy of early sixteenth-century humanism' (119–20), yet Marlowe, we might say, is a virus with attitude.

As the image of Victory in winged flight indicates, and as some of our examples anticipate, *1 Tamburlaine* keeps the sublime right at the surface of the verse. Earlier, we spoke of the play's two-phase plot, in which Tamburlaine begins as a republican freedom-fighter but then turns into the enemy of liberty – as if Marlowe were illustrating the Machivallian degeneration of liberty into empire. We may now see that each of these phases rehearses a distinct version of the sublime: what we might call *the sublime of divine beauty* and *the sublime of divine ambition*. As we shall see in the remainder of this section, Marlowe opposes the two versions, locates their opposition within the mind of Tamburlaine himself, and at the end seeks resolution between them. Tamburlaine's internal resolution of the sublime coincides with the romantic conclusion to the play: in the last line, the hero announces his marriage to Zenocrate, a character Marlowe invents from the Tamberlaine biographies of Pedro Mexia, Petrus Perondinus, and others. As editors remind us, the name 'Zenocrate' derives from the word *zenokratos*, 'might of Zeus' (J.S. Cunningham, ed. 110; Fuller, ed. 166). In Marlowe's play, Zenocrate is the subject of Tamburlaine's sublime of beauty and simultaneously his sublime of ambition, at once the source of his conflict and the site of their resolution.

From the Prologue onwards, Marlowe locates the sublime at the heart of the play. He does not use the word 'sublime' but instead relies on his own vocabulary, which he makes famous: in this theatre of war ('stately tent' [Pr.3]), the audience will 'hear the Schythian Tamburlaine: /Threat'ning the world with high astounding terms' (4–5). This last phrase forms Marlowe's principal vocabulary for the sublime: *high, astounding, terms*. As Longinus puts it, 'in poetry the aim is astonishment' (15.2: 159).[54] As in *Dido*, in *1 Tamburlaine* Marlowe's astounding language of the sublime becomes the play's principal legacy.[55]

The legacy is located primarily in the figure of Tamburlaine himself, whom Marlowe presents as a figure of the sublime. As Menaphon tells Cosroe,

> Of stature tall, and straightly fashioned,
> Like his desire, lift upwards and divine;
> So large of limbs, his joints so strongly knit,
> Such breadth of shoulders as might mainly bear
> Old Atlas' burden; 'twixt his manly pitch
> A pearl more worth than all the world is placed,
> Wherein by curious sovereignty of art
> Are fixed his piercing instruments of sight,
> Whose fiery circles bear encompassed
> A heaven of heavenly bodies in their spheres
> That guides his steps and actions to the throne
> Where honour sits invested royally.
> (*1 Tamburlaine* 2.1.7–18)

The portrait continues for another dozen lines, describing Tamburlaine's 'lofty brows' and his Achilles-like 'knot of amber hair', 'Betokening valour and excess of strength' (2.1.21–8). In response, Cosroe supplies us with an epithet, which speaks to the protagonist's sublime character: Tamburlaine is a 'wondrous man' (32). He is the icon of sublimity because he is 'tall', because his height (like his desire) 'lifts upward' to divinity, and because each step he takes soars to the height of moral excellence – even the man's eyebrows are up-lifting. Body hair, eyes, desire, flesh, motion – 'passion' (19): Marlowe reinvents the human as the sublime, including what is so important to Longinus, man's inner compulsion to domination ('Thirsting with sovereignty' [20]), which commits him innately to violence. It is as if Marlowe were answering Longinus, rendering in dramatic portraiture what the theorist described: 'It is our nature to be elevated and exalted by true sublimity' (7.2: 148).

From Burke, Kant, and their heirs, we are used to seeing the sublime as the antithesis of the beautiful. As Kant puts it in *Observations on the Feeling of the Beautiful and the Sublime*,

> Finer feeling ... is chiefly of two kinds: the feeling of the *sublime* and that of the *beautiful*. The stirring of each is pleasant, but in different ways. The

sight of a mountain whose show-covered peak rises above the clouds, the description of a raging storm, or Milton's portrayal of the infernal kingdom, arouse enjoyment but with horror; on the other hand, the sight of flower-strewn meadows, valleys with winding brooks and covered with grazing flocks, the description of Elysium, or Homer's portrayal of the girdle of Venus, also occasion a pleasant sensation but one that is joyous and smiling. In order that the former impression could occur to us in due strength, we must have a *feeling of the sublime*, and, in order to enjoy the latter as well, a *feeling of the beautiful*. Tall oaks and lonely shadows in a sacred grove are sublime; flower beds, low hedges and trees trimmed in figures are beautiful. ... The sublime *moves*, the beautiful *charms*. (Kant, *Observations on the Feeling of the Beautiful and Sublime* 46–7; trans. Goldthwait; his emphases)

Yet Kant goes on to allow for the entry of the beautiful into the sublime, when he divides the sublime into three kinds: (1) 'the terrifying sublime', characterized by 'a certain dread, or melancholy'; (2) 'the *noble* [sublime]', characterized by 'quiet wonder'; and (3) 'the *splendid* [sublime]', characterized by 'a beauty completely pervading a sublime plan' (47–8; his emphases).

Even though Kant equates the 'sublime' with male 'friendship' ('Friendship is Sublime' [66; see 52]), and 'love between the sexes' with 'the beautiful' (52), the binary between the beautiful and the sublime post-dates the early modern period. Long before, Longinus had used beauty as one of his many synonyms for the sublime, as revealed in his phrase 'splendour, grandeur, and beauty' (35.3: 178). He had also written that 'beautiful words are the light that illuminates thought' (30.2: 172), and argued that 'sublimity and emotion are a defence and a marvelous aid against the suspicion which the use of figures [of speech] engenders. The artifice of the trick is lost to sight in the surrounding brilliance of beauty and grandeur, and it escapes all suspicion' (17.2: 164).[56]

Marlowe clearly imagines beauty, including female beauty, as one of the primary progenitors of the sublime. Tamburlaine exhibits the sublime of divine beauty in Act 1, scene 2, when he first addresses his future wife by echoing the author's 'Passionate Shepherd': 'Come lady, let not this appal your thoughts' (1). When she resists the rhetoric of his invitation ('Disdains Zenocrate to live with me?' [82]), he renews his ardor.

> Zenocrate, lovelier than the love of Jove,
> Brighter than is the silver Rhodope,
> Fairer than whitest snow on Scythian hills,
> Thy person is more worth to Tamburlaine
> Than the possession of the Persian crown,
> Which gracious stars have promised at my birth.
> (*1 Tamburlaine* 1.2.87–92)

Critics often emphasize here the chilling lyric of Neoplatonic rhapsody, which shows the heightened male turning the lovely person of the female into a mere 'object of beauty' (Burnett, *'Tamburlaine'* 141, qting. Lisa Starks). While no doubt true, so is the literariness of the speech. The discourse does not simply re-play Marlowe's pastoral lyric but it refers to a myth about the poetic sublime, or the high-flying fame of the poet: the winged horse Pegasus, 'favourite steed to the Muses' (J.S. Cunningham, ed. 127). Tamburlaine invites Zenocrate to come live with him and be his love, but the terms of the invitation go beyond those offered by the Passionate Shepherd to the Nymph. In his speech, Tamburlaine declares the divine natural beauty of Zenocrate to be his highest value, more important than the 'Persian crown': she is lovelier than the 'love' of the highest deity, and more beautiful than earth's grandest snow-capped peaks – both images of the sublime for Longinus.

In the remainder of his speech, Tamburlaine inventories the gifts he will give Zenocrate if she will return his ardor:

> A hundred Tartars shall attend on thee,
> Mounted on steeds swifter than Pegasus;
> Thy garments shall be made of Median silk,
> Enchased with precious jewels of mine own,
> More rich and valurous than Zenocrate's;
> With milk-white harts upon an ivory sled
> Thou shalt be drawn amidst the frozen pools
> And scale the icy mountains' lofty tops,
> Which with thy beauty will be soon resolved;
> My martial prizes, with five hundred men,
> Won on the fifty-headed Volga's waves,
> Shall all we offer to Zenocrate,
> And then my self to fair Zenocrate.
>   (*1 Tamburlaine* 1.2.93–105)

Tamburlaine's sublime gifts include the luxurious leisure of exotic servants attending Zenocrate; equally exotic clothes 'Enchased' with precious stones; a magical ride on an 'ivory sled' pulled by white harts over frozen lakes and atop the snow-clad mountains, which her 'beauty' will 'resolve' or melt; the spoils of war protected by a small army under his own direction; and finally, Tamburlaine himself. Leisure, wealth, power, sexual energy, protection, a partner: Tamburlaine offers Zenocrate a masculine fantasy, embodied in his own divinely sanctioned person, if she will not disdain his love.[57]

Counterpoising Tamburlaine's sublime of divine beauty is his sublime of divine ambition, most famously represented in his speech on the Persian crown, and delivered to the newly deposed king of Persia, Bajazeth:

> The thirst of reign and sweetness of a crown,
> ...
> Moved me to manage arms against thy state.
> What better precedent than mighty Jove?
> Nature, that framed us of four elements
> Warring within our breasts for regiment,
> Doth teach us all to have aspiring minds:
> Our souls, whose faculties can comprehend
> The wondrous architecture of the world
> And measure every wand'ring planet's course,
> Still climbing after knowledge infinite
> And always moving as the restless spheres,
> Wills us to wear ourselves and never rest
> Until we reach the ripest fruit of all,
> That perfect bliss and sole felicity,
> The sweet fruition of an earthly crown.
> (*1 Tamburlaine* 2.7.12–29)

Those who malign the speech as bathos, because the exalted view of man degenerates into materialist desire for a rich object, underestimate the sublimity of the speech and misunderstand its political operation. The speech forms the play's set-piece because *1 Tamburlaine* is above all a drama about kingship and the material form that kingship takes. What has not been identified is the speech's republican ethos; for Tamburlaine delivers nothing less than an etiology of the republican king.[58]

To a royal monarch who reigns by hereditary succession, Tamburlaine delivers a myth of causality for why a base-born shepherd would be inclined to usurp his crown: it is built into the nature of things. Citing the originary myth of Jove usurping his father's throne as divine 'precedent' for his own imperial theft, Tamburlaine locates the origin of 'aspiring man' in 'Nature' – in our humoral character, composed of 'four elements', which, rather than mixing harmoniously to achieve equanimity, 'war[s]' for power 'within' us. Furthermore, says Tamburlaine, our naturally mobile physiology receives impetus from our 'soul', which 'climb[s]...after knowledge infinite' and 'Wills' our tireless ambition, itself 'always' desiring happiness created by an 'earthly crown'. Myth, body, soul – our classical heritage, our physiology, and even our spirituality: everything 'teach[es]' the common man to become a king. To put it another way, the notion of hereditary succession is *unnatural*, betraying both our human identity and our classical education. As the well-established allusion to the Book of Genesis in the last two lines indicates, that education undermines the central truth of Scripture, locating 'bliss' not in heaven but on earth, not in Christian faith but in classical politics. Tamburlaine's speech exhibits the triumph of the republican sublime: the impulse to infinity 'Move[s]' a shepherd to become a king.[59]

The Tamburlainian sublime of ambition and of beauty fuse in the play's only soliloquy. In Act 5, scene 1, the Scythian shepherd delivers his famous meditation on what seems to be the central idea behind the fiction of *1 Tamburlaine*: only the male's love of feminine beauty can civilize the peasant soul caught within a tyrannical warrior ideal. The structure of the plot supports this idea, for Tamburlaine begins by defeating kings we do not sympathize with (Mycetes and Cosroe), and he moves on to defeat kings with whom we do sympathize (Bajzaeth and his wife Zabina, the Soldan and Arabia). In this trajectory, Tamburlaine's soliloquy forms a hinge, as he works through a dramatic dilemma: whether to listen to the natural instinct outlined in his 'earthly crown' speech, that of carrying out his aspiration to kingship by killing Zenocrate's father and fiancé; or to listen to the authority of 'beauty', lodged in the 'person' of Zenocrate. In other words, Tamburlaine is caught in a dilemma over whether to follow the one or the other of the two versions of the sublime we are tracking.

In the first half of the soliloquy (lines 135–73), Tamburlaine entertains the authority of Zenocrate's divine beauty in political terms: 'Ah, fair Zenocrate, divine Zenocrate,/"Fair" is too foul an epithet for thee,/That, in thy passion for thy country's love/And fear to see thy kingly father's harm,/With hair dishevelled wipest thy watery cheeks' (135–9). Zenocrate's tears – and plea – result not simply from her fear for a parent's life but from her fear of the defeat of her 'country's' political leader. That politics, not just the family, is at the center of the dilemma becomes clear when Tamburlaine imagines a psychomachic war in heaven: 'There angels in their crystal armors fight/A doubtful battle with my tempted thoughts/ For Egypt's freedom and the Soldan's life' (151–3). In this 'battle', the dangerous rational power of Tamburlaine's political ambition to defeat a king is checked by an aesthetics-based conscience, grounded in the 'Beauty' of his beloved (144), which lends the king 'freedom'. The aesthetics is not a (Neoplatonic) theory of beauty pure and simple but a theory of poetry, made clear when Tamburlaine imagines 'Beauty' (rather than memory) as 'mother to the Muses' (a Marlovian invention) – that is, as an author 'comment[ing] ... volumes with her ivory pen' (144–5). While Tamburlaine attributes the creative power of poetry to the beauty of his tearful beloved, Marlowe self-reflexively pens a poetics of the sublime, inspired by thirst for political liberty.

As if to underscore such authorship, Tamburlaine returns to the 'poets' a few lines later, in one of the more torturous syntactical utterances of a notoriously difficult speech:

> What is beauty, saith my sufferings, then?
> If all the pens that ever poets held
> Had fed the feeling of their masters' thoughts
> And every sweetness that inspired their hearts,
> Their minds, and muses on admired themes;
> If all the heavenly quintessence they still
> From their immortal flowers of poesy,
> Wherein as in a mirror we perceive
> The highest reaches of a human wit;
> If these had made one poem's period
> And all combined in beauty's worthiness,
> Yet should there hover in their restless heads
> One thought, one grace, one wonder at the least.
> Which into words no virtue can digest.
> (*1 Tamburlaine* 5.1.160–73)

As the words 'admired', 'wonder', and 'highest' intimate, whatever these lines say, they register the sublime. Moving beyond rational speech, Marlowe renders the irrational character of the sublime of divine beauty syntactically, inventing an inexpressible poetry inspired by Zenocrate's beauty, one that he distills within the 'period' of his poetic sentence: both it and she are 'the highest reaches of the human wit'.

Having drawn this conclusion, in the second half of his soliloquy (174–90) Tamburlaine realizes that he has let the sublimity of beauty compromise his 'discipline of arms and chivalry': 'thoughts effeminate and faint' are 'unseemly' for his 'sex' (174–7). Yet the uncertainty remains short lived:

>   every warrior that is rapt with love
> Of fame, of valour, and of victory,
> Must needs have beauty beat on his conceits.
> (*1 Tamburlaine* 5.1.180–2)

In the end, Tamburlaine realizes that his love for Zenocrate is not incompatible with his military code but the inspiration for it: 'I ... /Shall give the world to note, for all my birth,/That virtue solely is the sum of glory/And fashions men with true nobility' (183–90). 'For all my birth' determines that we read Tamburlaine's conclusion not simply as humanist boilerplate but more specifically as humanist republican sentiment, as Machiavelli so often insists.[60] Tamburlaine does not say only that virtue leads to glory and allows men to be truly noble; rather, he situates the idea in the context of his lowly 'birth': 'Beauty' allows a shepherd to attain the state of manly *virtù*, resulting in 'nobility' and the telos of the Machiavellian life, 'glory'.[61] *1 Tamburlaine* concludes appropriately with the strange republican king's formulation of his new political empire:

> Cast off your armour, put on scarlet robes,
> Mount up your royal places of estate,
> Environed with troops of noble men,
> And there make laws to rule your provinces.
> (*1 Tamburlaine* 5.1.525–8)

Addressing monarchs in their 'royal places of estate', like the Soldan of Egypt, Tamburlaine presents himself as a king supported by counselor-friends, 'Environed with troops of noble men'. In this formation of a monarchical republic, Tamburlaine creates a free space to 'solemnise' the 'rites of marriage' with the sublime Zenocrate (535).

2 Tamburlaine

Readers often either neglect the sequel to *1 Tamburlaine* or express disappointment in it. Not simply does the narrative alter drastically, from the romantic story about a Scythian Shepherd becoming a mighty monarch to a story about this figure's tragic death, the death of his queen, and even the death of one of their three sons. And not simply does the play lose its admirable dramatic structure, which had been organized around Tamburlaine's meteoric ascent to sovereignty in both the political and the familial domains. Now the action foregrounds a series of opponents who lack the interest of a Bajazeth and a Zabina – such as their son Callapine, who fails dramatically to take over where his parents left off.[62]

More to the point here, *2 Tamburlaine* appears to lose its republican focus, as the technical language of liberty gives way to the language of empire. Whereas *1 Tamburlaine* uses cognates of the word 'liberty' seven times and 'freedom' six, bringing the total to thirteen, *2 Tamburlaine* uses cognates of 'liberty' only twice and of 'freedom' four times, making a total of six – less than half. In contrast, the 'imperial' discourse of 'empire' holds steady in the two Parts; once the freedom-fighter becomes a king, Marlowe appears to abandon interest in the central ideal of republicanism. Thus, *Part Two* becomes a story principally about the imperial aggression – and final death – of a 'tyrant' – a word that occurs only seven times in *Part One* but fifteen in *Part Two*. Repeatedly, Tamburlaine's enemies call him an 'injurious tyrant' (4.3.77), a 'vile tyrant' (5.1.133), 'tyrant of the world' (5.2.55), or just plain 'Tyrant' (5.1.54). Sometimes the full narrative of Tamburlaine's political career emerges succinctly, as when the King of Amasia calls him 'that base-born tyrant Tamburlaine' (5.2.18), or when Orcanes, King of Natolia, terms him 'slavish Tamburlaine' (3.5.175): this tyrant was born a slave, but now enslaves others. Repeatedly, Tamburlaine is accused of practicing 'taunts and bitter tyrannies' (4.3.56), 'barbarous damned tyranny' (4.1.141), and of being 'sent from hell to tyrannise on earth' (5.1.111).

When the discourse of liberty does appear, it does so only negatively: as the loss of freedom. In the play's second scene, for instance, Almeda tells Callapine, 'My sovereign lord, renowned Tamburlaine,/Forbids you further liberty than this' (1.2.7–8). In the next scene, Zenocrate attempts to free herself from her husband's tyrannical conduct: 'Sweet Tamburlaine, when wilt thou leave these arms/And save thy sacred person free from scathe' (1.3.9–10). Tamburlaine does not listen, and in Act 3, scene 1, Callapine reports on the outcome of his own conversation with Almeda, who has betrayed Tamburlaine: 'my friend/…freed me from the bondage of my foe' (69–70).

While the tension between empire and liberty slackens under Tamburlaine's ever-intensifying imperial whip, *Part Two* nonetheless continues to write republicanism in a significant way. This is evident in the opening line, in which the Prologue voices a populist paradigm of a common audience working in harmony with a communal theatre and an egalitarian author: 'The *general* welcomes Tamburlaine received/When he arrived last upon *our* stage/ Hath made *our* poet pen his second part' (1–3; emphasis added). The republican dynamic is in place also at the end of the play, when Marlowe relies on his source-texts to stage what the Elizabethan audience likely understood to be the failure of hereditary succession, as the technical republican discourse intimates: 'Let earth and heaven his timeless death deplore,/For both their worths will equal him no more' (5.3.253–4). In between these two moments, Tamburlaine continues to support his three newly royalized 'friends' – a word that recurs ten times, the identical amount to *Part One* – while he also continues to privilege the 'common soldiers' (4.3.67, 80, 91), most brutally when the 'tyrant' (77) gives the 'queens' (70) of the 'pampered Jades of Asia' (1) to his 'tall soldiers' (70) for their 'lust' (80): 'And let them equally serve all your turns' (73). This scene, which is Marlowe's invention, outstrips even the murder of the virgins of Damascus.

A similar travesty occurs in the next scene when the 'Governor of Babylon' (5.1.SD) initially emerges as 'the people's' savior (7), and refuses to surrender the city to Tamburlaine, despite advice to the contrary by the citizen Maximus:

> Villain, respects thou more thy slavish life
> Than honour of thy country or thy name?
> Is not my life and state as dear to me,
> The city and my native country's weal,
> As any thing of price with thy conceit?
> (*2 Tamburlaine* 5.1.10–14)

In this republican government, citizens are free to step forward to object to the Governor's will, as 'another [Citizen]' does by 'kneeling' in prayer (SD after line 23). In this non-aristocratic scene, Marlowe uses the debate between Governor and citizen over the 'secur[ity]' (16) of the city to stage a conflict between political resistance and 'servitude' (37). In the end, however, with the army of Tamburlaine laying siege, 'the sturdy Governor of Babylon' (81) sells out, begging Tamburlaine, 'Save but my life' (118), promising 'gold' (116). Tamburlaine takes the money, and orders the execution of 'Baghdad's Governor' (157), along with his equally nameless 'burghers' (160). From Baldwin's persuasion to Sigismund, King of Hungary, to break truce with the pagans – to protect 'Our liberty of arms and victory' (2.1.41) – to the most memorable travesty of republican values, the scene presenting the pampered kings of Asia drawing the base-born Tamburlaine's imperial chariot, Marlowe writes republicanism and troubles it. Such a project allows for a double ring in Orcanes' early comment about the tragic hero: 'He brings a world of people to the field. ... /All Asia is in arms with Tamburlaine' (1.1.67, 72).

We have some technical evidence that Marlowe writes republicanism self-consciously. Back in 1942, Paul Kocher argued that 4.1.93–113, the scene in which Tamburlaine kills his oldest son Calyphas, derives from a similar scene in Livy's *Rise of Rome*. As Livy narrates, the republican consul Manlius Torquatus orders his son Titus to be executed for violating orders. Titus had been lured by his Latin enemy Geminus Maecius into single combat, against the instructions of his father. Then, after Titus kills Geminus, Manlius is compelled to adhere to the discipline of arms: 'Since you, T. Manlius, have shown no regard for either the authority of a consul or the obedience due to a father, ... and have done your best to destroy the military discipline through which the Roman State has stood till now unshaken, and have forced upon me the necessity of forgetting either my duty to the republic or my duty to myself and my children, it is better that we should suffer the consequences of our offence ourselves. ... We shall be a melancholy example, but one that will be profitable to the young men of future' (8.7; trans. Roberts 2: 115).[63] Such a subtext shows Marlowe reworking the Tamburlaine narrative in terms of Roman republican history.

In addition to Livy, Lucan continues to find a voice in *Part Two*. Unlike with *Part One*, however, now Lucan appears only through verbal echo (rather than through direct reference). Nonetheless, modern editors have found several echoes of the *Pharsalia*, including *Lucan's First Book*. The play's opening conversation records the first echo, with the Viceroy of Byron, Gazellus, advising Orcanes to 'treat of peace' with the Christians, led by Sigismund because 'We all are glutted with the Christians' blood' (1.1.13–14). The phrasing recalls the opening of *Lucan's First Book*, when the narrator says, 'We plain not heavens, but gladly bear these evils/For Nero's sake: Pharsalia groan with slaughter,/And Carthage souls be glutted with our bloods' (37–9; see J.S. Cunningham, ed. 221). Not simply is the image similar but so is the thought, as Orcanes reproduces Lucan's complaint. The echo encourages us to view the international warfare through the Lucanian lens of civil war, but it also wryly equates the Christian spilling of blood with Nero's reign of terror.

In the most recent annotated edition of the play, Fuller records four more echoes of *Lucan's First Book*. In Act 1, scene 3, Techelles refers to the 'ugly Furies bearing fiery flags' (146), echoing *Lucan*'s image of the Furies carrying firebrands: 'foul Erinnys stalked about the walls,/Shaking her snaky hair and crooked pine/With flaming top, much like that hellish fiend' (570–2; Fuller, ed. 236). However graphic, the echo is more than incidental, for it picks up a striking image from classical literature to lend hyperbolic violence to a rather straightforward indictment of the enemy, as when Techelles reports how his defeat of the King of Fez confirms Jove's support of Tamburlaine. Similarly, in Act 2, scene 4, at the death of Zenocrate, Tamburlaine vents his grief (112) by recalling how he has broken his 'steeled lance, with which' he 'burst/The rusty beams of Janus' temple doors,/Letting out death and tyrannising war' (113–15), which recalls Lucan's infamous flattery of Nero as his 'god' (63): 'Peace through the world from Janus' fane shall fly,/And bolt the brazen gates with bars of iron' (61–2; Fuller, ed. 248). This echo is more important, because, as we shall see, the Lucanian discourse leads Tamburlaine to re-voice the sublime discourse of 'The Passionate Shepherd'.

More incidentally, in Act 4, scene 1, Tamburlaine indicts the kings he will later call the 'pampered Jades of Asia' (4.3.1) by comparing them to 'a herd of lusty Cimbrian bulls' (190), an echo of *Lucan*'s 'furious Cimbrians' (257; Fuller, ed. 266). The likelihood of an echo here increases, for L.C. Martin finds Marlowe glancing at *Lucan's First Book* just a few lines later (ed. 287). Earlier, we noted the similarity between a passage in *Dido* and Marlowe's translation in the image of the spear-like meteors (*LFB* 529–30), which recurs in *Part Two* at 4.1.202–5, when Tamburlaine says he will not relent in his tyrannical conduct 'till by vision or by speech' he hears 'Immortal Jove say "Cease, my Tamburlaine"' – retaining a vestige of Lucan's Caesar:

I will persist a terror to the world,
Making the meteors that, like armed men,
Are seen to march upon the towers of heaven.
          (*2 Tamburlaine* 4.1: 203–5)

Marlowe repeats the image yet a third time, in Act 5, scene 1, when Tamburlaine taunts the Governor of Babylon: 'Sirrah, the view of our vermilion tents,/Which threatened more than if the region/Next underneath the element of fire/Were full of comets and of blazing stars,/Whose flaming trains should reach down to the earth' (86–90; Fuller, ed. 274). For Marlowe, Lucan provides a resounding discourse of cosmic disaster that Tamburlaine deploys to assert his power over his enemy. Whereas Lucan records strange astral upheaval to 'presage the fall of kingdoms', Tamburlaine uses the Lucanian trope to demonstrate how his military action receives divine sanction.

Finally, Fuller allows us to see that even Marlowe's most infamous icon, the 'pampered Jades of Asia', most likely derives from Lucan, who, in Book 10 of the *Pharsalia*, refers to the Egyptian ruler 'Sesostris', who comes 'To the west and to the world's extremities…/And drove his Pharian chariot across the necks of kings' (276–7; Fuller, ed. 260).[64] Fuller adds one other gloss relevant here, which also alludes to Sesostris, although he does not refer to Lucan. In Act 5, scene 3, during the map-reading scene, Tamburlaine traces his military career to Egypt,

> And here, not far from Alexandria,
> Whereas the Terrene and the Red Sea meet,
> Being distant less than full a hundred leagues,
> I meant to cut a channel to them both,
> That men might quickly sail to India.
> (*2 Tamburlaine* 5.3.132–6)

According to Fuller, 'The construction of a canal from the Nile to the Red Sea was attributed to the semi-legendary Egyptian ruler Sesostris and to Pharaoh Ptolemy Philadelphus II (third century BC). Herodotus mentions such a canal constructed by Darius III (*Historia*, IV. 39). Marlowe may also have known of the attempts to construct a similar waterway by the Venetian republic in the early sixteenth century, which were revived by the Ottoman government of Egypt in 1586' (ed. 280). If we grant an echo of Lucan in the first Sesostris passage, perhaps we need to do so here as well.

Moreover, editors neglect Tamburlaine's Lucanian line in Act 3, scene, 5, about the way 'Heaven' protects his enterprise: 'And joined those stars that shall be opposite,/Even till the dissolution of the world' (80–2). The lines echo Marlowe's translation of the superb passage about cosmic dissolution discussed in earlier chapters: when 'Time ends, and to old Chaos all things turn,/Confused stars shall meet…/And…/Dissolve the engines of the broken world' (74–80). Whereas Marlowe's Lucan tells how cosmic dissolution heralds the atrocity of civil war, Tamburlaine recasts the trope to assert the longevity of his military success, all the way to the end of the world, even though the echo also equates his action with that of universal change. Repeatedly, Marlowe relies on Lucan – and his own translation of Lucan – to verify the divine authority of his sublime hero.

As we have intimated, Lucan's sublimity also finds its way into Marlowe's play.[65] Yet Tamburlaine is no longer the only one to re-voice 'The Passionate Shepherd'. Somewhat astonishingly, the first to use the Marlovian sublime is Callapine, who invites Almeda to come to war with him and be his friend:

> A thousand galleys, manned with Christian slaves,
> I freely give thee, ...
> The Grecian virgins shall attend on thee,
> Skilful in music and in amorous lays,
> As fair as was Pygmalion's ivory girl
> Or lovely Io metamorphosed.
> (*2 Tamburlaine* 1.2.32–9)

Embroidered with Ovidian 'metamorphos[is]', including the self-reflexive myth of Pygmalion transforming his 'ivory girl' into a real woman, Marlowe fuses the heterosexual to the homosocial, as one man lures another with fantasies of sexual union with beautiful young women. Perhaps Marlowe felt that Tamburlaine needed a serious rival, or perhaps Callapine's appropriation of Tamburlaine's high-astounding terms signals his own doom. Whatever the intent, the Marlovian sublime here becomes *transportable*.

Hence, in Act 3, scene 4, Tamburlaine's 'friend' Theridamas lapses into the discourse of 'The Passionate Shepherd' to address Olympia, who suffers from the death of her husband: 'But lady, go with us to Tamburlaine,/And thou shalt see a man greater than Mahomet,/In whose high looks is much more majesty/Than from the concave superficies/Of Jove's vast palace, th'empyreal orb' (45–9). Less a sexual invitation than a direct address, Theridamas' sublime discourse moves formally into the register of the Passionate Shepherd once he falls in love with a woman who longs to die: 'Leave this, my love, and listen more to me' (38):

> Thou shalt be stately Queen of fair Argier,
> And, clothed in costly cloth of massy gold,
> Upon the marble turrets of my court
> Sit like to Venus in her chair of state,
> Commanding all thy princely eye desires;
> And I will cast off arms and sit with thee,
> Spending my life in sweet discourse of love.
> (*2 Tamburlaine* 4.2.39–45)

Reminiscent of Tamburlaine's earlier courting of Zenocrate, Theridamas' 'sweet discourse of love' invites a captain's wife to metamorphose into the 'stately Queen of fair Argier' if only she will love him. Not just royal position but regal attire awaits the lucky woman who, in this masculine fantasy of the feminine, exalts her state as high as that of Venus, 'Commanding all thy precisely eyes desire'. The Marlovian sublime does not change here, but the result does: Olympia is not in the least tempted to become a royal idol of feminine beauty for the impassioned King of Argier; she is intent only to commit suicide (which she brings off decisively through enacting a page from Ariosto).

In the domain of sublime impotence, however, few can compete with Tamburlaine himself. In Act 2, scene 4, he attempts to talk Zenocrate out of dying: 'Live still, my love, and so conserve my life,/Or, dying, be the author of my death' (2.4.55–6). As in *Dido*, in *Part Two* Marlowe confers authorship on a royal female lying on the threshold of annihilation, as Tamburlaine marks off what he so powerfully renders here: in her demise as in her ascent, Zenocrate is the sublime inspiration for Tamburlaine's being. Even in her death, she remains a site for the sublime. Tamburlaine's sad exaltation spans the 142 lines of this scene, in long speeches of 38 lines, 40 lines, and a concluding 17. From the lyric refrain of the first, 'To entertain divine Zenocrate' (17, 21, 25, 29, 33), and the self-reflexive literary 'raving' (112) of the second, with its comparisons to Homer's Helen, Catullus' Lesbia, and Ovid's Corinna, to his final curse on the town where Zenocrate dies, Tamburlaine exhales the grandeur of his voice in service of his wife's beauty.

Most original is Marlowe's deployment of the Lucanian sublime to advance the art of resurrection:

> Behold me here, divine Zeoncrate,
> Raving, impatient, desperate, and mad,
> Breaking my steeled lance, with which I burst
> The rusty beams of Janus' temple doors,
> Letting out death and tyrannising war,
> To march with me under this bloody flag;
> And if thou pitiest Tamburlaine the Great,
> Come down from heaven and live with me again!
> 			(*2 Tamburlaine* 2.4.111–18).

Echoing *Lucan's First Book* (as we have seen), Tamburlaine weds the Lucanian and the Marlovian, the discourse of the *Pharsalia* with that of 'The Passionate Shepherd', epic civil war with pastoral invitation, breaking the sublime's generic boundaries.

No less sublime than *1 Tamburlaine*, the sequel exchanges its transcendent materiality for a grim counterpart: 'thou shalt stay with me,/Emblamed with cassia, ambergris, and myrrh,/Not lapped in lead, but in a sheet of gold,/And till I die thou shalt not be interred' (129–32). Andrew Hadfield, referring to Tarquin's rape of Lucrece, reminds us that the 'masculine phenomenon' of republicanism 'was established over the dead body of a woman, as the myth of the birth of the republic demonstrates' (174). With its own 'masculine phenomenon', *2 Tamburlaine* deploys this republican mythology through the death of Zenocrate, which uses the sublime from 'The Passionate Shepherd' to haunt the action, from Act 1 through Act 5.

Whereas *Part One* melds a sublime of divine beauty with a sublime of divine ambition (cf. Fuller, ed. xxiv), *Part Two* breaks the two asunder. If the first play charts Tamburlaine's dependence on Zenocrate's beauty for his argument of arms, the second traces the fall-out of her death on his imperial ambitions. Thus, in Acts 3 through 5 Tamburlaine goes on a rampage so excessive that even his friends warn him off (4.1.99–100) – unsuccessfully of course, as he ties the Jades of Asia to his chariot, gives their concubines to his soldiers, kills his eldest son, torches Babylon, and (somewhat anticlimactically) defeats Callapine. While engaged in these acts of atrocity, Tamburlaine creates what we might consider the penultimate chapter of his strange republican career; instead of celebrating Zenocrate's beautiful 'person' as the source of his imperial ambition, he worships the artificial relic of her mortal beauty: he turns Zenocrate into an artifact.[66] As in *Dido*, in *Part Two* a Marlovian hero deploys the sublime to exalt a beloved, yet in the process the author marks an unbridgeable gap between self and other: Tamburlaine and Zenocrate are not Romeo and Juliet.[67] Sacrificing intimacy between partners, Marlowe once more presents the sublime as a moment of authorship.[68]

Thus, as he lies dying, Tamburlaine calls for his wife's coffin, permitting a final sublimity:

> Now, eyes, enjoy your latest benefit,
> And when my soul hath virtue of your sight,
> Pierce through the coffin and the sheet of gold,
> And glut your longings with a heaven of joy.
> (*2 Tamburlaine* 5.3.225–8)

Lucan might be pleased, for Marlowe directs the sublime to its locus in the human body. Just as in Book 9 of the *Pharsalia* the poet witnesses the 'mighty ghost' of the deceased Pompey as it 'settled in the sacred breast/of Brutus and stationed itself in the mind of invincible Cato' (17–18), so Tamburlaine 'understands that his soul, freed of the limits of bodily sense, will be able to see Zenocrate's spirit' inside the coffin (Bevington and Rasmussen, eds., *Christopher Marlowe* 432).

Accordingly, *2 Tamburlaine* ends with the hero's attempt to secure his legacy. He does so through the act of hereditary succession, appointing his oldest surviving son, Amyras, as emperor: 'So reign, my son, scourge and control those slaves,/Guiding thy chariot with thy father's hand' (5.3.229–30), just as Phaethon did the chariot of Apollo (232–6). Yet the Ovidian allusion sounds ominously, and is intensified when Tamburlaine adds the tragic fate of another classical chariot-driver, Hippolytus (241). While on the surface the play ends amicably with the triumph of hereditary succession, the Ovidian references to Phaethon and Hippolytus remind the audience of the ending to the Tamburlaine source-texts, when the hero's attempt at hereditary succession ultimately fails, and his hard-won empire crumbles. In this way, Marlowe can be seen both to serve his country's political practice and to subvert it. Yet in subverting hereditary succession, the *Tamburlaine* plays rehearse a republican ethos operative in 1590s England. Along with *Dido, Queen of Carthage*, the resounding success of the *Tamburlaine* plays on the London stage unleashes a republican spirit of empire and liberty that looks forward grimly to the English Civil War.[69]

4
Machevill's Republican Monarchy: Civil War in *The Jew of Malta*, *The Massacre at Paris*, and *Edward II*

To complement his three plays of imperialism, Marlowe pens three plays about civil war: *The Jew of Malta* (1589); *The Massacre at Paris* (1592–3); and *Edward II* (1591–2). The last two are formally about civil war – the first treating the intestine broil in late sixteenth-century France, the second in fourteenth-century England. *The Jew* is set against the backdrop of a sixteenth-century Mediterranean war between Christians and Muslims on Malta but comes to focus on the island's civic turmoil, with a Jew at the eye of the storm. Traditionally, these three plays cohere in their 'Machiavellian policy', their deployment of a lead character's cunning political strategy popularly associated with Machiavelli's 'Prince', so that critics have termed the triad Marlowe's 'plays of policy'.[1] While the politics of policy in all three plays has been widely discussed, especially their debt to Machiavelli, European Machiavellianism, and the advent of the Machiavel on the Elizabethan stage, no one has situated the plays within the historical context of late Elizabethan republican discourse. That shall be the general goal of the present chapter.

In the last chapter, we discussed Machiavelli primarily with reference to his Sallustian paradigm of 'empire and liberty', as it appears in *Dido, Queen of Carthage* and the two *Tamburlaine* plays. This paradigm recurs in Marlowe's three plays of policy, and we shall discuss it when occasion permits. Primarily, however, the present chapter concentrates on a related paradigm, which more formally structures Machiavelli's political thinking in the *Discourses on Livy*: his recurrent transposition of the traditional three kinds of government (monarchy, aristocracy, democracy [*Discourses* 1.2: 23–8]) to two kinds – what Machiavelli habitually terms 'a Prince or a Republic' (chapter title to 1.21: 73). While recognizing a democracy or popular government, he instinctively discusses the manifold topics of the *Discourses* with respect to 'a republican or a monarchical form to civil life' (1.26: 80). For instance, he titles chapter 30 to Book 1 'What Means a Prince or a Republic May Employ to Avoid the Vice of Ingratitude' (86). Hence, everywhere we look, Machiavelli includes these two political options: 'Any state, whether republic or principality but especially a principality, that ... really believes it can win back with benefits the instant danger arises deceives itself' (1.32: 91). Such a discursive habit reminds us not simply that Machiavelli devotes a treatise to each form of government, the *Discourses* and *The Prince*, but that the two works interpenetrate, including when Machiavelli in one refers to the other (*Discourses* 3.42: 351; *Prince* 2: 4), and when in his treatise on the republic he addresses the 'prince' directly (*Discourses* 2.24: 221). We might, then, come to think of Machiavellianism proper – as distinct, say, from the early modern English definition of cunning dissembler – as a grid that intersects a principality with a republic.

It is across this grid, not simply the popular 'Machiavellian' one of crafty force, that we might view Marlowe's three Machiavellian plays of policy. In each play, Marlowe creates a fiction about civil war between the rights of a republic and the dictatorship of a principality. The general context for viewing these fictions emerges in Patrick Collinson's 'The Monarchical Republic of Queen Elizabeth I' (essay title; see Introduction): the late Elizabethan intersection of the two forms of government that Machiavelli emphasizes, yet carried out in English government policy (for Collinson, in the 1584 Bond of Association), in local practice (also for Collinson, in the city of Swallowfield), and (we may add) in such published treatises as Thomas Smith's *De Republica Anglorum* (1583) and Richard Beacon's *Solon his Follie* (1594).

In each play of policy, moreover, Marlowe situates the friction between 'prince and republic' within a more specific historical context, making each play distinct, invested with a different though related set of cultural ideas: in *The Jew of Malta*, the dynamic of liberty and wealth within what was called the *Respublica Hebraeorum*; in *The Massacre at Paris*, the civil war in France between Catholic monarchists and Republican Huguenots; and in *Edward II*, the civil war in England between absolutist monarchy and aristocratic republic, especially as viewed through the lens of Elizabethan Tacitism. As such, the presence of the three primary vectors we are tracking as intrinsic to Marlowe's republican authorship – 'Lucan, liberty, and the sublime' – undergoes fresh and important adjustment in these plays.[2]

The Jew of Malta: The *Respublica Hebraeorum* and the Maltese republic

For a play so often discussed for its 'competition, vengeance, and categorical hatred' (Engle, intro., *Renaissance Drama* 287) – or what T.S. Eliot long ago termed its 'savage comic humour' (64) – *The Jew of Malta* contains a remarkable discourse of republican authorship. As with his first three plays, this one includes a steady flow of *libertas*. The word 'liberty' itself occurs only once, yet cognates of 'freedom' occur thirteen times. For instance, the word 'free' recurs seven times – more than in any other Marlowe work – while the word 'freely' appears four times out of seven in his poems and plays, indicating this play's interest in concepts of liberty, civic and otherwise. Thus, it seems significant that *The Jew of Malta* includes two of Marlowe's six uses of the word 'liberal' (with its cognates) – his only work that includes more than one use. As the *OED* reports, at this time the word means 'the distinctive epithet of those "arts" or "sciences"... that were considered "worthy of a free man" ' (Def. 1). Marlowe had employed this definition formally in *Ovid's Elegies*: 'What man will now take liberal arts in hand' (3.7.1).

One of his six uses of 'liberal' comes from *Lucan's First Book*, within a specifically republican context, when the republican hero Pompey violates the party virtue of liberality, in part due to his vain commitment to one of Marlowe's twin arts: 'Pompey was strook in years,/And by long rest forgot to manage arms,/And being popular sought by liberal gifts/To gain the light unstable commons' love,/And joyed to hear his theatre's applause' (130–4). The concept of *liberal giving*, with commerce at its core, and here identified as a republican civic virtue, recurs throughout *The Jew of Malta*. Often we learn that characters 'freely give' (3.1.3), or purport to. Presently, we shall link freedom and commerce more directly, and not simply in the discourse of the play, but also in the discourse of European republicanism.

In fact, liberty is so important to *The Jew of Malta* that the word 'free' lies at the heart of Marlowe's dramatic narrative: 'Malta shall be freed' (5.5.112), declares Ferneze, the Governor of Malta, at the very end. The idea recurs three further times in Act 5, scene 2 alone, in a matter of a dozen lines (5.2.90, 5.2.95, 5.2.101), identifying Malta as a place of struggle between freedom and oppression, liberty and slavery. The reason is simple. For five Acts, we've been viewing a story about the loss of civic freedom. And it is not simply Barabas, the Jew of Malta, who loses his liberty, once Ferneze takes away his wealth to pay the tribute owed to the Turkish Emperor; nor is it simply Ferneze, who later loses his governorship to the scheming Barabas. Malta is an island oppressed from two opposing monarchical sides, by the Islamic Turks and the Christian Spanish, in a squabble over money and might.[3]

What has largely escaped attention is Marlowe's representation of Malta as a Christian republic.[4] Marlowe makes it clear that, unlike Spain or Turkey, Malta is no monarchy. Rather, it is run as a republic by the 'Governors of Malta', who are 'presided over by Ferneze, Chief Governor' (SD to Act 1, scene 1, in Bevington, ed., *Renaissance Drama* 298), a collectivity that conducts civic business by 'meeting in the senate-house' (1.1.166). The word 'senate' occurs ten times in the Marlowe canon, while the word 'senator' occurs two more, bringing the total to twelve. Of these, three occur in *The Jew of Malta*, and six in *Lucan's First Book* – a striking statistic, bringing early modern Malta into alignment with classical Rome, and Marlowe's tragedy into alignment with the central poem of the republican imagination. Not merely does the word 'senate' recur, but a crucial scene is set at the Maltese 'Senate-house' (1.2.236): at a public policy meeting, Ferneze demands that the Jews relinquish their wealth for the 'common good' (101).

As this meeting indicates, Marlowe's Republic of Malta is much like Rome's, as Machiavelli presents it in the *Discourses*: corrupt to the coffer. Critics of Marlowe have long complained that Machiavelli nowhere identifies Avarice as the cause of civil war or at issue in the battle between republics and monarchies. In fact, this is misleading. In an important essay titled 'The Republican Ideal of Political Liberty', Quentin Skinner sees one of the 'principal benefits' of a 'free state' (in classical republicans and Machiavelli alike) as 'civic greatness and wealth' (301), citing *Discourses* 2.2: 'It is easy to understand how this affection for a free way of life arose in those peoples, because experience demonstrates that cities have never enlarged or increased their wealth unless they have lived in liberty' (156). Here Machiavelli discusses his paradigm of 'empire and liberty' with reference to commerce: republics can succeed in the twin projects of enlarging their empire and increasing their wealth only through the practice of liberty. Wealth is the ally of empire, and the two can operate successfully only through political freedom. In Skinner's words, 'The people must set aside all personal and sectional interests, and learn to equate their own good with the good of the city as a whole' (*Foundations* 1: 44). This, I suggest, is the foundational idea of *The Jew of Malta*.[5]

Furthermore, Machiavelli scholars draw attention to 'one of his most original contributions to republican thinking' (Bondanella and Bondanella, eds. 363): since Rome's 'authority remained mixed [in its kinds], it created a perfect republic, and Rome came to this perfection through the discord between the plebeians and the senate' (*Discourses* 1.2: 27–8). As Skinner says, quoting *Discourses* 1.4, ' "all legislation favourable to liberty is brought about by the clash" between the classes, and thus ... class-conflict is not the solvent but the cement of a commonwealth' (*Foundations* 1: 181). Marlowe, I further suggest, understands Machiavelli's original contribution to republican thinking, but, rather than staging its comedic success, he turns the clash into a tragic farce, to create the theatrical achievement that Harold Bloom calls 'Marlowe's most vital and original play' ('Introduction' 2).

The republican dispute between civil liberty and commerce was afoot in Marlowe's London, not always in a formal Machiavellian guise. Robert Greene, for instance, in his 1590 *Royal Exchange*, refers to Cicero's key republican tract, *De officiis*, when writing that London is 'peopled with warlike Merchaunts, and politick Cittizens': to understand 'the calling of a Cittizen', we need to know 'the effects Tullie pende down in his *Offices*' (qtd. Peltonen,

'Citizenship' 89). In an essay on this topic, Markuu Peltonen discusses Elizabethan 'merchants as active citizens': 'the citizen's life of political action was often linked with an urban environment', even though 'seeing men of commerce as active citizens...demanded a public apology' (89). Peltonen finds an anonymous author making such an apology in a 1584 treatise titled *Breefe Discourse, Declaring...Laudable Customs of London*, in which citizens of London are 'profitable members of the common wealth, in transporting our commodities into other lands, and enriching us with the benefits and fruits of other countries' (qtd. Peltonen 89). Peltonen adds that the 'Ciceronian vocabulary was subtly used for defending the abilities of merchants *qua* active citizens' within a city government, which the anonymous author imagines as a republic modeled on classical Rome (89–90): 'The inescapable conclusion was that the inhabitants of a free town were expected to form a large and virtuous citizenry, to take care of the government of their hometown and to look after the well-being of their commonwealth' (92–3). This is the gold standard against which Marlowe writes *The Jew of Malta*. Removing the 'cittie' from London to Malta, injecting the 'urban environment' with outcast Jews, and presenting the 'free state' as the center of a geopolitical dispute over commerce, he puts before his own 'hometown' a displaced version of England's Machiavellian world.[6]

For Marlowe, however, the dynamic of liberty and commerce would also have had a Lucanian origin. In *Lucan's First Book*, for instance, he translates the Roman poet's political analysis about the impending doom of the Republic, which turns out to be caused by the commerce of greed: 'Poverty (who hatched/Rome's greatest wits) was loathed, and all the world/Ransacked for gold, which breeds the world decay' (166–8). One of the most famous exchanges in Marlowe appears on this topic, poised at the very center of *The Jew of Malta*, when Ferneze asks Callapine, 'What wind drives you thus into Malta road?' And Callapine replies, coolly, 'The wind that bloweth all the world besides: /Desire of gold' (3.5.2–4). For this utterance, we may detect a more specific Lucanian origin. In the lines leading up to the ones just quoted from *Lucan's First Book*, Marlowe translates the Latin original:

> this war's seed
> Was even the same that wracks all great dominions.
> When Fortune made us lords of all, wealth flowed,
> And then we grew licentious and rude;
> The soldiers' prey and rapine brought in riot;
> Men took delight in jewels, houses, plate.
> (*Lucan's First Book* 159–64)

As Lucan explains earlier, his larger 'purpose' is to 'unfold' the 'causes.../Of these garboils, whence springs a long discourse,/And what made madding people shake off peace' (67–9). In Book 1, he inventories several possibilities, from the envy of the gods, to the hungry power of Caesar and Pompey, to money itself. As we are anticipating, this last Lucanian etiology of civil war speaks to one of the major goals of European republics from Lucan's time to Marlowe's – and our own: 'reconciling commercial realities with republican hopes'.[7]

The Jew of Malta has other verbal links with *Lucan's First Book*. The first is in the Prologue, spoken by 'Machevill' himself, who allows us to see a crucial feature of this play: its fusion of the Lucanian with the Machiavellian.[8] Thus, in lines 18–19 Machevill refers to Julius Caesar:

> Many will talk of title to a crown.
> What right had Caesar to the empery?
> (*Jew of Malta* Pr.18–19)

Editorial commentary on the Prologue indicates how in Marlowe's imagination the early modern Italian political theorist cannot be extricated from the classical Roman epicist. Here is N.W. Bawcutt's Revels Play gloss: 'Machiavelli describes Caesar as a tyrant who seized power by force in the *Discourses*, I, 29, and Marlowe may have been influenced by the hostile portrayal of Caesar in Lucan's *Pharsalia*' (ed. 64). This gloss is at once useful and limiting: useful because it refers to both Machiavelli and Lucan, the *Discourses* and the *Pharsalia*; limiting because it neglects the historic invention here: an English author puts into the mouth of a stage presenter called Machevill the language of the arch-republican treatise, in order to refer to the central poem of the republican imagination.

If we return to the text Bawcutt cites, chapter 29 of Book 1 of the *Discourses*, here's what Machiavelli says,

> a city which lives in freedom has two goals, the first to acquire territory, the other to keep itself free, and it is likely to err in the pursuit of both of these goals through excessive love. As for the errors committed in acquiring territory, they will be discussed in the proper place. As for the errors committed in keeping itself free, there are, among others, the following: to injure citizens who should be rewarded; to be suspicious of those who should be trusted. Although these methods in a republic given over to corruption are the cause of great evils and quite often actually lead it to tyranny, as occurred in Rome with Caesar, who seized by force what ingratitude had denied him, they are nevertheless the cause of great benefits in an uncorrupted republic, and they cause it to live longer in liberty, since the fear of punishment makes men better and less ambitious. (Machiavelli, *Discourses* 1.29: 85)

If Bawcutt is right to gloss Marlowe's Machevill with this passage, we might wish to sort out just what Machiavelli says. First, notice the harmony between *this* Machiavelli and the one in *The Prince* – 'the dread of punishment will keep men better' – as well as the harmony between these Machiavellian voices and the one Marlowe invents. Second, notice the 'republican' context for the voice at this moment in the *Discourses*: Machiavelli does not simply 'describe...Caesar as a tyrant who seized by force in the *Discourses*, I, 29'; he situates his description of the tyrannical Caesar in terms of the larger republican dynamic of a 'free city', with its cardinal principle, 'liberty'. Specifically, Machiavelli contrasts the corrupt republic that Caesar capitalizes on with a republic 'not yet entirely corrupt'. For Machiavelli, Caesar's tyranny is always a civic violation of republican freedom. Put another way: from the perspective of Marlowe's works, Machiavelli's Caesar is always 'Lucanian'.[9]

Editors have turned up two other more incidental connections between *Lucan's First Book* and *The Jew of Malta*. First, in Act 3, scene 4, Bawcutt (ed. 135) glosses one of Barabas' most Machiavellian-sounding utterances, 'Repentance! Spurca! What pretendeth this?' (6), with line 625 of *Lucan's First Book*, 'And which (aye me) ever pretendeth ill', as the poet responds to the oracular power of oozing blood in a bull slaughtered by the augurer Arruns, which 'Did threaten horror from the host of Caesar' (621). Second, in Act 3, scene 5, Roma Gill (ed., *Works* 4: 115) glosses Ferneze's phrase 'more welcome is than wars' (36) with line 184 of *Lucan's First Book*, although we might include the preceding line, for its obvious application to *The Jew*: 'Hence interest and devouring usury sprang,/Faith's breach, and hence came war, to most men welcome' (183–4).

Gill also cites a passage from Lucan that Marlowe did not translate; in Act 1, scene 1, Barabas opens the play with reference to 'those Samnites, and the men of Uz' (1.1.4; Gill, ed., *Works* 4: 96), which she glosses with Book 2 of the *Pharsalia*, when Lucan refers to a battle at 'the Colline Gates.../...when the Samnites hoped/to inflict wounds on Rome exceeding the Caudine Forks' (135–8). According to Bawcutt, '"Samnites" appears to be meaningless (unless it was invented by Marlowe himself)' since 'there was no connection between the Samnites (a central Italian tribe conquered by the Romans, after a long struggle, in 295 B.C.) and the men of Uz (Job i.I)' (ed. 67). Yet Marlowe's conjunction between the Samnites and the men of Uz may be less meaningless if we recall the Lucanian republican genealogy: the Samnites are a perfect Lucanian tribe, a defeated republic who admirably fought the tyranny of Rome, only to fall into slavery when they were defeated, as Machiavelli recurrently records: 'Anyone...will not be amazed at the power the Samnites possessed when they were free and at their weakness when they subsequently fell into servitude' (2.2: 161; see 2.2: 156). Clearly, Marlowe attempts to link the classical example of oppression with the biblical one, so that Barabas can criticize both and offset his own commercial freedom.

If we return to the opening of the play's Prologue, we see something else Lucanian – what we might call Machevill's sublime:

> Albeit the world think Machevill is dead,
> Yet was his soul but flown beyond the Alps;
> And now the Guise is dead, is come from France
> To view this land and frolic with his friends.
> (*Jew of Malta* Pr.1–4)

Remarkably, editors have not glossed this opening with the famous opening to Book 9 of the *Pharsalia*, Lucan's most memorable representation of the sublime (see Chapter 1). Just as Lucan witnesses the 'mighty ghost' of the decapitated Pompey 'leap...up' and 'head...for the Thunderer's dome', only to return to earth to mock its headless torso and finally 'settle...in the sacred breast/of Brutus and station...itself in the mind of invincible Cato' (2–18), so does Marlowe present the 'soul' of Machevill transmigrating from Italy, 'beyond the Alps', to 'France', where first he took up residence in the body of 'the Guise', only now to visit England. Presumably for an Elizabethan audience, Marlowe's sublime photography of the *descent* of the Christian soul across nations had a shocking, even blasphemous, effect. The arrival of the Guise's Machiavellian soul in England, to 'view this land and frolic with his friends', measures an alarming metempsychosis, transmogrifying the notorious arch-republican, Niccolò Machiavelli, into a notorious monarchist, right in the London theatre. Yet Marlowe does not simply transplant and update Lucan's sublime; he converts it from the impotent to the impertinent. While the new Pompeian breast of Brutus and the great mind of Cato will lead the Roman Republic to suicide, the Machiavellian soul of the Guise will lead to merry gamboling among English 'friends'.[10]

Machevill's subsequent reference to 'Caesar' and his lawless 'right to the empery' identifies a Lucanian model for the play's presenter, who 'count[s] religion but a childless toy' and 'hold[s] there is no sin but ignorance' (14–15). Just as Caesar illegally stole 'the title to a crown', so Machevill presents himself as an opponent to the divine 'right' of 'kings'; he is the enemy of monarchy:

> Might first made kings, and laws were then most sure
> When like the Draco's they were writ in blood.
> Hence comes it that a strong-built citadel
> Commands much more than letters can import.
> (*Jew of Malta* Pr.20–3)

As Bawcutt's gloss allows us to see, line 20 is deeply implicated in European republican thought of the sixteenth century:

> It was long debated whether kingship originated through the violent seizure of rule by the most powerful, or through the voluntary surrender of power by the community to the man most fitted to rule. Machiavelli himself leant towards the second theory (*Discourses*, I, 2), but Jean Bodin strongly advocated the theory of force (*The Six Books of a Commonweal*, trans. R. Knolles, 1606, p. 47; earliest French edition, 1576). A plagiarized version of Bodin is in P. de la Primaudaye, *The French Academy*, trans. T. Bowes, 1586, pp. 585–6. (Bawcutt, ed., *Jew of Malta* 64)

We shall have more to say about the Huguenot Bodin shortly, when we turn to *The Massacre at Paris*, but for now we may recall simply that republican ideas such as the ones Marlowe versifies here were being translated into English during his lifetime. Even though paradoxically Machevill takes an un-Machiavellian view regarding the origins of kingship, his Bodinian view explodes the Tudor myth of hereditary succession familiar to Marlowe's audience, in the end aligning with Machiavelli himself.[11] Marlowe's maneuver is thus complex, but it will not do to pass it off simply as 'savage comic humour'.

As Bawcutt observes, 'Machiavelli did not mention Draco', the 'Athenian legislator who in 621 B.C. reformulated the Athenian legal code', becoming so 'proverbial' for his 'severity' that 'the orator Demades said that his laws were written in blood' (ed. 64). Reminiscent of Caesar in the Republic of Rome, however, Draco was a tyrant who polluted the democracy of Athens. Thus, this tyrant further illustrates how Machevill presents politics in terms of the Western conversation between the two kinds of government, monarchy and republic. For Machevill, Draco's power to write law in his own blood illustrates the grim notion that might makes kings, not divine right.

Just as editorial annotation shows Marlowe glancing at Lucan, it also shows him further glancing at Machiavelli in the *Discourses*. Bawcutt glosses Machevill's notorious quip that 'religion' is but a 'toy' this way: 'Machiavelli did not in fact dismiss religion in this way (see *Discourses*, I, 11–15), but his 16th c. opponents frequently described him as an atheist, or (with some justification) as one who believed in religion simply as a political tool (e.g., Hooker, *Of the Laws of Ecclesiastical Polity*, Book V, 1597, p. 7)' (ed. 63). In fact, what Machiavelli says is this: 'Just as the observance of divine worship is the cause of the greatness of republics, so the disregard of divine worship is the cause of their ruin, because where fear of God is lacking, that kingdom must either come to ruin or be sustained through fear of a prince who makes up for the shortcomings in its religion' (1.11: 52).[12] Machiavelli is chronically a political pragmatist, not an idealist, and he attacks anything violating his gold standard: 'a free civil state' (1.9: 46). Throughout the history of Western government, including Christian government, Machiavelli finds 'divine worship' the very 'cause' of 'greatness' in a republic, and its 'disregard' the cause of 'ruin'. In his own day, he goes on to say, Italy 'has lost all piety and religion', and – deploying the grim humor of Lucan and Tacitus – he adds, on the cusp of the Reformation, 'We Italians have, therefore, this initial debt to the church and to the priests, that we have become irreligious and wicked, but we have an even greater debt to them, which is the second cause of our ruin: that is, the church has kept and still keeps this land divided' (1.12: 55).[13]

Editors also gloss Machevill's next lines with the *Discourses*:

> Hence comes it that a strong-built citadel
> Commands much more than letters can import:
> Which maxima had Phalaris observed,
> H'had never bellowed in a brazen bull
> Of great ones' envy: o' the poor petty wights,
> Let me be envied and not pitied!
>   (Marlowe, *Jew of Malta* Pr.22–7)

In glossing the superiority of a 'citadel' over 'letters', Bawcutt cites Machiavelli's 'complicated, even contradictory' attitude as it varies from *The Art of War* to *The Prince* to the *Discourses*, with endorsements for the building of fortresses occurring in the first two works and criticism of such building in the third (ed. 65). In glossing Machevill's reference to the Sicilian tyrant Phalaris, Bawcutt observes further, 'Machiavelli expressed contempt for Phalaris (*Discourses*, I, 10)' (ed. 65). But Machiavelli did so more emphatically later when discussing the 'motive ... that drives men to conspire against a prince; this is the desire to free one's native city from the one who seized it. This motive moved Brutus and Cassius against Caesar; it also moved many others against Phalaris, Dionysius, and those who seized their native cities' (3.6: 258). Not simply is Phalaris a tyrant; he is a Sicilian correlate to the Roman Caesar, an oppressor of the republic and its primary value, liberty.[14] Finally, to gloss the most famous statement of all, Machevill's plea to be envied rather than pitied, Bawcutt cites only '*The Prince*, ch. 17' as the main example of an idea that was proverbial (ed. 65), when in fact Machiavelli also discusses the idea in the *Discourses* (3.21: 307).[15]

Bawcutt's glosses help us see the extent to which Machevill's Prologue is not based simply on the popular notion of the Machiavel but on Machiavelli's own republican treatise. Marlowe's dramatic scholarship underlying this portrait makes for a complex opening. Most visibly, Machevill is a

Machiavellian tyrant in the mold of Lucan's Caesar. But if we read the *Discourses* along with the English poet-playwright, we come to view 'the tragedy of a Jew/Who smiles to see how full his bags are crammed' (3–4) through the complicating lens of republican freedom and oppression. When Machevill closes his Prologue by entreating the audience to 'grace' Barabas 'as he deserves' (33), the presenter certainly encourages our complicity in the tragedy, but he also slyly grants the audience freedom to judge, in keeping with the acute artistic merit that Marlowe invests in the Jew.

In the play proper, Marlowe's memorable characterization of Barabas – Bloom calls him 'Marlowe's grandest character' ('Introduction' 2) – proceeds in two distinct phases pertinent here. In the first, exhibited at the beginning of the play, Barabas is a Republican Jew, living successfully in the Republic of Malta, benefiting cheerfully from its 'free' commercial system, and operating 'freely' without the oppression that historically had expelled the Jews from England in 1289, and from Malta in 1492. In the second phase, exhibited after Barabas loses his wealth to republican tyranny, the Jew metamorphoses from a successful republican merchant-citizen into what especially interests Marlowe: a new type of character, the Machiavellian man of theatre.[16] In other words, *The Jew of Malta* is not simply 'the tragedy of a Jew' (Pr.30); it is also a tragedy about one of the foundational myths of European culture, the *Respublica Judaeorum*. The 'Jewish Commonwealth' itself forms an 'analogue' to the more well-known foundational myth of early modern republics modeled by the Netherlands and by Florence: Republican Rome (Boralevi).[17] Let us look at each phase in turn.

In the first phase, Marlowe introduces Barabas as a free Republican Jew. In his opening soliloquy, Barabas outlines a commercial philosophy grounded in republican values. Occupying the minority position of a Jew, Barabas may be an outsider in the Christian community of Malta, but when we first see him, he has successfully used his business savvy to capitalize on Malta's unique standing, where 'if anywhere, East met West' (H. Levin, *Overreacher* 65; cf. Bartels 88; Hunter 202–3), where Christian meets Muslim, and where (I am suggesting) republic meets monarchy. Barabas appears to interest Marlowe because he is an outsider who can manipulate this geopolitical dynamic *freely*.

The word 'free' resonates in Barabas' soliloquy:

> Give me the merchants of the Indian mines,
> That trade in metal of the purest mould;
> The wealthy Moor, that in the eastern rocks
> Without control can pick his riches up,
> And in his house heap pearl like pebble-stones,
> Receive them free, and sell them by the weight.
> (*Jew of Malta* 1.1.19–24)

For his entrepreneurial models, Barabas selects the Indian merchant and the wealthy Moor, because each is 'free' to 'pick his riches up' and 'sell them by the weight', 'without control'.[18]

It is the power to exchange currency that Barabas finds liberating, expressed through the discourse of the Marlovian sublime:

> Bags of fiery opals, sapphires, amethysts,
> Jacinths, hard topaz, grass-green emeralds,
> Beauteous rubies, sparkling diamonds,
> And seld-seen costly stones of so great price,
> As one of them indifferently rated
> And of a carat of this quantity,
> May serve in peril of calamity
> To ransom great kings from captivity.
> This is the ware wherein consists my wealth.
> (*Jew of Malta* 1.1.25–33)

This is what Jonson saw as Marlowe's great achievement, his ability to locate the sublime in the beauty of the material, as rehearsed magnificently by Sir Epicure Mammon in *The Alchemist* (see Chapter 2). Yet what particularly excites Barabas himself about the sublimity of his precious stones is not simply their 'great price' but also their political currency. By hoarding 'wealth' freely, he positions himself strategically, able to escape 'the peril of calamity' and thus to 'ransom great kings from captivity'. This paradoxical project – *freeing kings* – speaks directly to the commerce between monarchical and republican values in Marlowe's play.

As a republican who frees kings, Barabas is no democrat. Critical of the 'needy groom' (12), he imagines himself serving the rich and powerful:

> And thus methinks should men of judgment frame
> Their means of traffic from the vulgar trade,
> And as their wealth increaseth, so enclose
> Infinite riches in a little room.
> (*Jew of Malta* 1.1.34–7)

To put himself in a position to free kings, a wise man needs to work above the common herd by keeping his treasure to himself. Yet his intense closeting of wealth turns out to have more than a political function; the commercial build-up is so intense it explodes into a stunning fantasy about *the sublimity of infinity*.

Barabas' sublime fantasy of eternal solitude, enclosing 'infinite riches in a little room', betrays a keen desire for what Machiavelli calls 'supreme greatness' (*Discourses* 2.6: 169), and thus social recognition – that is, both the imaginative state of the 'infinite' and the immortality of fame. In the *Discourses*, Machiavelli devotes a whole chapter to this topic: 'a man who keeps the company of honest companions acquires a good name'. To acquire a 'good reputation', a wise man must perform 'some extraordinary and noteworthy deed': 'Men who are born in a republic ... must strive to begin to distinguish themselves through some extraordinary deed', the fruit of which is infinite 'glory' and 'fame' (3.34: 335–6). A good student of Machiavelli, Barabas selects as his extraordinary deed – his ticket to glory – a commercial policy leading to political power. By enclosing infinite riches in a little room, he ransoms great kings from captivity.

Barabas' 'infinite' line may have an undisclosed Lucanian origin. A bit later in Book 9 of the *Pharsalia*, Lucan offers advance warning about the death of Cato, who has just inspired the republican cause with his renowned philosophy of stoicism, in which 'endurance in adversity rejoices', since 'happier is courage whenever it costs itself a great price' (403–4):

> So he fires
> their frightened minds with heroism and with love of toils
> and takes the journey not to be retraced on desert track;
> and Libya, soon to *shut his sacred name in a little tomb*,
> laid its hands upon the destiny of Cato, who was above worry.
> (Lucan, *Civil War* 9.406–10; trans. Braund; emphasis added)

Lucan's critique of Cato is visible in the irony of the final clause, but also in the italicized phrase that is his 'destiny': in the end, Cato will die far away from Rome, in the desert of 'Libya', where the exalted vastness of his 'sacred name' – his fame as a great martyr to the republican cause of stoicism – will be 'shut' in merely 'a little tomb'. Marlowe's 'Infinite riches in a little room' is more sublime than stoical: it is a form not of finite imprisonment but of 'infinite' freedom, the discovery of the eternal in the finite, and an expression of imaginative and political liberty, right within the local precinct of enclosure.

In a second soliloquy, delivered after the merchants report the success of his ships riding safe 'in Malta road' (1.1.50), Barabas voices a distinct republican thought more in a Judaic than a Roman register:

> These are the blessings promised to the Jews,
> And herein was old Abram's happiness.
> What more may heaven do for earthly men
> Than thus to pour out plenty in their laps,
> ...
> They say we are a scattered nation:
> I cannot tell, but we have scambled up
> More wealth by far than those that brag of faith.

> There's Kirriah Jairim, the great Jew of Greece,
> Obed in Bairseth, Nones in Portugal,
> Myself in Malta, some in Italy,
> Many in France, and wealthy in every one.
> *(Jew of Malta* 1.1.104–26)

Barabas may mis-locate 'old Abram's happiness' as lying in commercial 'plenty' rather than in religious 'faith', but he manages to give voice to a new type of Jewish 'nation', organized by entrepreneurial Jews around the globe who transact the utopian dream: 'wealth' for 'every one'.

Barabas goes on to distinguish between this Jewish commercial republic linking Greece, Portugal, Malta, Italy, France, and 'Bairseth' from the monarchy of 'kings', and he offers an apologia for his new collectivity:

> I must confess we come not to be kings.
> That's not our fault: alas, our number's few,
> And crowns come either by succession,
> Or urged by force; and nothing violent,
> Oft have I heard tell, can be permanent.
> Give us a peaceful rule, make Christians kings,
> That thirst so much for principality.
> *(Jew of Malta* 1.1.128–34)

As he confesses, 'echo[ing]...the early chapters of *The Prince*' (Bawcutt, ed. 74), the Jewish republic is fortunately too small to operate the way monarchies do, either won by 'succession/Or urged by force', and thus it is free from the violence that historically controls governments by kings. Replacing the 'thirst for principality' with the 'peace' of financial freedom, Barabas sculpts out a new east-west 'nation', and locates its capitol in the republic of Malta.

We need to take the idea of Barabas' Jewish Republic seriously because it appears to put on the stage what Quentin Skinner and Martin van Gelderen identify as one of the models for the solution to the 'two constitutional problems' confronted by 'republican theorists' of the early modern era: the first, 'how best to frame a mixed constitution, a *respublica mixta*, in such a way as to deploy power to balance power'; and the second, 'how to ensure that the people are able to make their voice heard – at least by representation – in the process of law-making, so that whatever laws are enacted may be said to reflect their wills'. According to van Gelderen and Skinner, republican theorists solved these two problems 'by reference to...local custom, classical theory and the exemplary instance of the Jewish commonwealth, a constitution widely believed to reflect God's own political preferences' ('Introduction' 1: 4). In her essay on this topic, Lea Campos Boralevi discusses how, during the late sixteenth century, the Dutch turned to two 'foundational myths' for their political model as a republic: 'the Batavian – mainly based on Tacitus's story of the revolt against the Romans – and the Israelite, referring to Holy Scripture' (248). Boralevi recalls that Tacitus 'presented the classical Batavians as the virtuous, republican and freedom-loving ancestors of the Hollanders' (251), a people from modern Zeeland and South Holland who revolted against Rome under the republican hero Claudius Civilis.[19]

For his part, Marlowe refers to a Lucanian (not simply a Tacitean) origin to the Batavian myth in *Lucan's First Book*, when he inventories the invisible 'cause' of the Roman civil war through reference to an array of tribes: 'and fierce Batavians,/Whom trumpets' clange incites' (432–3). Equally to the point, Marlowe experienced first hand the operation of the Dutch Republic, when he visited the Netherlands in 1592 as part of England's attempt to defeat the attacking army of imperial Spain – an episode that we know about because of Sir Robert Sidney's letter to Lord Burleigh announcing Marlowe's arrest on counterfeiting (rpt. Kuriyama 209–10). Significantly, the name 'Ferneze' seems implicated in the battle between the Dutch Republic and Spain. In her edition of the play, Gill observes that 'the name "Ferneze" seems to link Marlowe's character with the Farnese family – one of whose members was the Prince of Parma referred to at *Dr Faustus*, i. 93' (ed., *Works* 4: 94), while in her edition of *Doctor Faustus* she adds, 'From 1579 until 1592 the Prince of Parma was Spanish governor-general of the United Provinces of the Netherlands' (ed., *Works* 2: 59).

According to Boralevi, the Dutch Republic intertwined the Bativian republican myth with the *Respublica Hebraeorum* of the Hebrew Bible, finding in 'the Hebraic republic' a 'political model' (252): 'The Jewish state presented itself as a sacred model, a *respublica* of God's people, expounded in God's language: a state which had its roots in God himself' (254). Boralevi goes on to identify Flavius Josephus as the key dispenser of the Hebraic republic, presenting 'the history of the Jewish Commonwealth attractively in the language of classical political philosophy' (255). The central event in the myth, Boralevi emphasizes, is the 'Exodus paradigm', since it 'spoke of the liberation from Egyptian slavery and of the Covenant' (256).

This is the very 'myth' to which Barabas refers, first when he mentions 'old Abram's happiness' and the 'scattered nation', and later when he refers to the Exodus story directly, during his balcony scene soliloquy, spoken in the sublime register: 'O thou, that with a fiery pillar led'st/The sons of Israel through the dismal shades,/Light Abraham's offspring' (2.1.12–14). We have some evidence that Marlowe was even reading Josephus, for Bawcutt glosses two passages with *Antiquities of the Jews*. In Act 2, scene 3, Barabas says that the 'Unchosen nation, never circumcised,/... were ne'er thought upon/Till Titus and Vespasian conquered us' (8–10) – referring to the 'Jews of Palestine [who] revolted against their Roman masters in

A.D. 66, but were gradually suppressed by the Roman commander Vespasian. He became emperor in A.D. 69, leaving his son Titus to complete operations by the siege and capture of Jerusalem in A.D. 70' (ed. 105). Later in this scene, Barabas, in an aside to Abigail, calls Lodowick 'This offspring of Cain' (303), 'possibly alluding to the Jewish tradition that the descendents of Cain were all wicked', as Josephus records at *Antiquities* 1.2.2 (ed. 121).[20]

Yet if early modern political theorists solve the problems of mixed constitution and popular representation through reference to the Jewish Commonwealth, Marlowe finds in their solution a dramatic occasion for savage farce. He assembles all the details of a republican comedy, and resolutely refuses to perform it. *The Jew of Malta* is not about Barabas' enactment of his sublime fantasy of using infinite riches to ransom kings but its exact inversion. No sooner does he give voice to his fantasy than the imperial Turks arrive to demand the tribute, and the republican governor decides to exact it: on the freedom-seeking Jew. The potential for a republican comedy metamorphoses into an imperial tragedy, with Barabas the prize victim of political tyranny.

Thus, in the second phase of his characterization, the Jew resorts to Machiavellian policy, and most of the rest of the play concentrates on a single idea: when dealt with unjustly through the levying of the tax, Barabas transfers his republican business acumen to an imperious theatricality, grounded in the bitterness of deception, trickery, and falsehood:

> No, Barabas is born to better chance,
> And framed of finer mould than common men,
> That measure naught but by the present time.
> A reaching thought will search his deepest wits,
> And cast with cunning for the time to come.
> (*Jew of Malta* 1.2.222–6)

In this scene, Barabas adopts the 'counterfeit profession' (294) of a theatrical man, turning to 'dissembl[ing]' (291, 292, 293) to contend with the corruption of Ferneze's island republic. Effectively, Barabas metamorphoses into Lucan's Caesar, the imperial victor, 'framed of finer mould than common men', because he does not tie himself to the present but uses his 'cunning' to invent the future.

Marlowe's design is historic for English literature, for the new Marlovian theatrical figure specifically invents his Machiavellian-Lucanian character out of disillusionment with the republican ideal of commercial freedom. In keeping with such disillusionment, *The Jew of Malta* contains Marlowe's most detailed – and famous – parody of the sublime discourse from 'The Passionate Shepherd to His Love', when the Islamic slave Ithamore, freed by

Barabas to help him transact his revenge plot, courts the prostitute Bellamira:

> we will leave this paltry land,
> And sail from hence to Greece, to lovely Greece:
> I'll be thy Jason, thou my golden fleece;
> Where painted carpets o'er the meads are hurled,
> And Bacchus' vineyards overspread the world:
> Where woods and forests go in goodly green,
> I'll be Adonis, thou shalt be love's queen:
> The meads, the orchards, and the primrose lanes,
> Instead of sedge and reed, bear sugar-canes:
> Thou in those groves, by Dis above,
> Shalt live with me and be my love.
> (*Jew of Malta* 4.2.101–11)

Here Marlowe presents a freed slave singing a sublime discourse to a courtesan whom scholars intriguingly trace to the republic of Venice (Bawcutt, ed. 128). By underwriting Ithamore's courtship with a story about slavery and freedom, Marlowe makes clear the politics of the sublime, even as he parodies it. Serving as the model for Sir Epicure Mammon's courtship of Doll Common in *The Alchemist*, who uses the sublime to imagine a voyage to the republican 'free state', Ithamore fantasizes a voyage from the 'paltry land' of Malta to 'lovely Greece', home to Athenian democracy, where the lovers can re-enact a classical myth of wealth, epitomized in Jason's capture of the Golden Fleece, to relax in a natural world of beauty, comfort, and intoxication, as Adonis did with Venus. In his exalted imagination, Ithamore experiences the eternizing fantasy of the godhead, within time, released through the bliss of sexual 'love'.

Marlowe allows Ithamore to have his fantasy only to nip it in the bud, for the slave's overreaching betrayal of his master leads to a wry floral death, when Barabas, 'with a lute, disguised' (SD after line 34) as a 'French musician' (4.4.35), offers the carousing couple a poisoned 'posy' (41) – a word that at this time means both *nosegay* and *poesy*. Whereas the Passionate Shepherd had offered the Nymph 'a thousand fragrant posies' (10) if she would be his love, Barabas gives the Islamic passionate lover a posy of death, during a remarkable moment of self-conscious literary authorship, evoking Marlowe's career not just as a dramatist but as a poet.[21]

But it is with drama that the play closes: 'As Barabas, hammer in hand, constructs the machinery for this climactic falsehood, it is difficult not to equate him with the playwright himself, constructing the plot, and Marlowe appears consciously to encourage this perception' (Greenblatt, 'Marlowe, Marx' 52). In out-foxing Ferneze – by everyone's account, the play's singular Machiavellian (e.g., Cartelli, *Marlowe, Shakespeare* 171) – Barabas becomes

Governor of the Republic of Malta. For a moment, Marlowe stages a republican comedy, only to offer two twists. In the first (and most surprising), Barabas returns the republic to the rightful Governor, as if his model of freedom lies outside the body politic, within the rapture of commerce, the paradise he had lost. In the second twist, Ferneze pursues his own counterplot, trapping Barabas in the very cauldron that the Jew had set to entrap the Turks, and using this festive occasion to imprison Calymath and his army, under guard of Martin Del Bosco and the Spanish empire.

In this grim tragedy of a Jew, the Christian republican West, conspiring with Christian monarchical Spain, triumphs over the imperial Eastern Turk. While we might situate Ferneze as Republican Governor within sixteenth-century political thought, especially circles in England during the 1590s favoring republican values, Marlowe does not idealize anything. Ferneze is no hero, as he himself reveals to Calymath in the play's final speech:

> for come all the world
> To rescue thee, so will we guard us now,
> As sooner shall they drink the ocean dry,
> Than conquer Malta, or endanger us.
> So march away, and let due praise be given
> Neither to fate nor fortune, but to heaven.
> (*Jew of Malta* 5.5.118–23)

Curiously, there is no sense here – or anywhere – that Ferneze wants power, money, or anything in particular, beyond governing the republic of Malta, just as he has long done. That is, no evidence suggests that he plans or even wants to turn himself into a tyrant or a monarch. Everything he does protects the civility of the Maltese Christian Republic: 'Malta shall be freed' (5.5.112). Accordingly, as editors reveal, Marlowe pierces his notorious final line through with the republican thought of Machiavelli: 'Early patristic writers attacked the pagan concept of fortune, and asserted that events are brought about by divine providence. But Machiavelli ignored providence and laid great stress on fortune (*The Prince*, ch. 25), for which Gentillet rebuked him (pp. 139–41)' (Bawcutt, ed. 190; see also Bawcutt, 'Machiavelli' 46–7). Thus, Ferneze's final line gestures to three alternatives for political agency, and organizes them into a climactic idea: the play officially privileges Christian heaven over classical fate, yet in the end it dramatizes Machiavelli's notion of 'fortune'. Thus, only through sheer 'policy' does the Machiavellian-Lucanian Governor secure the dubious freedom of a Christian Republic.[22]

The fortune of Marlowe's play during the seventeenth century speaks to its original republican representation. As is well known, *The Jew of Malta* was not published until 1633 (Gill, ed., *Works* 4: xvi) – on the eve of the English

Civil War. In his recent study of this topic, Zachery Lesser shows how the publisher Nicholas Vavasour positioned the printing of Marlowe's play as 'Laudian', in opposition to 'the more "forward" Protestants who demanded a further Reformation' (83). While emphasizing this 'confessional divide' (82), Lesser concludes that it 'in large part determined how the debates of the 1630s would be redrawn as the battle lines of the 1640s': 'Before the Civil War, Laudians and puritans waged a paper war, and people like Vavasour were at the center of it, providing the books that helped to define each side. If Vavasour's understanding of *The Jew of Malta* strikes us now as conservative, this only underscores how much our world has been transformed since the play's publication. In its own time, and by that I mean the 1630s and not the 1590s, *The Jew* participated in the religious polemics that helped bring early Stuart society to an end' (114). Such a view leads Lesser so suggest that this particular 'Marlowe book ... may have been the most subversive' of all his works (114; his emphasis).

Lesser does not refer to republicanism directly, but in a note he quotes the historian Peter Lake: 'For many the choice between the king and Parliament may have devolved into a choice between popery or a populist Puritanism as the greater threat to order' (qtd. 114n93). From the perspective of the present study, Vavasour may have appropriated Marlowe's *Jew* for a royalist cause, but that cause responded decisively to a radical republican opposition. Such an opposition, we have seen, is right at the surface of *The Jew of Malta*. Finally, perhaps, it is to Marlowe's credit that his complex representation was appropriated for one side when it well could have been appropriated for the other.[23]

The Massacre at Paris, Huguenot republicanism, and the Caesarian guise

In the Prologue to *The Jew of Malta*, we have seen, Marlowe links Barabas with the Duke of Guise from *The Massacre at Paris*. The stage-presenter Machevill tells the English audience that his 'soul' has migrated out of Italy to France and taken up residence in the Guise – a metempsychosis, we have also seen, modeled on the Lucanian sublime in Book 9 of the *Pharsalia*. This authorial link between the two plays makes discussion of their shared republican discourse more than natural.[24]

Indeed, *The Massacre* contains the discourse of republican thought that we have traced in *The Jew*. Yet the notoriously mangled state of the text makes discussion of the play especially challenging. Unlike *The Jew*, and such plays as *Tamburlaine* or *Edward II*, *The Massacre* survives in only half the length of a typical Elizabethan play, and scholars unanimously identify the 1250-line text as the product of memorial reconstruction.[25] Until recently, critics were largely content to agree with Wilbur Sanders, who in 1968 (in a chapter ominously titled 'Dramatist as Jingoist') accused Marlowe of being a 'brutal, chauvinist propagandist' and his play a 'nasty piece of journalistic bombast' (22), an outright 'prostitution of art' (36). During the 1990s, however, a backlash set in, producing a remarkable series of historically grounded essays defending the play. Today, we can applaud *The Massacre* for its accurate historical view of 'one of the most infamous and most publicized of sixteenth-century international events', the St. Bartholomew Day's Massacre (Poole, '*Massacre*' 2), a 'defining moment in English Protestant consciousness' (Hadfield, *Literature, Travel* 201).[26] As critics point out, Marlowe narrates two stages to the traumatic event: the massacre itself, which occurred in August and September 1572 (scenes 1–12), and the assassination of Henry III in 1587, followed by the accession of Navarre as Henry IV in 1589 (scenes 13–24; see J. Briggs 262–3).

Moreover, recent criticism is nearly unanimous in identifying *The Massacre* as an uncanny dramatic rehearsal of the late-sixteenth-century battle between French Catholics and Huguenots, a tragic instance of 'the burning question of the late sixteenth century throughout Europe': the 'relation of state religion and the individual conscience' (J. Briggs 259). As Julia Briggs reminds us, for Marlowe's English audience the Huguenots 'were not merely persecuted co-religionists whose wrongs at the hands of the Catholics, the international conspiracies of Spain, the Jesuits, and the Pope, required rectification. They were also rebels against their lawful king, and were gradually evolving a theory of justified political resistance, which had developed among the refugees from Mary Tudor, and would be remembered by the opponents of Charles I' (260). Even though recent critics disagree about the effect of Marlowe's feat – some argue that he elicits 'sympathy' for both the Huguenots and the Catholics, including the Guise, while most insist that the play is 'rabidly anti-Catholic' in its 'militant Protestantism' (White 79) – critics today tend to agree that *The Massacre* is best understood as a biting critique of monarchy, including English monarchy under Queen Elizabeth.[27]

Only during the past few years, however, has Andrew Hadfield connected Marlowe's critique of monarchy with republican thought, especially through hereditary succession, and noticed the links between the stage tragedy and Marlowe's translation of the *Pharsalia*.[28] We can build on Hadfield's brief analysis by looking further into the republican underpinnings of *The Massacre*, including the remnants of its republican discourse, its surprisingly detailed connection with *Lucan's First Book*, the historical context for this connection – the battle between Catholics and Huguenots – and finally, Marlowe's republican signature, his discourse of the sublime.

Perhaps not surprisingly for a text mangled by memorial reconstruction, *The Massacre* contains little formal discourse of republican liberty. The word 'free' occurs only twice, in back-to-back sentences, although the scene is an important one, since it alone survives in manuscript, and perhaps even in Marlowe's hand (Nicholl, 'Marlowe, Christopher'). In scene 19, an unnamed soldier enters to assassinate Mugeroun, who has committed adultery with the Duchess of Guise, and in the process engages in some richly evocative discourse, not all of it purely sexual, as appears in the Folger manuscript version:

> Now sir, to you that dares make a Duke a cuckold, and use a counterfeit key to his privy-chamber: though you take out none but your own treasure, yet you put in that displeases him [the Guise], forestall the market, and set up your standing where you should not. But you will say you leave him room enough besides. That's no answer; he's to have the choice of his own free land. If it be not too free – there's the question. (*Massacre at Paris* 19.1–8; rpt. Burnett, ed. 575)

In the soldier's metaphorical mind, Mugeroun deserves to be killed because he has violated the commercial gold standard at the center of the republic (his own language for Mugeroun's tilling of the Duchess' 'ground' that only the Duke has the right to 'occupy' *freely*). That is to say, the soldier equates the wife with the husband's 'free land'.[29]

For a play set during a civil war in monarchical France, we can expect the concept of tyranny to emerge, from beginning to end. In scene 1, the Prince of Condé sets the pace by accusing the Guise of 'tyranny' (1.40), while in scene 4 King Charles fears that the plan for the massacre at Paris will be 'noted through the world/An action bloody and tyrannical' (5–6). Finally, in scene 23 the Guise's brother, the Duke Dumaine, charges the next king, Henry III, of possessing a 'tyrant's pride' (22). The ironies abound, for in this play nearly every political leader behaves like a tyrant, with the Guise simply the leader of the pack. Accordingly, characters talk a lot about 'rights' – a word that recurs four times, with each focusing on 'the right of France' (1.55; see 10.28, 13.48, 14.5). On this note, the phrase 'country's good' occurs three times (4.19, 14.58, 16.11), while 'common good' appears once (2.37) and 'common profit' once more (14.59) – more than in any Marlowe work. Since this is a play about 'civil broils' – a phrase that occurs three times (16.33, 21.104, 21.113) – we should expect a staging of what is at stake in a French monarchy: hereditary succession. Thus, not simply does kingship change hands twice – from Charles to Henry III to Navarre – but characters carry on a dialogue about 'due descent' (10.20), 'just succession' (13.35), and 'true succession of the faith' (16.18).

We have to take such monarchical discourse seriously, and Marlowe invites us to view it in terms of republican Rome. Thus, in scene 14 he inserts the words 'senate' and 'senator' when the Queen Mother, Catherine, welcomes

Henry III back to France for his coronation, outlining a government that looks suspiciously like a French monarchical republic:

> Here hast thou a country void of fears,
> A warlike people to maintain thy right,
> A watchful senate for ordaining laws.
>   (*Massacre at Paris* 14.4–6)

In this speech, one royal addresses another by locating the king at the center of a government that includes both the 'people' and a 'senate', the former to maintain the king's 'right', the latter to 'watch' over the 'ordaining' of 'laws'. Later, in scene 19 Henry tells the Guise, in bitter jest,

> wear our crown, and be thou King of France,
> And as dictator make or war or peace,
> Whilst I cry *'placet'* like a senator.
>   (*Massacre at Paris* 19.55–7)

Editors gloss the Latin word *'placet'* as 'it pleases me', and see Marlowe evoking 'the old Universities when a question is put to the vote' (Esche, ed. 396; see Oliver, ed. 143). Yet the word 'senator' also suggests a more formal political context, recalling the original senate in classical Rome, and perhaps the republic of Cicero (as subsequent references make clear). Thus, the play presents a king jestingly handing over his crown to a 'dictator', while the king idles by with consent, like the representative of a dead republic.

These remnants of republican discourse speak to a neglected context for viewing *The Massacre at Paris*: the 'Huguenot Republic'.[30] The Huguenots *were* republicans. Not simply Protestants fighting the Catholic monarchy in the late sixteenth century, they followed John Calvin in privileging 'resistance theory', which allowed magistrates to depose a tyrant lawfully. As we have seen in the Introduction, the central Huguenot text was *Vindiciae, Contra Tyrannos, or, concerning the legitimate power of a prince over the people, and of the people over a prince* (1579).[31] Written in the aftermath of the St. Bartholomew Day's Massacre by Philippe du Plessis Mornay, friend to Sir Philip Sidney, *Vindicae* relies on the dual authority of classical republicanism and Scripture to pursue a single conviction (McLaren 35): that all individuals should be able to live free of tyranny, acting to 'preserve and protect...life and liberty – without which life is scarcely life at all' (3: 149; qtd. McLaren 42).[32] In particular, the goal of the Huguenots was to follow the United Dutch Republic in setting up a republic in France (Herman 252).

Complexly, *Vindiciae* does not rely only on a principle of republican liberty to attack the tyranny of the French monarchy; it foregrounds an attack on 'the evil arts, vicious counsels, and false and pestiferous doctrines of Niccolò Machiavelli the Florentine' (ed. 8): 'it was chiefly through the study of the books of Machiavelli that some were sharpening their minds so that they might embrace the artifces of disrupting the commonwealth on the basis of the authority of those who rule it' (ed. 9). Defining 'Machiavellians' as 'slaves of tyrants' (ed. 10), *Vindiciae* presents its author as a republican hero aptly named Stephanus Junius Brutus, who 'clearly and necessarily follows what the duty of the prince is towards the people, what the right and office of the people is towards the prince; and that these obligations are distinct from one another, although they are mutual and reciprocal' (ed. 11). Brutus' main charge is that Machiavelli has 'educated' 'tyrants' to 'evaluate everything according to their own desires, rather than public utility' (ed. 12). Throughout, Brutus tells the reader, 'subjects are not obliged to obey kings, if they order anything against the law of God' (1: 33). Not simply is 'the consent of the whole people ... required' for political action (2: 41), but 'officers' of the state are 'superior' to the 'king' (2: 47). In a chapter titled 'Kings are Made by the People' (2: 68–74), Brutus insists not only that 'God institutes kings' but more precisely that 'the people constitutes kings, confers kingdoms, and approves the election by its vote' (2: 68). Rejecting 'hereditary' succession ('absolutely no-one is born a king' [2: 71]), the author recalls that 'all kings were wholly elected from the beginning' (2: 74). While Brutus draws on biblical and contemporary example, repeatedly he cites Roman precedent, with Julius Caesar emerging as an arch-Machiavellian tyrant (2: 81): 'the friends of Caesar serve Caesar, the friends of the king or emperor serve the kingdom' (2: 88), 'the liberty of the people' (2: 91): 'There is no trade in free men' (2: 124).

While drawing an implicit equation between Caesar and Machiavelli, Brutus complicates his republican discourse even further by occasionally stitching in Lucan's *Pharsalia*. Near the beginning, in a chapter titled 'The Convenant Between God and Kings' (1: 21–34), Brutus grants both God and Caesar his 'tribute' or 'fisc', to conclude, 'In short, anyone who confuses these mixes up heaven and earth and wants to reduce everything to primordial Chaos' (1: 27).[33] On the surface, Brutus looks to be criticizing Lucan, who inscribes the topos of political chaos more famously than anyone: 'Time ends, and to old Chaos all things turn,/Confused stars shall meet', reads Marlowe's translation. Yet readers of Lucan know how savagely he mourns the state of chaos. Later, Brutus relies on a second influential Lucanian trope when defining a tyrant: 'So a tyrant – who is more destructive than any enemy – forces those whom a king protects and defends against the attacks of enemies to plunge their swords into their own innards' (3: 144–5), referring to the *Pharsalia*'s opening image of civil war as a form of suicide: 'Wars worse than civil on Thessalian plains,/And outrage strangling law, and people strong/We sing, whose conquering swords their own breasts launched' (1–3). Shortly afterwards, Brutus quotes 'Pompey' on the topic of Roman 'liberty' and 'zeal for the preservation of the country', referring to the freedom-fighter 'Camillus' as an example to be emulated (3: 153), as derived from a speech by Lentulus in Book 5 of the *Pharsalia* (27–9; see Garnett, ed. 154–5n570). Finally, in the 'Postscriptal Poem' concluding *Vindiciae*, another pseudonymous author, Alphonsus Menesius Benavides, the Aragonese, refers again to the opening of the *Pharsalia* and its image of civil suicide: 'Why has the citizen sharpened cruel swords against his very own entrails?' (186). In this way, Lucan supplies Mornay with a sharp rhetorical tool for condemning tyrannical violations of the republican value of liberty. In Mornay's hands, the *Pharsalia* becomes a Huguenot text of French resistance theory.

To my knowledge, scholars have never considered whether Marlowe knew *Vindiciae*, although his interest in the French civil wars and its corresponding republican discourse suggests in all likelihood that he did. What he could have found is a strange mix of Lucan, Machiavelli, and French republican discourse, all connected to what prompted the treatise in the first place: the St. Bartholomew Day's Massacre.[34]

Huguenot scholars locate Mornay's 1579 treatise in a genealogy that traces to Theodore Beza's 1574 *De Jure Magistratuum* and François Hotman's 1573 *Francogallia*, the latter being what Quentin Skinner calls 'the greatest and most radical Huguenot treatise on the fundamental constitution of France' (*Foundations* 2: 304).[35] As Marlovians know, in 1941 Paul Kocher demonstrated that Marlowe borrowed much of his plot material for *The Massacre* from another work by Hotman, the 1574 *True and Plain Report of the Furious Outrages of France*, which Vivien Thomas and William Tydeman print as the primary source of the play.[36] Both Kocher's research and Thomas and Tydeman's extracts are misleading, however, because neither allows us to gauge the republican agenda of Hotman's work. Kocher, for instance, calls Hotman simply the 'renowned Huguenot lawyer and author of the *Francogallia*', and takes no interest in the historical context of 'probably the account of the St. Bartholomew massacre which was most popular with Englishmen' ('Hotman' 350). Similarly, the extracts of Thomas and Tydeman largely cull those moments of plot in the source text which Marlowe seems to be using: 'About noon, when he [Admiral Cologni] was returning home from the council, ... behold, a harquebusier ... out of a window of a house near adjoining shot the Admiral with two bullets of lead through both the arms' (eds. 263). Only a single passage, the first extracted, intimates Hotman's republican agenda:

> And so was the third civil war ended [1570], and the peace concluded with the same conditions that were before, that every man should have free liberty to use and profess the religion [Protestantism]. (Hotman, *A True and Plain Report of the Furious Outrages of France* (1574), fol. 4r; rpt. Thomas and Tydeman, eds. 261)

Here may we peer through the political window of the source text, to see Hotman's commitment to the people of France's 'free liberty'.[37] Kocher argues that Hotman, not European Machiavellianism, constitutes the primary source for *The Massacre*, but in fact the two avenues of political thought were often intertwined, and are, I suggest, in Marlowe's tragedy.[38]

Thus, by writing *The Massacre at Paris*, Marlowe stages one of early modern Europe's most important political battles. This battle is between a republic and a monarchy, and it leads to 'the first full-scale revolution within a modern European state' (Skinner, *Foundations* 2: 241).[39] By putting this battle center stage, Marlowe writes republicanism for the new English theatre. However, rather than following Hotman, Mornay, and other Huguenots polemically, to champion republican liberty outright, Marlowe selects a more complex design, which intersects two major strands of thought. First, in the face of Catholic monarchical savagery, he celebrates Huguenot virtue, figured in the virtuous Navarre; and second, he simultaneously expresses fascination with the savage theatrical man *par excellence*, the Duke of Guise. The mangled state of the text may not present a fully coherent account of this intersection, but with the 'Huguenot' features of the text at least highlighted, we may turn to the play's central figure, the Huguenots' arch-antagonist: the Guise.[40]

Marlowe's portrait of the Guise is challenging because this arch-monarchist, who murders French republicans to secure the French crown, derives not just from Hotman and European Machiavellianism but also from Lucan's *Pharsalia*.[41] As critics and editors have long established, the Guise models himself on Julius Caesar – no fewer than three times. First, during his long, and deservedly famous soliloquy, the Guise points to his sword,

> First let's follow those in France
> That hinder our possession to the crown.
> As Caesar to his soldiers, so say I:
> Those that hate me will I learn to loathe.
> (*Massacre at Paris* 2.93–6)

Writing in the 1940s, Kocher argued that the Guise's Caesarian identity originates in the Catholic League writers, who 'were fond of drawing' an 'analogy between Guise and Julius Caesar' ('Pamphlet Backgrounds' 155). Yet in 1956 William Blissett determined that the Guise models himself specifically on Lucan's Caesar.[42] Although the Guise's quotation of Lucan's anti-hero 'does not appear to have been identified' (Esche, ed. 373), it looks distinctly Lucanian; as Blissett glosses the passage, 'This is the Caesar of Lucan'. We shall return to the Guise's soliloquy presently.

The Guise's other two references to 'Caesar' frame his death. In scene 21, the Third Murderer tells the Duke not to go into the 'next room' because the other murderers await him; the Guise refuses to heed him:

> Yet Caesar shall go forth.
> Let mean conceits and baser men fear death:

> Tut, they are peasants. I am Duke of Guise;
> And princes with their looks engender fear.
> *(Massacre at Paris* 21.68–71)

At once nobly fearless and foolishly naïve, the Guise models his decision to enter the assassination room on Caesar's decision to attend his own assassination on the Ides of March.[43] While the Guise's reference to Caesar's assassination is not strictly Lucanian (Blissett 565), his anti-populist contempt for 'mean conceits', 'baser men', and 'peasants' is consistent with Lucan's portrait of the imperial-minded Caesar in the *Pharsalia*. Finally, after receiving his death-wound, the Guise reiterates his contempt for the commons, 'To die by peasants, what a grief is this!' (85), revising his line about Caesar: 'Thus Caesar did go forth, and thus he died' (91). Effectively, the Guise dies announcing a Lucanian heritage at once political and literary.

As is well known, Marlowe veers from historical veracity – including as represented in source texts like Hotman's – in making the monarchically minded Guise the instigator of the massacre of the Huguenot republicans in Paris (Kocher, 'Hotman' 366–7). While much of the play-text foregrounds the religious character of the dispute, Marlowe tends to use the speeches of the Guise to insert the political dynamic driving it. As the Guise's adoption of a Caesarian identity indicates, the play's fundamental strategy is to use the Roman civil war as the historical backdrop to – and literary origin for – the civil war in France. Thus the Guise meditates on his power over King Henry III before the murderers arrive to assassinate him:

> As ancient Romans over their captive lords,
> So will I triumph over this wanton king,
> And he shall follow my proud chariot's wheels.
> *(Massacre at Paris* 21.53–5)

The comparison sets up the Guise's two references to the assassination of Caesar immediately following, but it also underscores Marlowe's desire to connect the battle between the Roman Empire and Republic with the battle between the French Empire and Huguenot Republic. The Guise imagines himself marching in a formal Roman 'triumph' after his military victory over 'captive lords', and he adds a distinct Marlovian twist, which he will amplify in *Edward II*: the Guise betrays his contempt for a 'wanton' sovereign, Henry III, flagrantly committed to minions like Epernoun.[44]

As the mangled text might further lead us to expect, *The Massacre at Paris* is also unusual in Marlowe's dramatic canon because it does not contain a clear echo of 'The Passionate Shepherd'.[45] Nonetheless, the Marlovian sublime still appears, and right where we should expect it, in the primary speech in the tragedy that unequivocally bears the author's signature: the Guise's long soliloquy. According to Blissett, what 'Lucan adds' to the history of Caesarism is what we find the Guise voicing: 'darkness, a dimension of evil, a sense of spiritual wickedness in high places. Everything is heightened with all the arts of rhetorical emphasis: Caesar's ambition is to rule the world; his impiety is active and defiant; his cruelty is only disguised by apparent clemency; his personal courage and daring is superhuman, springing from a demonic impatience; and his success is such as to make one doubt the moral order of the world' ('Lucan's Caesar' 560).

Right before adopting Lucan's Caesar as his model, the Guise communicates to the audience his plan to become King of France:

> Now, Guise, begin those deep-engendered thoughts
> To burst abroad those never-dying flames
> Which cannot be extinguished but by blood.
> Oft have I levelled, and at last have learned
> That peril is the chiefest way to happiness,
> And resolution honour's fairest aim.
> What glory is there in a common good
> That hangs for every peasant to achieve?
> That like I best that flies beyond my reach.
> Set me to scale the high Pyramides,
> And thereon set the diadem of France,
> I'll either rend it with my nails to naught,
> Or mount the top with my aspiring wings,
> Although my downfall be the deepest hell.
> 			(*Massacre at Paris* 2.31–44)

To my knowledge, this speech has never been discussed in terms of the Lucanian sublime.[46] We need to discuss the Lucanian sublime here because the Guise so self-consciously presents himself as Lucan's Caesar.

In particular, there may be a Lucanian recollection in line 40, 'Set me to scale the high Pyramides'. In Book 9 of the *Pharsalia*, Pompey's son Gnaeus uses language we have seen forming an origin for 'The Passionate Shepherd': 'Shall not Amasis, torn out from the pyramid tombs,/and the other kings go floating down the rushing Nile for me?' (155–6). Unlike Lucan in this speech, however, Marlowe voices the sublime through technical images of flight – images for which Lucan elsewhere is famous. What the Guise likes 'best' is to 'fl[y]...beyond [his]...reach', to 'scale the high Pyramides', or 'mount the top with [his]...aspiring wings'. As he makes clear, he loves the *violence* of sublime flight, just as Lucan represents it (and Longinus theorizes it).[47] Yet Marlowe overgoes Lucan by *thinking through* the violence of the sublime: only through seeking out 'peril' can he attain real 'happiness'; only through 'resolution' can he attain 'honor'. Committed to both a private and a public goal, the interior state of contentment and the social achievement of 'glory', the Duke finds his only route in acts of danger. Rather than fearing danger, he seeks it as the surest track to the sublime, a state of exaltation at once psychological and political. Yet, instead of entering the sublime to experience the freedom of the republic, the Guise pursues the 'crown' of a king (101), and he does so by highlighting his monarchical thirst through contempt for a republican based-value, the common man's attempt to find 'glory' in 'the common good'. As for Tamburlaine, for the Guise the sublime constitutes an imaginative space for fantasizing kingship, above 'every peasant'.

Each of Marlowe's plays writes republicanism strangely, but *The Massacre at Paris* overgoes the author himself. Everything republican is in place, enough to excite the constitutional enthusiast – the discourse of freedom, the Huguenot political context, Lucan, and even the sublime – but to what avail? While the mangled text prohibits a definite answer, we may nonetheless note how consistently Marlowe's republican authorship is designed to tantalize, not fulfill.[48] Rather than a lucid narrative about the triumph of republican freedom, or even its tragedy, we find a truncated text that, to quote the Guise, refuses 'To bring the will of our desires to end' (2.84). This authorial situation improves only slightly in the last play we shall discuss in this chapter.

The sodomitical sublime: *Edward II* and the Tacitean republic

Like *The Massacre at Paris*, *Edward II* is one of Marlowe's two plays formally about civil war. Instead of narrating the French civil wars during his own lifetime, he turns to the fourteenth-century civil war in his own country. In both cases, the author invites his audience to apply the theatrical fiction to the context of Elizabethan politics, as recent historical criticism demonstrates.[49] Arguably Marlowe's most mature play, and maybe his last, *Edward II* affords an especially sturdy example of Marlowe's republican authorship toward the end of his literary career.[50] While most recent criticism concentrates on the sexual politics of *Edward II* as a 'gay classic' (Wiggins and Lindsey, eds. xvii), we may initially emphasize the government politics itself, to place the play in a fresh context: the shift in religio-political thought occurring at the time that Marlowe writes, from the providentialist model for regulating language based on Christian *iniuria*, advanced by Raphael Holinshed and other English chroniclers, to a political model of Tacitism.[51]

According to Debora Shuger, Tacitism 'sanctioned representational tactics fundamentally at odds with the habits of charitable reticence shaping the Tudor chronicle histories and history plays…, in part because it rested on such very different assumptions about human nature and knowledge. Tacitus [along with Suetonius]…take[s] for granted that a person's moral character is essentially fixed', so that his historiography 'track[s] this core selfhood, disclosing its presence beneath stately masks which power uses to conceal its guilt'. Whereas chroniclers like Holinshed kept 'within the bounds of charitable representation' and thus 'ratified the bonds of trust and respect that weave the fabric of the Christian community', Tacitism 'depicts a world in which such bonds have been replaced by the politics of the gaze' (*Censorship* 206–7). Shuger summarizes the shift this way: Taticism 'provided the main channel through which a hermeneutic of suspicion ... entered the discourses of mainstream legitimate history, and in so doing worked to delegitimate the whole system of language regulation based on the Christian *iniuria* model' (210). She goes on to identify both Sir Walter Ralegh and Ben Jonson as Taciteans, and Shakespeare as a member of the Christian model, since he 'consistently allows the characters in the history plays to die in the odor of sanctity, or at least with the saving grace of ambiguity'. However, when she briefly includes *Edward II* in this latter camp (194), she misses a genuine opportunity to see Marlowe's tragedy strung across precisely this historical divide.

Editors identify the 'source' material of *Edward II* as deriving from the English chronicles, primarily the second or 1587 edition of Holinshed's *Chronicles*, but also Fabyan, Stowe, and Grafton. In his recent Revels play edition, for instance, Charles R. Forker devotes some 25 pages to this topic (ed. 41–66), and prints excerpts of these chronicles (along with Churchyard) (ed. 327–63).[52] In his detailed discussion of the Marlowe-Shakespeare relation, however, Forker reports that the 'providential concept of historical process ... gets scant or no emphasis in Marlowe', whose 'universe continues to look morally darker and psychologically more tormented' (ed. 34) – without offering an explanation for why Marlowe might be darkening the providentialist project of the chroniclers: 'Marlowe transformed the cluttered narrative of Holinshed into an eloquent drama of character and ideas – a tragedy built upon the politics of weakness, of naked aggression, of willful selfishness, of savagery, of miscalculation, of sexual rejection and magnetism, and of civil chaos' (ed. 45–6).[53]

Forker's inventory of the psychological, sexual, and political landscape of *Edward II* is basically what Shuger and others mean by Taciticism. In the primary statement on this topic, Peter Burke calls Taciticism 'a fashion, a craze, a movement, which lasted some hundred years, *c.* 1580–c.1680'; it was originally inspired in the Netherlands by Justus Lipsius and by his disciple in France, Marc-Antoine Muret; and it is divisible into four 'strands': style; historicism; ethics; and politics ('Taciticism', Dorey, ed. 150–1). As a style, Taciticism is characterized by an eloquent, epigrammatic, anti-Ciceronian prose that is 'weighty, concise, and ... "sententious"', and it became associated with the 'loose' style of Seneca (151–2). As a historicism, Taciticism is concerned with 'causes and motives' and 'penetrating analyses of them', with special attention to 'hidden motives' (154–5). As an ethics, Taciticism is committed to 'moral judgments' of character and motive, including an obsession with 'dissimulation' (156). Finally, as a politics, Tacitism can be divided into what Giuseppe Toffanin in the 1920s famously termed 'red' and 'black' versions: red Tacitism is 'disguised republicanism', emphasizing the importance of individual 'liberty' in a historical narrative about the way 'the Empire destroyed Roman culture' through the 'tyranny' of kingship, while teaching the subject to live prudently in the state; conversely, black Tacitism is 'disguised Machiavellianism', teaching kings how to be tyrants (Burke 163–5). Burke adds a third type, '"pink" Tacitists', who were 'supporters of limited monarchy in an age of absolutism', with François Hotman serving as an 'early example' (163). As Burke goes on to discuss, Machiavelli and Tacitus are 'frequently linked by writers between 1580 and 1680': 'There are cases in the commentary-literature where a maxim is ascribed to Tacitus which is not quite like anything he wrote, but very close to a specific passage in Machiavelli' (165). Sometimes, writers 'attack Tacitus in order to attack Machiavelli' (166).[54] Although Tacitism 'declined in the later seventeenth century' (169), it marks a watershed in early modern history: the 'enthusiasm for Tacitus coincides approximately with the age of religious wars in Europe, 1559–1648, and with the longer-term rise of courts and of absolute monarchy', for in both of his major works, the *Annals* and the *Histories*, 'Tacitus described a period of civil war, and emperors with unlimited power; he was also interested in dissimulation' (168).[55]

In Elizabethan England, the precipitating event of Tacitism was Henry Savile's 1591 translation of Books 1–4 of the *Histories* and another Tacitean work, the *Agricola*. Since the *Annals* stops at AD 66, and the *Histories* do not begin until 1 January 69, Savile supplies his own prefatory essay to bridge the three-year gap, titled 'The Ende of Nero and Beginning of Galba'. This essay, writes David Womersley, aims to 'vindicat[e] ... a political, not a moral, charge against the emperor[, Nero]' (321–2), a view that turns out to be 'Machiavellian', since Nero falls because he 'lack[s] ... the creative, amoral energy which Machiavelli, and Machiavelli alone, had argued was peculiar to successful politicians'. In Savile's hands, Nero becomes 'a dramatized antitype of the political figure Machiavelli had analysed and idealized in *The Prince*' (325–6): 'Savile seems to have pursued the ends of what Toffanin called "red Tacitism" (veiled republicanism) through the means of the "black Tacitism" (disguised Machiavellianism)' (326).

In his astonishing essay, Savile tells the story of Julius Vindex, the hero who had the courage to inaugurate the rebellion leading to Nero's fall, and the bloody year 69 that saw four men successively become Emperor of Rome: Galba, Otho, Vitelius, and Vespasian. Even though Vindex commits suicide when Nero discovers his revolt, Savile presents him as a republican freedom-fighter, 'more vertuous then fortunate', who 'first entred the lists, chalenging a prince upholden with thirty legions, rooted in the Empire by fower descents of ancestors'. In Savile's narration, Vindex rebels 'not to establish his owne soveraignety, ... but to redeeme his cuntrey from tyranny and bondage'. According to Savile, Vindex deserves to be recalled as a hero because he 'first stirred the stone, which rowling along tumbled Nero out of his seate' (6–7).

In a prefatory epistle to his volume, Savile dedicates his translation to Queen Elizabeth, because she herself held Tacitus' *Histories* in 'great acount'. Savile even goes so far as to wish her majesty not simply 'leasure' but 'a Tacitus to describe your most glorious raigne' (para. 2–3) – indicating just how seamless republicanism and monarchism could be at this time.[56] More remarkably, Savile follows his royal dedication with a second epistle, titled 'A.B. to the Reader', which Ben Jonson claimed was written by Robert Devereaux, earl of Essex – a conclusion modern historians do not dispute (Womersley 316; Smuts, 'Roman Historians' 25). Whoever wrote the epistle, it indicates how members of the Essex circle read Tacitus in the 1590s: 'thou shalt see all the miseries of a torne and declining state: The Empire usurped; the Princes murthered; the people wavering; the soldiers tumultuous; nothing unlawfull to him that hath power, and nothing so unsafe ase to bee securely innocent'. In the four emperors who grimly follow Nero within the space of a year, the reader will see 'the calamities that follow civill warre, where lawes lie a sleepe, and all things are judged by the sword' (para. 3–4).

Although Elizabethan Tacitism was centered at Oxford, and specifically at Merton College, where Savile was Warden, it had an immediate reach outside the academy. For Savile was a friend of Henry Cuffe, an Oxford professor of Greek who became Essex's personal secretary. Consequently, 'Savile's volume provides suggestive evidence about the way Tacitus was being used in the Earl's circle' (Smuts, 'Roman Historians' 25). Like many on the Continent, Savile and this circle link Tacitus with Machiavelli (Womersley 316), and they follow 'Huguenot resistance' theory to laud an individual's 'desire to free one's country from "tyranny and bondage" – the same emphasis with which Machiavelli had concluded *The Prince*' (319) – in a 'challenge' to the 'prevailing political orthodoxies of late sixteenth-century England' (329), as Mornay emphasizes in *Vindiciae* (326–30).

While historians and literary historians identify Tacitism as a major force of late Elizabethan political culture, literary critics rarely connect Marlowe with it. As indicated in Chapter 1, the only critic I have seen do so is Michael Hattaway, who writes briefly that Tacitus' 'great themes were ancient liberty, what his translator [Savile], almost certainly invoking *Tamburlaine*, called "higher aspiring minds", and modern servitude': 'Tacitus delighted in exposing the hypocrisy of courtiers: his target was absolutism and its handmaid, theatricality. His tone was sardonic and his characters could be theatricalized and fantastical. Marlowe's politics ... are in this mould' ('Ideology and Subversion' 208–9).[57] What is notable here is a series of intriguing inferences: that the academic translator of Tacitus might have 'invoked' Marlowe's only play in print in 1591; that Savile equates Tacitus' great theme of liberty with the Marlovian sublime, through the notion of the high aspiring mind; that Savile locates Tacitus' attack on absolutism in *Tamburlaine*; and finally, that he finds in Marlowe's play a Tacitean fascination with theatricality. Like Machiavelli, Tacitus is a blood relative of Christopher Marlowe.

Curiously, however, modern editors of Marlowe's works provide no evidence that he read Tacitus. Yet is this because Marlowe did not read Tacitus, or because Tacitus, like Savile, has 'dropped below our intellectual horizon' (Womersley 313)? I would find it more remarkable that Marlowe had not read Tacitus than if he did, especially since the Roman historians were part of the English curriculum, part of the culture, with recent Marlowe biographers mentioning especially Livy and Sallust, along with Cicero and Polybius.[58]

Until the topic is studied in detail, we cannot settle the question for certain, but we might wish to follow up on Hattaway's comment, to see Marlowe writing within the Tacitean 'moment', especially since Tacitus becomes inseparable from Machiavelli, who is a staple of *Edward II* criticism. Rather than locate specific Tacitean borrowings in *Edward II*, we might attend to Tacitism more broadly. For instance, we might recall the play's patronage context, especially the Tacitean earl of Essex. According to Park Honan, Marlowe's young patron, Thomas Walsingham, 'had cause to follow Essex's career' at Scadbury in spring 1593 (332). Yet very little research has been done on the Marlowe–Essex connection.[59] Richard Rowland reports that Francis Bacon in 1601 used the story of Edward II as a backdrop for the Essex rebellion, and he finds an anticipation in Sir Francis Walsingham's 1583 use of the King Edward story to lecture King James VI of Scotland, a lecture based on *Vindiciae* (ed. xx–xxi). We cannot be certain that Marlowe's narrative about the dangers of a royal favorite, Piers Gaveston, specifically targets the Tacitean Essex in the early 1590s, but we also might not wish to exclude the possibility.[60]

More confidently, we know that Marlowe infuses his re-telling of Holinshed's historical narrative of fourteenth-century English kingship with recurrent references to classical Rome.[61] For instance, in a much-cited passage at the end of Act 1 of *Edward II*, when the barons plot to murder Gaveston, Mortimer Senior counsels tolerance on the grounds that 'The mightiest kings have had their minions' (1.4: 390), citing not simply Alexander and Hephaestion, Hercules and Hylas, Achilles and Patroclus, and Socrates and Alcibiades, but also Cicero and the young Augustus: 'The Roman Tully loved Octavius' (395).[62] In addition to many representations of classical mythology (e.g., 1.1: 60–6: Diana and Actaeon; 1.4.178–80: Juno, Jove, and Ganymede; 2.2.53–5: Jove and Danae; 2.5.15–17: Helen of Troy), and references to such historical figures as Plato and Aristotle (4.7.10), Aristarchus (5.4.52), and Julius Caesar (to be discussed below), in Act 4, scene 6, Mortimer's henchman Rice Ap Howell likens the father of Edward's later favorite, Spencer Junior, to 'the lawless Catiline of Rome' because he has 'Revelled in England's wealth and treasury' (51–2). Since we have no evidence that Catiline revelled in Rome's treasury, editors tend to pass the reference off as either inept scholarship, stylistic flourish, or both, without recognizing how it contributes to Marlowe's republican authorship.[63]

Forker recalls that Catiline was 'the Roman nobleman whose famous conspiracy against the republic failed through the opposition of Cicero and who was killed in battle' (ed. 258), while Rowland reminds us that 'Sallust had made Catiline's name synonymous with the provocation of civil strife and [that] English renderings of his history invariably concentrated on his "lewde conspiracies"', citing Kyd's *Cornelia* 3.2.58 (ed. 115; see Chapter 1). In other words, Catiline is that member of a republic who acts out a conspiracy against the republic, to become the arch-enemy of the arch-republican, Tully.

Catiline might not have robbed the Roman treasury, but Sallust provides recurrent details to trick Marlowe into remembering that he did. In *The Conspiracy of Catiline*, Sallust reports that Lucius Catiline '[f]rom his youth...had delighted in civil war, bloodshed, [and] robbery', and that his 'monstrous ambition hankered continually after things extravagant, impossible, beyond his reach', and even more specifically that he had a 'love of luxury and love of money' (178). Sallust is particularly drawn to the topic of 'Avarice' and the role it plays in Rome's 'change' from a republic to an empire: 'Growing love of money, and the lust for power which followed it, engendered every kind of evil.... As soon as wealth came to be a mark of distinction and an easy way to renown, military commands, and political power, virtue began to decline' (181–3). In fact, Catiline 'planned a revolution' precisely by 'looking back regretfully to the loot which past victories had brought them [he and his men] and longing for civil war' (185). Thus, what Catiline and Company really want is 'superfluity of riches' (189), 'affluence' (190), and 'personal aggrandizement' (205). Later, when the Senate deliberates over the conspirators' fate, and Caesar advises the state to 'confiscate' the conspirators' 'goods' (220), the great stoic republican, Cato, counsels to the contrary, calling for capital punishment and taunting Caesar bitterly: 'let Romans be liberal, if they want to, at the expense of our subjects, let them be merciful to plunderers of the exchequer' (222). It is this last phrase, I propose, 'in furibus aerari' (52.12: 'plunderers of the treasury'), that Marlowe likely remembered when he associates Catiline with reveling wealth and treasury.

Presumably, Marlowe also knew what is so patently obvious, that Tacitus habitually draws on Sallust, 'not simply verbal reminiscences...but sometimes entire episodes' (Fyfe, ed. xi). For instance, Tacitus' portrait of the

Flavian commander Antonius Primus 'is closely modelled on Sallust's description of the rebel Catiline at his final battle (*Catiline* 60)' (Fyfe, ed. 270). Even though Sallust himself had been a hapless client of Julius Caesar, he presents himself as the champion of Roman liberty and thus as a critic of tyranny (*Catiline*, 'Preface' 179). Tacitus understands the Sallustian program, and uses the earlier historian as a model for his own historiography. In this way, the syncretic imagination of Marlowe's day could naturally include Sallust's story of Catiline as part and parcel of what went under the rubric of Tacitism.[64]

Marlowe's Tacitean reference to Catiline formally invites the audience to view the drama about the fourteenth-century English civil war in light of the first-century BC Roman civil war, the metamorphosis of the Republic into the Empire. In particular, Marlowe's injection of Tacitism into Holinshed warrants pause. Whereas Marlovians have been largely content to register the play's rejection of the chronicler's providentialist model (Forker, ed. 34, 61, 82; Rowland, ed. xxv; Romany and Lindsey, eds. 32), the opposition between Tacitus and Holinshed is not as transparent as it might seem.[65] In our most recent, authoritative study of Holinshed, Annabel Patterson argues for the 'demystifying spirit of the *Chronicles*' (*Chronicles* 213), which is based on an 'egalitarian principle' (214). Reminding us that the syndicate of men who compiled both the 1577 and the 1587 editions were middle-class writers aiming to address middle-class readers (3–7), Patterson highlights the work's 'protoliberalism', based in 'rights theory, specifically in constitutional and legal rights', and even more particularly in 'rights of writing and reading' (7) – to foreground what she calls social 'equality' (106), 'consent' (108–13), and 'freedom of consultation and speech' (123). To offset this 'preeminently...citizen project' (198), Patterson recurrently turns to Savile's elitist and Tacitean critique of Holinshed (e.g., 5, 10, 20, 104, 188, 190). She does so to locate the cultural work of the *Chronicles* as lying most potently in its 'populism' (187–214), not in Savile's aristocratic republicanism. Yet she also allows us to see a further complication, for at one point she shows that Holinshed himself relies on Tacitus. To narrate the story of Boadicea, or Voadicea, the British heroine who in AD 62 led a revolt against the Romans, 'Holinshed paused to permit Voadicea to deliver a long speech on the subject of "ancient liberty," a speech that he had troubled to unearth in Dion Cassius, despite the fact that it duplicates a briefer one translated directly from Tacitus, his primary source at this point' (104). What this moment tells us is how complicated it is to unravel Tacitism from English national history in the late Elizabethan era.

Patterson refers only once to Holinshed's story of Edward II, concluding that 'Edward's deposition was a crucial step in the self-definition of Parliament because, although it had been accomplished by force, both houses had been involved in legitimizing the change' (111). Marlowe's staging of this story, about the people's legal right to depose a king of England, as enriched by Tacitism, creates a unique political drama toward the end of Elizabeth's reign. *Edward II*, I suggest, rather than being either a simple Holinshedian story of parliamentary populism or a Tacitean story about the imperial loss of liberty, is a complicated tragedy about this very 1590s predicament.[66]

To modify or at least supplement Shuger's historical trajectory, and the place of *Edward II* in it, we need to turn to the one Roman writer whom we know Marlowe uses throughout his canon, the very figure whose death Tacitus himself memorializes, although not without approbation: antiquity's greatest poet of civil war, Lucan. In the *Annals*, Tacitus records Lucan's importation of 'an intensely keen resentment' into the Pisonian conspiracy against Nero: 'Lucanus had the stimulus of personal motives, for Nero tried to disparage the fame of his poems and, with the foolish vanity of a rival, had forbidden him to publish them' (15: 332). Nowhere is this imperial opposition to the poet's liberty more starkly animated than here, along with its dark shadow, authorial republican resentment. When the Pisonian conspiracy is discovered, and the emperor orders his former friend to commit suicide, Lucan orchestrates his last act to counter imperial censorship and to promote his legacy of authorial liberty:

> Next he [Nero] ordered the destruction of Marcus Annaeus Lucanus. As the blood flowed freely from him, and he felt a chill creeping through his feet and hands, and the life gradually ebbing from his extremities, though the heart was still warm and he retained his mental power, Lucanus recalled some poetry he had composed in which he had told the story of a wounded soldier dying a similar kind of death, and he recited the very lines.[67] (Tacitus, *Annals* 15: 343)

We might wonder whether Marlowe could have found here a Lucanian license for his well-known habit of self-quotation.

Editors of *Edward II* identify two substantive passages that echo *Lucan's First Book*.[68] In Act 3, scene 2, Edward indicts the barons as 'traitors all' (30):

> Rather than thus be braved,
> Make England's civil towns huge heaps of stones.
> (*Edward II* 3.2.30–1)

The lines are similar to lines 25–6 in Marlowe's translation (W.D. Briggs, ed. 161–2; Forker, ed. 233): 'That rampires fallen down, huge heaps of stone/Lie in our towns, that houses are abandon'd all'. The echo again shows how Marlowe's imagination links the architectural and 'civil' upheaval of the English civil war with that of the Roman civil war.

Even more substantively, in Act 4, scene 4, Isabella welcomes her 'loving friends and countrymen' (1) after they return to England, and she laments their 'heavy case' (4):

> When force to force is knit, and sword and glaive
> In civil broils make kin and countrymen
> Slaughter themselves in others, and their sides
> With their own weapons gored. But what's the help?
> Misgoverned kings are cause of all this wrack.
> (*Edward II* 4.4.5–9)

Isabella evokes the opening of the *Pharsalia* (W.D. Briggs, ed. 171; Forker, ed. 251) – especially, according to editors, line 3 – which we have seen Marlowe translate as

> Wars worse than civil on Thessalian plains,
> And outrage strangling law, and people strong
> We sing, whose conquering swords their own breasts launched,
> Armies allied, the kingdom's league uprooted,
> Th' affrighted world's force bent on public spoil,
> Trumpets and drums like deadly threat'ning other,
> Eagles alike displayed, darts answering darts.
> (*Lucan's First Book* 1–7)

Like Mornay in *Vindiciae*, Lucan outlines the grim 'outrage' of civil war to lie in 'public' self-slaughter – 'people' launching their 'own breasts'. Isabella locates a Lucanian outrage in the 'civil broils' of England, where 'kin and countrymen' slaughter themselves by using their 'weapons' to 'gore' their own 'sides'. Yet Isabella's remark ranges beyond Lucan's Prologue to a passage later in Book 1, when the poet introduces his real goal: not simply to narrate the Roman civil war between Caesar and Pompey but to anatomize the *cause* of their civil broil: 'The causes first I purpose to unfold/Of these garboils' (67–8). While Lucan inventories as a major cause the envy of the Fates (70), and as a secondary cause the 'wrack' of 'all great dominions', 'wealth' (160–1), he emphasizes the cause identified by Isabella: 'Misgoverned kings are the cause of all this wrack'. Marlowe might well have taken Mornay's cue, for in *Vindiciae* the French resistance writer uses Isabella's parliamentary resistance to Edward as an example of republican rule, a parallel to Lucius Junius Brutus, who rebelled against the Tarquins to form the Roman Republic (3: 161): 'In the kingdom of England, Elizabeth [Isabella], the wife of Edward II, appealed to the parliament of the kingdom against him, and by its authority he was judged unworthy of the kingdom on account of tyranny against his subjects, especially the leading men, whom he executed without any case having been heard' (3: 163).

In addition to editors, W.L. Godshalk claims that 'Lucan was in the back of Marlowe's mind as he wrote this play', finding Edward echoing Book 2 of the *Pharsalia* during a soliloquy when the king wonders, 'Why should a king be subject to a Priest', only to prompt reflection on 'Proud Rome, that hatchest such imperial grooms' and to attack the papacy:

> I'll fire thy crazed buildings and enforce
> The papal towers to kiss the lowly ground,
> With slaughtered priests make Tiber's channel swell,
> And banks raised higher with their sepulchers.
> (*Edward II* 1.4.100–3)

In the *Pharsalia*, Lucan tells of the lament by the elders of Rome at the proclamation of civil war, and specifically of the fall-out of Sulla's revenge:

> The Tyrrhenian flood
> received in a heap all the Sullan corpses.
> The first fell down into the river, the last on top of bodies.
> (Lucan, *Civil War* 2.209–11; trans. Braund)

Once more, Marlowe's echo of Lucan encourages the Elizabethan audience to see England re-enacting the Roman civil war, apprising them of a potentially grim future.

Additionally, William Blissett identifies the play's one reference to Caesar as a Lucanian allusion. In Act 1, scene 1, Edward and Gaveston engage in an exchange with deep republican implications, when the king bestows new titles on his friend:

> *Edward.* Thy worth, sweet friend, is far above my gifts;
>   Therefore, to equal it, receive my heart.
>   ...
>   Save or condemn, and in our name command
>   Whatso thy mind affects or fancy likes.
> *Gaveston.* It shall suffice me to enjoy your love,
>   Which whiles I have, I think myself as great
>   As Caesar riding in the Roman street
>   With captive kings at his triumphant car.[69]
>   (*Edward II* 1.1.160–73)

Here a king *equalizes* himself with one of his subjects, and this is what especially galls barons like Mortimer, as critics observe. The play opens on this note, when Gaveston in soliloquy quotes Edward's entreaty in the language of 'The Passionate Shepherd': 'come, Gaveston,/And share the kingdom with thy dearest friend' (1.1.1–2). Generously (yet, as it turns out, naïvely), Edward extends the notion of freedom to the 'mind' and 'fancy' of his friend, an inner state of the beloved's desire that can 'command' royal action – in this case, the acquisition of political titles and power. Effectively, Marlowe presents Edward as a king with a republican cast of mind; this is one way of viewing the tragedy that ensues. Gaveston responds with a correspondingly ambiguous simile: enjoying the freedom of Edward's 'love', he feels like imperial Caesar riding into Rome in his chariot to form a ritual triumph over 'captive kings'. At the beginning of the play, it is not the hero but his 'sweet friend' who assumes the identity of Lucan's anti-republican villain.

We need to read Marlowe's Lucanian authorship into the play's opening because the continuation of Gaveston's soliloquy alludes to other works in the Marlowe canon:

> Sweet prince, I come; these, these thy amorous lines
> Might have enforced me to have swum from France
> And, like Leander, gasped upon the sand,
> So thou wouldst smile and take me in thine arms.
> The sight of London to my exiled eyes
> Is as Elysium to a new-come soul.
> (*Edward II* 1.1.6–11)

Strategically 'positioned in the role of the play's Presenter' (Cartelli, *Marlowe, Shakespeare* 123–4), Gaveston follows up his re-voicing of Marlowe's pastoral lyric with echoes of both *Hero and Leander* and *Doctor Faustus*.[70] As we shall see in *Doctor Faustus* (Chapter 5), Marlowe uses his Prologue to inventory poems and plays he himself has penned, inviting the audience to read into the chronicle narrative of Edward, his favorite, and Lucanian civil war the republican authorship of Christopher Marlowe.

The Lucanian channel in *Edward II* runs deeper than scholarship and criticism allows. In Act 1, scene 2, the Lucanian Isabella tells Warwick that she would rather 'endure a melancholy life' without her husband than 'be oppressed by civil mutinies' (65–6), evoking Lucan's central theme, the loss of civil liberty to tyranny. Later, talking with his wife, Edward accuses Mortimer of growing 'so brave/That to my face he threatens civil wars' (2.2.231–2), once more evoking Marlowe's translation of Lucan's prologue. Curiously, however, it is Isabella who serves as the play's Lucanian spokesperson, accusing her husband of allowing 'Unnatural wars, where subjects brave their king' (3.1.86). One memorable Lucanian image has especially escaped notice, that of the oak tree, when Mortimer Junior soliloquizes that he 'stand[s] as Jove's huge tree,/And others are but shrubs compared to me' (5.6.11–12).[71] If editors supply an intertext, it is the *Georgics* 3.332 (W.D. Briggs, ed. 202; Rowland, ed. 126), but Virgil's image turns out to have an afterlife that includes both his own *Aeneid* and Spenser's *Februarie* eclogue in *The Shepheardes Calender*, with the *Pharsalia* serving as the principal intermediary, when Lucan likens Pompey to a falling oak, as Marlowe translates it:

> Like to a tall oak in a fruitful field,
> Bearing old spoils and conquerors' monuments,
> Who though his root be weak, and his own weight
> Keep him within the ground, his arms all bare,
> His body (not his boughs) send forth a shade;
> Though every blast it nod, and seem to fall,
> When all the woods about stand bolt upright.[72]
>
> (*Lucan's First Book* 137–43)

Since Lucan associates Pompey with the fallen oak, Mortimer's use of the arboreal image is consistent with his republican self-presentation, while his arrogance about his royal power looks forward to his own Pompey-like fate.

Finally, we might suggest a Lucanian echo in a recurrent image in this play about civil war: that of the headless body. In Book 8 of the *Pharsalia*, Lucan gestures to Book 2 of the *Aeneid*, with its graphic image of Pyrrhus beheading Priam, when narrating Pompey's decapitation: 'his headless corpse is tossed/this way and that by shallow waters' (698–9) – a harrowing image that typologically fulfills the prophecy of the Bacchic Roman matron at the end of Book 1, who envisions (in Marlowe's translation) 'This headless trunk that lies on Nilus' sand' (684).[73] The image recurs twice in *Edward II*: first at the midpoint, when Mortimer anticipates Gaveston's beheading by referring to the Frenchman's 'senseless trunk' (2.5.52), a discourse that is reiterated afterward by Arundel, who tells how 'Warwick in an ambush lay/And bare him to his death, and in a trench/Strake off his head' (3.1.118–20); and second at the play's close, when the head of Mortimer Junior is brought on stage before the new king, Edward III: 'here is the head of Mortimer' (5.6.92). While the source texts include both beheadings, the recurrent Lucanian intertextuality makes the Lucanian provenance of this image palpitate.

In addition to recalling Lucan, Marlowe appears to have been reading other literary works about the Roman civil war. For instance, editors have found him reading other civil war plays (see also Chapter 1), especially Lodge's *Wounds of Civil War* and Kyd's translation of Robert Garnier's *Cornélie* (Forker, ed. 173, 194, 234, 235, 294; Rowland, ed. 113; Wiggins and Lindsey, eds. 110).[74] Most notably, in Act 5, scene 3, when Matrevis and Gurney wash Edward in puddle water and shave his beard, Edward addresses 'Immortal powers, that knows the painful cares/That wait upon my poor distressed soul,/O level all your looks upon these daring men' (37–9) – an address likely plagiarized by Lodge: 'Immortal powers that

160 Marlowe's Republican Authorship

know the painful cares/That weight upon my poor distressed heart,/O bend your brows and level all your looks/Of dreadful awe upon these daring men' (4.2.87–90). Since Lodge's play depends so acutely on Lucan's concept of civil war, his act of counterfeiting reads the *Pharsalia* back into *Edward II* formally.[75]

Like *The Massacre at Paris* and *The Jew of Malta*, *Edward II* also includes a broader discourse of republican freedom. Given the high quality of the play, we can expect it to outstrip the other two in the technical terminology of its republican discourse. The word 'liberty' occurs twice, both with reference to Edward, who 'casts to work his [own] liberty' (5.2.57; see 5.2.70), while 'liberal' occurs once, associated appropriately with Gaveston: 'The liberal earl of Cornwall is the man' (2.1.10). Moreover, the word 'free' appears three times, as when Edward himself 'laid a plot/To set his brother [Kent] free' (5.2.32–3), while the word 'freely' occurs once, when Edward says of his crown, 'I would freely give it to his [Gaveston's] enemies' (1.4.308). Such discourse reminds us that *Edward II* is a tragedy about freedom, foregrounding the bondage of a king – as well as his final assassination. Yet Marlowe's primary project is more complex than simply unleashing anti-royalist feeling, for toward the end the play sympathizes with Edward – and, I am suggesting, with a paradox we have found in Tamburlaine: a republican-minded king. As to be expected, the word 'tyrant' recurs five times (with cognates), as Edward threatens to 'be cruel and grow tyrannous' (2.2.205), even as he finds himself subject to the 'tyrant...hand' of Mortimer (5.3.36).

Less surprisingly, *Edward II* uses the word 'parliament' four times (Marlowe's only other use occurs in *1 Tamburlaine* [see Chapter 3]), drawing attention to an institutional authority different from the king's prerogative.[76] In Act 1, scene 1, Gaveston announces Edward's arrival in the play, 'Here comes the King and the nobles/From the parliament' (71–2), while later in this scene the Bishop of Coventry threatens to 'incense the parliament' (183) if Gaveston does not leave England for France. In Act 4, scene 6, Mortimer Junior voices the sentiment behind Queen Elizabeth's monarchical republic, when responding to Kent's question about what the barons will do with the king: "Tis not in her [Isabella's] controlment, nor in ours,/But as the realm and parliament shall please' (35–6). Finally, in Act 5, scene 1, Sir William Trussel demands of the king, 'My lord, the parliament must have present news' (84). Throughout, the barons and the clergy present themselves as the protectors of the parliament in their 'stand against [the] King' (1.1.96). As the Archbishop of Canterbury puts it, 'We and the rest that are his counselors/Will meet, and with a general consent/Confirm his banishment with our hands and seals' (1.2.69–71). When Lancaster replies, 'What we confirm the King will frustrate', Mortimer Junior retorts, as if taking a page out of *Vindiciae*, 'Then may we lawfully revolt from him' (72–3). Especially in the first part of the play, Marlowe follows Holinshed in dramatizing a legal problem between king and parliament.

The barons' parliamentary pressure on the king helps explain Marlowe's attention to a concept that must have aroused suspicion in an audience serving the daughter of Henry VIII: an elected king. In Act 1, scene 4, Mortimer speaks an aside to the Archbishop of Canterbury when Edward refuses to 'subscribe' to Gaveston's banishment (53): 'Curse him if he refuse, and then may we/Depose him and elect another king' (54–5). Then, in Act 5, scene 1, when the earl of Leicester and the Bishop of Winchester try to persuade Edward to abdicate, the king fears that they will 'make a new elected king' (78), exclaiming, 'Elect, conspire, install, do what you will' (88).[77] The topic of election is opposed to that of 'hereditary succession', as Mornay reveals in *Vindiciae*: 'absolutely no-one is born a king' (3: 71). In *Edward II*, the 'basely born' Gaveston (1.4.402) bitterly turns the tables on the barons who attack him: 'Base leaden earls, that glory in your birth,/Go sit at home and eat your tenants' beef' (2.2.74–5).

Hence, at least three times in the opening Act alone, Marlowe uses a dramatic speech to write the traditional three forms of government coming out of Aristotle's *Politics* and especially Polybius' *Rise of the Roman Empire*, but appearing most authoritatively for Elizabethan England in Sir Thomas Smith's *De Republica Anglorum*. In the opening scene, in the second half of his soliloquy, Gaveston announces to the audience,

Farewell base stooping to the lordly peers;
My knee shall bow to none but to the King.
As for the multitude, that are but sparks
Raked up in embers of their poverty,
Tanti!
              (*Edward II* 1.1.18–22)

Lordly peers, King, multitude: these terms evoke aristocracy, monarchy, and democracy, but they also take a dramatic stance on them, distinctive of their speaker. Gaveston rejects a government based on either aristocracy or democracy to favor a government based on monarchy – with a twist, since he goes on to report that he will 'draw the pliant king which way' he 'please[s]' (52). According to scholars, his subsequent declaration that he 'must have wanton poets,/Musicians, ... /... Italian masques by night,/Sweet speeches, comedies, and pleasing shows' (50–5), evokes two famous events: the earl of Leicester's staging of pageants for Elizabeth at Kenilworth Castle in 1575; and the Roman emperor Tiberius' rehearsal of pastimes on the island of Capri.[78]

Similarly, in the second scene of the play, Mortimer echoes Gaveston's scripting of the three forms of government when announcing his contempt for the upstart Frenchman:

> Were all the earls and barons of my mind,
> We'll hale him from the bosom of the King,
> And at the court-gate hang the peasant up,
> Who, swoll'n with venom of ambitious pride,
> Will be the ruin of the realm and us.
> (*Edward II* 1.2.28–32)

In Mortimer's eyes, a commoner leaning on the bosom of the king unsettles the delicate balance between king and aristocracy. In particular, the king's disordered desire for a common person dismantles the foundation of English government itself.

Finally, in the play's fourth scene, when the barons and clergy confront Edward about Gaveston, the king candidly encourages them to turn England from a monarchy into a republic, organized around aristocratic power:

> Make several kingdoms of this monarchy,
> And share it equally amongst you all,
> So I may have some nook or corner left
> To frolic with my dearest Gaveston.
> (*Edward II* 1.4.70–3)

As clearly as anywhere in his canon, Marlowe writes republicanism; but as so often, he tarnishes the ideal through Edward's erotic irresponsibility: the king will allow his monarchy to become a republic only if he can 'frolic' with his friend.

The barons hold the king to his word, and Mortimer Junior takes the lead as the spokesman for a new English republic:

> 'Tis treason to be up against the King.
> So shall we have the people of our side,
> ...
> And when the commons and the nobles join,
> 'Tis not the King can buckler Gaveston;
> We'll pull him from the strongest hold he hath.
> My lords, if to perform this I be slack,
> Think me as base a groom as Gaveston.
> (*Edward II* 1.4.281–91)

Mortimer's plan to grab power is clear. To dethrone the royal lover of Gaveston, he will ensure that the 'common' people 'join' the 'nobles';

again, the plan is right out of *Vindiciae*. Yet, as his theatrical word 'perform' hints, he will only pretend to be the liberating republican. The pretense works even on Edward, who tells Gaveston that he cannot commit Mortimer to the Tower because 'the people love him well' (2.2.234). Yet it is Kent who peers through the curtain of Mortimer's republican theatre:

> O, miserable is that commonweal, where lords
> Keep courts and kings are locked in prison.
> (*Edward II* 5.3.63–4)

Suggestively, only when Edward becomes locked in prison does Marlowe's discourse of the sublime begin to soar. Intimations do appear earlier. As we have seen, Gaveston opens the play by echoing 'The Passionate Shepherd', although Mortimer re-deploys this discourse to trap Gaveston: wherever the Frenchman 'shall live and be beloved/'Tis hard for us to work his overthrow' (1.4.261–2). Just previous to this, Edward himself tells Mortimer, 'Ere my sweet Gaveston shall part from me,/This isle shall fleet upon the ocean/And wander to the unfrequented Inde' (1.4.48–50). The language recalls the sublime rhetoric of Dido and to an extent Tamburlaine, with their forceful use of passionate speech to imagine an exotic (and violent) future. Later, after Mortimer has Gaveston murdered, Edward turns his invitational homoerotic discourse to draw his new friends to 'philosophy' and the 'life contemplative': 'Come Spenser, come Baldock, come sit down by me' (4.7.16–20).

Recently, much has been made of the role of the 'passions' in *Edward II*, yet without registering its connection to the sublime.[79] Indeed, the word that appears in the title to Marlowe's pastoral lyric, 'passionate', recurs more in *Edward II* than in any other of his works (three of six uses), while the allied term 'passions' similarly recurs (three of seven uses). According to Thomas Cartelli, Marlowe presents the passions of both Edward and the barons as equally impeding 'the good of the kingdom' ('*Edward II*' 162).[80] Cartelli goes on to follow the formulation of Jonathan Goldberg (164), who goes so far as to claim that 'sodomy is the name for all behavior in the play' (*Sodometries* 123), not simply Edward's homoerotic passion for Gaveston, Spencer, and Baldock, but also the heterosexual passion of Isabella for both Edward and Mortimer. While true, these formulations miss the way that the play's increasingly 'passionate' discourse of 'sodomy' soars into the Marlovian sublime.

Marlowe's historic invention of the sublime wedded to sodomy emerges viscerally in the concluding act, which opens with the king's meditation before Leicester over the difference between the 'griefs' of 'private men' and 'kings' (5.1.8–9). The invention becomes graphic in the self-image of the 'imperial lion' (11) reacting to its goring with such horrific violence (including drinking hot blood) that he 'mounts into the air' (14):

> For such outrageous passions cloy my soul
> As with the wings of rancour and disdain
> Full often am I soaring up to heaven,
> To plain me to the gods.
> (*Edward II* 5.1.18–22)

Edward's language is complex, but evidently he means that his extreme passions pierce or weigh down his soul just as when, complaining to the gods, he lets his anger pull him down. Referring to the genre of the complaint, Marlowe makes clear his discursive understanding of the passions firing the sublime, from Longinus forward.[81]

Such discourse recurs too often at the end to dilate fully here, but one last example is especially pertinent, when Edward finally gives his crown to Winchester:

> Now, sweet God of heaven,
> Make me despise this transitory pomp
> And sit for aye enthronised in heaven.
> Come, death, and with thy fingers close my eyes,
> Or if I live, let me forget myself.
> (*Edward II* 5.1.107–11)

Like both Tamburlaine and Faustus, Edward yearns for the eternal, here Christianized through prayer – 'Or' its pagan opposite, oblivion. As the end draws near, the king's passionate sorrow becomes heroic – and eloquent: 'I feel a hell of grief' (5.5.89). In the end, Marlowe's republican authorship turns the freedom of sublimity not into a political state for the liberated citizen but rather into a tragic form of passionate language. In the famous last 'cry', which we are told has the power to 'raise the town' (5.5.113), Marlowe boldly rehearses the Elizabethan age's most harrowing political language: a new sodomitical sublime.

5
'Make man to live eternally': The Skeptical Sublime in *Doctor Faustus*

In this concluding chapter, I wish to find the apex of Marlowe's republican authorship in *Doctor Faustus*, and to locate its historic achievement in a literary economy I call *the skeptical sublime*. The phrase yokes two major topics of early modern thought typically separated in modern scholarship: the philosophical problem of skepticism and the aesthetic principle of sublimity. Like sublimity (which we have discussed at length in previous chapters), skepticism is a complex topic that has produced a vast wealth of commentary, not just by historians of early modern philosophy but recently by early modern literary critics.[1] While literary critics have long recognized Marlowe as an iconoclastic and dissident writer, and found *Doctor Faustus* to be his most profound exploration of the skeptical habit of mind, only as late as 2005 has William Hamlin produced a full-length study, *Tragedy and Scepticism in Shakespeare's England*, which focuses on the drama (as its title indicates), including a brief chapter on *Faustus* (144–54).[2]

Labeling *Doctor Faustus* a 'sceptical play' (144), imbued with the discourse of classical and early modern skepticism, Hamlin argues that Faustus exhibits a 'complex interaction of doubt and desire, a paradoxical reciprocity between the two that hints...at genuine "philosophical preoccupations" of the culture in which Marlowe...lived'. Although never mentioning sublimity, Hamlin suggests that 'Faustus' habit of casting doubt is preempted by an experience of euphoric ravishment that yields in turn to new casting of doubt' (148). As these terms reveal, Hamlin finds an 'experience' in the play that resembles what I am calling the skeptical sublime.[3]

In particular, Hamlin's pioneering history of skepticism from antiquity through to the Tudor and Stuart era foregrounds 'two basic configurations'. First, 'Pyrrhonism, named after Pyrrho of Elis and carefully delineated in the treatises of Sextus Empiricus, suggested that we have inadequate grounds for claiming certain knowledge about anything; we should therefore suspend judgement on all matters where conflicting perceptions and opinions may be advanced'. Second, 'Academic scepticism', which derives from Plato but finds its most important spokesman in Cicero, especially his *Academica*, 'argued that epistemological certainty is impossible to attain, and that we should rather seek to develop forms of probable knowledge based on the scrupulous study of appearances'. Despite the distinction between Pyrrhonism and Academicism, for many Renaissance writers 'the two traditions of scepticism were seen as fundamentally akin...in their common engagement with epistemological doubt and their shared emphasis on the radical situatedness of individual humans' (3).

For Hamlin, 'the essence of skepticism' is thus 'an irrepressible spirit of questioning: an abidingly critical attitude towards all dogmatic or doctrinaire positions conjoined with an implicit and unceasing defence of open-minded enquiry'. The twin values of such a humane 'temper of mind', he suggests, are first 'what the Pyrrhonists call *epochē*', the 'deliberate withholding of assent or dissent', and, second, what they call *ataraxia*, 'cerebral tranquility, freedom from anxiety' (5–6), which could also take the form of 'freedom of thought and expression' (143). Although the topic of liberty remains incidental to Hamlin's discussion of skepticism, he allows us to determine just how palpably early modern skepticism came to value inner freedom.[4]

Hamlin goes on to track the migration of classical skepticism into early modern humanism (his chapter 1), and specifically into Elizabethan England (his chapter 2), filtered through such figures interested in republicanism as George Buchanan, Philippe de Mornay, and Michel de Montaigne, including such English writers as Gascoigne, Lyly, Ralegh, Spenser, Fraunce, Bacon, and Florio: 'the English, too, had their doubts' (53). Hamlin even claims that 'writers of all sorts exhibit a sensitivity to epistemological questions, distinctions and anxieties which I believe to be a crucial feature of the age' (70). But it is in his chapter on the 'kinds', 'paradigms', and 'values' of skepticism (120) that Hamlin briefly delineates what he calls 'applied scepticism': 'scepticism about the practice of standard human activities like writing history or wielding political power'. Observing that 'No one insists that Machiavelli read Sextus or inclined towards Pyrrhonism', he suggests nonetheless that Machiavelli's 'studies of political morality have often been characterized as profoundly sceptical of earlier ideals of governments', and he goes on to connect Machiavellian skepticism with what in Chapter 4 we called Tacitism: 'The Tacitean exposé of imperial Rome, so popular in the late sixteenth century, thus combines with the attitude of detachment implicitly promoted by scepticsm, and together the two encourage an analysis of "policy", or *realpolitik*, which in turn surfaces in many contemporary literary works' (123). In other words, during the Elizabethan era, Tacitism, like Machiavellianism, became inseparable from skepticism.

Fundamentally, this is the topic of Richard Tuck's 1993 *Philosophy and Government 1572–1651*. In this nuanced (and influential) historical study,

Tuck tells the story of the advent of modern political theory as a story about the migration of skepticism from a 'Ciceronian' to a 'Tacitean' humanism: 'the most important difference of all was the much greater role accorded to *scepticism* in the late sixteenth century: that behind *raison d'état* lies scepticism, and that it should not surprise us – for after all, a scepticism about the validity of moral principles is almost a necessary condition for a thoroughgoing confidence in the need to override the ethical and legal norms of a society'. 'All across Europe at this time', Tuck continues, 'writers' understood skepticism not as *'epistemological'* but rather as *'psychological'*, because the skeptic, like the stoic, 'was searching for "wisdom", ... and he believed that he had found it in the complete elimination from his mind of the beliefs which cause harm – namely all beliefs which, if acted upon or expressed, would bring him into some kind of conflict with other men or with the world itself' (xiii; his emphases).

Nonetheless, Tuck traces the way in which the two versions of republicanism, Ciceronian and Tacitean, played out in Renaissance political thought, with his own interest lying in the victory of Tacitism over Ciceronianism (his chapter 2). In the 1570s, 'a new kind of humanism became a central and familiar feature of the intellectual landscape', with its 'undeniable links with the Machiavellian tradition': Tacitism replaced Ciceronianism because 'no other Roman writer was such a sceptical and disenchanted commentator on political events' (40). What emerged from the two leaders of this movement, Justus Lipsius and Montaigne (45), was the recognition 'that the only secure basis for conduct was an acceptance of the force of *self-interest*, or *self-preservation*. But the self could only be preserved by a kind of emotional horticulture, in which certain passions were allowed to blossom and others kept firmly under control' (62; his emphases). Such a tradition spread to England in the 1580s and 90s, blossoming with Henry Savile's translation of Tacitus, and crowning in the work of Francis Bacon, a member of the Essex circle (104–19). Unlike Montaigne, Bacon insists on skepticism's utility for 'a *public and active life'*, and repeatedly he 'attacked the "despair" which stemmed from scepticism' (112; his emphasis).

Like Hamlin, Tuck never mentions the sublime; but in another 2005 monograph, *Sublimity and Skepticism in Montaigne and Milton*, David L. Sedley brings the two terms into alignment. Responding to the critical tradition that separates them, Sedley argues that 'the story of skepticism, the dominant problem of modern philosophy, is also the story of sublimity, the preeminent modern aesthetic category. By recognizing that these stories must be told together, we may begin to move beyond trying to tell them apart' (153). In particular, Sedley develops two arguments that he aims to dovetail. First, 'sublimity motivated skepticism: the sense that a force existed outside the aesthetic categories conventional in the Renaissance drove authors into a skeptical frame of mind'. Second, 'skepticism created sublimity: the skeptical mind-set offered alternative resources of aesthetic power and enabled authors to fashion a sublime style'. Sedley proposes that his two 'claims' are significant because they 'revise standard views of skepticism and the sublime, suggesting a mandate for an enriched aesthetics behind late-Renaissance loss of belief and exposing the Renaissance impulse behind the modern career of sublimity', but also because the claims 'contribute to ongoing discussion of the origins of modernity and genealogies of modern habits of criticism' (8). Sedley chooses to foreground Montaigne, a late sixteenth-century French essayist, and Milton, a late seventeenth-century English poet, because 'Montaigne holds an important place in histories of skepticism as the first Renaissance thinker to absorb deeply the ideas of ancient doubters', while 'Milton wrote the first postclassical poetry consistently considered to be sublime'. Sedley concludes by arguing that 'Montaigne cultivated skepticism...in order to produce sublimity. Milton forged sublimity...through his encounter with skepticism' (15). While Sedley discusses both skepticism and sublimity as part of a single early modern phenomenon, he does not enter the critical terrain traversed by Hamlin: the Elizabethan era of Marlovian tragedy. Nonetheless, by mapping Sedley's argument onto Hamlin's (and Tuck's), we may determine that Marlowe joins his contemporary Montaigne, and preempts Milton, by putting sublimity and skepticism into a distinct literary economy.

Accordingly, in this chapter I argue broadly that Marlowe rewrites the Faust story from the *Faust Book* to be a play about the literary encounter between the philosophical problem of skepticism and the aesthetic category of sublimity. In particular, I argue that Marlowe produces his famed sublimity out of his titanic engagement with skepticism, creating (as Sedley allows us to see) a sublimity that retains the residue of skepticism. The details of this economy require patience to sort out, but at stake for Marlowe, I suggest, is the form that a third concept will take, the one announced in the title-quotation to this chapter: immortality. As is well known, Marlowe's tragedy expresses skepticism about the truth-value of Scripture's central tenet, grace, or what the Prologue calls Faustus' 'chiefest bliss' (27): God's providential care for humankind, the soul's immortality in the kingdom of bliss.[5] Out of a profound doubt about Christian immortality, the play's tragic hero produces an epiphanic discourse that we are calling the sublime, a visionary language of immortality that reaches its erotic apotheosis in Helen of Troy, 'the beautifull'st [woman] in all the world' (A-text 5.1.10–11). In some of the most rhapsodic poetry in English, Helen becomes Marlowe's icon of the skeptical sublime, at once a gripping erotic alternative to the immortality of the Holy Spirit and a new dubitative figure of literary rapture. In this way, *Doctor Faustus* does two things simultaneously: it presents a haunting spiritual tragedy about the Christian truth of the universe; and, out of this tragedy, it invents what is finally most memorable about the play: its exhilarating literary exaltation about the value of Marlovian authorship.[6]

In the fiction of Marlowe's play, Helen may be no more than a succubus, a grand illusion that takes Faustus to the brink of damnation, but I shall emphasize the need to move beyond the fiction to take account of the character's effect on the audience. As Marlowe knew, there is an afterlife, but not (just) the one Scripture imagines. Rather, it is the afterlife of Marlovian authorship itself; 400 years later, *Faustus* is still playing in theatres around the world, being printed in publishing houses across the globe: '*Terminat hora diem; terminat author opus*' (Burnett, ed. 389: 'The hour ends the day; the author ends his work'). The skeptical sublime is the historic form that the Marlovian afterlife takes.[7]

Lucan, republicanism, and the sublime

We may call this authorial afterlife 'republican' because Marlowe's invention of the skeptical sublime in *Doctor Faustus* (as indeed in many of his works) participates in the discourse of political thought called republican by modern scholars.[8] At the center of this discourse, we have seen, is the republican value of liberty, as foregrounded by theorists from Cicero and Sallust, to Livy and Tacitus, to Machiavelli and Montaigne.[9] As we have also seen, however, the principal writer of republican liberty for Marlowe was none other than the counter-Virgilian epicist he himself translated, author of the tragic narrative about the imperial defeat of the Roman Republic by Julius Caesar: Lucan. In *Doctor Faustus*, I shall finally propose, the skeptical sublime is fundamentally Lucanian, in ways we have not yet determined.

While literary historians of republicanism have only recently connected Lucanian liberty with the sublime as an ideal of the early modern state, they continue to overlook the role that skepticism plays in this dynamic.[10] In turn, even though literary historians of skepticism overlook the role of sublimity, they offer cues for connecting Lucan and liberty with Tacitean skepticism. For instance, Tuck quotes the Dutch political thinker Hugo Grotius on the Batavi, whom we have discussed in Chapter 3:

> A passage in Tacitus...shows that the Germain tribes were under the rule not of individuals, but of *plures* at all periods: in it he refers to the oldest expulsions of the Germans, 'since the liberty of the Germans was bitter to the kingdom of Arsacis'; and Lucan says, 'liberty has receded beyond the Tanais and the Rhine'... In these contexts *liberty* is opposed to *kingship* properly so called – as is shown by the beginning of the *Annals*: 'the city of Rome at first had kings. L. Brutus instituted liberty and the consulate'. (Grotius, *De antiquitate*; qtd. Tuck, *Philosophy and Government* 165)

Among other things, in the early modern discourse of republican thought, Grotius exhibits the link between Tactitus and Lucan, skepticism and liberty. What remains is to follow the lead of Sedley in putting skepticism into play with sublimity, and to track the way that Marlowe could have found a literary precedent for such play in Lucan's *Pharsalia*.[11]

Luckily, the notorious question of Marlowe's text encourages us to pursue this line of investigation, for *Doctor Faustus* exists in two quite different editions: the A-text of 1604, and the B-text of 1616. Today, most editors and critics privilege the A-text as 'both aesthetically preferable to the B-version and more authentic, in the sense of being closer to what Marlowe actually wrote' (Keefer, 'Verbal Magic' 324).[12] In 1996, Leah Marcus invaluably distinguished between the two texts on 'ideological' grounds: 'The A-text places the magician in "Wertenberg" and within a context of militant Protestantism; the B text situates him instead in "Wittenberg," within a less committedly Calvinist, more theologically conservative and ceremonial milieu' ('Textual Instability' 41).[13] Marcus emphasizes the B-text's 'proimperial' agenda (58): 'the A text could be described as more nationalist and more Calvinist, Puritan, or ultra-Protestant, the B text as more internationalist, imperial, and Anglican, or Anglo-Catholic' (42). In arguing that 'B's political agenda brings it very close to imperial Catholicism' (59), she recalls that 'The duchy of Würtemberg took a consistently anti-imperial stance during the last sixteenth century' (45). She also situates the A-text's antiimperial 'Wertenberg' within the wars against Catholicism both in France and in the Netherlands. Finally, Marcus accounts for the 'shift' from the A-text to the B-text by reference to 'the earl of Essex's fall from favor in 1598' (59).[14] What Marcus allows us to remember is that Essex fell from favor because he was enacting an anti-imperial and specifically republican agenda, and that the wars in both France and the Netherlands were fought between imperial Catholicism and republican Protestantism (see Chapter 4). Furthermore, by recalling 'the monarchical republic of Queen Elizabeth I' (in Patrick Collinson's phrase), we can see how Marcus' argument about the A-text leads us to re-classify the play's ideology: for all intents and purposes, it is republican.[15]

Irrespective of whether we cite the A- or the B-text (in this chapter, I am using the former, with occasional references to the latter), *Doctor Faustus* is unique in Marlowe's dramatic canon, in that modern editors have never glossed it with Lucan or with *Lucan's First Book*. This is surprising, in part because Mephistopheles refers to Lucan's anti-republican hero, Julius Caesar (to be discussed below); and in part because several passages warrant reference to the *Pharsalia*. In Act 1, scene 3 of the A-text, for example, Faustus charges Mephistopheles to do what he commands, 'Be it to make the moon drop from her sphere' (39). Michael Keefer supplies the following gloss: 'This and similar feats were ascribed to sorceresses and magicians by various ancient writers: Virgil, *Eclogues* VIII.69; Horace, *Epodes* V.45–6 and XVII.57–8; Ovid, *Metamorphoses* VII.192ff.; and Apuleius, *Metamorphoses* (*The Golden Ass*) I.iii' (ed. 18). In Book 6 of the *Pharsalia*, however, Lucan pauses to narrate 'the most horrific of all descriptions of necromancy in ancient writers' (Braund, ed. 282), when Pompey's son Sextus consults the Thessalian witch Erichtho about the outcome of the battle on the fields of Pharsalus. In the lines right before he introduces Erichtho, Lucan describes powers held by Thessaly's witches: 'By them the stars/were first drawn down from the racing sky and Phoebe clear,/assailed by dreadful poisonous words, grew dim/ and burnt with black and earthy fires' (499–502). Like Lucan's witch, Marlowe's magician imagines an occult incantation calling the moon out of her orbit. Surely, then, a work that Marlowe translated deserves inclusion in modern annotation.

For critics surprisingly neglect the origins of Faustus' 'cursed necromancy' (Pr.25) in the necromancy of Lucan's Erichtho. The reasons for not connecting the two figures are clear: whereas Faustus is a male magician, Erichtho is female; she is an old, ugly, and brutal hag who inhabits the rural countryside in Thessaly, Greece, unlike Faustus, who is a learned theologian living at an urban German university. Indeed, the origins of Faustus can be traced to the learned Renaissance magic of such historical magicians as Henricus Cornelius Agrippa von Nettesheim (1.1.119) and Giordano Bruno.[16] Yet, as Keefer's gloss above makes clear, Marlowe injects into his portrait of the learned Renaissance magician the demonic female necromancy of classical poets, the most detailed and famous of whom is Lucan's Erichtho. Technical details further connect the witch with the magician. In Act 1, scene 3, Faustus christens himself 'conjuror laureate' (33), leading Keefer to say, 'crowned with laurel; of proved distinction' (ed. 17). While the idea of Faustus' self-crowned laureateship is natural enough in Marlovian authorship, the link between conjuring and the laurel crown appears somewhat gratuitous. Until, that is, we recall Book 6 of Lucan's epic: 'From here the Python, the enormous/snake, came down and glided into the lands of Cirrha/ – and that is why Thessalian laurels come to the Pythian games' (407–9). Right afterwards, Sextus is 'goaded' by 'fear' to 'know ahead of time Fate's course', so he 'consults not Delos' tripods' (423–5) but Erichtho. Marlowe, too, overgoes the magic at Delphi, when Faustus says he will be 'more frequented for this mystery/Than heretofore the Delphian oracle' (1.1.144–5).[17]

Most obviously, though, the scene of Faustus' inaugural incantation recalls that of Lucan's witch:

> Now that the gloomy shadow of the earth,
> Longing to view Orion's drizzling look,
> Leaps from th'Antarctic world unto the sky,
> And dims the welkin with her pitchy breath,
> Faustus, begin thine incantations.
>
> (*Doctor Faustus* A-text 1.3.1–5)

Editors and critics cite various intertexts for this speech, ranging from Lucretius and Virgil to Macrobius (Keefer, ed. 16) and Spenser (*MCP* 193–201). Yet the image of the female earth 'longing' and 'leap[ing]' to 'dim' the sky with 'her pitchy breath' is in the Erichthoan mode, and Marlowe is likely glancing at her:

> Sinking almost to the dark and hidden caves of Dis
> the ground falls steep, a place oppressed by a forest
> colourless with drooping leaves and shaded by the yew
> impenetrable to Phoebus and with no crown facing heaven.
> Within, the withered darkness and the colourless decay
> from long night cavern-bound have no light unless spell-conjured.
> (Lucan, *Civil War* 6.642–8; trans. Braund)

As Vivien Thomas and William Tydeman note in their anthology of Marlowe's dramatic sources (quoting Johannes Birringer), 'the highly charged atmosphere at the beginning of the scene, set by its magnificent opening lines, does not derive from the *English Faust Book*' but 'has much in common with the expansive rhetoric and "strange aura of the supernatural" which Marlowe would have found in Lucan's *Pharsalia*' (eds. 178).[18]

Other Lucanian moments spring to life in Marlowe's tragedy. One of the most innovative emerges during the scene of the blood pact, Act 2, scene 1, when Faustus tries to write his name in blood, only to see it 'congeal' (62), leaving him to wonder what it means:

> What might the staying of my blood portend?
> Is it unwilling I should write this bill?
> Why streams it not, that I may write afresh?
> 'Faustus gives to thee his soul' – ah, there it stayed.
> Why shouldst thou not?
> (*Doctor Faustus* A-text 2.1.64–8)

When Mephistopheles brings in a chafer of coals, Faustus sees his 'blood begin...to clear again' (71); after finishing the bill, however, an 'inscription' mysteriously appears on his arm: ' "*Homo fuge!*" Whither should I fly?' (76–7). In this mini-narrative, Marlowe lends agency to blood, gives it volition, a character of its own – even the power of high-flying authorship:

> My senses are deceived; here's nothing writ.
> I see it plain. Here in this place is writ
> '*Homo fuge!*' Yet shall not Faustus fly.[19]
> (*Doctor Faustus* A-text 2.1.79–81)

Similarly, in Book 1 of the *Pharsalia* the augurer Arruns slays a bull to read the text of a Roman prophecy, which reads in Marlowe's translation:

> from the yawning gash,
> Instead of red blood, wallowed venomous gore.
> These direful signs made Arruns stand amazed,
> ...; a dead blackness
> Ran through the blood, that turned it all to jelly,
> And stained the bowels with dark loathsome spots;
> The liver swelled with filth, and every vein
> Did threaten horror from the host of Caesar:
> ... and from the gaping liver
> Squeezed matter; through the caul the entrails peered,
> And which (aye me) ever pretendeth ill,
> At that bunch where the liver is, appeared
> A knob of flesh.
> (*Lucan's First Book* 613–27)

Lucan's fascination with blood re-appears in Marlowe's play, especially its free agency and its portent: its fundamental theatricality.[20]

These Lucanian underpinnings remind us that *Doctor Faustus* is a play about liberty – a word that occurs importantly in the B-text in a passage sounding distinctly Marlovian. Faustus tells Mephistopheles,

> Whilst I am here on earth; let me be cloyed
> With all things that delight the heart of man.
> My four and twenty years of liberty
> I'll spend in pleasure and in dalliance.
> (*Doctor Faustus* B-text 3.1.58–61)

By 'liberty', of course, Faustus means freedom to pursue his desires, specifically for the purpose of 'pleasure'. Although the word 'free' and its cognates appear only two times (A-text 4.1.52; 4.2.76), of all Marlowe's plays this one is most viscerally about the idea of freedom: 'Adders, and serpents, let me breathe awhile!' (5.2.120), Faustus gasps at the end, when the devils take him off to hell.[21] The image of the attacking adders may record another Lucanian memory; more graphically than any Western author, Lucan narrates a horrific story about a republic of serpents devastating the republican military ranks of Cato, caught in the desert: 'Look – from afar a savage serpent, called by Africa/the Jaculus, ... / pierces through the head of Paulus and his temples and escapes. ... / In place of Caesar, Dipsads/fight; Cerastae finish off the civil war' (9.822–4, 850–1).

In Marlowe, not surprisingly, the devil himself refers to Caesar, when Faustus travels to Rome:

> Besides the gates and high pyramides
> Which Julius Caesar brought from Africa.
> (*Doctor Faustus* A-text 3.1.42–3)

The reference is a curious one, since the 'pyramides' are, as John Jump long ago put it, 'the obelisk which the emperor Caligula brought from Heliopolis in the first century A.D. and which was moved to the Piazza San Pietro, where it still stands, in 1586' (ed. 49). Even so, Marlowe invites the audience to view his tragedy in light of classical Rome. As such, the reference to Caesar is consistent with the others we have examined in previous chapters, especially in its linking of Lucan's anti-republican hero with aspiration (see, e.g., *MP* 2.43–6).

Moreover, two of Lucan's most infamous Caesarian moments bear on *Doctor Faustus*: the future emperor's trip to the ruins of Troy, and his subsequent visit to the tomb of Alexander the Great. In Book 9 of the *Pharsalia*, Caesar departs victorious from Pharsalus, and sails by the Hellespont – 'water swum/in love, and Hero's towers on the melancholy shore' (954–5) – only to arrive at 'burnt-out Troy', where his travel guide repeatedly chastises him for sacrilege against the site's 'memorable name' (964), as 'all of Pergamum/is veiled by thickets: even the ruins suffered oblivion' (968–9): 'Have you no respect for the Hercean altars' (979). Caesar's hapless violation of Troy's sacred ruins prompts the poet to intervene, in one of Lucan's most sublime (and shocking) self-representations of authorship:

> O how sacred and immense the task of bards! You snatch everything
> from death and to mortals you give immortality.
> Caesar, do not be touched by envy of their sacred fame;
> ...
> The future ages will read me and you, our Pharsalia
> shall live and we shall be condemned to darkness by no era.
> (Lucan, *Civil War* 9.980–6; trans. Braund)

Here, writes David Norbrook, Lucan counterpoises the themes of 'imperial monumentality and republican sublimity', reminding us that 'no regal monument...will endure for ever', and offering 'a threat' to 'Caesar' (32) – not simply Julius but perhaps Nero – to establish 'a very ironic kind of equality' between 'poet and emperor': 'if Lucan does gain his poetic fame it will be because he has had the opportunity of narrating the eclipse of the political values he holds most dear', especially 'Rome's liberties' (32). In *Doctor Faustus*, Marlowe resurrects the myth of Troy, in the iconic figure of Helen, to achieve a dramatic effect that bears on Lucan's counterpoising of republican sublimity with imperial monumentality. As we shall see, Faustus does not follow Caesar in choosing to return to Troy, but he does conjure up the greatest spirit of Trojan eros on record.

Equally eerily, in Book 10 Caesar leaves Troy for Egypt to meet with Cleopatra, but along the way he stops to visit a 'cavern hollowed out for a burial-place': 'There the crazy offspring of Pellaean Philip/lies, the lucky bandit' (20–1). Savagely, Lucan goes for Alexander's jugular, indicting him for his monarchical tyranny, in the form of his own hapless republican fantasy: 'For if Liberty had ever restored the world to itself,/he had been kept for mockery, born as an example/not serviceable to the world – to show that lands so many/could be under one man's sway' (25–8). While we cannot say whether in *Faustus* Marlowe remembered Caesar's twin visits to the ruins of Troy and the grave of Alexander, we can register an intriguing intertext for the appearance later in the play of both the shade of Alexander and the spirit of Helen.

Several details further connect Marlowe's tragedy with Roman republican culture. The play opens with a flurry of activity right in this territory, when the Chorus begins the Prologue:

> Not marching now in fields of Trasimene,
> Where Mars did mate the Carthaginians,
> Nor sporting in the dalliance of love,
> In courts of kings where state is overturned,
> Nor in the pomp of proud audacious deeds.
>   (*Doctor Faustus* Pr.1–5)

Editors typically find here an inventory of previous Marlowe plays, with line 3 referring to *Dido, Queen of Carthage,* line 4 to *Edward II,* and line 5 to *Tamburlaine* (see Keefer, ed. 3), as 'Marlowe announces his intention of turning away from the heroic and political themes that had occupied his attention' (Bevington and Rasmussen, eds., *DF* 106). This authorial approach, however, creates a problem for lines 1–2, since 'We have no evidence that he wrote a play about Hannibal' (Bevington and Rasmussen, eds. 106). In 1959, however, John P. Cutts argued that Marlowe refers to a lost play that he wrote on Hannibal's Carthaginian defeat of the Romans at Lake Trasimenus in 217 BC (72). Keefer adds that the Prologue's 'mention of Mars is an allusion to Livy's *Historiae* XXII.1.8–12, according to which the battle was preceded by terrifying portents in which the war-god figured prominently. Since these portents demoralized the Romans, Livy's text could suggest either that Mars had allied himself with the Carthaginians or that he had rivaled them in destroying the Roman army' (ed. 3). As we have seen in Chapter 3, Hannibal is a recurrent figure in republican discourse, from Polybius to Machiavelli. The opening lines of *Doctor Faustus* introduce a lost play on this topic for the Marlowe canon – yet they also introduce a specific republican lens for viewing the play itself. As Philip Hardie reminds us, in Silius Italicus' *Punica*, 'Hannibal is a hero in the mould of Lucan's Caesar'; he is 'a fairly close relative also of Milton's Satan', since he claims to be '"made equal with the gods" (IV.810)' (64, 96). If Marlowe did write a play on Hannibal, almost certainly it would have been in this Lucanian vein.

Finally, *Doctor Faustus* will also go on to refer to such Roman images as 'Ovid's flea' (2.3.117) and 'Maro's golden tomb' (3.1.13), as well as to such classical myths as Daedalus and Icarus, Paris and Oenone, Amphion and Thebes, Diana and Actaeon, Jove and Semele, Jove and Arethusa, and Achilles and Paris. Such references encourage us to view Marlowe's rendering of the Faust myth as a tragedy about authorship, including republican authorship.[22]

In the remainder of this chapter, we shall locate the skeptical sublime of Marlowe's republican authorship in four principal areas: Faustus' opening monologue, in which he turns from the books of traditional learning to the book of magic; his subsequent imagining of what he hopes to accomplish through magic; his later use of magic to conjure up Helen of Troy; and his final monologue renouncing magic.

The opening monologue: 'be eternized'

In his opening monologue, Faustus turns from the four cornerstones of humanist learning – Aristotelian philosophy, Galenic medicine, Justinian law, and the scripture of Saint Jerome – because they fail to secure a satisfying form of immortality.[23] First, although quoting the Huguenot Republican Ramus rather than 'Aristotle's...Sweet *Analytics*' (1.1.5–6; Bevington and Rasmussen, eds., *DF* 110), Faustus rejects Aristotelian philosophy because it 'affords...no greater miracle' than to 'dispute well' (8–9). According to Faustus, that is, the 'chiefest end' (8) of Aristotle is purely mundane, rather than miraculous, for it views power as a rational language rather than as a super-rational energy capable of changing matter. To conclude his doubt about such orthodox learning, Faustus appropriately quotes Sextus Empiricus: '*On kai me on*' (12: 'being and not being'; Jump, ed. 7).

Second, Faustus rejects Galenic medicine because its greatest 'end' is only to preserve the 'body's health' (17); it is limited, in other words, by its ability to make the 'physician' famous simply for 'some wondrous cure' (14–15). Faustus claims that he has already 'be[en] eternized': 'monuments' of 'bills' have been 'hung up' around 'cities', whom he has helped to 'escape...the plague' (15–21). Such power of 'physic' (17), he suggests, may help 'ease' the 'desp'rate maladies' of others, but it can do nothing to affect what really matters to him – his mortality: 'yet art thou still but Faustus, and a man'

(22–3). It is here that Faustus pauses to fantasize the alternative to Christian grace that I believe drives the play:

> Wouldst thou make man to live eternally,
> Or, being dead, raise them to life again?
> Then this profession were to be esteemed.
>   (*Doctor Faustus*, A-text 1.1.24–6)

As the last line indicates, Faustus wants to be famous, but the first two lines introduce two alternatives to an esteemed profession that we need to distinguish. The conventional gloss here is misleading: 'Faustus longs for the divine power to grant eternal life, or the power of Christ (who raised Lazarus from the dead: St John ii.1–44)' (Gill, 'A-text', ed. 8). In the second line, Faustus clearly seeks a Christ-like power to resurrect a dead (Lazarus-like) body, but, given the context of necromancy, we need to remember Lucan's Erichtho, who raised to life a dead body.[24] Yet it is the first line that interests me (and, I think, the play), for which we need to recall the 1979 comment of R.W. Ingram: 'what he lusts after is eternal living rather than the life-eternal' (75). Faustus does not long for the immortality of the soul promised by Christianity but rather the immortality of the body, nowhere more grimly envisaged than by Lucan: a body that does not die.

Third, Faustus rejects Justinian law for this very reason: it locates immortality in 'external trash' – 'too servile and illiberal' for him (35–6). In this branch of knowledge, immortality exists only in the form of 'paltry legacies' (30), the succession of the father through the agency of the son. According to Faustus, the study of Justinian's law 'fits a mercenary drudge'.[25]

Finally, Faustus rejects 'divinity' (37) as represented in 'Jerome's Bible' (38). As is well known, here he fixes on the Christian problem of death as the consequence of sin, notoriously neglecting to mention that the very passage he quotes from Scripture, 'The reward of sin is death' (41) – from Romans 6.23 – continues by promising life-eternal: 'the gift of God is eternal life through Jesus Christ our Lord' (Geneva Bible). Nonetheless, Marlowe registers, I suggest, a genuine complaint against Christianity, which posits death as the prerequisite for immortality. For Faustus, death is 'hard' (41), and thus he can imagine only an eternal state of annihilation: 'everlasting death' (48).[26]

As an antidote to the failures of orthodox learning, Faustus' fantasy of eternal living is neither as sophomoric nor as 'desp'rate' (83) as it at first might sound. Presciently, he articulates the goals of modern medicine and science, which in the twenty-first century continues to double the human life-expectancy from the Elizabethan era. In the late 1580s or early 1590s, modern science did not yet exist, yet *Doctor Faustus* indicates that Galenic medicine was making little in-road on life expectancy.[27] Out front here (as so often), Marlowe anticipates our current obsession with eternal living; but, lacking access to a form of learning that might bring it about, he resorts to a dark alternative: 'ravish[ment]' by 'magic' (112).[28]

'Metaphysics of magicians': The republican sublime

Faustus is ravished by magic precisely because he believes it is an art of immortality, a philosophical science of eternal living:

> These metaphysics of magicians,
> And necromantic books are heavenly:
> ...
> O, what a world of profit and delight,
> Of power, of honour, of omnipotence
> Is promised to the studious artisan!
> ...
> A sound magician is a mighty god.
> Here, Faustus, try thy brains to gain a deity.
> (*Doctor Faustus* A-text 1.1.51–65)

For Faustus, magic is the true metaphysical art because it promises 'omnipotence' to the 'studious artisan', allowing a mortal to become immortal: 'a mighty god', a 'deity'. Notably, Faustus embeds his desire for metaphysical 'power' within a critique of political power, and in particular monarchical power: 'Emperors and kings/Are but obeyed in their several provinces,/Nor can they raise the wind or rend the clouds' (1.1. 59–61). From the outset, Faustus expresses dissatisfaction with monarchy as a form of power, because it limits authority to earthly rule; it cannot affect the grim Christian default of 'everlasting death'.

Consequently, once he is in command of 'that famous art' (1.1. 76) Faustus imagines a new political philosophy, governed by 'spirits' who can 'fetch' him 'what' he 'please[s]' (81). This philosophy is the skeptical sublime, appearing for the first time in the play:

> I'll have them fly to India for gold,
> Ransack the ocean for orient pearl,
> And search all corners of the new-found world
> For pleasant fruits and princely delicates.
> I'll have them read me strange philosophy,
> And tell the secrets of all foreign kings.
> I'll have them wall all Germany with brass,
> And make swift Rhine circle fair Wittenberg.
> I'll have them fill the public schools with silk;

Wherewith the students shall be bravely clad.
I'll levy soldiers with the coin they bring,
And chase the Prince of Parma from our land,
And reign sole king of all our provinces:
Yea, stranger engines for the brunt of war
Than was the fiery keel at Antwerp's bridge,
I'll make my servile spirits to invent.
             (*Doctor Faustus* A-text 1.1.84–99)

Through this familiar Marlovian rhetoric, re-deployed from 'The Passionate Shepherd' (as well as from *Dido* and the *Tamburlaine* plays), Faustus imagines a political application for his newly discovered 'metaphysic[al]' art. Certainly, he will acquire money and wealth, food and bounty, learning and wisdom, academic costume and university elegance, but he will also create national pride and distinction, political power, even kingship. Like Tamburlaine (or Dido, and to an extent Edward), Faustus uses the skeptical sublime to transact a monarchical goal. What lends his project a distinct republican cast is its implied challenge to hereditary birth: for this sole king is 'born' from 'parents base of stock' (Pr.11). Magic supplies the common man with the monarchical power he lacks, so he can combat political injustice (such as that transacted by the Prince of Parma on Germany) and thus treat subjects fairly, especially poor 'students'. Faustus may want kingship, but his altruistic goals approximate those of the Western ideal of a monarchical republic.

This becomes especially clear when Faustus calls in Valdes and Cornelius, two republican-minded 'friends' (1.1.113) who generously share with him 'The miracles that magic will perform' (138).[29] In particular, Valdes' detailed speech promising that 'all nations' will 'canonise' them for their 'wit' and 'experience' (121–2) *republicanizes* the sublime achievement of magic doubly: first in the form of their venture tripartite; second in the form of an imagined community of admiring nations:

As Indian Moors obey their Spanish lords,
So shall the subjects of every element
Be always serviceable to us three.
...
From Venice shall they [the spirits] drag huge argosies,
And from America the golden fleece,
That yearly stuffs old Philip's treasury.
             (*Doctor Faustus* A-text 1.1.123–34)

As we have seen, in the sixteenth century Venice was renowned as a republic (cf. 3.1.6), and here Marlowe provides a republican backdrop to the action of his tragedy, one based on the economic freedom we have discussed with respect to *The Jew of Malta* (see Chapter 4). Yet the magicians' collectivity also imagines itself jointly performing their art with reference to the battle being waged between the monarchy of Philip II of Spain against the Dutch Republic, as indicated by the reference to the 'Prince of Parma' and 'Philip's treasury', and supported by Faustus' earlier reference to 'Antwerp's bridge' (quoted above).

Faustus' sublime fantasy, in other words, displays skepticism not just about the Christian godhead ('I think hell's a fable', he later tells Mephistopheles [2.1.129]) but also about the godhead's principal minister on earth, the monarch. Yet, as we have also seen, Marlowe tends to extricate himself from such a monopoly not through democracy but through a different form of monarchy:

> Had I as many souls as there by stars,
> I'd give them all for Mephistopheles.
> By him I'll be great emperor of the world,
> And make a bridge through the moving air
> To pass the ocean with a band of men;
> I'll join the hills that bind the Afric shore,
> And make that land continent to Spain,
> And both contributory to my crown.
> The Emperor shall not live but by my leave,
> Nor any potentate of Germany.
> (*Doctor Faustus* A-text 1.3.104–13)

Marlowe critiques monarchy here, whether potentates in Germany or Charles V, the Holy Roman Emperor. For, despite Faustus' humble origins (or perhaps because of them), the magician cannot tolerate political subjection, and he finds in magic the power to trump the authority of a king: the magical power of immortality, the power to perform feats of superhuman strength, such as building a bridge across the ocean or joining bodies of lands separated by water. To his credit, Faustus does not want to depose (or even assassinate) the Emperor or the German potentates; he wants to be free of subjection to them, and to have a power he believes they lack, including the power of the Longinian sublime ('raise the wind or rend the clouds').[30]

In Acts 3 and 4, Marlowe formally stages the political economy of the skeptical sublime. In the Chorus to Act 3, Faustus' student Wagner reveals that his master takes a journey right into the very sphere of the sublime:

> Learned Faustus,
> To know the secrets of astronomy,
> Graven in the book of Jove's high firmament,
> Did mount himself to scale Olympus' top,
> Being seated in a chariot burning bright,
> Drawn by the strength of yoky dragons necks.

> He is now gone to prove cosmography,
> And, as I guess, will first arrive at Rome,
> To see the Pope and manner of his court.
>   (*Doctor Faustus* A-text 3.Chorus 1–9)

Whereas Tamburlaine and the Guise only imagine scaling the heights of the gods, Faustus makes the actual trip, relying on a sublime technology worthy of Longinus: a chariot drawn by dragons able to fly atop Mount Olympus.[31] To 'prove cosmography', however, Faustus descends to earth, where he visits a series of monarchical 'court[s]', and demonstrates his metaphysical power: first the Pope, then later, back in Germany, both Charles V and the Duke and Duchess of Vanholt.[32]

For our purposes here, Faustus' most important visit is to the Emperor, who announces publicly the political success that Faustus earlier voiced privately: 'I have heard strange report...that none in my empire, nor in the whole world, can compare with thee for the rare effects of magic' (4.1.1–4). To verify Faustus' singular achievements, Charles asks Faustus to conjure up one of his 'ancestors' (21), Alexander the Great, 'chief spectacle of the world's preeminence' (27–8):

> If, therefore, thou, by cunning of thine art,
> Canst raise this man from hollow vaults below,
> Where lies entombed this famous conqueror,
> And bring with him his beauteous paramour,
> Both in their right shapes, gesture and attire
> They used to wear during their time of life,
> Thou shalt both satisfy my just desire,
> And give me cause to praise thee whilst I live.
>   (*Doctor Faustus* A-text 4.1.33–40)

In the last line perhaps gesturing to Marlowe's 'Come live with me, and be my love', the Emperor engages in superb Lucanian intertextuality, combining the episode of the witch Erichtho with that of Julius Caesar's at Alexander's tomb. Marlowe overgoes Lucan, as Faustus conjures up 'the right shapes' of Alexander and even his paramour, prompting the Emperor's wonder: 'Sure, these are no spirits but the true substantial bodies of those two deceased princes' (4.1.72–3). Like Erichtho, Faustus restores the dead to life. Unlike Caesar, he draws Alexander out of his tomb to live again, adding the touch of the paramour to bring the Lucanian sublime to its height of rapture.

Helen of Troy and the skeptical sublime

In Act 5, Faustus' stunning vision of Helen of Troy, 'the face that launched a thousand ships' (A-text 5.1.89), becomes the premier moment of skeptical sublimity in the Marlowe canon.[33] While critics have long expressed rhapsody over this moment, they neglect its Lucanian origins, its political operation, and thus its connection to the history of republican authorship in English:

> Was this the face that launched a thousand ships,
> And burnt the topless towers of Ilium?
> Sweet Helen, make me immortal with a kiss.
> [Faustus and Helen kiss.]
> Her lips suck forth my soul – see where it flies!
> Come, Helen, come give me my soul again.
> [They kiss again.]
> Here will I dwell for heaven be in these lips,
> And all is dross that is not Helena!
> (*Doctor Faustus* A-text 5.1.89–95)

In this version of the skeptical sublime, Marlowe stages the male's imaginative vision of the beautiful female face (see also 5.1.10, 106), which he imagines creating catastrophic annihilation, national destruction, and apocalyptic burn-out: a revelatory holocaust in a quintessence of fire. Marlowe also presents the female's beautiful face not as passive and superficial but as active and exalting: Helen uses her 'lips' to 'kiss' Faustus into subliminal lift-off. Indeed, her erotic action sends the male soul flying into the thrill of imaginative ecstasy, so that he enters the condition of the eternal: 'make me immortal with a kiss. ... /Her lips suck forth my soul – see where it flies!' Faustus' discourse of the sublime fulfills his organizing post-Christian passion from the opening monologue: to 'make man to live eternally'.[34]

Faustus' last lines in the Helen speech especially require pause, because they are so philosophically precise. To approach them, we initially need to recall their origin in the Longinian hero Plato, and specifically the *Symposium*, glanced at earlier in the scene. For, after an academic 'conference about fair ladies – which was the beautifull'st in all the world' – the First Scholar requests to 'see' Helen of Troy, 'that peerless dame of Greece, whom all the world admires for majesty' (5.1.9–15).[35] In the *Symposium*, Plato had outlined the famous ladder of desire:

> The man who has been guided thus far in the mysteries of love, and who has directed his thoughts towards examples of beauty in due and orderly succession will suddenly have revealed to him as he approaches the end of his initiation a beauty whose nature is marvelous indeed, the final goal, Socrates, of all his previous efforts. This beauty is first of all eternal: it neither comes into being nor passes away, neither waxes nor wanes. (Plato, *Symposium* 93; trans. Hamilton)

According to Plato, the lover's epiphany of 'absolute beauty' (94) transcends his love of materiality altogether: 'nor ... will this beauty appear to him like the beauty of a face or hands or anything else corporeal' (93): 'it is absolute, existing alone with itself, unique, eternal, and all other beautiful things as partaking of it' (94). The Christian afterlife of Plato's theory of beauty as an eternal form is well known, from St. Augustine's Platonic vision with his mother in Book 9 of the *Confessions* (Augustine 171, trans. Chadwick) to Cardinal Bembo's Platonic vision in Book 4 of Castiglione's *Courtier*: 'And thus shall [the lover] beholde no more the particular beautie of one woman, but an universall, that decketh out all bodies' (Castiglione 318; trans. Hoby).

Faustus' speech on Helen taps into the Platonic tradition, and does so via the Lucanian sublime. We need to recall Lucan because of Marlowe's startling phrase, 'Her lips suck forth my soul', which suggests *necrophilia*, the kiss of death. In the act of kissing, Helen sucks Faustus' life-force, his soul, out of his body, leaving his corpse spiritless. Marlowe evokes necrophilia, as Spenser had done with his witch Acrasia in Book 2, canto 12 of *The Faerie Queene*, with her victim, Verdant: 'And all that while, right over him she hong,/With her false eyes fast fixed in his sight,/.../And oft inclining downe with kisses light,.../And through her humid eyes did sucke his spright' (73). This striking image – a witch sucking a man's soul out of his body – does not have precedent in the literary tradition to which Spenser is thought to be indebted: Homer, the Greek tragedians, Virgil, Ovid, Seneca, Dante, Petrarch, Chaucer, Boiardo, Ariosto, Tasso, Trissino (see, e.g., Hamilton, ed. 283–4).

Yet the image bears on a Lucanian signature, located in the chronic gyrations of Erichtho from Book 6 of the *Pharsalia*:

> Often, too, the hag has straddled a corpse – her own kin –
> her witch's limbs writhing atop his cherished body;
> affixing kisses, she severs the head, prises its sealed mouth
> open, nips off the tip of the tongue pasted onto his dry
> palate; between his icy lips she pours murmurs,
> sending through him an evil message to Stygian shades.
> (Lucan, *Pharsalia* 6.564–9; trans. Joyce)[36]

Erichtho literalizes her daemonic gyration when she erects the cadaver of the unknown solider on the fields of Pharsalus, so he can deliver a prophecy of the military battle for Pompey's son, Sextus. As Erichtho herself puts it,

> A soul I ask for, ...
> ... a soul on its way down,
> life's light just fled, a soul still hesitating at the door,

to pallid Orcus' chasm, a soul which, though he drain these drugs,
will join the dead once only.
(Lucan, *Civil War*, 6.712–16; trans. Braund)

In his apostrophe to Helen, Faustus transposes this horrific version of the Lucanian sublime to its ecstatic opposite. Helen's kiss, rather than taking his soul away demonically, as the necrophilic language intimates, elevates him to the eternal sublime, as if he were experiencing a life-after-death moment, with his soul lifting out of his body to fly toward the heavens: 'see where it flies!' Perhaps only by understanding Helen's kiss as the immortalizing power of the Lucanian sublime may we account for Faustus' next line: 'Come, Helen, come give me my soul again'.[37]

What makes Faustus' sublime Lucanian, rather than simply Platonic or Augustinian or Neoplatonic, is Marlowe's insistence on the literary authenticity of corporeality, of sexuality, and finally of the darkness of magic rapture. As David Norbrook reminds us, Longinus theorized the sublime in opposition to a principle of 'easy, specious harmony' (137). As Longinus himself says, 'Sublimity...produced at the right moment...tears everything up like a whirlwind' (1.4: 144).

Accordingly, Faustus' acquisition of spiritual power through the phantom of Helen makes him feel superior as a military hero, as his continuation of the speech reveals:

> I will be Paris, and for love of thee,
> Instead of Troy shall Witternberg be sacked;
> And I will combat with weak Menelaus,
> And wear thy colours on my plumed crest:
> Yea, I will wound Achilles in the heel,
> And then return to Helen for a kiss.
> O, thou art fairer than the evening air,
> Clad in the beauty of a thousand stars.
> Brighter art thou than flaming Jupiter,
> When he appeared to hapless Semele,
> More lovely than the monarch of the sky
> In wanton Arethusa's azured arms,
> And none but thou shalt be my paramour.
> (*Doctor Faustus* A-text 5.1.96–108)

In this magnificent discourse of the sublime, Marlowe represents masculine ecstasy over the beauty of the feminine, and the male's acquisition of military violence. We witness the creation of a new inward condition, mobilized for martial action – a new kind of national leader, as the references to 'Troy' and 'Wittenberg' indicate.

In the Helen scene, Marlowe appears to be struggling with what Kant will later call the sublime. In the *Critique of the Power of Judgment*, Kant defines sublimity broadly as 'that which is absolutely great' (2.25: 131), but specifically he defines it as that which 'is to be found in a formless object insofar as limitlessness is represented in it': 'for what is properly sublime cannot be contained in any sensible form, but concerns only ideas of reason' (2.23: 128–9). For Kant, in other words, 'the sublime is...not to be sought in the things of nature but only in our ideas': 'It is the disposition of the mind resulting from a certain representation occupying the reflective judgment, but not the object' (2.25: 26). In turning from the traditional bodies of knowledge in Faustus' opening monologue, Marlowe appears to be rehearsing an early modern version of the Kantian sublime. The difference is that Marlowe does give form to the sublime, whereas Kant insists that the sublime is 'unbounded', 'formless' (Shaw 80, 78). For Kant, the sublime is 'greater even than either nature or imagination' (Shaw 82), whereas for Marlowe the sublime is tied to an imagination free of nature. This helps explain why the sublime in Faustus' hands takes the form of Helen of Troy. Kant does assert that 'the formless phenomenon can be grasped as a totality in terms of a rational idea' (qtd. Shaw 83); as Philip Shaw summarizes: 'Sublimity...resides in the human capacity to think beyond the bounds of the given' (83). Marlowe grasps the Kantian sublime, and fails to grasp it, since Helen is and is not a product of imagination, is both a form and formless, at once known and given, and precisely beyond the known and given. Shaw goes on to show that German Romantic poets like Schiller and English Romantic poets like Coleridge re-grab 'the primacy of imagination', to insist on 'the unity of mind and world', the very unity Kant had failed to discover. Thus, Coleridge's model of imagination 'yoke[s] the human to the divine' (93). Whereas Coleridge succeeds in using 'imagination to regard objects of sense as symbolic of the eternal' (94), Marlowe can only represent a dark and tragic version.

Marlowe is careful to juxtapose Faustus' pre-Kantian sublime not simply with Christian Neoplatonism but also with the orthodox Christian harmony of the Old Man, including through images of flight (A-text 5.1.109–17). Such a dramatic strategy suggests that Marlowe displays 'the Tudor play of mind' outlined by Joel Altman (book title), according to which a disputant at Oxford or Cambridge learns to argue both sides of a question but remains aloof from both – a practice at one with philosophical skepticism. That we need to read the play within this frame is clear at the outset, when Faustus evokes it: 'Is to dispute well logic's chiefest end?' (1.1.8). As a Renaissance scholar, Faustus has been trained in the (classical and) medieval art of disputation, and yet it is this art that he finds so objectionable: 'Affords this art no greater miracle?/Then read no more' (9–10).

From Altman's model, we might wish to offer two follow-up points. First, Marlowe introduces an alternative to the discourse of disputation in the discourse of the sublime. Second, his achievement lies not in the latter but in the former: in an innovative theatre not of disputation but of sublimity.[38] His legacy to English literature is the Lucanian sublime, a form of republican authorship. We might then see in *Doctor Faustus* a second narrative voice emerging from the orthodox one at the surface of the play: the sublime republican voice of *textual apotheosis*.

Time, solitude, and sublimity: Faustus' final monologue

As we have been surmising, the sublime is the ultimate form of solitude, an exalted state of consciousness in which the human imagination is truly alone, cut off not just from nature but from community, heroically at one with the tyranny of time. What makes Faustus' final monologue so sublimely terrifying is that he is alone with God:

> *Exeunt SCHOLARS. The clock strikes eleven.*
> FAUSTUS.   Ah, Faustus,
> Now hast thou but one bare hour to live,
> And then thou must be damned perpetually.
> (*Doctor Faustus* A-text 5.2.SD, 66–8)

According to Edmund Burke, 'Few things are more aweful than the striking of a great clock' (2.18: 76). Burke may not have Faustus in mind, but well he could have. In the history of the godhead, Marlowe's theatrical presentation of the sublime constitutes the ultimate wrestling match with the Western spirit of Christianity:

> And see where God
> Stretcheth out his arm and bends his ireful brows!
> Mountains and hills, come, come and fall on me,
> And hide me from the heavy wrath of God!
> ...
> O soul, be changed into little waterdrops,
> And fall into the ocean, ne'er be found!
> (*Doctor Faustus* A-text 5.2.83–118)

No longer are the mountain and the ocean the supreme sites of the sublime but rather its devouring engines.

Consequently, Faustus' final utterance forms a dark shadow to the one Coleridge reports when he goes into a Gothic cathedral:

> Gothic art is sublime. On entering a cathedral, I am filled with devotion and with awe; I am lost to the actualities that surround me, and my whole being expands into the infinite; earth and air, nature and art, all swell up into eternity, and the only sensible expression left is, 'that I am nothing!' (Coleridge, 'European Literature'; qtd. Shaw 97)

In Faustus' final monologue, Marlowe manages an unprecedented feat: through theatrical poetry, the author makes the sublime consciousness of damnation appear, and the reality of the Christian godhead disappear.[39] This is the real 'magic' of *Doctor Faustus*, a horrific rather than a comedic 'translation of object into subject, of the Gothic Church transformed by an operation of mind into a fit emblem of the eternal and thus, by sleight of hand, into a symbol of the unbounded power of imagination' (Shaw 97).[40]

Marlowe's concluding narrative about sublime authorship does not proceed only through its well-documented Ovidian moments, or even its transcription of the Ovidian text that he himself translates at the outset of his literary career: 'O lente, lente currite noctis equi' (5.2.75).[41] For, alongside the Ovidian narrative of political resistance, a corresponding Lucanian narrative resists the tyranny of empire through sounding the death cry of republican freedom:

> My God, my God, look not so fierce on me!
> *Enter [Lucifer, Beelzebub, Mephistopheles, with other] Devils.*
> Adders, and serpents, let me breathe a while!
> Ugly hell, gape not, come not, Lucifer!
> I'll burn my books, ah, Mephistopheles!
> (*Doctor Faustus* A-text 5.2.119–22)

Here at the end of *Doctor Faustus*, Marlowe's authorship inscripts a narrative about the loss of freedom, the collapse of the divine into the demonic, the closure of political space that finds optimum expression in the sublime. Yet from *Ovid's Elegies* through *Edward II*, we have been seeing that Marlowe's legacy to English literature lies outside the bounds of this model; and inside what survives, in the works of future English authors, and perhaps in the history of audience reception, is a new, dramatic Lucanian language, the skeptical sublime. This language is the 'greater miracle' – the radical voice of eternal immanence: the apex of Marlowe's republican authorship.

Terminat hora diem; terminat author opus.[42]

Afterword: The Afterlife of Marlowe's Republican Authorship – Nashe to Milton

This book has not argued that Marlowe was a 'republican'. Rather, it has attempted to situate Marlowe's poems and plays within a long history of republican thought, stretching from Polybius and Tacitus, to Machiavelli and Thomas Smith, to Algernon Charles Swinburne and David Norbrook. The book has argued that Marlowe's authorship *is* 'republican', in the sense that his literary works vigorously engage classical Roman and early modern European republican writing, both historical and literary.

Scholarship and criticism has long connected Marlowe's works with such important writers of republicanism as Cicero, Livy, Tacitus, Machiavelli, Françoise Hotman, and Smith, without contextualizing the connection within the republican tradition. This professional situation, we have seen, contrasts sharply with that regarding several Elizabethan authors surrounding Marlowe: Sidney, Spenser, Shakespeare, and Jonson, all of whom have an important if recent body of work. Equally to the point, twentieth- and twenty-first-century commentary neglects the figure of republican authorship most important to the Marlowe canon: Lucan. Marlowe is not simply the first Englishman to translate Lucan; he is the first English author to make Lucan a keystone to a new sixteenth-century model of authorship, which combines poems and plays within a single literary career. While critics have long identified Lucan's Caesar as an important model for the Marlovian superhero, no one has studied the topic in detail, and located the results within the history of republican thought.

As we have also seen, Lucan is central to Marlowe's republican authorship because he so profoundly links two principles often separated in modern scholarship: the political principle of liberty and the aesthetic principle of the sublime. From Lucan, Marlowe could have learned to tell a story about the tyrannical oppression of liberty as the crucible of the high-soaring literary imagination. In the present book, we have tracked the presence of such a story in Marlowe's poems and plays, from 'The Passionate Shepherd' and *Lucan's First Book* through *Edward II* and *Doctor Faustus*. While critics have produced numerous studies of Marlowe as an Ovidian author – Ovid being the other great Roman dissident poet committed to *libertas* – *Marlowe's Republican Authorship* is the first book to present Marlowe as also fundamentally Lucanian.

In particular, we have inserted Marlowe's Lucanian authorship into a history of the sublime, to suggest that he forms an unacknowledged bridge between the classical sublime at one end and the Miltonic sublime at the other. Marlowe's achievement here is to pioneer an *author-based* aesthetic of the sublime that precedes the *subject-based* aesthetic analyzed by modern theorists from Burke and Kant to Lyotard and Žižek.[1] For Marlowe, as for Lucan and Longinus, the sublime is not simply rhetorical but literary: not simply a discourse about the subject but an intertext about the author. By studying moments of the sublime in Marlowe's poems and plays, we have seen that we may discover not 'the man in his work' but the author who makes the work. We learn that the author's violent vortex utterance is divine in origin, born out of an agon with rival authors, exalted in literary quality, emotional in effect, potentially liberating in political operation, and finally eternizing in its telos of fame. By reading the Marlovian sublime, then, we witness the author in his literary workshop, offering a record for the making of the literary itself. In this way, his penning of an intertextual sublime constitutes a profound, often neglected communication between author and reader. Above all, the author communicates a paradox at the heart of recent critical theory not just about the sublime but about the author and about intertextuality: self-consciously, the author puts himself at the center of his work precisely to disappear in the exalted enigma of divine afflatus: to enter the condition of the eternal.[2]

Not only does Marlowe write a sublime liberating republicanism, but his contemporaries were quick to identify him as doing so. The 1594 portrait that serves as the epigraph to this book, by Thomas Nashe in *The Unfortunate Traveler*, presents Marlowe just as we have witnessed him here:

> His pen was sharp pointed lyke a poinyard. ... His sight pearst like lightning into the entrails of all abuses. ... He was no timorous servile flatterer of the commonwealth wherein he lived. ... Princes hee spard not, that in the least point transgrest. His lyfe he contemned in comparison of the libertie of speech.[3] (Nashe, *The Unfortunate Traveler*, McKerrow 2: 264–5)

Nashe portrays Marlowe as an author whose commitment to free speech led him to transgress the authority of 'Princes' – whenever they stepped over the line of *libertas*. In particular, Nashe's Marlowe both lives in a 'commonwealth' and refuses to be its slave. In his hand, Marlowe wields an instrument of literary power that we have called sublime, as the Lucanian (and Longinian) metaphor of the 'lightning' bolt indicates. Finally, Nashe's troping of the

Marlovian sublime looks distinctly Lucanian, for he identifies Marlowe's powers of literary 'sight' as a lightning bolt able to pierce what fascinates the author who narrates the fall of the Roman Republic: its 'entrails'.[4]

Among contemporaries, Nashe is not alone in penning Marlowe in this way. We have examined instances in the works of Lodge, Kyd, and especially Jonson, as well as in such lesser known writers as J. Paulin. While the topic needs to be studied in greater detail – like most topics introduced in this book – we may end with the most important: Milton.[5]

In one of the most renowned literary appropriations during the English Renaissance, Milton's Satan re-voices Mephistopheles' formulation of an *inward hell*. In *Doctor Faustus*, Marlowe's demon responds to the magician's inquiry about the location of hell:

> Why this is hell, nor am I out of it.
> Think'st thou that I, who saw the face of God,
> And tasted the eternal joys of heaven,
> Am not tormented with ten thousand hells,
> In being deprived of everlasting bliss?
> (*Doctor Faustus* A-text 1.3: 78–82)

Significantly, the first line of Mephistopheles' speech, which intimates the trauma of his inward hell, gives way to a celebrated speech often regarded as exposing the rib of Marlovian biography (for, like the demon, the Matthew Parker scholar fell from grace). The passionate authorial cry of paradise lost, prefaced by the demonic torment of inward hell, might help explain a phenomenon we have had occasion to review: the longstanding equation of Christopher Marlowe with satanic character, from Robert Greene and Gabriel Harvey to today.

Later, Mephistopheles adds,

> Hell hath no limits, nor is circumscribed
> In one self place, for where we are is hell,
> And where hell is must we ever be.
> (*Doctor Faustus* A-text 2.1: 123–5)

Mephistopheles voices a version of what we might call the demonic republican sublime – almost certainly the first major statement in English literature.[6] Hell is at once a geographical place and a state of mind, but what is most important here is the way Mephistopheles' inward hell *grounds* the sublime fantasy of republican flight.

For his part, Satan in Book 1 of *Paradise Lost* publicly confronts his own loss of Heaven and his entry into Hell with a famous declaration of independence:

> fardest from him [God] is best
> Whom reason hath equall'd, force hath made supreme

> Above his equals.
> ...
> The mind is its own place, and in itself
> Can make a Heav'n of Hell, a Hell of Heav'n.
> ...   Here at least
> We shall be free;
> ...
> Here we may reign secure, and in my choice
> To reign is worth ambition though in Hell:
> Better to reign in Hell, than serve in Heav'n.
>   (Milton, *Paradise Lost* 1.247–63)

According to Satan, it is 'best' to be 'fardest' from God, and he asserts that his own rational power 'equall[s]' that of the deity, who has resorted to superior force in placing himself 'above' those angels 'equal' to him. In other words, Satan justifies his freedom from God through equality with God. He then declares that his justification originates in and depends on a mental gold standard: the angels are 'free' to use their 'mind' to create their own imaginative 'place', and thus free to 'choose' personal 'ambition though in Hell'. Important to the present book, Satan invents his famed theological discourse of mental hell through the discourse of republican liberty.[7]

Later, in Book 4, the Miltonic narrator pauses to describe the tragic fallout of Satan's republican discourse, and in the process of foregrounding the demon's 'troubl'd thought' (19) slips into the sublime:

> The Hell within him, for within him Hell
> He brings, and round about him, nor from Hell
> One step no more than from himself can fly
> By change of place: Now conscience wakes despair
> ...
> Which way I fly is Hell; myself am Hell.
>   (Milton, *Paradise Lost* 4.20–3, 75)

Here Milton doubly renders his most famous version of demonic republican sublimity, imping the exuberant motion of flight onto the despairing stasis of consciousness. Satan may discover the freedom to soar through the cosmos, but he finds himself bound inside the globe of his own distraction.[8] As Neil Forsyth allows us to see, Milton presents Satan reducing the episteme of Christian exterior 'place' to the emergent episteme of modern secular interiority.[9]

In Marlowe, Milton found a profound insight: once the republican-minded intellectual discovers the liberty of conscience, he is tempted to free himself from the bond of inequality. Thus, Satan attempts to justify the ways of the Devil to men by crafting out the freedom of a hell within, happier far, liberated from the tyranny of the monarchical God.[10] Officially, thereby, Satan's project constitutes a photographic negative of Milton's, which aims to 'justify the ways of God to men' (1.26) by asserting the freedom of a 'paradise within ... , happier far' (12.587). While critics connect Milton's inward paradise with Satan's inward hell, they do not always record the follow-up insight: Milton's formulation of paradise as a sublimely republican state of mind also traces to Marlowe's formulation of hell as a demonic republican state.

We might conclude, then, by suggesting that Marlowe is Milton's predecessor in a distinct historical achievement: the founding of English authorship on the political dynamic of classical liberty and Christian freedom. Contrary to Milton's vast corpus, however, Marlowe's truncated corpus of five poems and seven plays voices the first radical authorship in English precisely by severing classical liberty from Christian freedom.[11] Milton, I believe, grasped Marlowe's 'atheist' republican authorship as a threat to his republican Christianity, and equated Satan, 'the Author of all ill' (2.381), with Marlowe's English authorship. By modeling Satan on the tragic Marlovian superhero, and then opposing the author of evil to the authors of good, God and the Son, Milton locates Marlowe within a distinct literary genealogy in the formation of Christian republican authorship. From Milton's perspective, Marlowe did not simply squander a unique historical moment; by equating the sublimity of liberty with irreligion, Marlowe dangerously contaminated the English republican enterprise as the political hope of Christianity.

This authorial genealogy differs from the mainstream one of English national poets that begins with Chaucer and Spenser, finds its bridging figure in Milton, and continues with Blake, Shelley, and the Romantics.[12] In Milton criticism, it has long been a commonplace to agree or disagree with Blake, who said that Milton was of the devil's party without knowing it, or with Shelley, who turned Milton's Satan into the great champion of Romantic freedom combating political tyranny (Forsyth 65–8). Yet we might wish to recall the place that Christopher Marlowe occupies in this narrative. For it was precisely after Milton that Marlowe slipped into obscurity on stage and page, and precisely during the Romantic era when he was restored to the English canon.[13] Whether Blake or Shelley knew it, what they found in Milton's Satan was the imprisoned ghost of Christopher Marlowe, the sublime spirit of tragic liberty who first dared, in the days of Queen Elizabeth, to voice the Lucanian *agon* of republican authorship in English.

Notes

Introduction: Was Marlowe a Republican?

1. On Marlowe as a pioneer author in Elizabethan England, see Cheney, 'Introduction', *Cambridge Companion to Marlowe*.
2. Wall mentions Marlowe only once in passing, seeing 'The Passionate Shepherd to His Love' as an instance of the 'social dimension of Renaissance writing', where 'texts' could 'travel' and were 'open to inscription by readers', spawning 'verse replies' such as Ralegh's 'The Nymph's Reply' (71). See also Wall, *Imprint of Gender*.
3. On Spenser as England's first laureate, see Helgerson, *Self-Crowned Laureates* 100; on the laureate as 'the servant of eternity', see 8. According to Helgerson, Marlowe is a 'professional' writer who 'made play writing a part of an amateur career' (36; see 112, 147, 167n62, 217). In *Forms of Nationhood*, Helgerson includes Marlowe in a group of playwrights who write a nationhood of the common people (1, 197, 199–200, 204, 225, 242, 243). I go on to counter both classifications.
4. Marcus, 'Textual Indeterminacy'; Healy, *Marlowe* 1–9. This is also the collective project of *Constructing Christopher Marlowe*, ed. Downie and Parnell. In 'Authorship and Collaboration', Masten includes the incident when an atheist tract said to be owned by Marlowe got 'shuffled' in with Kyd's papers in order to 'resist categories of singular authorship' (360–1); see also Masten, *Textual Intercourse*. On the way Marlovian identity and authorship have been falsely 'constructed' by others, not by the author himself, see Dutton. More recently, see Erne, 'Biography'.
5. Foucault, 'What is an Author?'; Barthes, 'Death of the Author'. For a recent, authoritative version of this post-structuralist model for English Renaissance drama, with important reference to Marlowe, see Wall, 'Dramatic Authorship', esp. 3–5 on *DF*.
6. For a thorough review of the two-text situation, see Bevington and Rasmussen, eds., *Doctor Faustus* 62–102.
7. Greene speaks of Marlowe 'daring God out of heaven with that Atheist Tamburlan' (rpt. MacLure, ed., *CH* 29), echoing *1 Tamb* 1.2.156: 'His looks do menace heaven and dare the Gods'. For my review of this author-in-his-works model, see Cheney, 'Biographical Representations'. For theoretical rejections of the post-structuralist model, and vigorous attempts to revive the notion of the Marlovian author, see esp. Shepherd, 'Criticism, Fantasy'; Wilson, 'New Historicists'.
8. Greenblatt, *Renaissance Self-Fashioning* 220. For a belated rebuttal to this line of criticism, see Harraway, who observes that 'a common concern with the figure of the author characterizes Marlovian scholarship to its detriment' (2). For my review of Harraway, see Works Cited under Cheney.
9. For Marlovian *intratextuality*, I am indebted to Genette's model of intertextuality as a palimpsest: 'on the same parchment, one text can become superimposed upon another, which it does not quite conceal but allows to show through' (398–9).
10. For this methodology applied to Shakespeare, see Cheney, *Shakespeare's Literary Authorship*, 'Introduction'.

194 Notes

11. See Forsythe; Henderson 120–66; Bruster. On this intratextuality as inaugurating Marlowe's dramatic career, see *MCP* 68–87.
12. See *MCP*, which aims to re-classify 'Marlowe, Christopher, the Dramatist' (General Catalogue, British Library, London) as the author of both poems and plays (see 259–64). See also Cheney, *Poet-Playwright*, for this model of authorship as the invention largely of the sixteenth century, with Marlowe preceding Shakespeare and Jonson, among others (17–48). Marlowe's seven plays are (in the order to be discussed in this book) *Dido*, *1* and *2 Tamburlaine*, *The Jew of Malta*, *The Massacre at Paris*, *Edward II*, and *Doctor Faustus*. The five poems are (also in the order to be discussed) *Ovid's Elegies*, 'The Passionate Shepherd', *Lucan's First Book*, *Hero and Leander*, and the Latin epitaph on the sixteenth-century jurist Sir Roger Manwood. This particular chronology of Marlowe's plays and poems follows the one outlined in *MCP*, with one exception convenient to make here: I discuss *MP* before *E2*. On the poems as a body of work in their own right, complementing the plays, see Cheney, 'Introduction', *Collected Poems*, ed. Cheney and Striar. To Marlowe's poems, we may add the 1592 Latin dedicatory epistle that Marlowe wrote to Mary Sidney Herbert, the Countess of Pembroke, prefacing Thomas Watson's *Amintae Gaudia* (rpt. Cheney and Striar, eds. 291–2; discussed 23–5).
13. See *MCP* 42–7, 91–6. For detail on Jonson, see Cheney, 'Biographical Representations'. Livius Andronicus and Ennius precede Ovid in the composition of both poems and plays; see Farrell.
14. The key spokesman for the received wisdom is Pocock.
15. See also N. Smith 204; Burrow 186.
16. For Norbrook's commentary on Lucan, see esp. 23–62, 83–92, 439–67.
17. Like Norbrook, Hadfield mentions Marlowe in passing as the translator of Lucan: 'Was Spenser a Republican?' 170. On Spenser as well, see Wilson-Okamura; Hadfield, 'Reply'; Hammill.
18. Hadfield is here responding to my own published work on Marlowe and republicanism (*Republicanism* ix, 260n24). Other recent work includes Perry's 2006 chapter on *E2* in *Favoritism*, to be taken up in chapter 4.
19. According to J. Scott, writing in 2004, 'This is a literature still in a rapid state of development' (*Commonwealth Principles* 4).
20. He was, of course, accused of sedition against the Queen's monarchy, as we shall see.
21. For a critique of Norbrook – and Peltonen – see Worden, 'Republicanism, Regicide and Republic', esp. 308–14. Worden criticizes Norbrook and Peltonen for bridging the gap between 'two approaches' to republicanism that he believes need to be separated: Skinner's model of 'constitutional republicanism', which depends on 'kingless government' and emerges historically during the Interregnum (307); and Pocock's model of 'civic republicanism', which depends on 'political action and civic virtue' and emerges before the Interregnum (308). Worden is especially critical of Skinner's model of 'negative republicanism', which consists simply of 'the repudiation of monarchy', offering instead his own model of 'positive republicanism', which consists of a 'commitment to the introduction of republican architecture' (327n16). I return to Worden later.
22. On Gorges and May as Marlowe's successors in translating Lucan, see Steane 266–71. Norbrook makes clear how carefully (and widely) seventeenth-century Englishmen read classical texts to help process the trauma of political upheaval, as Milton does on the title page of *Areopagitica* (1644) when he quotes Euripides'

The Suppliant Women in Greek and provides an English translation: 'This is true Liberty when free born men/Having to advise the public may speak free' (qtd. Norbrook 126).
23. Norbrook quotes Fink x, who himself defines 'a "classical republican"' as 'a person who advocated or admired a republic, and also took his ideas for such a government whole or in part from the ancient masterpieces of political organization, their supposed modern counterparts, or their ancient and modern expositors' (x). The *OED* traces the word 'republic' to Drayton's Lucanian *Baron's Wars* of 1603 (Def. 1), and subsequently defines the term thus: 'A state in which the supreme power rests in the people and their elected representatives or officers, as opposed to one governed by a king or similar ruler; a commonwealth. Now also applied loosely to any state which claims this designation' (Def. 2a).
24. For a superb collection of the biographical archive, see Kuriyama, 'Appendix: Transcriptions and Translations of Selected Documents' (173–240).
25. Even though never referring to Norbrook, Walker's magisterial 2005 *Writing under Tyranny* provides a fresh occasion for examining Marlowe's republican authorship, since Walker demonstrates how a generation of Henrician writers, including Wyatt and Surrey, use their humanist training to resist the tyrannical regime of Henry VIII. Only at the end, however, and in an endnote, does Walker situate his argument with respect to republicanism: 'In this way the Henrician poets and prose writers pre-empted a phenomenon that historians of ideas have tended to see as a development of the later sixteenth-century, the revival of classical republicanism', citing Pocock and Peltonen (536n2). Walker's study forms an important bridge both to Helgerson's *Forms of Nationhood* (which covers the later sixteenth and early seventeenth centuries, foregrounding six forms of nationhood countering absolutist royalism) and to Norbrook's *Writing the English Republic* (which covers the later seventeenth century and foregrounds republicanism in dialogue with royalism). Read together, these three monographs offer detailed contextual work for the present argument.
26. Hadfield adds, 'This is one reason why republicanism seems to have appealed as much to imaginative writers of literature as political theorists and historians' (*Republicanism* 51–2). On the way censorship influences authorship during the early modern period, see Patterson, *Censorship*.
27. In his superb overview on 'The Author' (book title), Bennett demonstrates, first, that 'the problem of criticism *is* the problem of authorship' (112); and, second, that 'The history of authorship is yet to be written' (31). Usefully, he identifies Barthes' 'The Death of the Author' and Foucault's 'What is an Author?' as 'the two most influential essays on authorship in twentieth-century criticism' (5). He also shows that for the foundational theorist, Barthes, two key topics within the present study, *intertextuality* and *reception*, operate to supplant the notion of individuated authorship (9–19), and later he discusses recent work on early modern 'collaboration' by Masten, Wall, and others as support for the Barthesian model (94–107). Yet Bennett himself argues that 'There is no great difficulty in accommodating collaboration to conventional understandings of autonomous literary production': 'the logic [of collaboration studies] is rather to confirm than to question or disturb the notion of the individuality and autonomy of the author' (97, 99). In the chapters following, I operate from the following model of authorship, outlined in more detail in *Shakespeare's Literary Authorship* (see esp. the 'Introduction'): I accept the Barthesian (and Foucauldian) model, but follow Bennett and other scholars in granting agency to the author, and attempt

to re-imagine both intertextuality and reception in terms not just of collaboration but of individuation. That is, the intertextuality and reception that I trace take the form of an exchange between verifiable authors and their texts.
28. As Shapiro observes, both Turbervile and Googe attempted translations but gave the enterprise up (316–17). On Marlowe as the first English translator of Lucan, see Bolgar 530–1; MacLure, ed., *Poems* xxxv.
29. This was the major idea that I took away from the International Lucan Conference, organized by Denis Feeney and Nigel Smith at Princeton University in October 2003. Of course, Lucan does more than mourn the loss of Republican liberty; for instance, he fixates on the awesome tyranny of Julius Caesar.
30. For publication details, see MacLure, ed., *Poems* xxxiv–vi; Gill, ed., *Works* 1: 87–92.
31. On the late dating of *LFB*, see Lewis 486; Shapiro 323–4. The question is also longstanding whether Marlowe completed *Hero and Leander*, although today most prefer to follow Martz in believing that the work is complete (ed.); see also Campbell; Gill, ed., *Works* 1: 185.
32. See *MCP*, esp. 221–6. On *LFB* as epic, see H. Levin, *Overreacher*, who calls the translation 'a glance in the direction of the epic' (10), concluding that 'Marlowe learned the epic mode from Lucan' (165; see 17, 32). Gill also observes that Marlowe 'made out of the first book of the *Pharsalia* the beginning of an epic poem worthy of notice in itself' ('Sulpitius' 406).
33. Martindale, *Redeeming the Text* 71; Lewis 486. On the excellence of Marlowe's translation for classicists, see W.R. Johnson xii, 3, 14–16, 57n23, 75; Joyce, trans., xvi.
34. Steane 249–79; Gill, 'Sulpitius'; Shapiro; Ronan. More recently, see *MCP* 227–37, and Cheney, 'Introduction', in Cheney and Striar, eds. 12–17; Brown, 'Marlowe's Poems' 120–4.
35. On the 'temperamental kinship' between Marlowe and Lucan, see H. Levin, *Overreacher* 10; Steane, who emphasizes their 'violent and early deaths' (254), their reputations as 'bold, independent mind[s], given to strong antipathies and enthusiasms, with an irreverent and ironical streak which courted danger' (255), their 'partisan' works hopelessly backing the defeated (255–6), their commitment to 'hyperbole' (257), their 'unorthodoxies in artistic and religious matters' (257), and 'the most striking affinity', their 'sadis[m]' (258).
36. In the words of Steane, 'Marlowe's Lucan is in fact an English poem' (270). See also Leech 34–5; Gill, 'Sulpitius' 403–4.
37. This topic needs to be studied; to my knowledge, no one has looked into the Marlovian underpinnings of either Gorges' or May's translations. As Steane's printing of the prologue by all three translators allows us to see (266–7), Gorges does not appear to need Marlowe, while May appears to imitate Marlowe's opening line, changing only one important word (italicized below), perhaps borrowed from Gorges:
    Marlowe: 'Wars *worse* then civill on Thessalian plains'
    Gorges: 'A *more* then civill warre I sing'
    May: 'Warres *more* then civill on Aemathian plaines'.
38. For details, see *MCP* 23–4. On the importance of patriotism to early modern republicanism, see Skinner, *Foundations* 1: 175–6. More recently, Sedinger calls 'love of one's country' the 'very ground of republicanism' (73).
39. For classicist commentary on Book 1, see Fantham, ed. 23–34.
40. *LFB* 684–5: 'Hunc ego, fluminea deformis truncus harena/Qui iacet, agnosco'. As Henry Day reminds me, this image recurs throughout the *Pharsalia* (1.140, 3.413,

6.584, 8.698, 9.966), and is distinctly intertextual, reaching back to Virgil's *Aeneid* (2.557–8) and outward to Seneca's *Agamemnon* (e.g., 901–3). For authoritative commentary, see Hinds, *Allusion and Intertext* 8–10.
41. Blissett, 'Lucan's Caesar' 563–5.
42. Thomas and Tydeman, in their useful anthology of 'sources' for Marlowe's plays, neglect Lucan, mentioning him only twice in passing (eds. 178, 258–9).
43. Our most important study of militarism in Marlowe – Shepard – does not mention Lucan.
44. The most famous study is by Skinner himself, *Liberty before Liberalism*.
45. Greenblatt, *Renaissance Self-Fashioning* 212; Dollimore 112. As the epigraph to this book indicates, the history of commentary linking Marlowe with liberty traces to Nashe's 1594 *Unfortunate Traveler*: 'His life he contemned in comparison of the liberty of speech' (McKerrow 2: 265). In 1753, Theophilus Cibber fears that Marlowe was 'inclined to free-thinking' (rpt. MacLure, ed. *CH* 56); and in 1880, A.C. Bradley says that Marlowe 'lived in a free and even reckless way' (rpt. MacLure, ed. *CH* 126). In 1892, James Russell Lowell identifies Marlowe as a 'liberal thinker' (rpt. MacLure, ed. *CH* 158), and in 1893, an unsigned article situates *DF* within the context of the 'Reformation and the Renaissance', which 'had granted the people from a double slavery, from a corrupt system of religion on the one hand, on the other, from ignorance' (rpt. MacLure, ed. *CH* 194). Then, in 1896–1910, W.J. Courthope finds in Marlowe 'Seneca's exaltation of the freedom of the human will, dissociated from the idea of Necessity, and joined with Machiavelli's principle of the excellence of *virtù*' (rpt. MacLure, ed. *CH* 195).
46. The first full-length study of Marlowe's politics, Shepherd's 1986 *Marlowe and the Politics of Elizabethan Theatre*, builds on Greenblatt and Dollimore to present Marlowe as a dissident iconoclast, and subsequent critics follow suit. For recent accounts, see White, 'Politics of Religion'; Wilson, 'Tragedy, Patronage'. For representative comments on Marlowe and freedom, still authoritative, see H. Levin, *Overreacher*, who says that Marlowe 'boldly asserted the values of freedom' (163); Altman, on *DF*: 'Essentially, Marlowe is testing the viability of an imagination that seeks to liberate itself from the trap of a fallen history and reassert its dominion over nature' (375). Kott adds, 'Marlowe [is] one of the most radical and independent minds of his day' (20).
47. The major study of the sublime grand style is Shuger, *Sacred Rhetoric*, discussed further in Chapter 1.
48. The next two paragraphs attempt to digest Shaw's complex history and his corresponding taxonomy (esp. his unit titled 'The Sublime Has a History' [4–10]). The critic who most influentially theorizes the sublime as a form of 'discourse', de Bolla (book title), emphasizes the subject-based form of the sublime (see, e.g., 6), not the author-based literary sublime that I emphasize.
49. Shaw mentions both Augustine (20–1, 150) and Dante (21–3, 25, 150) but, surprisingly, not Shakespeare – nor any other Elizabethan or Jacobean. In Chapter 5, I discuss Sedley's *Sublimity and Skepticism*, which foregrounds not simply Milton but Montaigne.
50. According to Vickers, in his anthology of English Renaissance literary criticism, 'The organic, transforming or metabolizing power of *imitatio*, when correctly practiced, was expressed in slightly different terms by the unknown author – usually called "Longinus" – of the treatise *On Sublimity* (first century AD), one of the most intelligent works of literary criticism ever produced, which was just beginning to be known in the late sixteenth century. One of the "roads

to excellence" that he recommends the budding writer to follow is "imitation and emulation of the great prose writers of antiquity". Such an encounter is in no way a routine or mechanical one, but a creative stimulus. ... This process is imitation, Longinus concludes, but not plagiarism: "such a proceeding is not theft; it is like obtaining a pattern from beautiful forms or images or other works of art"' (25–6).
51. We could add a fourth feature, Longinus' discussion of the way in which 'figures are natural allies of sublimity' (17.1: 163; on the sublimity of metaphor, see also 16.1–4: 162–3).
52. Cf. Russell and Winterbottom: Longinus 'holds that in an almost mystical way the composer is identified with what he describes; and it is because of the excitement of that moment of inspiration that the hearer or reader too is stunned by a sudden conviction of the sublimity of the passage' (eds. xvii).
53. Both Burke and Kant are notorious for gendering the sublime masculine, and the beautiful feminine. Usefully, Shaw presents the Burkean sublime as 'nothing other than a textual performance', a 'reality "effect", a semblance of the real woven from a tissue of citations' – a charge, Shaw notes, that Tom Paine makes against Burke in his *Rights of Man*: 'I consider Mr Burke's book in scarcely any other light than a dramatic performance ... a stage effect' (qtd. Shaw 70–1).
54. Cf. Shaw on the sublime as 'dictatorial', and the beautiful as 'democratic' (9).
55. Shaw traces Longinus' treatise to the republicanism of Cicero: '*On Sublimity* [is] linked to the republican ethos of political speech' (12). Shaw also shows how E. Burke does not formally take up the politics of the sublime in his *Philosophical Enquiry* but rather later in his career: 'For Burke, the [French] Revolution is an event of sublime theatricality' (64; see 63–71).
56. Day, *Neronian Sublime* MS 1.
57. For drawing my attention to Swinburne's republicanism, I am indebted to my former student James Goodwin (personal communication). On 'Swinburne's Republican Aesthetics', see Kuduk (essay title).
58. Shaw helps me see that Swinburne's model of the Marlovian sublime is theoretically informed, built right into the etymology of the word: '*sub* (up to) and *limen* (lintel, literally the top piece of the door)': 'there is no sense of the unbounded that does not make reference to the placing of a limit or threshold. Yet, by the same token, there is no limit which does not assume the existence of the unlimited': 'It would be impossible to conceive of the unlimited without the limited' (119).
59. Cf. H. Levin, *Overreacher*: 'Though Marlowe would not be Marlowe without a cosmic prospect, he seems to be moving centripetally through a descending gyre toward a core of self-imposed limitation' (80). Cf. Shaw: 'The modern sublime is defined not by its intimations of transcendence but rather by its confirmation of immanence, the sense in which the highest of the high is nothing more than an illusion brought about through our misperception of reality. Uncoupled from the Judeo-Christian concept of the divine, the sublime is figured in postmodern thought as immanent rather than transcendent' (3–4).
60. Swinburne's is only the fourth statement on *LFB* recorded in MacLure's *Critical Heritage* volume; the first is by Warton in 1781, the second by Bradley in 1880, and the third by Saintsbury in 1887 – all brief.
61. For H. Levin's famous comments on Marlovian flight, see *Overreacher* 22, 23–4, 40, 52–3, 96, 108, 112, 119, 134, 157, 159–61, 164.
62. In passing, Leech cites '*Peri Hupsous*, Chapter 3' (230n5) as a gloss on *1 Tamb* 1.1.57–61: Marlowe's 'imagery, in a way that Longinus talks of, falls into the puerile and frigid' (69).

63. Benston neglects both the politics of the Marlovian sublime and the contribution Lucan makes to it, but his analysis of the *Tamburlaine* plays opens the topic up to other works from the Marlowe canon, including the poems.
64. Qtd. Moore 341.
65. On Marlovian 'firstness', see Cheney, 'Introduction', *Cambridge Companion to Marlowe*, ed. Cheney.
66. For the Essex-Raleigh context, see esp. Nicholl, *Reckoning*.
67. In addition to Hadfield and Hammill on Spenser, and Hadfield on Shakespeare, see Sedinger on Sidney, and esp. J. Sanders on Jonson, an important book-length study. On Sidney and liberty, see Woods.
68. Long ago, H. Levin identified the overreacher of Marlowe as 'a mouthpiece for his epoch': 'His protagonist is never Everyman but always *l'uomo singolare*, the exceptional man who becomes king, because he is a hero, not hero because he is a king; the private individual who remains captain of his fate, at least until his ambition overleaps itself; the overreacher whose tragedy is more of an action than a passion, rather an assertion of man's will than an acceptance of God's' (*Overreacher* 24). Levin also sees Marlowe himself in the overreacher-figure (30, 104–5). Yet he does not take the next step: to see the exceptional man of the plays as a signature of Marlovian authorship, and especially to ground Marlovian authorship in Machiavelli's republican thought from the *Discourses*. In the following chapters, we shall take this step.

1 Republican Representation: Marlowe, the Age of Elizabeth, and *Lucan's First Book*

1. In this first section, I depend on the three recent Marlowe biographies: Kuriyama; Riggs, *World*; Honan. Neither Kuriyama nor Honan mentions republicanism, although Riggs mentions the topic once: 'Lucan's masterpiece depicts the civil war between Caesar and the Republicans from the Republican point of view. As the great Republican poet in the epic tradition, Lucan addresses his work to the Roman counterparts of Northumberland and Strange' (*World* 305–8). Thus the following account is intended as a preliminary analysis, and begins with the recognition that we know precious little about Marlowe's life, with much of the archive 'at one remove from his own voice': 'The facts of his adult life are few, scattered, and of doubtful accuracy. He is an irretrievably textual being' (Riggs, 'Marlowe's Life' 24). Readers may also consult the four essays on Marlowe in Mulryne and Kozuka, eds.: by Nicholl, 'Atheism'; Hopkins, 'Scotland'; Cheney, 'Biographical Representations'; Riggs, 'Poet in the Play'.
2. James, 'Erotic Elegy', shows that in early modern England 'Ovidian elegy approaches its political commitments' as 'a mode of engagement: it takes up the expressive liberties of classical republicanism' (126).
3. Skinner, 'Classical Liberty' 2: 9–10. For Skinner, this Elizabethan print practice is part of the origin of seventeenth-century republicanism.
4. We shall return to Hotman in chapter 4 when discussing *MP*.
5. Elsewhere, Skinner devotes an entire essay to the role of classical republican translations in early modern England, concluding that 'Anyone who had received a university education would have been required to study these texts ["Cicero, Sallust, Livy, and Tacitus" on "civil liberty"] in their original Latin',

and repeating his inventory of Elizabethan and early Jacobean translations ('Renaissance Translation' 313–4).
6. Baldwin's classic study, *Shakespeare's Small Latine & Lesse Greeke*, supports the conclusions not just of Riggs and other Marlowe biographers but also of Skinner, Peltonen, and other historians regarding the presence of classical republican texts in the English school and university curriculum, including at Canterbury and at Cambridge. To cite just one example: in 1517, students at Corpus Christi College, Oxford studied Sallust on Mondays, Wednesdays, and Fridays, and Lucan on Tuesdays, Thursdays, and Saturdays (Baldwin 1: 104). On Livy, see Baldwin 1: 105, 352, 388, 2: 30, 566; Tacitus, 1: 103, 190; Cicero's *De officiis*, 1: 105, 367, 371, 406.
7. On Machiavelli and England, including Marlowe, see Praz; Babb; Minshull, 'Sound Machevill'; M. Scott (as well as *MCP*, chpt. 6).
8. For detail, see Bawcutt's recent essay, 'Gentillet Reconsidered'.
9. For the importance of Bodin, see Skinner, *Foundations* 2: 284–301; Hadfield, *Republicanism* 247, 256, 262. On Harvey's reading of Livy, see Jardine and Grafton.
10. According to the Oxford editors of Machiavelli's *Discourses*, Bondanella and Bondanella, 'Much scholarly effort during the last few decades has been spent upon trying to resolve the apparent paradox [between] the author of a treatise on absolute rulers [and] the progressive republican theorist. There is no doubt about which political system Machiavelli preferred under the best of circumstances – a republican form of self-government. To pigeon-hole Machiavelli as either the counsellor of tyrants or the republican theorist simply obscures [his] overriding concern': 'to maximize independence and internal self-government' (xiv–xv).
11. On the Marlovian politics of Elizabethan Christianity, see, most recently, White. For a Reformation focus on early modern republicanism, see esp. J. Scott, *Commonwealth Principles*, esp. x–xi, 6–7.
12. On the Dutch Republic, see Velema; J. Scott, 'Classical Republicanism'; Tilmans; van Gelderen.
13. For recent intriguing detail, see Rowland, ed. xx–xxiii. On the ramifications of Marlowe's interest in going to Scotland for a 'profound shift in his literary aesthetic', see Hopkins, 'Scotland' 167.
14. Beacon's 1594 *Solon His Follie* takes as 'a matter of so great importance' the need to 'defende the multitude from the oppression of the mighty', discussing 'the meanes whereby we may abate the greatnes of the Lordes and Nobles, as also deliver the multitude from their oppressions' (3.6: 102; see also 3.5: 101–2).
15. In Chapter 4, I discuss Patterson's egalitarian reading of Holinshed.
16. Most critics writing on Elizabethan republicanism build on Collinson's paradigm. See, for example, Norbrook 11–14; Hadfield, *Renaissance Politics*, chpt. 3, and *Republicanism* 17, 49; Perry, *Favoritism* 186. For historians, see J. Scott, *Commonwealth Principles* 64; Peltonen, *Republicanism* 6, 19, 48, 55–6. Recently, Collinson follows up on his own essay, to argue that Elizabethan England was a 'Monarchical Commonwealth' (title). For a collection responding to Collinson, titled *The Monarchical Republic of Early Modern England*, and demonstrating the ongoing importance of his concept, see McDiarmid, ed., which appeared too late for me to make use of it.
17. For detail on these treatises, see Peltonen, *Republicanism*, chpts. 1–2; Hadfield, *Republicanism*, chpt. 1. On the three forms of government in Beacon, see 2.20: 84–6, esp. his summarizing comment: 'a Monarchie governed popularlie is then

secure and voide of perill: for in the multitude of the people consisteth the strength and force of every kingdome' (3.6: 105).
18. For recent commentary on *Vindiciae*, see McLaren, who responds to Skinner's classical model of early modern republicanism emphasizing Roman law by focusing instead on religion and Christianity.
19. On Sidney's link between 'forward Protestantism and Ciceronian republicanism', see Sedinger 49; she cites Worden, *Sound* 23–37; Stewart, *Philip Sidney* 202–12.
20. Hadfield's survey continues, and is extensive, considering non-Roman plays that depict 'Literary republicanism' (80), such as Lyly's *Compaspe*, Chapman's other tragedies, Sidney's *Arcadia*, Spenser's *Faerie Queene*, and Greville's tragedies, *Mustapha* and *Alaham* (80–95). Berek, in his discussion of contemporary plays that 'show clear debts to *Tamburlaine*' (58), neglects *Caesar's Revenge*, despite its overwhelming debt to Marlowe (Boas, ed. vi). Berek does discuss Lodge's *Wounds of Civil War* (58, 60–3); for his belief that Lodge is imitating Marlowe, not the other way around, see 61n15.
21. For details on freedom and slavery in *De officiis*, and its importance, see Skinner, 'Renaissance Translation' 314–16.
22. Perry's excellent essay on the play is forthcoming; building on Erne, he argues that '*Cornelia* is a play that is centrally about Roman republicanism as a coded language for native liberties and limited monarchy, but it seems also to be in some ways about the idea that this language might not be appropriate for the contemporary situation': through this 'uneasy tension', Kyd, 'like us, is actually divided about the appropriateness of republicanism for English constitutional thought' (MS 25–6). If true, Kyd's 'uneasy' republicanism joins what I am calling his roommate's *troubled* republicanism. I am grateful to Professor Perry for sending me his essay before publication.
23. On the early modern debate between aristocratic and popular republicanism, always in opposition to monarchy, see Skinner, *Foundations* 1: 159. On the term 'commonwealth', see J. Scott, *Commonwealth Principles* 34–9: during the early modern period, the term refers to the idea that 'government must be directed to the public good' – an 'English rendering of the Latin *res publica*, meaning "public thing"' (34). Sixteenth-century writers argued 'that the kingdom was also a commonwealth', with 'two principles' informing their 'commonwealth discourse': 'government must be directed to the public good'; and government 'must be legal and constitutional' (36). Scott singles out More's *Utopia* for demonstrating the 'potential' of English government to be operated by 'a republican constitution' (38). See also Collinson, 'Monarchical Commonwealth', for the 'resonance' of the term 'commonwealth' as 'a genuine and instrumental ideology of membership, participation, common interest': '"Commonwealth" was interchangeable with "republic", at least in Latin' (93).
24. Although Marlowe never uses the word 'sublime', he does translate Lucan's 'sublimis' at *Pharsalia* 1.137 as 'tall', using a famous simile to describe Pompey as a tall oak subject to lightning. Taking this instance as a cue, we can add that Marlowe uses the word 'tall' 15 times in his canon; 'lofty', 25 times; and cognates of 'high', 62 times. This is just the tip of a sublime iceberg in Marlowe's language, as the famed phrase 'high astounding terms' intimates (*1 Tamb* Pr.5).
25. Shuger's *Sacred Rhetoric*, about 'The Christian Grand Style in the English Renaissance' (subtitle), periodically discusses both Longinus and sublimity.

Arguing that 'the Christian grand style is one of the most far-reaching and innovative developments in Renaissance rhetoric' (6), Shuger demonstrates that the 'sacred rhetorics of the Renaissance emphasize the passion, sublimity, and grandeur of sacred discourse, grounding these qualities in the Classical grand style and in the principles of Renaissance theology and psychology' (7). She singles out Longinus for presiding over a 'shift' in classical rhetoric from 'ornament to passion and sublimity' that 'conferred a new importance on the inner life': for Longinus, 'Sublimity is the echo of a great soul' (29). Consequently, 'Longinian sublimity possesses strong sacral overtones', 'spiritualiz[ing] the grand style' (38; see also 157–63). In foregrounding religious prose, rather than political poetry and drama (7), Shuger does not mention figures important to the present study: Lucan and Marlowe (she does mention Philip Sidney in passing [204, 210]).

26. See also John Lane's 'Alarum to Poets' (first published 1648, but written in the late sixteenth century): 'Now all these Laureats standing at her gate,/Own offices did, and her love dilate,/In straines, conceits, and stile alike sublime,/As love could ravish nature up divine!' (267–70).

27. The word 'sublime' was also an alchemical term, as Jonson would render it in *The Alchemist*; Marlowe could have come across the alchemical usage in Sidney's *Astrophil and Stella*, Sonnet 77, as part of a Petarchan blazon: 'Those words that doe sublime the quintessence of blisse' (8). In the *Defence of Poesy*, Sidney recurrently describes poetry in terms of freedom and the sublime, what he calls 'that high flying liberty of conceit proper to the poet' (rpt. Vickers, ed. 341): 'The poet goeth hand in hand with nature, not enclosed within the narrow warrant of her gifts, but freely ranging only within the zodiac of his own wit. The poets only deliver a golden' (rpt. Vickers, ed. 343). See also the following phrasings: 'the free course of his own invention' (rpt. Vickers, ed. 346); 'the senate of poets hath chosen verse as their fittest raiment' (rpt. Vickers, ed. 347); 'the gates of popular judgement' (rpt. Vickers, ed. 340); 'to lift up the mind to the enjoying of his own divine essence' (rpt. Vickers, ed. 348); 'the poet is the right popular philosopher' (rpt. Vickers, ed. 353); as well as this on the genre of tragedy: it 'maketh kings fear to be tyrants' (rpt. Vickers, ed. 363).

28. Williams, *Modern Tragedy*, in Drakakis and Liebler, eds. 154; see also 161–2. Drakakis and Liebler recall the idea that 'tragedy is a liberated form' goes back to Aristotle's *Poetics*, with its idea of catharsis: 'Tragedy can be said to liberate its audience through a recognition and an articulation of those very forces which conspire to undermine civic identity' (ed. 4). On the politics of tragedy with reference to freedom, see Boal (Drakakis and Liebler, eds. 126–31). In linking tragedy with the sublime, I have benefited from conversations with Michael Silk, a classicist specialist on the topic.

29. The principal study of the sublime in advance of the Longinian vogue remains Nicolson. For the debate over whether Montaigne knew Longinus, see Sedley 21, 58–9, who concludes, 'Sublimity for Montaigne does not depend on any references to Longinus, which may or may not exist' (58). Not surprisingly, Sedley expresses detachment from the principle of intertextuality (15), and in so doing veers from the methodology of the present study.

30. On Lucan in the Middle Ages, see Crosland. For the most wide-ranging study of Lucan in English literature – from Chaucer to Robert Graves – see Dilke, who briefly discusses Marlowe, primarily to criticize his translation (86–7). According to Dilke, the principal precursor to a Lucanian Marlowe in Renaissance England

is Thomas Hughes in *The Misfortunes of Arthur*, which largely purloins 'whole sections from Seneca's tragedies and Lucan' (85).
31. The subtitle of MacLean's book is 'Historical Representation in English Poetry, 1603–1660'.
32. Lodge, in his 1579 *Defence of Poetry*, speaks to the Elizabethan political interpretation of Lucan: 'Beleeue mee the magestrats may take aduise (as I knowe wisely can) to roote out those odde rymes which runnes in euery rascales mouth, sauoring of ribaldry. Those foolishe ballets that are admitted make poets good and godly practices to be refused. I like not of a wicked nero that wyll expel Lucan, yet admit I of a zealous gouernour that wil seke to take away the abuse of poetry' (in G.G. Smith, ed. 1: 76).
33. Cf. Norbrook: Book 1 describes 'the breakdown of the republican system' (27).
34. See Feeney: 'Unlike the poems of Homer, Vergil, even Apollonius, this epic has nothing to say about the wishes or designs of any deity in its proem. There is no Muse' (272–3, 275).
35. MacLure says that 'trumpets and drums' is Marlowe's 'lively elaboration of "signa", standards' (ed., *Poems* 223). See also Gill, ed., *Works* 1: 247. Gorges writes 'conquering hand' and 'ensignes', and May 'victorious swords' and 'Ensignes' (qtd. Steane 266–7).
36. See Ahl: 'In book 1...Lucan has taken some pains to make his criticism [of Caesarism] oblique by attributing these words [ll. 668–72] to one of his characters. [T]he *Pharsalia* is hostile to Caesarism. ... [In t]he invocation of Nero in 1.33–66 ... every element admits of double entendre. ... At the opening of the epic, the work's final nature is not manifest; the reader does not yet know that this is to be an epic without gods, in defiance of tradition. Thus only the more playful aspects of the satire would be noticeable. ... [T]here is no compelling reason to assume ... that the *Pharsalia* is favorable to *princeps* and principate. But there is much to suggest the opposite. Even if one does not concede the satirical nature of the apotheosis [of Nero] in book 1, we ought to bear in mind that dedications to kings and emperors are part and parcel not only of Roman, but of Elizabethan and Jacobean poetry. To renounce one's emperor in the opening book of an epic would be ill-advised, possibly even fatal to both poet and poem' (44, 46, 47, 48, 49, 54).
37. Gill adds: 'Some of the best writing in *Lucan's First Booke* speaks directly to the Elizabethans, warning of the horror of civil war'; the translation thus has a 'grim topicality' (ed., *Works* 1: 89).
38. As Striar helps us see, Marlowe changes Lucan's original: 'MacLure and Martin both note that Marlowe seems to have taken "Phoebe's wain" as the subject of the transitive verb "Dissolve", whereas the Latin makes "engines" the subject of what would then be the intransitive verb "Dissolve" (*machina divolsi trubabit foedera mundi*). If, however, we recall the image of Nero balancing the world in 53–8 and then breaking of the world in 70–3, the constructions of "engines" as the subject (as per Lucan's text) would make more sense. That is to say, this passage, along with 70–3, implies a criticism of Nero that is ludicrously exploited in 53–8 and that culminates in 81 with "all great things crush themselves"' (Cheney and Striar, eds. 173).
39. On Marlowe as the Lucanian 'poet of dissolution', see Brennan, to whom I am indebted for compelling me to see the startling beauty of this passage. See also Lapidge.
40. Caesar's illegal crossing of the Rubicon is the event that historically embodies this dark parody of republicanism.

41. As Hardie puts it, 'recent criticism has dragged into the light the shadow of the epic poet Lucan lurking behind characters engaged in acts of prophecy': 'the frenzied matron whose apocalyptic visions close the first book of the *Bellum Civile* inspired by Apollo, and compared to a Maenad filled with the god Bacchus, two gods considered (before being rejected) as sources of poetic inspiration by Lucan in the prologue of book I' (107–8; see Feeney 275).

2 Authorship, Freedom, and Rapture in Marlowe's Ovidian Poems

1. The following details come from the annotated editions by L.C. Martin; MacLure; Gill. For a recent survey, see Cheney and Striar, eds. 1–5.
2. The Loeb edition has 49 poems, inserting an elegiac dream vision as 3.5, which was missing from Marlowe's source-text. This omission affects the numbering of *OE* for the poems following; thus Marlowe's concluding elegy, 3.14, is 3.15 in the Loeb.
3. Even the Manwood epitaph, which I shall not discuss further, participates in a kind of republican ethos, presenting the dead jurist as an egalitarian hero, 'whose face awed/Thousands of men' (8–9): 'Rejoice, Offspring of crime' (3). A similar ethos emerges in the Latin dedicatory epistle to Mary Sidney Herbert, 'born of a race of poets', and said to be like 'Philomela [who] once fled from the Thracian tyrant' (1–4).
4. Two recent, authoritative examples include Brown, 'Marlowe's Poems'; Sinfield, whose title is 'Marlowe's Erotic Verse'.
5. James, 'Ovid and the Question of Politics', and 'Marlowe and Erotic Elegy'.
6. The two examples that follow both appear in James, but she quotes them for what they say about Ovid, not Lucan. Earlier, she does recall the important criticism done recently on the politics of Lucan, commenting, 'Long before Lucan *railed*, however, Ovid *toyed*, with the lost prerogative of bold and open speech' ('Erotic Elegy' 106; her emphasis).
7. See, for example, Hardie, esp. 105–11 (where Ovid and Lucan *rebel* against Virgil, while Statius and Silius Italicus *revere* him); Martindale, *Redeeming the Text*, esp. 48–53, 54–74 (with 56–60 on Marlowe and Ovid). For fuller bibliographies on both Ovid and Lucan, see *MCP*, chpts. 1–2 and 10.
8. In 'The Poet's Toys' James titles her penultimate section 'Marlowe's Ovidian Raptures' (120), observing, 'It is surprising, in fact how often Marlowe presents Ovid as a poet whose imaginative, rhetorical, and moral license is worth dying for': 'Marlowe shares with Ovid the wanton reverie, in which the body goes slack while the mind ranges in the zodiac of its own capricious wit' – what she calls the 'Ovidian fantasy of ravishment' (120–1). James cites Goldman's 'Marlowe and the Histrionics of Ravishment' (121n40), in which Goldman outlines 'a histrionic pattern' depicting 'Marlowe's heroes' as 'ravished men' (22). Goldman defines ravishment as an emotional condition in which the hero is 'aroused by a single source to the possibility of entire bliss' (22), even though in all cases but Tamburlaine's ravishment leads to 'suffering' (35). Consequently, the hero's histrionic ravishment commits him to 'a state of dissolution' (36).
9. As Shaw summarizes, 'All that remains essential to the sublime is a state of feeling, which may be loosely described as wonder, awe, rapture, astonishment, ecstasy, or elevation' (14).

10. Shaw relies on recent criticism to subject Longinus' analysis of Sappho to a feminist critique: 'Longinus' stress on the mastery of excess contrasts with Sappho's openness to "self-shattering"' (25).
11. As we will recall from Chapter 1, Longinus even exemplifies the sublime through one of the myths that critics identify as a Marlovian signature: Phaethon (H. Levin, *Overreacher* 52, 112, 160). In particular, Longinus quotes two passages from Euripides' *Phaethon* (extant only in fragments), the first of which voices the messenger's report on the young man's death: 'Drive on, but do not enter Libyan air – /it has no moisture in it, and will let/your wheel fall through – ' (15.4: 160). On the second, similar passage, Longinus comments, 'May one not say that the writer's soul has mounted the chariot, has taken wing with the horses and shares the danger' (15.4: 160).
12. Details for the reading in this paragraph, as well as scholarship and criticism, appear in *MCP*, chpts. 1–2; more recently, see Cheney, 'Introduction', *Poems of Marlowe* 7–10.
13. See, for example, Stapleton, who reads the collection as a work about the *desultor amoris*.
14. On the importance of equality in a republic, see, for example, Machiavelli, *Discourses*: 'The founder of a republic should, therefore, organize it where there exists or has existed great equality' (1.56: 138).
15. For Cupid's 'desert empire', see 2.9.52. Throughout *OE*, the poet deploys militarism, often as a metaphor for love; for instance, this is the topic of 2.12.
16. Jonson's translation is printed alongside Marlowe's in the first extant edition of all 48 elegies.
17. We cannot idealize Ovid's authorship of slavery, but neither should we simply criticize it, for he candidly presents himself entangled in the slave system.
18. For other Longinus examples about the sublime power of water, see 9.5: 151, 10.5: 155.
19. Elsewhere, the Ovidian poet can use the king's leverage to his own advantage, as when he cites the sex lives of sovereigns as precedent for his own erotic commitment: 'Greater than these myself I not esteem;/What graced kings, in me no shame I deem' (2.8.13–14).
20. During the sixteenth century, only the *Amores* among Ovid's major works was not allowed into the school curriculum.
21. For the most recent book on this phenomenon, see Montrose, *Subject of Elizabeth*.
22. See Montrose, 'Perfecte paterne of a Poete' 50.
23. For details, see Cheney, 'Teaching Marlowe's Translation of Ovid's *Amores*'.
24. According to Moulton, the Bishops banned these poems for their subversive attack on 'social norms of gender identity and behavior' (86): 'although epigrams can be seen to have a conservative, regularly function – mocking vice and folly in order to encourage conformity to a "rational" and "natural" order – Davies' epigrams, like much satire in the 1590s, were seen by the Bishops and others concerned with policing public morals as provoking the vices they condemned' (85). On the Bishops' Ban, see also McCabe. For my discussion of Davies, see Cheney, 'Introduction', *Poems of Marlowe* 8–10.
25. The editions of Brooke, L.C. Martin, MacLure, Orgel, and Gill miss the connection; for the only exception, see Cheney and Striar, where Striar glosses the passage, 'The language of "The Passionate Shepherd"' (ed. 37).

26. The passage in *OE* thus joins the documented origins to 'PS': Theocritus, Idyll 6 and 11; Virgil, Eclogue 2; Ovid, *Metamorphoses* 13.623–969 (Polyphemus and Galatea); Spenser, *Januarye* 55–60. See *MCP*, chpt. 3, including for scholarship and criticism; more recently, see Cheney, 'Introduction', *Poems of Marlowe* 10–12.
27. On the 'eternizing conceit never made fully explicit by Marlowe's shepherd', to which we shall return, see Bruster 52.
28. Riggs joins most critics in believing that 'The Passionate Shepherd' had to have been written, circulated, and widely known for parodies such as we find in his plays to work (*World* 107–10). In *The Compleat Angler* (1653, 1655), Izaak Walton recalls 'that smooth song which was made by Kit Marlow, now at least fifty years ago' (qtd. MacLure, ed., *CH* 6).
29. Eliot 75. Maus refers to the commonplace that Jonson records the Marlovian sublime to lend voice to the great dreamer of gold: Mammon's 'gullibility arises not from a failure of imagination but from a lurid excess: Jonson gives him impressive blank verse lines, full of mythic resonances and exotic allusions, modeled upon the language spoken by Christopher Marlowe's magniloquent heroes. In London as Jonson depicts it, grand appetites make one all the more susceptible to chicanery' (intro., *Renaissance Drama*, ed., 862). Quotations of the play come from this edition.
30. See J. Sanders on 'Ben Jonson's Theatrical Republics' (book title), esp. 68–88 on *The Alchemist*. Although Sanders situates Jonson's play within early seventeenth-century republican discourse, she does not recall that Mammon's 'remarkable style of speech' (82) is foundationally Marlovian, or connect it with the sublime; nor does she discuss in any detail the conversation between Mammon and Doll on the 'free state'.
31. On Doll and the republic, see J. Sanders 73–6.
32. For a succinct reception history, see Evans: 'Mammon has been called a great imaginative creation, the best non-Shakespearean comic figure in English drama, a reflection of Jonson's own enormous imagination, a parody of Christopher Marlowe's over-reachers' (196).
33. To this extent, we may need to modify J. Sanders' excellent work on Jonson's 'theatrical republics' by recalling Eliot's remark that Jonson is Marlowe's legitimate heir.
34. According to Forsythe, other poems in *Hesperides* imitate 'The Passionate Shepherd': 'The Wake' (705) and 'The Apparition of His Mistress Calling Him to Elysium' (705), the last of which presents a lady inviting her lover to die with her in the company of famous poets from antiquity through the Renaissance, including Lucan (706). Forsythe adds that 'Related to Herrick's [poem], is Carew's "The Rapture"' (706). To my knowledge, the topic has never been studied in any detail; major studies of Herrick by Marcus, Coiro, and DeNeef do not discuss 'To Phillis', nor Marlowe's presence in Herrick's verse.
35. The image of the 'urn' with its 'mixed dust' may gesture to the closing of Shakespeare's 'Phoenix and Turtle'. Paulin's lines feel Donnean as well.
36. For an early critic who catches the borrowing, see Forsythe 714. For more recent commentary, see Hurley 70–83. The following discussion abbreviates that in Cheney, 'Milton, Marlowe, and Lucan'.
37. As both Shaw and Sedley reveal, the Miltonic sublime is among the most renowned in English.
38. Marloweism appears as early as line 24, 'So buxom, blithe, and debonair', said of Lady Mirth, echoing Marlowe's description of Hero in *Hero and Leander*: 'So

young, so gentle, and so debonair' (1.288); cited in volume 2 of the 6-volume *A Variorum Commentary: The Poems of John Milton*, on *The Minor English Poems*, ed. Woodhouse and Bush 2.1: 276.
39. Some may think the companion poems too early in Milton's career to represent his republicanism, but Dzelzainis cites evidence to the contrary; see 'Milton's Politics', esp. 71 for Milton's 1640–42 remark that a 'commonwealth is to be preferred to a monarchy'.
40. As we have seen, in the 1650s Walton knows that Marlowe wrote 'The Passionate Shepherd'.
41. The classic study of the sublimity of mountains in the Western literary tradition is by Nicholson, although she argues (mistakenly, I think) that mountains do not become sublime till the late seventeenth and early eighteenth centuries. For instance, she refers to Lucan only once in passing (304), neglecting the sublimity of the landscape examined in the Introduction, which relies on the analysis of H. Day.
42. For details, see *MCP* 78–87, from which some phrasing here is borrowed.
43. For an inventory of scholarship, see *MCP*, chpt. 11. The major studies foregrounding Ovidianism in *HL* include Keach; Hulse; most recently, Brown, *Redefining*.
44. See *MCP* 221–6.
45. Lucan's Latin does not explicitly make the ocean speak, but both Braund and Joyce translate it as if it does. Much has been made of Marlowe's anti-Platonic 'naturalism' in *Hero and Leander*, grounded in Lucretian materialism, in Ovid, and in others (Neuse; Turner; Altieri), but rarely in Lucan.
46. See Wheeler: 'Lucan does not avoid Ovidian eroticism altogether: Caesar's love for Cleopatra recalls that of Pygmalion for his statue (cf. 10.71–72 and *Met* 10.252)' (379n57). For Lucan on the tragic loveliness of erotic female beauty, see his sensitive portrait of Phemonoe, the Delphic priestess of Apollo, in Book 5.
47. Joyce's translation makes explicit the detail of Lucan's paved floor: 'Every floor in the whole house was paved/with slabs of onyx' (10.116–17).
48. Joyce's translation is especially exquisite: 'Dazzling white, her breasts gleamed through Sidonian chiffon' (10.141).
49. Otis calls Ovid 'the West's first champion of true, normal, even conjugal love' (277); while Segal adds that such love in Ovid is often tragic (67). For my discussion of the conjugal Ovid, especially in the exile poetry, see *MCP* 57–8. See also Getty (a former student), who follows up with the influence of the conjugal Ovid on Spenser's *Amoretti*.
50. See Brown: 'The epyllion challenges the Petrarchan model of the relationship between the sexes, of the silent, passive female object of desire who is pursued by the dominant male and it does so by acknowledging the erotic equality of the sexes' (*Redefining* 139). *Hero and Leander* thus contrasts with Shakespeare's *Venus and Adonis*, which Hadfield discusses as 'republicanesque' (*Republicanism* 133), with Venus functioning as a figure for Elizabeth's erotic monarchical dominance over male aristocrats (132–6).
51. On the poem's 'repudiating femininity', with attention to the masculine exposure of the shamed Hero, see Miller 782. On the 'literariness' of the epyllion genre, see Brown, *Redefining* 116, for whom Hero and Leander function as 'synecdoches for literature' (140; see esp. 106–7) and thus a 'literary community' (176). Rather than emphasizing rapture, however, Brown foregrounds Marlowe's willingness to equate his male authorship with female shame (157–64): Hero's 'description

provokes extreme poeticism from the narrator' (163). It is this 'poeticism' in particular, I believe, that readers take away with them.

3 'Defend His Freedom 'Gainst a Monarchy': Empire and Liberty in *Dido, Queen of Carthage* and *Tamburlaine, Parts One* and *Two*

1. For earlier discussion of the dilemma of empire and liberty in Machiavelli and Sallust, see Skinner, *Liberty before Liberalism* 61–5. Skinner situates this dilemma within 'the neo-roman theory of free states' (59), which argues that 'it is only possible to be free in a free state' (60) against critics like Hobbes, who in *Leviathan* insists that Roman theorists like Sallust discuss only the freedom of cities, not of men (59–60).
2. We have some evidence that Marlowe knew Sallust; in *E2*, he refers to Catiline's conspiracy against Republican Rome (4.6.51; see Chapter 4).
3. Armitage also identifies Machiavelli's debt to Polybius (34): 'The Machiavellian compound of Sallust's moral account of Roman decline and Polybius's constitutional analysis provided an enduring model for later republicans to understand the competing pressures of liberty at home and expansion abroad' (35).
4. For Machiavelli's direct reference to 'the conspiracy of Catiline described by Sallust', see *Discourses* 3.6: 273.
5. On empire and liberty in Beacon's *Solon his Follie*, see 2.20: 86–7; 3.6: 105–6. For detailed commentary on Beacon's treatise as 'perhaps the most important as well as the most radical exponent of classical humanist discourse in England before the 1650s', including its 'develop[ment] of many central themes of classical republicanism', see Peltonen, *Republicanism* 76–102 (76). See also Hadfield, *Republicanism* 28–31.
6. Philip Hardie helps me see that the justification for reading political enslavement into Dido's erotic remark comes from the fact that she is bound to the hero of empire (personal communication).
7. On 'emperie' as 'Marlowe's preferred form of "empire"', see Fuller, ed. 171.
8. The most important works include Dollimore 109–19 (on *DF*); Goldberg; Shepherd, *Politics*. For a useful overview of historical criticism indebted to Greenblatt, see Burnett, 'Marlowe and the Critics', ed. 617–18.
9. For my review of criticism on *Dido*, see *MCP* 100–2, to which the information following is indebted.
10. For details, see *MCP* 102–5.
11. Not much has changed since my review of scholarship in *MCP* 295–6n5.
12. Cornelia's set-complaints recall – and may be indebted to – those of Ovid's women, including Dido, in the *Heroides*. See Leigh on the similarity between Cornelia's 'mental state' at 8.43–54 and Hero's 'around *Her.* 19.59' (291n1).
13. For commentary, see Cheney, *Poet-Playwright* 117.
14. To these echoes, we can add Oliver's three uses of *LFB* to gloss *Dido*: (1) 4.1.25 on 'whist': see *LFB* 262 (ed. 59); (2) 4.4.117–9, following Brooke: see *LFB* 527–30 (ed. 71); (3) 5.1.159 on 'Hircania': see *LFB* 327–30 (ed. 82). There may also be a connection between Lucan's passage on dissolution and Juno's claim to 'make the clouds dissolve their watry works' (3.2.90).
15. This inventory does not include incidental versions, such as Dido's 'Come in with me' at 1.2.42.

16. Not all of Marlowe's sublime discourse re-voices 'The Passionate Shepherd'; some of the most eloquent utterances operate more broadly in that formal register of the sublime, spiritual flight, as in Dido's cosmic soaring at 3.4.51–3: 'What more than Delian music do I hear,/That calls my soul forth from his living seat/To move unto the measures of delight'.
17. Deats adds, 'The ambiguous treatment of the two antagonists, elevated through heroic rhetoric while deflated through prosaic action, foreshadows the equivocal development of all Marlowe's protagonists – Tamburlaine, Barabas, Faustus, Edward, and the Guise' (195). The present discussion re-routes the usual track into the tragedy from 'passion' (196) to the sublime. Gibbons sees *Dido* foregrounding 'the inner complexities of the sublime and the heroic' (46), without amplifying.
18. Logan shows that '*Antony and Cleopatra* was strongly affected by the Marlovian style of epic grandeur, majestic amplitude, hyperbole, and sharp emphasis', particularly from *Dido* (176): 'Shakespeare apparently finds Marlowe impressively successful at awing his audience' (177). Logan's sensitive analysis of 'resounding grandiloquence' as one of Marlowe's mightiest (Shakespearean) 'legacies' (176) can be strengthened, I believe, through access to Marlowe's inscription of the early modern sublime.
19. Presumably, the author of *On Sublimity* would not be amused at Marlowe's blasphemous burlesque.
20. The phrase 'boy eternal' comes from *The Winter's Tale* 1.2.65, when Polixenes describes to Hermione the carefree life he led with her husband, Leontes, when they were young. For my use of this phrase to characterize what I'm now calling the Marlovian sublime, see *MCP* 82–7.
21. The first passage grows out of lines cited previously as Lucanian, when Dido says her 'empery' will not be 'Presage[d]' by 'bloody spears, appearing in the air,/Nor blazing comets' (4.5.118–19) but only by 'Aeneas' frown' (120), leading into the lines about his immortalizing kiss.
22. On the psychology of disfunctionality in Marlowe's own Canterbury family, see Proser.
23. Logan 176. Logan calls Marlowe's grand style 'more cerebral, less directly emotional and less emotionally engaged than Shakespeare's' (172), and emphasizes that language's 'impersonality' and 'depersonalization' (174).
24. The tradition of imagining Dido as an author figure begins with Ovid, who presents her writing a letter in the *Heroides* (*MCP* 109).
25. Later, Achates will make Dido's effeminizing project explicit when compelling Aeneas to leave Carthage for Rome (4.3.33–6).
26. In *HL*, writes Brown, 'Marlowe challenges the concept of chaste literature by suggesting parallels between female sexuality and the behavior of male authors. Marlowe's narrator identifies himself with women' (*Redefining* 157–8). Like Tamburlaine, Dido is prone to talking about 'our poets' (4.4.144).
27. On Dido's 'artful court-ship' here, see Henderson: 'As in "The Passionate Shepherd", lyric poetry envisions an erotic paradise whose time and place exist only in language' (127–8).
28. On Elizabeth in the play, especially Spenser's Elizabeth, see *MCP* 99–106. Henderson is esp. useful on Elizabeth and Dido (146–8) and on Elizabeth and the old Nurse (150).
29. Bowers re-conceives the play's burlesque in terms of 'camp': 'all meanings are converted from a straight, public, conventional meaning to a zany, private, unusual experience' (96).

30. The link between Icarian soaring and poetry is made clearer at *MP* 2.34–47 and at *DF* Pr.15–22. On Icarus in Ovid, see Wise; Carrubba; Ahern. On the Icarus myth in the Renaissance, see Ashton. For a broader survey, from antiquity through modernity, see Rudd 21–53.
31. Cf. Logan: 'in Marlowe's passage, we are made more aware of the cleverness of the style than the frustrations of the speaker because they are overarticulated' (178–9).
32. On Hannibal as the 'public enem[y] of Rome', see Hardie 62: 'The conflict between Carthage and Rome is to a large extent a war between the families of Hannibal and of Scipio Africanus' (96). On Scipio as a 'republican hero', see Hadfield, *Republicanism* 27. In the *Discourses*, Machiavelli presents Scipio as 'the supreme Roman republican hero' (Bondanella and Bondanella, ed. 366; see 1.10: 48), and Hannibal as the Roman Republic's arch-enemy (3.22: 308).
33. Since Livy had had a lot to say about Hannibal, Gabriel Harvey in his commentary on Livy ends up discussing the Carthaginian general repeatedly, as Jardine and Grafton show; for Harvey's sympathy for Hannibal, see Jardine and Grafton 72.
34. Later, Hardie reports of Silius' Hannibal, 'There is more than a hint of Lucan's Caesar in him, and he is a fairly close relative of Milton's Satan' (80). In Chapter 5, we will remember that *DF* intimates that Marlowe himself likely wrote a play on Hannibal, a dramatic kinsman (we shall see shortly) to Tamburlaine. For editorial dispute about whether Marlowe refers to Hannibal again at *LFB* 39 (the reference is to 'Carthage souls'), see Gill, ed., *Works* 1: 249. In *De officiis*, Cicero helps us understand what might have attracted Marlowe to Hannibal professionally: the Carthaginian superman is a theatrical man, a figure of 'guile, adept at concealment, tight-lipped, [a] dissembler laying traps' (1.108: 37).
35. As we might imagine, historians link Tamburlaine with Hannibal; in one of the main source texts for Marlowe's plays, Perondinus writes, 'Both physically and in other respects Tamerlane was very similar to Hannibal of Carthage as described by several ancient writers' (Thomas and Tydeman, eds. 118). Similarly, John Shute's 1562 translation of Andreas Cambinus' 1529 *Libro* also compares Tamburlaine with Hannibal (Thomas and Tydeman, eds. 130). For additional links, see Voegelin 161–2.
36. Riggs discusses 'Marlowe's cosmography syllabus' with respect to 'Polybius' account of how "almost the whole inhabited world was conquered and brought under the dominion of the single city of Rome"', an account which 'proceeds along a geographical axis that runs from west to east, from conflicts in Italy to North Africa to Egypt. *1 Tamburlaine* proceeds from east to west, from Persia to Egypt' (*World* 162).
37. For excellent historical criticism lacking access to republicanism but supportive of it nonetheless, see Burnett, '*Tamburlaine*': Tamburlaine is a commoner imitating a magistrate' who operates through 'fellowship' and 'communality' in order to construct 'narratives of egalitarian glory', a 'joint rule that is distinguished by its classical antecedents' (134–5).
38. Hadfield has been instrumental in seeing the *Tamburlaine* plays as attacking 'hereditary monarchy': 'Tamburlaine's behaviour shows that royal status is not a birthright, but something that can be earned. *Tamburlaine* is not a work of republican ideology or propaganda. It is, however, a spectacular and relentless assault on received values, in particular hereditary kingship, which is shown time and again to be an illusion that fails to protect the monarch in question from being overthrown' (*Republicanism* 61).

His brief analysis (59–61) warrants further detail and context. For Machiavelli's critique of 'hereditary succession', the antithesis of 'adoption' or 'election', see *Discourses* 1.10: 49. Without referring to republicanism, K. Cunningham discusses Marlowe's obsession with 'treason': 'Throughout his plays, Marlowe dramatizes a consistent pattern of imagining the death of the king' (142).

39. For details on the contemporary reception of the *Tamburlaine* plays, see Berek; R. Levin; Cartelli, *Marlowe, Shakespeare*. More recently, see L. Potter, 'Theatre and Film'; Hopkins, 'Reception'.
40. Curiously, Burnett's text contains a typo right at the key word, mistakenly printing 'kingdom' instead of 'freedom' (personal communication).
41. We might wonder how the printer Richard Jones' cutting of 'some fond and frivolous jestures', which, during performance, 'some vain conceited fondlings greately gaped at' (rpt. Burnett, ed. 3), affected the conflict between republican and monarchical values.
42. Compared with 33 times in *E2*; 6 in *Dido*; 10 in *2 Tamb*; 5 in *JM*; 8 in *MP*; and 7 in *DF*. The total of 21 uses of 'friends' in the two *Tamburlaine* plays reveals how important this concept is to Marlowe at the outset of his London theatrical career.
43. On friendship within the context of early modern republicanism, see Shannon, who says that friendship at this time is 'Neither democrat nor republican', but that the term did undergo politicization in response to monarchical necessities: 'Before a conception of rights, it grounds itself instead on a virtually Stoic emphasis on self-possession and acts of will' (19). On the incompatibility of friendship and monarchy in *E2*, see her chpt. 5: 'Where friendship rules, kingship fails, and participation in friendship exacts the price of sovereign status' (159). *1 Tamb* seems to entertain the opposite view, and to do so (I would argue) within a republican dynamic. Recently, Gillies situates the play's friendship in terms of Deleuze and Guattari's 'world of the tribe or pack or band' (42).
44. See also Machiavelli on the change 'from the kings to consuls' (*Discourses* 3.7: 277). In the prose Argument to the 1594 *Rape of Lucrece*, Shakespeare records the narrative that ends the Roman Empire and gives birth to the Republic: Lucrece's suicide is so charged that it 'changed' the 'state government from kings to consuls' (Argument 45); see Cheney, *Poet-Playwright*, chpt. 4.
45. For this line as the 'motto' of the play, because it speaks to the audience's own 'perplexity' regarding Tamburlaine, see Barber 59.
46. Most critics have their own way of expressing the play's strangeness; Gillies' recent formulation of 'ludic anarchy' is particularly apt here (43). Here is Barber's formulation from a previous generation: 'there was nothing new about blasphemous defiance, tyranny, self-idolatry, cruelty. What was new was that *Tamburlaine* presents these things, programmatically and unqualifiedly, as heroic achievements. There is no stable, moral, eschatological framework' (51).
47. On Tamburlaine's 'very sane cruelty', see Engle, intro. to *Tamburlaine, Renaissance Drama*: 'on the whole [he is] cheerful, rational, and rewarding to be close to', having 'little in common with the unhinged tyrants of later Renaissance drama or with those of both Renaissance and modern history' (ed. 188). Tamburlaine's loyalty to his friends is legendary, as is his refusal to engage in 'Machiavellian' fraud. On both commonplaces, see the recent formulation by Gillies: 'The refusal of any dissimulation or qualification is completely un-Machiavellian. So too is the absolute fidelity with which he rewards loyalty' (42).
48. Marlowe goes beyond all the source texts excerpted in Thomas and Tydeman by foregrounding Damascus as a republic. Perondinus, for instance, narrates the

event but never mentions the Governor, just 'citizens' (and no virgins) (113–14; see also 115–16).
49. It as if Marlowe parodies the Machiavellian idea of the patriot king articulated 150 years later by Bolinbroke, turning his republican ideal into a republican tyrant. As such, Marlowe's response to Machiavelli resembles William Gladstone's biting critique of 'Bolinbroke's admirer, Disraeli': 'Liberty for ourselves, Empire over the rest of mankind' (qtd. Armitage 42). Can we imagine a better slogan for Marlowe's Tamburlaine?
50. The idea is commonplace, but see esp. Voegelin, who sees Machiavelli influencing the sixteenth-century biographies of Tamburlaine and thus, at least indirectly, Marlowe: 'While Machiavelli himself did not reflect on Asiatic events, the image of Timur, shaped by the preceding generations, is very noticeable as an influence on his own image of the Prince' (155). See J.S. Cunningham, ed. 10, 15, including Machiavelli's Titus Livius as an origin for Marlowe's Tambulaine (ed. 15). We should not forget that Machiavelli periodically refers to 'Bajazet' (*Discourses* 1.19: 72; 3.6: 259).
51. Cf. Engle, introd. to *Tamburlaine, Norton Anthology*: 'Tamburlaine focuses on the political process that most fascinated Machiavelli: the combination of luck and skill that permits an obscure person to establish himself as a new prince' (185). For an origin to Machiavelli's singular man, see Polybius, *Histories* 6.5: 305–7: 'The one man who excels in physical strength and courage should lead and rule over the rest' (6.5: 305). In *Solon his Follie*, Beacon cites Machiavelli's *Discourses* in arguing that 'the action of reformation' – his major topic in the treatise – 'is to be given into the hands of some man of race and excellent vertues', citing Lucius Junius Brutus as an example (2.13: 64).
52. Masters 9–10; Blissett, 'Lucan's Caesar' 652–4.
53. In the *Discourses*, Machiavelli calls Caesar 'the first tyrant of Rome, after which the city was never again free' (1.37: 101).
54. See Burnett, '*Tamburlaine*', which probes the ways in which the two plays *astound*: '*Tamburlaine, Parts One* and *Two* are indeed "astounding", both in terms of their dramaturgy and their social and cultural reverberations' (141).
55. On Tamburlaine as 'Marlowe's test case for the idea of man as a sublime poet', see McAdam 76, who concludes nonetheless that Tamburlaine fails the test: Tamburlaine's 'imagination' produces merely 'a narcissistic fantasy of omnipotence, and the sense of tragedy is oddly qualified from the start by a sense of parody and comic deflation' (77). The major study of the Tamburlainian sublime remains that of Benston (see chpt. 1), although I disagree with his conclusion about 'the central truth': 'that Tamburlaine is a transcendentally solipsistic poet of the Sublime' (207). Today, most critics identify Tamburlaine with the sublime, although typically only in passing; see, for example, Fuller, who speaks of Tamburlaine's 'poetry of sublime aspiration' and its opposition to brutality (ed. xxxvii).
56. E. Burke also acknowledges that 'the qualities of the sublime and beautiful are sometimes found united' (3.27: 114; see also 4.24: 142).
57. Tamburlaine's second speech on Zenocrate's beauty, at 3.3.317–31 ('Zenocrate, the lovelist maid alive'), repeats some of this discourse, but adds Zenocrate's power to 'clear the darkened sky' with her 'looks' and 'calm the rage of thund'ring Jupiter'. Effectively, she brings serenity to Tamburlaine's unruly militarism.
58. In *Philosophical Enquiry*, E. Burke identifies ambition with the sublime, citing Longinus: 'God has planted in men a sense of ambition, and a satisfaction arising

from the contemplation of his excelling his fellows in something deemed valuable amongst them. It is this passion that drives men to all the ways we see in use of signalizing themselves. Hence proceeds what Longinus has observed of that glorying and sense of inward greatness, that always fills the reader of such passages in poets and orators as are sublime' (1.17: 46–7).

59. Tamburlaine's speech on the 'crown' may derive in part from Machiavelli's *Discourses*, which emphasize 'The thirst to rule' (3.4: 254), and man's natural ambition and warlike nature, relying on the same vocabulary, as the following italics demonstrate: 'It is a saying of ancient writers that whenever the necessity for fighting is taken away from [men], they fight for the sake of *ambition*, which is so powerful a passion in the human *breast* that, no matter the *rank* to which a man may *rise*, he never abandons it. The reason is that *nature* has created men in such a way that they can *desire* everything but are unable to obtain everything, so that their desire is always greater than their power of acquisition, and discontent with what they possess and lack of satisfaction are the result' (1.37: 99; see also 2.Preface: 151, and 2.20: 211; his emphases).

Greenblatt esp. emphasizes the Marlovian hero's restless nature, his 'unsatisfied longing' (*Renaissance Self-Fashioning* 221).

60. Fuller's annotation on 'virtue' in this passage reads: 'Vertue] manly excellence, courage (*OED sb.* 7), but with some colouring of *virtù*, the fully developed powers of the human intellect and will. As Marlowe would probably be aware, *virtù* is a key but shifting term in the vocabulary of Machiavelli' (ed. 220).

61. Throughout the *Discourses*, Machiavelli demonstrates his commitment to the glory of the noble man of *virtù*, making it his signature. Beginning with the idea that 'the Romans were great lovers of glory' (1.36: 98), continuing to the notion that 'ancient religion beatified only men fully possessed of worldly glory' (2.2: 159), to a full chapter devoted to 'Fame' (3.34: 334–7), Machiavelli argues that the best way to achieve 'a good reputation' in a 'republic' is to 'distinguish' oneself by 'some extraordinary deed' (335). For detailed commentary on the humanist and Machiavellian ideal of '*vir virtutis*' achieving 'honour, glory and fame', see Skinner, *Foundations* 1: 118–28.

62. Most critics express their own version of the change; see, for example, R. Martin, who emphasizes the 'romance' of Tamburlaine: 'The quest seems shabby and vicious. Throughout Part II, Marlowe appears less decisively in favor of Tamburlaine than he does in Part I, and the dramatic world of Part II hangs more precariously on the brink of tragedy. The ideal seems to shrink. The reader feels a growing repugnance toward Tamburlaine's excessive brutality' (58). Fuller notes that 'Marlowe does adumbrate the loss of empire in Part 2 in so far as the unity of his action allows' (ed. xxi).

63. Fuller supports this argument: 'Kocher shows that the incident was often cited by Renaissance writers on military affairs as an exemplum' (ed. 263).

64. Fuller follows criticism in attributing the image primarily to Diodorus Siculus, adding that 'Marlowe may have known this either directly, or through a reference in Lucan' (ed. 260). I suggest that we probably need to put Lucan at the head of the list in annotation here.

65. Gillies responds to recent criticism by separating 'the "spatial" dimension' from 'the "imperial" dimension and the sublime', arguing that 'the spatial and imperial sublime might have actually required the subversive (atheism, blasphemy) in order to work its elusive chemistry with the audience' (36).

66. Critics have noticed this tendency before but not in the present terms. See, for example, McAdam: 'Tamburlaine turns real people into artifacts' (100).
67. We might recall the commonplace that Shakespeare in the balcony scene of *Romeo and Juliet* responds to the balcony scene in the *Jew of Malta*.
68. Burnett, '*Tamburlaine*', speaks of the hero 'aestheticiz[ing] Zenocrate', but he understands this as 'rob[bing]' her of 'a meaningful sexuality' (136). Cf. Greenblatt's version, which refers to Tamburlaine's burning of the town where Zenocrate dies: 'For experiencing this limitlessness, this transformation of space and time into abstractions, men do violence as a means of marking boundaries, effecting transformation, signaling closure' (*Renaissance Self-Fashioning* 197). Greenblatt calls Tamburlaine's project 'an act of radical freedom' but concludes that 'the blasphemy pays homage to the power it insults' (212).
69. On the role of the new commercial theater of Marlowe, Shakespeare, and colleagues in the English Civil War, see esp. Dollimore 3–5.

4 Machevill's Republican Monarchy: Civil War in *The Jew of Malta*, *The Massacre at Paris*, and *Edward II*

1. See Ellis-Fermor 18–22; Cartelli, *Shakespeare, Marlowe* 121–3; MCP 11, 26, 136, 137.
2. Cf. Chedgzoy, who briefly links *LFB* with *JM*, *MP*, and *E2* along the route of 'civil war' and its fall-out, 'political disorder' (248).
3. Cf. Engle, who describes the plot this way: 'At the geopolitical level, Spanish Christians and Turkish Muslims vie for control of the island of Malta as part of an ongoing struggle in the Mediterranean between these powers. The Knights of Malta, caught in the middle, play one side against the other with the canniness that is demanded by their minor economic and military status as a Christian monastic order that rules only one small island' (Intro, *Renaissance Drama* 287).
4. The only critic I have seen who identifies Malta as a republic is Borot: 'This play, far from being a virtuous call to the people to create a republic, repeats Machiavelli's judgement that the three forms of regime are equal; but Marlowe is convinced that they are equally evil. The Maltese island-state is nothing but a parody of the ideal forms of government dreamt of by the humanists. Even Machiavelli's notion of the steadfastness of republics is not spared' (10). This view, however, forgets Machiavelli's own savaging of any republic that violates its ideals. For the most part, critics discuss the island this way: 'Malta itself is a little room, cramped and urban, a fortified Mediterranean island which draws Turks, Christians and Jews alike, all blown in by "Desire of gold"' (Romany and Lindsey, eds. xxvi).
5. Skinner has been discussing this idea for a long time; see *Foundations* 1: 170: 'Machiavelli and his contemporaries...outline a full-scale programme devoted to securing the value of political liberty. One suggestion they make – arising out of their fears about private wealth – is that freedom and poverty tend to go together'. Hence the need for the free state to 'enlarge'. For more on republican fears of 'private wealth', see Skinner, *Foundations* 1: 162; on Machiavelli's vehemence against 'luxurious habits' as an impediment to republican liberty, see 1: 163; on 'usury' as inimical to a republic, see 1: 44. On 'republican liberty and commerce', see also Armitage 39–43 (40).

6. Mullaney influentially discusses Malta as London, specifically discussing the scene (5.1) when Barabas is thrown outside the city walls as a reminder to the audience that the play is being performed in what Mullaney terms 'the topology of early modern London and its Liberties' (59). Grady sees a pertinent analogue in Shakespeare's Athens: 'Republics are associated in Shakespeare with commerce, wealth, and commodities, and with power, warfare, and politics – in brief with emerging modernity and its constituent institutions, a capitalist economy, and nation state/empire system. Athens in this play is a site for all these associations, and they are interconnected' (433).
7. Winch 310. The topic is so important that van Gelderen and Skinner devote three Parts of volume 1 of their monumental two-volume study, *Republicanism*, to 'Republicanism and the Rise of Commerce', which includes no fewer than six essays. Winch's essay concludes the volume, and I've quoted from his last sentence.
8. Machiavelli scholars do not discuss Lucan; neither *The Prince* nor the *Discourses* ever refers to the *Pharsalia*. For a register, see an important recent collection of essays, edited by Skinner and others, *Machiavelli and Republicanism*, which does not include an index entry on 'Lucan'. So far, I have failed to find discussion of these two authors together.
9. Earlier in Book 1, in chapters 17–19, Machiavelli takes up the topic of 'whether or not it is possible to maintain a free government in a corrupt city' (1.18: 67), concluding that it would be difficult or impossible to 'maintain ... a republic in corrupt cities' (1.18: 70), and referring to characters who appear in Marlowe's *Jew* and *Tamburlaine*. Specifically, Machiavelli is discussing whether 'After an Excellent Prince, a Weak Prince Can Maintain Himself' (Book 1, chapter 19 title: 71), and he cites two examples of successful father–son governments, the second of which reads: 'Bajazet, sultan of the Turks, although a man who was more a lover of peace than of war, was able to enjoy the fruits of his father Mahomet's labours; his father, like David, having beaten down his neighbours, left his son a secure kingdom that could easily be maintained with the arts of peace. But if the present ruler, his son Selim, had resembled his father and not his grandfather, that kingdom would have come to ruin, and it is evident that Selim is about to surpass the glory of his grandfather. Let me say with these examples, therefore, that after an excellent prince it is possible to maintain a weak prince, but after a weak prince, it is impossible to maintain any kingdom with another weak prince' (1.19: 72). In Marlowe's *Jew*, Selim-Calymath, or 'Selim II (1566–74), is the son of sultan Suleyman the Magnificent (1527–66), ruler of Turkey during the siege of Malta in 1565' (Gill, ed., *Works* 4: 94). In other words, Selim-Calymath is the son of the 'Selim' discussed by Machiavelli. Selim-Calymath is basically a virtuous person in the play; in this, Marlowe's characterization is consistent with Machiavelli's.
10. For the republican dynamic of friendship, see Chapter 3.
11. For Machiavelli's republican critique of 'hereditary succession', see *Discourses* 1.10: 49.
12. Machiavelli's idea of religion as state theater has an origin in Polybius, *Rise of the Roman Empire* 6.56: 349.
13. Skinner discusses this 'heterodoxy' from the *Discourses*: the rituals of the Catholic Church fail to protect the civic freedom of the republic (*Foundations* 1: 182–3).

14. Phalaris is a common subject for Roman republican writers like Livy (which is why Machiavelli discusses him). See also Cicero, *De officiis* 2.26: 63; 3.29: 94; 3.32: 94. In *The Republic*, Cicero presents Scipio Africanus demarcating the 'defects' of the three types of government, and, after selecting a mixed government, he cites Phalaris as an example of the monarchical tyrant (1.44: 20–1).
15. Skinner shows that the idea was at the center of Italian debate between city republics and principates (*Foundations* 1: 41).
16. My word 'Machiavellian' here retains its meaning of *cunning* but includes Machiavelli's historical commitment to a republican empire.
17. This argument complements Lupton's reading of Marlowe's 'rezoning' project, which clears space for the 'artist' to 'imagine a universe' of 'limited autonomy' on the 'stage' out of 'the civil society of the Jews' ('*Jew of Malta*' 155–6). In *Citizen-Saints*, Lupton recalls, 'In [historical] Malta, the Jewish community, in evidence since Roman times, bore the name *Universitas Judeorum*' (53). In *Commonwealth Principles*, J. Scott adds 'the republic of Israel' to the 'exemplar republics' of 'Athens, Sparta and Rome; Venice, Switzerland and the United Provinces' as actual early modern republics (22).
18. Cf. Greenblatt, *Renaissance Self-Fashioning*: 'A victim at the level of religious and political power, ... [Barabas] is, in effect, emancipated at the level of civil society' (204).
19. For more on Tacitus, see the final section below on *E2*.
20. For the link in Milton between 'Radical Politics and Biblical Republicanism', see Lim (book title).
21. For further detail, see *MCP* 154–5.
22. We probably also need to recall that providence was a key part of Calvinist resistance theory in sixteenth-century English political thought. See Skinner, *Foundations* 2: 166–7, 70, 95, 139–40, 161, 195–6, and esp. 202–5; for providence versus fortune, see 1: 95–6, 145–6; 2: 278.
23. Hence Lesser's apology for Vavasour's royalist appropriation, and the implication: for most critics today, *The Jew* operates in the 'radical' or republican camp.
24. Comparison between the two plays is a staple of *Massacre* criticism, esp. with reference to the similarity between the Guise and Barabas. For a recent example, see Deats, '*Dido* ... and *The Massacre*': 'like his prototype Barabas in *The Jew of Malta*, the Guise revels in his atrocities' (202).
25. In the most recent authoritative analysis, Maguire includes *The Massacre* as one of only four plays out of forty-one typically suspected of being the product of memorial construction (*Suspect Texts* 325). See also Maguire, 'Marlovian Texts' 44–7. For detail of the three most recent modern editions, see Bennett, ed. 170–5; Oliver, ed. lii–lxi; Esche, ed. 293–305.
26. The most authoritative statement of 'the historical veracity of the play' comes from a historian, P. Roberts (431). Weil's 1977 analysis paved the way for subsequent criticism, claiming 'a central position' for *The Massacre* in Marlowe's dramatic canon: 'enough of Marlowe's art has survived to hint that his irony could have been a response to the contradictions of religious warfare, a defence against pain, and an attack upon the very sources of political disorder' (85).
27. In addition to Briggs, see esp. Hadfield, *Literature, Travel* 205, 212, 216–17; P. Roberts 440–1; Kirk 196–77, 209; Hillman 72–111; Deats, '*Dido* ... and *The Massacre*' 201. For other essays consistent with this argument but not focusing specifically on monarchy, see Poole, '*Massacre*' 5.

28. Hadfield, *Republicanism* 61–5: 'Marlowe's connection to this later republican tradition seems to have gone largely unnoticed – as does the link between *The Massacre at Paris* and the history narrated in Lucan's poem' (63). See also Hadfield, *Literature, Travel* 209–12.
29. The quarto version of this speech differs in many particulars, most of them incidental to the present discussion, except one phrase. Whereas the quarto reads 'which is his own free land', the manuscript reads 'the choice of his own free land'.
30. I borrow the phrase from Herman, whose title is 'The Huguenot Republic'.
31. According to Hadfield, *Vindiciae* 'advertise[d] the link between republicanism and Protestant resistance theory' (*Republicanism* 31).
32. Skinner influentially pursues the model of classical republicanism in *Vindiciae*, but just recently McLaren challenged his model by demonstrating the presence not simply of Roman law but of the law of God: 'liberty consists pre-eminently in the freedom to find and follow God, whether or not any given individual avails him or herself of the opportunity: it is the all-important freedom to follow the light within' (42). Thus, McLaren does not deny the presence of Skinner's republican model but argues for the preeminence of the biblical one. I suggest the need to include both.
33. In his edition of *Vindiciae*, Garnett glosses this passage with 'Lucan, *Pharsalia*, 1, 74–5' (ed. 27n97). The following discussion of the presence of Lucan in *Vindiciae* is indebted to Garnett.
34. For the many references to the massacre in Garnett's edition, see his index entry under 'St Bartholomew's Day Massacre' (ed. 218).
35. On this genealogy, see also Giesey, who calls Hotman, Beza, and Mornay 'The Monarchomach Triumvirs' (title).
36. See Kocher, 'Hotman', as well as 'Pamphlet Backgrounds' and 'Pamphlet Backgrounds...Part Two'. *The True and Plain Report* is an English translation of the French original, which appeared in 1573.
37. According to Hadfield, Hotman 'cited Polybius as a key plank in his attack on the tyranny of the French monarchy, arguing...that the "mixed constitution" was the best form of government', and thus revealing 'the close links many made between religious – in this case, Protestant – political thought and republican texts' (*Republicanism* 26). As Wright recalls, the 'origins of republicanism in France' trace to 'the most famous text of the Huguenot resistance, Hotman's *Francogallia* (1573)', which 'attacked royal "tyranny" in the name of a traditional constitution explicitly described as a "mixed" or "blended" government, as expounded by Cicero and Polybius' (290). As J. Scott put the case recently, Hotman's *Francogallia* joins Buchanan's *De Jure Regni apud Scotos* and Hugo Grotius's *Treatise of the Antiquity of the Batavian now Hollandish Republic* as 'the most important' Protestant texts for 'English republicans' of the seventeenth century (*Commonwealth Principles* 192). Scott also calls Tacitus Hotman's 'key classical source' (199), showing how later republican theorists like Harrington remember Hotman's contribution to their political thought (114, 199, 347), including Milton (114).
38. Velema says that the political theorists of the Dutch Republic 'liberally used French Huguenot theories of resistance during the sixteenth-century struggle with Philip II', and that 'they borrowed from Machiavellian republicanism' (10).
39. Skinner further defines the significance of the massacre as bringing 'the French people to the limits of political obligation' (*Foundations* 2: 328); his two-chapter

study (2: 239–348) emphasizes how the massacre forms the precipitating event of Huguenot resistance: 'After 1572 the main task of the Huguenot revolutionaries was to call the natural leaders of the people to arms' (2: 337).
40. The text has a number of names for the religious sect the Guise targets ('Protestants', 'Lutherans', 'Puritans'), but the most recurrent is 'Huguenots'. See, for example, 5.50: 'There shall not be a Huguenot breathe in France'.
41. See Brown, 'Marlowe's Poems': 'France served as a formative intertext between Marlowe and Lucan. The Duke of Guise, from *MP*, is modeled on Lucan's Caesar, and Marlowe read widely in the French and English propaganda produced at the time of the French wars of religion from the late 1580s onwards' (121).
42. Blissett, 'Lucan's Caesar' 565. Oliver cites Kocher's emphasis on the contemporary pamphlets but adds that 'the comparison may have had special interest for Marlowe, who had translated, or was translating, Lucan's account of Caesar's civil wars' (ed. lvii).
43. Editors point out that the Guise's 'Yet Caesar shall go forth' appears verbatim in Shakespeare's *Julius Caesar* 2.2.28 (Oliver, ed. 149; Esche, ed. 398), indicating an intriguing afterlife for Marlowe's Caesarian Guise. For recent commentary, see Logan 32–5.
44. On this topic, see esp. D. Potter, who emphasizes Marlowe's 'contradictory' portrait of Henry III as 'a victim of circumstance as well as a participant in massacre' (88).
45. Two vague echoes – or perhaps remnants of echoes – appear at 3.24, when Navarre says of the mother who has just died in his arms, 'That I with her may die and live again!'; and at 15.35, when the Guise says to the duchess who has just betrayed him, 'fly my presence, if thou look to live'.
46. For my analysis of the soliloquy, emphasizing Spenserian intertextuality, see *MCP* 181–5.
47. Later, the Guise adopts Longinus' most famous image for the violence of the sublime, the whirlwind (1.4: 144), telling Queen Catherine, 'Madam,/I go as whirlwinds rage before a storm' (12.28–9). For post-Renaissance figures like Kant, the pyramids naturally become a subject of the sublime (Shaw 118).
48. For a book-length study of this topic, see Tromly.
49. The topicality of *E2* is a commonplace of criticism. See, for example, White 79–81; Shepherd, *Politics* 118, 122; Sales 113, 123–4, 126; Archer 73; Zunder 53. According to Rowland, ed., 'The topicality of *Edward II* is, paradoxically, central to the way in which [Marlowe's]...distancing effects are achieved' (xxvii). As we shall see, the most important recent study comes from Perry, *Favoritism* 185–202.
50. See Bakeless: 'All critics are generally agreed that this is the maturest of Marlowe's plays and...the latest' (2: 4). As Forker put it more recently, '*Edward II* would seem to mark the high point in Marlowe's dramatic career of emotional complexity subtly and powerfully rendered' (ed. 82). For a dating of 1591–2, see Merchant, ed. xi–xii; Forker, ed. 14–17; Rowland, ed. xiv–xv; Wiggins and Lindsey, eds. xiii–xiv.
51. On the 'political struggle' in *E2* as 'paramount', see Wiggins and Lindsey, eds. xxviii: 'the play's overall unity lies in its political action', which focuses on 'the clash between monarch and nobility' (xxx). Critics writing on *E2* neglect Taciticism.
52. For excerpts from Holinshed, Stowe, and Fabyan, see also Thomas and Tydeman, eds. 341–81.
53. For similar commentary, see Rowland, ed. xxiv–v.

54. On how Tacitus became 'a surrogate for Machiavelli', see also Smuts, 'Roman Historians' 25.
55. See also P. Burke, 'Tacitism, Scepticism'. There is currently no sustained study of Tacitism in Renaissance England but rather a number of important essays. For a book on Tacitus in European Renaissance political thought, see Schellhase. For essays on the Jacobean era, see Bradford; Salmon. On the Elizabethan and Jacobean eras, see Smuts, 'Roman Historians', *Culture and Power*; Levy; Hadfield, *Republicanism* 23, 26, 43–52. On the Elizabethan era alone, see Womersley. On the Elizabethan translation of Tacitus, see also Skinner, 'Classical Liberty' 9–10.
56. Primarily because Taciteans like Savile, and his friends William Camden and Ben Jonson, use Roman historiography not to topple the monarchy but to reform it. See Worden, 'Jonson', esp. 82–3.
57. Recently, Hattaway repeats this argument and adds that the Tacitean 'moment of politic history ... can be located about the time of the composition of Marlowe's translation of Lucan's *Pharsalia* and the publication of Sir Henry Savile's translation of Tacitus' *Histories* in 1591, printed with an epistle that, according to Jonson, was written by the Earl of Essex himself' ('History Play' 18). Hattaway recalls that Savile joined Mornay in arguing that 'it was right to resist a tyrant' (19), effectively transplanting the thesis of *Vindiciae* to English soil during Marlowe's prime.
58. Among the three recent Marlowe biographies, Riggs is most attuned to Marlowe's classical education, focusing on Virgil, Ovid, and Lucan (*World* 44–96), while mentioning Livy (88–9), Cicero (78–83), and Polybius (88–9). For a brief reference to Tacitus, to be discussed below, see 305–6. Editorial citation of Sallust will also be discussed presently.
59. Although Honan mentions the connection, he does not amplify; neither does Kuriyama nor Riggs. Of course, Nicholl argues that in May 1593 Marlowe got caught in the crossfire between the Ralegh faction, to which he belonged, and the Essex faction, which had him murdered (*Reckoning* 195, 295–7, 299, 301, 307, 320, 323, 325) – a conclusion that Kuriyama, Riggs, and Honan all reject.
60. On the strong association between the 'Essex circle' and 'Tacitean commentary' in the 1590s, and the way in which 'the earl's high-profile flame-out focused national attention on the volatility of political intimacy and on the career paths of favorites', see Perry, *Favoritism* 246. In his study of the Edward II fable in the Elizabethan, Jacobean, and Caroline eras, Perry observes that Elizabeth Cary's *History of the Life, Reign and Death of Edward II* (composed 1627, printed 1680) is a 'Tacitean history' (185; see 217).
61. On the 'sheer abundance of classical references' in *Edward II*, see Rowlands, who sees the references as evidence simply of Marlowe's 'university education' (ed. xxvi). Holinshed's story of Edward II does not include classical references (see *Holinshed's Chronicles* 2: 546–88), even though elsewhere such references do occur (e.g., to Cicero at 1: 522, to Caesar at 1: 401, and to Nero at 6: 124).
62. There is no historical evidence of this 'love' relationship but simply of Cicero's loyalty to Octavius (Forker, ed. 181). Yet the representation reminds us that the great republican politician is also a premier theorist of friendship (cf. Stewart, '*Edward II*' 84, 89–90).
63. See Forker, ed. 258; Rowland, ed. 115–16. Forker adds, 'MacLure (in his manuscript notes) suspects that "Marlowe wrote 'Catiline' when he meant 'Sejanus'"' (ed. 258).

64. Womersley discusses the joint publication in 1557 of Alexander Barklaye's translation of Sallust's other work, *Bellum Iugurthinum*, and Thomas Paynell's 'translation of Constantius Felicius' account of the conspiracy of Catiline' (317).
65. Levy, for instance, argues that Daniel, Bacon, Greville, and others turn from Holinshed's providentialism to Tacitus and Machiavelli to 'create ... a new, English political history' (3).
66. Perry's important work on favoritism in *Edward II* supports this argument, situating the play within Collinson's 'monarchical republic' (*Favoritism* 186) to identify the Edward II story as 'a fable about the over-extension of royal prerogative and the resulting precariousness of the monarchical republic' (187): 'Marlowe's innovation' is to 'transform' the 'Edward II story into the preeminent literary vehicle for weighing the shifting native languages of prerogative and dissent' (202).
67. G. Brown, 'Marlowe's Classicism', reminds us that Cuffe inspired Essex to rebellion by discussing Lucan with him (122).
68. Additionally, Forker records an incidental echo of *LFB* 121–2, 'that late deeds would dim/Old triumphs', at 2.1.46: 'Mine old lord' (ed. 186).
69. Editors since W.D. Briggs gloss this passage only with reference to Peele's *Edward I* and of course *2 Tamb* (e.g., Forker, ed. 152).
70. For commentary and criticism, see *MCP* 160–3.
71. P. Burke says that 'an oak tree standing firm against the buffeting of the winds' was a 'favourite' image of the stoics ('Tacitism, Scepticism' 491).
72. On Lucan's oak simile, see W.R. Johnson 73–4. For Lucan's imitation of Virgil's simile, see Ahl 157, 224; Rosner-Siegel 166n5. For the genealogy tracing to Spenser, see L.S. Johnson 69; Cheney, '*Februarie*'.
73. At 4.2.12, Isabella says to her son, Edward III, 'Whither, O whither dost thou bend thy steps', echoing the Roman matron at *LFB* 677–82: 'Paean, whither am I haled? ... /Whither turn I now?'
74. Forker also glosses 5.4.50 ('Feared am I more than loved; let me be feared') with two arch-republican texts: Cicero, *De officiis* 1.28.97; Machiavelli, *Prince*, chpt. 17 (ed. 299).
75. On the republican dynamic of Lodge's play, see Hadfield, *Republicanism* 66–73; for the connection between the play and Lucan, see esp. 71–3.
76. Perry emphasizes this paradigm: Marlowe 'seems to offer up a condensed and exaggerated version of the tension between ... competing conceptions of royal authority as embodied in the ideological conflict between the king and his peers' (*Favoritism* 189–90).
77. As we have seen, in *Vindiciae* Mornay focuses Question 3 on the election of a king: 'God institutes kings. ... [T]he people constitutes kings, confers kingdoms, and approves the election by its vote' (68). Mornay recalls that in ancient Rome 'kings would be chosen by the votes of the people with the approval of the senate' (71). In the *Annals*, Tacitus uses the striking phrase 'imperial election' early on (1: 11), prompting his modern editor to comment: 'a sarcastic oxymoron: the term "election" was not used of selecting imperial heirs, but was the republican word for when a magistrate was voted in by a citizens' assembly. Even under the Empire, such elections were largely in the hands of the Senate, not the Emperor alone' (ed. 252). For commentary on the historical context of Marlowe's phrase 'elected king', see Perry, *Favoritism* 190.
78. Forker cites both events (ed. 144); for commentary, see Perry, *Favoritism*: 'We are invited to think of Gaveston simultaneously in terms of the Earl of Leicester – Elizabeth's controversial favorite who had died in 1588 – and in terms of

Sejanus – Tiberius's favorite, the man responsible for arranging his retreat to Capri' (192–3).
79. Perry titles his unit on the play 'Marlowe's Edward II and the Politics of Passion' (189), while Cartelli in his essay on the play in the *Cambridge Companion to Marlowe* focuses on 'the passions' (158): 'in *Edward II* the passions embodied in the acts and lines of specific characters operate within a very narrow, yet volatile, field of reference, one whose "murky materiality" manifests fewer ties to humoural theory or physiology than to "affective economies" of anger and desire that refuse to accommodate themselves to a moral economy of restraint or control' (159).
80. The concept of the country's good or cause recurs in the discourse of the play, beginning to end (1.4.257; 2.3.1–3; 2.5.23; 2.6.10; 4.4.18; 4.6.65; 5.1.38).
81. See Mortimer's warning to Isabella, 'You must not grow so passionate in speeches' (4.4.15).

5 'Make man to live eternally': The Skeptical Sublime in *Doctor Faustus*

1. The primary historians of skepticism are Schmitt; Popkin; Floridi. I discuss the literary critics below.
2. As Hamlin reveals, the linking of Marlowe with skepticism is a commonplace that has never been studied historically. Although Hamlin focuses on tragedy, he has 'no hesitation discussing several plays which lie outside the conventional bounds of this genre', such as Shakespeare's *Troilus and Cressida* (7).
3. As Hamlin's analysis makes clear, he focuses primarily on moments of 'doubt' in the play, opening space for the present analysis, which tries to get at doubt's sublimity.
4. On 'interior freedom', see also P. Burke, 'Tacitism, Scepticism' 491.
5. Jump, ed., glosses 'chiefest bliss' as 'hopes of salvation' (5); Gill, ed., *Dr Faustus* (New Mermaid, 'A-text') glosses the phrase as 'hope of life after death' (6); Burnett, ed., specifies: 'eternal life' (577). Editors also gloss Marlowe's *polyptoton* of 'graced' in lines 15–17 of the Prologue, which refers both to conferment of the doctor's degree and to entry into the Grace Book at Cambridge University: 'So soon he profits in divinity,/The fruitful plot of scholarism graced,/That shortly he was graced with doctor's name'. See esp. Gill, ed., *Works* 2: 50–1. Finally, the word 'grace' intensifies at the end of the tragedy when Faustus talks with the Old Man, who sees an angel offering Faustus 'a vial full of precious grace' (5.1.53), prompting the magician to express his agon powerfully: 'Hell strives with grace for conquest in my breast' (5.1.63).
6. Although critics used to take the morality play structure at its word, finding an orthodox play about the Christian damnation of an unrepentant sinner, today most identify the morality structure as an ingenious strategy for getting past the censors, a heterodox critique of Christianity. On *DF* as such a 'radical tragedy', see Dollimore 109–19. For a lucid overview of the play's complex rendering of specific 'theological contradictions', see Poole, '*Dr. Faustus*' 103: 'The strident division between ... orthodox and heterodox views in part reflects the conflicted biography of Christopher Marlowe himself' but also the 'Elizabethan era' (106). For the most recent attempt to situate *DF* in terms of Western Christianity, and esp. medieval drama, see J. Parker 228–45.

7. As we have seen (esp. Chapter 1), Longinus identifies the sublime utterance in a literary work as a site of authorship, when the author speaks through his character. Few texts more formally exhibit this principle than *DF*.
8. New Historicists and cultural materialists emphasize the 'politics' of *DF*, including the politics of its theology: Greenblatt, *Renaissance Self-Fashioning*; Dollimore; Shepherd, *Politics*; Sinfield, *Faultlines*; Marcus, 'Textual Indeterminacy'. The argument most pertinent here comes from Minshull: Marlowe 'constructs an ironic subtext which points to his awareness of the Faust myth as a political construct shoring up absolutist rule, with Faustus's fate mirroring that of dissidents who fell foul of state authority' ('Dissident Subtext' 194). Thus, Mephistopheles is a state 'informer' (201) and hell 'State imprisonment' (199): Marlowe 'portrays the exercise of absolutist authority as repressive, entrenched, unjust, and implacable' (205). Like many political critics, Minshull does not discuss what *DF* posits as an *alternative* to absolutist rule.
9. Critics have long understood the importance of liberty in *DF*, as well as its inversion, bondage and limitation: for example, H. Levin, *Overreacher* 134, 162. The seminal study comes from Garber, 'Enclosure', esp. 11–12, 17–18, 20–1. For a recent account of the play's rehearsal of Elizabethan 'debates over free will and predestination', see Poole, '*Dr. Faustus*' 97.
10. The most influential example is Norbrook.
11. Sedley mentions 'liberty' in passing (125), and he shows how Montaigne came to fix on Tacitus (144). In his discussion of Elizabeth Cary's *Mariam*, Hamlin refers to Montaigne's observation about Lucan's criticism of Julius Caesar (197), while Sedley discusses Du Bellay's use of the *Pharsalia* in his *Antiquitez de Rome*: 'Like Lucan, Du Bellay organizes his description around a paradox that challenges the opposition between grandeur and ruin' (38–9; see also 128).
12. See esp. Bevington and Rasmussen, eds., *DF* 62–70; Gill, ed., *Works* 2: xv–xxi; Keefer, ed. lx–xlix. Critics are divided over the question of authorship, with many arguing that Marlowe worked with a co-author (esp. Bevington and Rasmussen, eds. 70), although some argue that Marlowe wrote the whole play (Eriksen 19). Finally, critics remain divided over the date of the play, with some arguing for an earlier date, 1589, and some a later one, 1592, with most today arguing for the former (Bevington and Rasmussen, eds. 1–3; Gill, ed., *Works* 2: xii; Keefer, ed. lv–lx). I argue for a dynamic process of authorship, which allows for Marlowe's penning of the play across his career (*MCP* 192–3).
13. Marcus originally presented her findings in a 1989 article, 'Textual Indeterminacy'.
14. Marcus sees *DF* functioning along the '"ravishing" razor edge between exaltation and transgression' ('Textual Indeterminacy' 5) – perhaps her version of sublimity and skepticism. She also suggests that the various revisions of the play kept 'Marlowe sounding like himself even decades after his physical demise' (15).
15. I am grateful to Professor Marcus for encouraging me to say so (personal communication).
16. On the background of learned Renaissance magic in the play, see esp. Mebane; Gatti (on Bruno); Eriksen; *MCP* 194–201; G. Roberts.
17. Following Ellis-Fermor, Fuller glosses 'Thessalian drugs' at *1 Tamb* 5.1.133 with '*Pharsalia* (Book 6)' (ed. 217). Moreover, Hardie cites Greenblatt on Marlowe to discuss Lucan's Erichtho (109n36).
18. Barber discerns a hint of orgasm in Marlowe's sexualized imagery – 'an almost unutterable desire' (108) – thus bringing the representation into alignment with

the gripping fornication that Erichtho is wont to perform on spiritless cadavers (*Pharsalia* 6.564–9), as we shall see.
19. Garber, 'Here's nothing writ', finds her title phrase here to emphasize Faustus' role as 'a writer' (310).
20. I also discuss this Lucanian fascination with the theatricality of blood in Shakespeare's *Rape of Lucrece*; see *Poet-Playwright*, chpt. 4. On *DF*'s use of magic as a metaphor for 'theater', see Orgel, 'Tobacco and Boys' 569. In *World*, Riggs sees 'the mutilated body that never appears at the end of *Doctor Faustus*' as an instance of what Marlowe 'shared' with Lucan: a 'commitment to a narrative strategy of deferral', by which the 'narrator actively resists any interpretation that would predetermine the outcome of his story' (308).
21. See Hattaway, 'Theology': after the opening monologue, Faustus 'spends the rest of the play coming to grips with his intellectual freedom' (59).
22. On 'Ovidian Physics' in *DF*, see Poole (essay title), by which she means 'an understanding of the world in which matter and space are perceived as fluid and plastic' (207): 'Ovidian physics is at once poetic, a product of the imagination, and material, a new way of experiencing the world' (210); it is 'a mode of thought and perception that does not recognize a division of imagination and reality' (212).
23. Conventionally, critics do not read the opening monologue for its discourse of immortality, but rather as 'a short treatise on a familiar Renaissance theme, the vanity of human knowledge' (Hattaway, 'Theology' 54). For an excellent recent close analysis, see Halpern 467–71, who nonetheless skips over immortality to concentrate on capital.
24. As Hardie puts it, 'Erictho is not content to call up ghosts, but instead brings the corpse itself back to life' (108).
25. Skinner, *Foundations*, includes a unit on the humanist attack on Justinian law that bears on Faustus' complaint: 'Justinian's code began to appear under the sustained philological gaze of the humanists as little more than a "battered relic" – a loosely assembled and poorly transmitted series of enactments designed for a long-defunct Empire' (1: 207). Later, Skinner adds that Justinian's Code blocks civic liberty by equating the *princeps* with the Holy Roman Emperor (2: 351).
26. On death as annihilation as a model for Renaissance England, see Watson.
27. On *DF* occupying 'an intermediate space between Agrippa and Bacon', see Halpern 482.
28. In *Foundations*, Skinner calls the Florentine model of '*vir virtutus*' (1: 92) as exemplified in Pico's *Oration on the Dignity of Man* a 'Faustian figure' who possesses 'godlike qualities' and a thirst for 'honour, glory and praise' (1: 98–9). Critics have long situated Marlowe's play in the 'ebb and flow of exultant individualism and despairing fatalism' as represented in the opposition of Pico and Calvin (Mahood 64; see *MCP* 199–200), without considering the larger republican context indicated by Skinner.
29. On friendship and republicanism, see Chapters 3 and 4.
30. According to Skinner, in 1527 Charles V 'smashed' the 'attempts of the Republicans to re-establish a popular government in Rome' by sacking the city; three years later, the Emperor sacked the Republic of France (*Foundations* 1: 186).
31. In *Sacred Rhetoric*, Shuger helps us understand that Marlowe might be deploying the Longinian sublime as a response to Calvinism: 'Longinian sublimity…possesses strong sacral overtones. It lifts its hearers "near the mighty mind of God" (36.1) and intimates "the object of our creation" (35.3)' (38). Shuger reminds us that Longinus

cites the Book of Genesis as an example of the sublime (38), and she notes similarities between 'Longinus and Augustine', for both of whom 'emotion is...the mind's response to the divine', and for whom 'passion or sublimity' becomes 'the sole criterion' for the grand style (9).
32. There might be a Machiavellian context for Faustus' critique of the Pope and subsequent valuation of Helen of Troy. As Skinner observes, in the *Discourses* Machiavelli criticizes the Vatican in favor of classical Greece (*Foundations* 1: 167).
33. Critics routinely see the sublime operating in the Helen scene. See Barber 105, 111: here, 'Marlowe's poetry is sublime' (123).
34. Worden, 'English Republicanism', helps contextualize Marlowe's representation here: 'The republicans' confidence in "reason" seems to contrast markedly with the Calvinist pessimism of the Puritans and nonconformists with whom they often found themselves in alliance. Equally, republican enthusiasm for classical and pagan civilization looks barely compatible with Puritan fundamentalism' (471). Worden adds, 'Republicanism always had affinities with the Arminian and Socinian criticism of Calvinist theological rigour' (474).
35. On the *Symposium* as a subtext here, see *MCP* 195–201.
36. I quote Joyce's translation because it is so graphic.
37. Kott gets at the paradox of the Helenian sublime: 'All of us who are old enough to know: life with Helen is a disaster, but life without her is a void' (17).
38. Healy reports that in all the productions he's seen, 'Even if you agree with the old man's endeavours, visually, when placed beside Helen, the emotional and aesthetic sympathy was with her', and he goes on to wonder whether 'it was the same in early modern productions' ('*Doctor Faustus*' 183). Similarly, Halpern concludes, 'Faustus's death-drive, his capacity for self-cancellation, is a mark of strength.... Marlowe's theater of night makes something out of the void': 'a repository of emptiness' (490).
39. Cf. Weiskel: 'The Sublime...revives as God withdraws from an immediate participation in the experience of man' (qtd. Phillips in E. Burke xi).
40. Theorists of the sublime, from Burnet and Burke, to Kant and Žižek, focus on the human *subject*, his or her experience, whether divine or doubtful, Romantic or post-Romantic. Yet Longinus is unusual in that he operates free of the later philosophical obsession with subjectivity to emphasize a larger literary process, which begins with the *object* of the subject's art, an imitated author's work, and with what we might call the *post-object*, the subject's *reader*. Coleridge's concern with the infinite is one thing, and Longinus, Lucan, and Marlowe share it. But Longinus is the first to insist on *fame* as an afterlife for the sublime, and this literary process, I suggest, moves beyond the subject as a site for the sublime. Thus, Marlowe does not solve the problem of the sublime, but he does discover in Lucan (and in Ovid) a way out – evidently, the only way he had available: poetic immortality.
41. Cf. *Amores* 1.13.40; *OE* 1.13.40. See *MCP* 217–20. Marlowe did not need to wait for the post-Kantian wave, the German and English Romantics, to know that 'Poetry...will enable us to comprehend the sublime', or discover in the art of poetry the missing 'bridge' to the 'gulf between noumena and phenomena,...idea and reality, mind and world' (Shaw 92). For a different, though complementary, model of authorship in *DF*, see Halpern, who emphasizes that 'Faustus's metaphysical yearnings...are clearly haunted' by 'Marlowe's wish to be adequately reimbursed for his labor' as a 'playwright' (459–60): '*Doctor Faustus* constructs an

implicit but carefully weighed parallel between Faustus's selling of his soul and Marlowe's selling of his play', so that finally '*Doctor Faustus* is in part an exploration of "dispossessive authorship"' (462).
42. See Barber on this line: 'the author is still alive. ... Marlowe has earned an identity apart from his hero's – he is the author' (126)

Afterword: The Afterlife of Marlowe's Republican Authorship – Nashe to Milton

1. In addition to Sedley, and Norbrook (137), for Milton's historic role in the history of the sublime, see Shaw 33–6: 'For Milton the sublime is identified with the transformational power of language', so 'in *Paradise Lost* poetic speech has the power to make or unmake a world', and 'Christian language has the power to raise poet and reader above the merely pagan' (33), including a 'Longinian emphasis on rhetorical flight' (34). For, as Milton writes: 'my advent'rous Song.../...with no middle flight intends to soar/Above th' Aonian Mount' (*PL* 1.13–15).
2. On this 'paradox or tension', see Bennett: through a 'discourse of the sublime', the author puts himself at 'the centre of aesthetic discourse while at the same time removing or annulling his or her autonomy and authority with an experience of divine afflatus, of inspiration' (66).
3. The first to identify Nashe's subject here, 'Aretine', as Marlowe, were L. and E. Feasey. For recent commentary on the validity of the identification, see Honan 362–3. On Marlowe and Nashe more broadly, see Bednarz, esp. 95–9.
4. See *LFB* 531 and 605 for 'lightning', and *LFB* 624 for 'entrails'. For my commentary on Lucan's commitment to the grim national truth of the body's entrails at *LFB* 613–28, see Cheney, *Poet-Playwright* 118–20.
5. The following discussion of Milton re-works material in Cheney, 'Milton, Marlowe, and Lucan'. For Marlowe in the seventeenth century, see L. Potter, 'Civil War'; Shawcross; Riddell. For Marlowe's reception more broadly, see L. Potter, 'Theatre and Film'; Hopkins, 'Reception'.
6. In his influential edition of Milton, Hughes comments: 'The most famous of many assertions of the doctrine is by Marlowe's Mephistophelis', quoting *DF* 2.1.117–19, and citing St. Bonaventura, who 'said (*Sentences* II, d, vi, 2, 2) that "the devils carry the fire of hell wherever they go"' and St. Thomas Aquinas, who 'declared (*Summa Theol.* I, q. 64, art. 4) that they are "bound with the fire of hell while they are in the dark atmosphere of this world"' (ed. 277–8). Honan adds Calvin's *Commentary on 1 John*: 'we shall always carry hell about within us', since 'hell reigns where there is no peace with God' (211).
7. Blissett, 'Caesar and Satan', identifies Satan's speech as Lucanian in character (232). Studies of Milton's republicanism are legion, but I have been most influenced by Norbrook: on Lucan, see chpt. 1, and on Milton see esp. chpts. 3 and 10. See also *Milton and Republicanism*, ed. Armitage, Himy, and Skinner, which, despite its groundbreaking research, does not include Marlowe in its index and refers to Lucan only twice (145, 224).
8. Gorecki demonstrates that Satan's eight-day astronomical journey in Book 9 of *Paradise Lost* (63–7) is indebted to Faustus' eight-day journey in the Prologue to Act 3.
9. At least eight times in his award-winning 2003 monograph, Forsyth charts this episteme by turning to Milton's 'deliberate echoes' of the Marlovian concept of

an inward hell (56–7, 60–1, 65–6, 133, 149–51, 152–5 [a section titled 'Faustus and the Abyss'], 165, 316 [qt. from 153]), even though Forsyth does not link the topic with Milton's republicanism.
10. Cf. Norbrook: 'While he [Milton's God] enjoys the panoply of kingship, he is ready to undergo sacrifice for the general good.... Milton's God, then, is a king with distinct overtones of a republican founding legislator.... Satan is using a republican language for a speech-act designed to consolidate his personal power' (474, 477, 478).
11. For help in formulating this idea, I am indebted to Laura Knoppers (personal communication).
12. For Milton as the center of this genealogy, see Teskey 1.
13. According to Dabbs, the 'Marlowe' we know today is fundamentally a nineteenth-century invention.

Works Cited

Ahern, Charles F., Jr. 'Daedalus and Icarus in the *Ars Amatoria*'. *Harvard Studies in Classical Philology* 92 (1989): 273–96.
Ahl, Frederick M. *Lucan: An Introduction*. Ithaca: Cornell UP, 1976.
Altieri, Joanne. '*Hero and Leander*: Sensible Myth and Lyric Subjectivity'. *John Donne Journal* 8 (1989): 151–66.
Altman, Joel B. *The Tudor Play of Mind: Rhetorical Inquiry and the Development of Elizabethan Drama*. Berkeley: U of California P, 1978.
Anonymous. *Tragedy of Caesar and Pompey or Caesar's Revenge*. Ed. F.S. Boas. Oxford: Malone Society, 1911.
Archer, John Michael. *Sovereignty and Intelligence: Spying and Court Culture in the English Renaissance*. Stanford: Stanford UP, 1993.
Aristotle. *The Basic Works of Aristotle*. Ed. Richard McKeon. New York: Random House, 1941.
Armitage, David. 'Empire and Liberty: A Republican Dilemma'. Van Gelderen and Skinner, eds. *Republicanism*. 2: 29–46.
Armitage, David, Armand Himy, and Quentin Skinner, eds. *Milton and Republicanism*. Cambridge: Cambridge UP, 1995.
Ascham, Roger. *The Scholemaster*. London, 1570.
Ashton, J.W. 'The Fall of Icarus'. *Renaissance Studies in Honour of Hardin Craig*. Stanford: Stanford UP, 1941. 153–9.
Augustine, St. *Confessions*. Trans. Henry Chadwick. Oxford World's Classics. Oxford: Oxford UP, 1991.
Babb, Howard S. 'Policy in Marlowe's *The Jew of Malta*'. *ELH* 24 (1957): 85–94.
Bakeless, John. *The Tragicall History of Christopher Marlowe*. 2 vols. 1942, Hamden, CT: Archon Books, 1964.
Baldwin, William. *William Shakespere's Small Latine & Lesse Greeke*. 2 vols. Urbana: U of Illinois P, 1944.
Bancroft, Richard. *A Survey of the Pretended Holy Discipline*. London, 1593.
Barber, C.L. *Creating Elizabethan Tragedy: The Theater of Marlowe and Kyd*. Ed. Richard P. Wheeler. Chicago: U of Chicago P, 1988.
Bartels, Emily C. *Spectacles of Strangeness: Imperialism, Alienation, and Marlowe*. Philadelphia: U of Pennsylvania P, 1993.
Barthes, Roland. 'The Death of the Author'. *The Norton Anthology of Theory and Criticism*. Ed. Vincent B. Leitch, et al. New York: Norton, 2001. 1466–70.
Bawcutt, N.W. 'Machiavelli and Marlowe's *The Jew of Malta*'. *Renaissance Drama* 3 (1970): 3–49.
——. 'The "Myth of Gentillet" Reconsidered: An Aspect of Elizabethan Machiavellianism'. *Modern Language Review* 99 (2004): 863–74.
——, ed. '*The Jew of Malta*': *Christopher Marlowe*. Manchester: Manchester UP, 1978.
Beacon, Richard. *Solon His Follie, or a Politique Discourse Touching the Reformation of Common-Weales Conquered, Declined or Corrupted* (1594). Ed. Clare Carroll and Vincent Carey. Binghampton: MRTS, 1996.
Bednarz, James P. 'Marlowe and the English Literary Scene'. Cheney, ed. *Cambridge Companion to Marlowe*. 90–105.
Bennett, Andrew. *The Author*. New Critical Idiom. London: Routledge, 2005.

Bennett, H.S., ed. *'The Jew of Malta' and 'The Massacre at Paris'*. New York: Dial P, 1931.
Benston, Kimberly. 'Beauty's Just Applause: Dramatic Form and the Tamburlanian Sublime'. Bloom, ed. *Christopher Marlowe*. 207–27.
Berek, Peter. '*Tamburlaine*'s Weak Sons: Imitation as Interpretation Before 1593'. *Renaissance Drama* 13 (1982): 55–82.
Berry, Philippa. *Of Chastity and Power: Elizabethan Literature and the Unmarried Queen*. London: Routledge and Kegan Paul, 1989.
Bevington, David, ed. *English Renaissance Drama: A Norton Anthology*. New York: Norton, 2002.
Bevington, David, and Eric Rasmussen, eds. *Christopher Marlowe: 'Tamburlaine, Parts I and II', 'Doctor Faustus', A- and B-Texts, 'The Jew of Malta', 'Edward II'*. Oxford: Clarendon, 1995.
——, eds. *'Doctor Faustus': A- and B-texts (1604, 1616)*. Revels Plays. Manchester: Manchester UP, 1993.
Blissett, William. 'Caesar and Satan'. *Journal of the History of Ideas* 18 (1957): 221–32.
——. 'Lucan's Caesar and the Elizabethan Villain'. *Studies in Philology* 53 (1956): 553–75.
Bloom, Harold, ed. *Christopher Marlowe*. New York: Chelsea House, 1986.
Bolgar, R.R. *The Classical Heritage and Its Beneficiaries*. Cambridge: Cambridge UP, 1954.
Boralevi, Lea Campos. 'Classical Foundational Myths of European Republicanism: The Jewish Commonwealth'. Van Gelderen and Skinner, eds. *Republicanism*. 1: 247–62.
Borot, Luc. 'Machiavellian Diplomacy and Dramatic Developments in Marlowe's *Jew of Malta*'. *Cahiers Elisabethains* 33 (1988): 1–11.
Bowers, Rick. 'Hysterics, High Camp, and *Dido Queene of Carthage*'. Deats and Logan, eds. *Marlowe's Empery*. 95–106.
Braden, Gordon. *The Classics and English Renaissance Poetry*. New Haven: Yale UP, 1978.
Bradford, Alan T. 'Stuart Absolutism and the "Utility" of Tacitus'. *Huntington Library Quarterly* 46 (1983): 127–55.
Brennan, Alicia. 'Marlowe's Discourse of Dissolution in *Lucan's First Book*'. Honors Thesis. Pennsylvania State University, 2004.
Briggs, Julia. 'Marlowe's *Massacre at Paris*: A Reconsideration'. *Review of English Studies* 34 (1983): 257–78.
Briggs, William Dinsmore, ed. *Marlowe's 'Edward II'*. London: David Nutt, 1914.
Brooke, C.F. Tucker, ed. *The Works of Christopher Marlowe*. Oxford: Clarendon, 1910.
Brown, Georgia E. 'Marlowe's Poems and Classicism'. Cheney, ed. *Cambridge Companion to Marlowe*. 106–26.
——. *Redefining Elizabethan Literature*. Cambridge: Cambridge UP, 2004.
Bruster, Douglas. '"Come to the Tent Again": "The Passionate Shepherd", Dramatic Rape and Lyric Time'. *Criticism* 33 (1991): 49–72.
Burke, Edmund. *A Philosophical Enquiry into the Origin of Our Ideas of the Sublime and Beautiful*. Oxford World's Classics. Oxford: Oxford UP, 1990.
Burke, Peter. 'Tacitism'. *Tacitus*. Ed. T.A. Dorey. New York: Basic Books, 1969. 149–71.
——. 'Tacitism, Scepticism, and Reason of State'. *The Cambridge History of Political Thought 1450–1700*. Ed. J.H. Burns. Cambridge: Cambridge UP, 1991. 479–98.
Burnet, Thomas. *The Sacred Theory of the Earth*. Intro. Basil Willey. Carbondale: Southern Illinois UP, 1965.
Burnett, Mark Thornton. '*Tamburlaine the Great, Parts One* and *Two*'. Cheney, ed. *Cambridge Companion to Marlowe*. 127–43.

——, ed. *Christopher Marlowe: The Complete Plays*. Everyman Library. London: Dent; Rutland, VT: Tuttle, 1999.

Burrow, Colin. *Epic Romance: Homer to Milton*. Oxford: Clarendon, 1993.

Campbell, Marion. '"Desunt Nonnulla": The Construction of Marlowe's *Hero and Leander* as an Unfinished Poem'. *ELH* 51 (1984): 241–68.

Carrubba, Robert W. 'The White Swan and Daedalian Icarus'. *Eranos* 80 (1982): 145–9.

Cartelli, Thomas. '*Edward II*'. Cheney, ed., *Cambridge Companion to Marlowe*. 158–73.

——. *Marlowe, Shakespeare, and the Economy of Theatrical Experience*. Philadelphia: U of Pennsylvania P, 1991.

Castiglione, Baldassare. *The Book of the Courtier*. Trans. Sir Thomas Hoby. London: Dent, 1974.

Chapman, George. *The Works of George Chapman: Plays*. Ed. Richard Herne Shepherd. 3 vols. London: Chatto and Windus, 1911–24.

Chaucer, Geoffrey. *The Riverside Chaucer*. Ed. Larry D. Benson, et al. Boston: Houghton Mifflin, 1987. Based on *The Works of Geoffrey Chaucer*, ed. F.N. Robinson. 2nd edn. Boston: Houghton Mifflin, 1957.

Chedgzoy, Kate. 'Marlowe's Men and Women: Gender and Sexuality'. Cheney, ed. *Cambridge Companion to Marlowe*. 245–61.

Cheney, Patrick. 'Biographical Representations: Marlowe's Life of the Author'. Mulryne and Kozuka, eds. *Shakespeare, Marlowe, Jonson*. 183–204.

——. 'Introduction: Authorship in Marlowe's Poems'. Cheney and Striar, eds. *Collected Poems of Christopher Marlowe*. 1–25.

——. 'Introduction: Marlowe in the Twenty-First Century'. Cheney, ed. *Cambridge Companion to Marlowe*. 1–24.

——. *Marlowe's Counterfeit Profession: Ovid, Spenser, Counter-Nationhood*. Toronto: U of Toronto P, 1997.

——. 'Milton, Marlowe, and Lucan: The English Authorship of Republican Liberty'. *Milton Studies* 49 (2008): 1–19.

——. '"Novells of His Devise": Chaucerian and Virgilian Career Paths in Spenser's *Februarie* Eclogue'. Cheney and De Armas, eds. *European Literary Careers*. 231–67.

——. Review of Harraway, *Re-Citing Marlowe*. *Renaissance Quarterly* 54 (2001): 1666–72.

——. *Shakespeare, National Poet-Playwright*. Cambridge: Cambridge UP, 2004.

——. *Shakespeare's Literary Authorship*. Cambridge: Cambridge UP, 2008.

——. 'Teaching Marlowe's Translation of Ovid's *Amores*'. *Approaches to Teaching Ovid and Ovidianism*. Ed. Cora Fox and Barbara Boyd. New York: Modern Language Association, 2008, forthcoming.

——, ed. *The Cambridge Companion to Christopher Marlowe*. Cambridge: Cambridge UP, 2004.

——, and Brian J. Striar, ed. *The Collected Poems of Christopher Marlowe*. New York: Oxford UP, 2006.

——, and Frederick A. de Armas, eds. *European Literary Careers: The Author from Antiquity to the Renaissance*. Toronto: U of Toronto P, 2002.

Cicero. *On Obligations*. Trans. P.G. Walsh. Oxford World's Classics. Oxford: Oxford UP, 2000.

——. *The Republic* and *The Laws*. Trans. Niall Rudd. Oxford World's Classics. Oxford: Oxford UP, 1998.

Collinson, Patrick. 'The Monarchical Republic of Queen Elizabeth I'. *The Tudor Monarchy*. Ed. John Guy. London: Arnold, 1997. 110–34.

——. '"The State as Monarchical Commonwealth": "Tudor" England'. *Journal of Historical Sociology* 15 (2002): 89–95.

Cope, Jackson I. *Dramaturgy of the Daemonic*. Baltimore: Johns Hopkins UP, 1984.
Coiro, Ann Baynes. *Robert Herrick's 'Hesperides' and the Epigram Book Tradition*. Baltimore: Johns Hopkins UP, 1988.
Crosland, Jessie. 'Lucan in the Middle Ages'. *Modern Language Review* 25 (1930): 32–51.
Cunningham, J.S., ed. *'Tamburlaine the Great': Christopher Marlowe*. Revels Plays. Manchester: Manchester UP; Baltimore: Johns Hopkins UP, 1981.
Cunningham, Karen. ' "Forsake Thy King and Do but Join with Me": Marlowe and Treason'. Deats and Logan, eds. *Marlowe's Empery*. 133–49.
Cutts, John P. 'The Marlowe Canon'. *Notes and Queries* ns 6 204 (1959): 71–4.
Dabbs, Thomas. *Reforming Marlowe: The Nineteenth-Century Canonization of a Renaissance Dramatist*. London: Associated UP, 1991.
Day, Angel. *The English Secretary or Methods of Writing Epistles and Letters*. London, 1599.
Day, Henry. *The Neronian Sublime*. D Phil. Cambridge U, forthcoming.
Deats, Sara Munson. *'Dido, Queen of Carthage* and *The Massacre at Paris'*. Cheney, ed. *Cambridge Companion to Marlowe*. 193–206.
——, and Robert A. Logan, eds. *Marlowe's Empery: Expanding His Critical Contexts*. Newark: U of Delaware P; London: Associated UP, 2002.
De Bolla, Peter. *The Discourse of the Sublime: Readings in History, Aesthetics, and the Subject*. Oxford: Basil Blackwell, 1989.
DeNeef, A. Leigh. *'This Poetick Liturgie': Robert Herrick's Ceremonial Mode*. Durham: Duke UP, 1974.
Dilke, O.A.W. 'Lucan and English Literature'. *Neronians and Flavians: Silver Latin I*. Ed. D.R. Dudley. London: Routledge, 1972. 83–112.
Dollimore, Jonathan. *Radical Tragedy: Religion, Ideology and Power in the Drama of Shakespeare and His Contemporaries*. Chicago: U of Chicago P, 1984.
Downie, J.A., and J.T. Parnell, eds. *Constructing Christopher Marlowe*. Cambridge: Cambridge UP, 2000.
Drakakis, John, and Naomi Conn Liebler, eds. *Tragedy*. London: Longman, 1998.
Dutton, Richard. 'Marlowe: Censorship and Construction'. *Licensing, Censorship and Authorship in Early Modern English: Buggeswords*. Basingstoke: Palgrave, 2000. 62–89.
Dzelzainis, Martin. 'Milton's Politics'. *Milton, Rights, and Liberties*. Ed. Christophe Tournu and Neil Forsyth.
Eliot, T.S. *Elizabethan Dramatists*. London: Faber and Faber, 1963.
Ellis-Fermor, U.M. *Christopher Marlowe*. Hamden, CT: Archon Books, 1967.
——, ed. *Tamburlaine the Great*. New York: Dial P, 1930.
Elyot, Thomas, Sir. *Bibliotheca Eliotae Eliotis librarie*. London, 1542.
Engle, Lars. 'Introduction'. *Jew of Malta*. Bevington, ed. *English Renaissance Drama*. 287–92.
——. 'Introduction'. *Tamburlaine the Great , Part 1*. Bevington, ed. *English Renaissance Drama*. 183–8.
Eriksen, Roy T. *'The Forme of Faustus Fortunes': A Study of 'The Tragedie of Doctor Faustus' (1616)*. Oslo: Solum Forlag A.S.; Atlantic Highlands, NJ: Humanites P International, 1987.
Erne, Lukas. *Beyond 'The Spanish Tragedy': A Study of the Works of Thomas Kyd*. Manchester: Manchester UP, 2001.
——. 'Biography, Mythography, and Criticism: The Life and Works of Christopher Marlowe'. *Modern Philology* 103 (2005): 28–50.
Esche, Edward J., ed. *'The Massacre at Paris with the Death of the Duke of Guise'*. Vol 5 of Gill, ed., *Works*. Oxford: Clarendon, 1998.

Evans, Robert C. 'Johnson's Critical Heritage'. *The Cambridge Companion to Ben Jonson.* Ed. Richard Harp and Stanley Stewart. Cambridge: Cambridge UP, 2000. 188–201.
Fantham, Elaine, ed. *Lucan: 'De Bello Civili': Book II.* Cambridge: Cambridge UP, 1992.
Farrell, Joseph. 'Greek Lives and Roman Careers in the Classical *Vita* Tradition'. Cheney and de Armas, eds. *European Literary Careers.* 24–46.
Feasey, Lynette, and Eveline Feasey. 'The Validity of the Baines Document'. *Notes and Queries* 194 (1949): 514–17.
Feeney, D.C. *The Gods in Epic: Poets and Critics of the Classical Tradition.* Oxford: Clarendon, 1991.
Fehrenbach, Robert J., Lea Ann Boone, and Mario A. Di Cesare, eds. *A Concordance to the Plays, Poems, and Translations of Christopher Marlowe.* Ithaca: Cornell UP, 1982.
Fink, Zera S. *The Classical Republicans: An Essay in the Recovery of a Pattern of Thought in Seventeenth Century England.* Evanston: Northwestern UP, 1945.
Forker, Charles R., ed. *'Edward the Second': Christopher Marlowe.* Revels Plays. Manchester: Manchester UP, 1994.
Forsyth, Neil. *The Satanic Epic.* Princeton: Princeton UP, 2003.
Forsythe, R.S. *'The Passionate Shepherd*; and English Poetry'. *PMLA* 40 (1925): 692–742.
Foucault, Michel. 'What is an Author?' *The Foucault Reader.* Ed. Paul Rabinow. New York: Pantheon Books, 1984. 101–20.
Friedenreich, Kenneth, Roma Gill, and Constance B. Kuriyama, eds. *'A Poet and a Filthy Play-Maker': New Essays on Christopher Marlowe.* New York: AMS P, 1988.
Fuller, David. *'Tamburlaine the Great, Parts 1 and 2'.* Vol 5 of Gill, ed., *Works.* Oxford: Clarendon, 1998.
Garber, Marjorie. '"Here's Nothing Writ": Scribe, Script, and Circumspection in Marlowe's Plays'. *Theatre Journal* 36 (1984): 301–20.
——. '"Infinite Riches in a Little Room": Closure and Enclosure in Marlowe'. Kernan, ed. *Two Renaissance Mythmakers.* 3–21.
Gatti, Hilary. *The Renaissance Drama of Knowledge: Giordano Bruno in England.* London: Routledge, 1989.
Genette, Gerard. *Palimpsests: Literature in the Second Degree.* Trans. Channa Newman and Claude Doublinsky. 1982; Lincoln: U of Nebraska P, 1997.
Geneva Bible: A Facsimile Edition. Ed. Lloyd E. Berry. Madison: U of Wisconsin P, 1969.
Getty, Laura J. 'Circumventing Petrarch: Subreading Ovid's *Tristia* in Spenser's *Amoretti*'. *Philological Quarterly* 79 (2000): 293–314.
Gibbons, Brian. 'Unstable Proteus: Marlowe's *The Tragedy of Dido Queen of Carthage*'. *Christopher Marlowe.* Ed. Brian Morris. New York: Hill and Wang, 1968. 27–46.
Giesey, Ralph E. 'The Monarchomach Triumvirs: Hotman, Beza and Mornay'. *Bibliotheque d' Humanisme et Renaissance* 32 (1970): 41–56.
Gilbert, Allan H., ed. *Literary Criticism: Plato to Dryden.* Detroit: Wayne State UP, 1962, 1967.
Gill, Roma. 'Marlowe, Lucan, and Sulpitius'. *Review of English Studies* 24 (1973): 401–13.
——, ed. *The Complete Works of Christopher Marlowe.* 5 vols. Oxford: Clarendon, 1987–1998.
——, ed. *'Doctor Faustus'*: A-Text. London: A and C Black; New York: Norton, 1965.
——, ed. *'The Jew of Malta'.* Oxford: Clarendon, 1995. Vol. 4 of Gill, ed., *Works.*
——, ed. *Poems and Translations and 'Dido, Queen of Carthage'.* Oxford: Clarendon, 1987. Vol. 1 of Gill, ed., *Works.*
Gillies, John. *'Tamburlaine* and Renaissance Geography'. Sullivan, Cheney, and Hadfield, eds. *Early Modern English Drama.* 35–49.

Godshalk, William L. 'Marlowe and Lucan'. *Notes and Queries* 18 (1971): 13.
Goldberg, Jonathan. *Sodometries: Renaissance Texts and Modern Sexuality*. Stanford: Stanford UP, 1992.
Goldman, Michael. 'Marlowe and the Histrionics of Ravishment'. Kernan, ed. *Two Renaissance Mythmakers*. 22–40.
Gorecki, John. 'A Marlovian Precedent for Satan's Astronomical Journey in *Paradise Lost* IX. 63–7'. *Milton Quarterly* 17 (1983): 45–7.
Gosson, Stephen. *The School of Abuse*. London, 1579.
Grady, Hugh. '*Timon of Athens*: The Dialectic of Usury, Nihilism, and Art'. *A Companion to Shakespeare's Works: The Tragedies*. Ed. Richard Dutton and Jean Howard. Oxford: Blackwell, 2003. 430–51.
Grantley, Darryll, and Peter Roberts, eds. *Christopher Marlowe and English Renaissance Culture*. Aldershot, Hampshire: Scolar P, 1996.
Greenblatt, Stephen. 'Marlowe, Marx, and Anti-Semitism'. *Learning to Curse: Essays in Early Modern Culture*. New York: Routledge, 1990. 40–58.
——. *Renaissance Self-Fashioning: More to Shakespeare*. Chicago: U of Chicago P, 1980.
Greene, Robert. 'To the Gentlemen Students of Both Uniuersities.' *Menaphon*. London, 1589.
Greville, Fulke. *A Treatise on Monarchy*. London, 1670.
Guy, John. 'The 1590s: The Second Reign of Elizabeth I?' *The Reign of Elizabeth I: Court and Culture in the Last Decade*. Ed. John Guy. Cambridge: Cambridge UP, 1995. 1–19.
Habermas, Jürgen. 'The Public Sphere: An Encyclopedia Article (1964)'. *New German Critique* 3 (1974): 49–55.
Hadfield, Andrew. *Literature, Travel, and Colonial Writing in the English Renaissance 1545–1625*. Oxford: Clarendon, 1998.
——. *Shakespeare and Renaissance Politics*. New York: Thomson Learning, 2003.
——. *Shakespeare and Republicanism*. Cambridge: Cambridge UP, 2005.
——. 'Was Spenser a Republican?' *English* 47 (1998): 169–82.
——. 'Was Spenser Really a Republican After All? A Reply to David Scott Wilson-Okamura'. *Spenser Studies* 17 (2003): 275–90.
Hall, John. *Peri Hypsous, or Dionysius Longinus of the Height of Eloquence*. London, 1652.
Halpern, Richard. 'Marlowe's Theater of Night: *Doctor Faustus* and Capital'. *ELH* 71 (2004): 455–95.
Hamilton, A.C., ed. *Edmund Spenser: 'The Faerie Queene'*. 2nd edn. London: Longman, 2001.
Hamlin, William M. *Tragedy and Scepticism in Shakespeare's England*. Basingstoke: Palgrave, 2005.
Hammill, Graham. ' "The Thing / Which Never Was": Republicanism and *the Ruines of Time*'. *Spenser Studies* 18 (2003): 165–83.
Hardie, Philip. *The Epic Successors of Virgil: A Study in the Dynamics of a Tradition*. Cambridge: Cambridge UP, 1993.
Hardison, O.B., Jr. 'Blank Verse before Milton'. *Studies in Philology* 81 (1984): 253–74.
Harraway, Clare. *Re-Citing Marlowe: Approaches to the Drama*. Aldershot, Hampshire: Ashgate P, 2000.
Hattaway, Michael. 'Christopher Marlowe: Ideology and Subversion'. Grantley and Roberts, eds. *Christopher Marlowe*. 198–223.
——. 'The Shakespearean History Play'. *Cambridge Companion to Shakespeare's History Plays*. Ed. Michael Hattaway. Cambridge: Cambridge UP, 2002. 3–24.

——. 'The Theology of Marlowe's *Doctor Faustus*'. *Renaissance Drama* 3 (1970): 51–78.
Healy, Thomas. *Christopher Marlowe*. Plymouth, England: Northcote House in Association with the British Council, 1994.
——. '*Doctor Faustus*'. Cheney, ed. *Cambridge Companion to Marlowe*. 174–92.
Helgerson, Richard. *Forms of Nationhood: The Elizabethan Writing of England*. Chicago: U of Chicago P, 1992.
——. *Self-Crowned Laureates: Spenser, Jonson, Milton and the Literary System*. Berkeley: U of California P, 1983.
Henderson, Diana E. *Passion Made Public: Elizabethan Lyric, Gender, and Performance*. Urbana: U of Illinois P, 1995.
Herman, Arthur. 'The Huguenot Republic and Antirepublicanism in Seventeenth-Century France'. *Journal of the History of Ideas* 53 (1992): 249–69.
Herrick, Robert. *The Complete Poetry of Robert Herrick*. Ed. J. Max Patrick. New York: Norton, 1968.
Hillman, Richard. *Shakespeare, Marlowe and the Politics of France*. Basingstoke: Palgrave, 2002.
Hinds, Stephen. *Allusion and Intertext: Dynamics of Appropriation in Roman Poetry*. Cambridge: Cambridge UP, 1998.
Holinshed, Raphael. *Holinshed's Chronicles of England, Scotland and Ireland* (1587). Ed. Henry Ellis. 6 vols. London, 1807–8.
Honan, Park. *Christopher Marlowe, Poet and Spy*. Oxford: Oxford UP, 2005.
Hopkins, Lisa. 'Marlowe's Reception and Influence'. Cheney, ed. *Cambridge Companion to Marlowe*. 282–96.
——. 'Was Marlowe Going to Scotland when He Died, and Does it Matter?' Mulryne and Kozuka, eds. *Shakespeare, Marlowe, Jonson*. 167–82.
Hughes, Merritt Y., ed. *John Milton: Complete Poems and Major Prose*. Indianapolis: Bobbs-Merrill, 1957.
Hulse, Clark. *Metamorphic Verse: The Elizabethan Minor Epic*. Princeton: Princeton UP, 1981.
Hunter, G.K. 'The Theology of Marlowe's *The Jew of Malta*'. *Christopher Marlowe's 'The Jew of Malta'*. Ed. Irving Ribner. New York: Odyssey P, 1970. 179–218.
Hurley, C. Harold. *The Sources and Traditions of Milton's 'L'Allegro' and 'Il Penseroso'*. Lewiston: Edwin Mellen, 1999.
Ingram, R.W. '"Pride in Learning Goeth before a Fall": Dr. Faustus' Opening Soliloquy'. *Mosaic* 13 (1979): 73–80.
James I, King of England. 'The Translators Invocation'. *The Poems of King James VI of Scotland*. Ed. James Craigie. 2 vols. Edinburgh: Blackwell, 1955–8.
James, Heather. 'Ovid and the Question of Politics in Early Modern English'. *ELH* 70 (2003): 343–73.
——. 'The Poet's Toys: Christopher Marlowe and the Liberties of Erotic Elegy'. *MLQ* 67 (2006): 103–27.
Jardine, Lisa, and Anthony Grafton. ' "Studied for Action": How Gabriel Harvey Read His Livy'. *Past and Present* 129 (1990): 30–78.
Johnson, Lynn Staley. '*The Shepheardes Calender*': *An Introduction*. University Park, PA: Pennsylvania State UP, 1990.
Johnson, W.R. *Momentary Monsters: Lucan and His Heroes*. Ithaca: Cornell UP, 1987.
Jonson, Ben. *The Alchemist*. Bevington, ed., *English Renaissance Drama*. 861–99.
Joyce, Jane Wilson, trans. *Lucan: 'Pharsalia'*. Ithaca: Cornell UP, 1993.
Jump, John, ed. *Marlowe: 'Doctor Faustus'*. Revels Plays. London: Macmillan, 1969.
Kant, Immanuel. *Critique of the Power of Judgment*. Ed. Paul Guyer. Trans. Paul Guyer and Eric Matthews. Cambridge: Cambridge UP, 2000.

Kant, Immanuel. *Observations on the Feeling of the Beautiful and Sublime*. Trans. John T. Goldthwait. Berkeley: U of California P, 1960.
Keach, William. *Elizabethan Erotic Narratives: Irony and Pathos in the Ovidian Poetry of Shakespeare, Marlowe and Their Contemporaries*. New Brunswick: Rutgers UP, 1977.
Keefer, Michael. 'Verbal Magic and the Problem of the A and B Texts of *Doctor Faustus*'. *Journal of English and Germanic Philology* 82 (1983): 324–46.
——, ed. *Christopher Marlowe's 'Doctor Faustus': A 1604-Version Edition*. Peterborough, Ontario: Broadview P, 1991.
Kernan, Alvin, ed. *The Alchemist*. New Haven: Yale UP, 1974.
——. *Two Renaissance Mythmakers: Christopher Marlowe and Ben Jonson*. Baltimore: Johns Hopkins UP, 1977.
Kirk, Andrew M. 'Marlowe and the Disordered Face of French History'. *Studies in English Literature 1500–1900* 35 (1995): 193–213.
Kocher, Paul H. 'Contemporary Pamphlet Backgrounds for Marlowe's *The Massacre at Paris*'. *Modern Language Quarterly* 8 (1947): 151–73.
——. 'Contemporary Pamphlet Backgrounds for Marlowe's *The Massacre at Paris*. Part Two'. *Modern Language Quarterly* 8 (1947): 309–18.
——. 'François Hotman and Marlowe's *The Massacre at Paris*'. *PMLA* 56 (1941): 349–68.
Kott, Jan. *The Bottom Translation: Marlowe and Shakespeare and the Carnival Tradition*. Trans. Daniela Miedzyrzecka and Lillian Vallee. Evanston: Northwestern UP, 1987.
Kuduk, Stephanie. ' "A Sword of a Song": Swinburne's Republican Aesthetics in *Songs before Sunrise*'. *Victorian Studies* 43 (2001): 253–78.
Kuriyama, Constance Brown. *Christopher Marlowe: A Renaissance Life*. Ithaca: Cornell UP, 2002.
Kyd, Thomas. *The Works of Thomas Kyd*. Ed. Frederick S. Boas. Oxford: Clarendon, 1901.
Lane, John. *Alarum to Poets*. London, 1648.
Lapidge, Michael. 'Lucan's Imagery of Cosmic Dissolution'. *Hermes* 107 (1979): 344–70.
Leech, Clifford. *Christopher Marlowe: Poet for the Stage*. Ed. Anne Lancashire. New York: AMS P, 1986.
Leigh, Matthew. *Lucan, Spectacle and Engagement*. Oxford: Clarendon P, 1997.
Lesser, Zachary. *Renaissance Drama and the Politics of Publication*. Cambridge: Cambridge UP, 2004.
Levin, Harry. 'An Introduction to Ben Jonson'. *Ben Jonson: A Collection of Critical Essays*. Twentieth-Century Views. Ed. Jonash Barish. Atlantic Highlands: Prentice-Hall, 1963. 40–59.
——. *The Overreacher: A Study of Christopher Marlowe*. Cambridge, MA: Harvard UP, 1952.
Levin, Richard. 'The Contemporary Perception of Marlowe's Tamburlaine'. *Medieval and Renaissance Drama in England* 1 (1984): 51–70.
Levy, F.J. 'Hayward, Daniel, and the Beginnings of Politic History in England'. *Huntington Library Quarterly* 50 (1987): 1–34.
Lewis, C.S. *English Literature in the Sixteenth Century Excluding Drama*. 1954; London: Oxford UP, 1973.
Lim, Walter S.H. *John Milton, Radical Politics, and Biblical Republicanism*. Newark: U of Delaware P; Cranbury NJ: Associated UP, 2006.

Livy. *The History of Rome*. Trans. Canon Roberts. Everyman's Library. 6 vols. London: Dent; New York: Dutton, n.d.
——. *The Rise of Rome, Books 1–5*. Trans. T.J. Luce. Oxford World's Classics. Oxford: Oxford UP, 1998.
Lodge, Thomas. *The Defence of Poetry*. Smith, G.G., ed., *Elizabethan Critical Essays*. 1: 61–86.
——. *The Wounds of Civil War*. Ed. J.W. Houppert. London: Arnold, 1970.
Logan, Robert A. *Shakespeare's Marlowe: The Influence of Christopher Marlowe on Shakespeare's Artistry*. Aldershot, Hampshire: Ashgate P, 2007.
Longinus. *On Sublimity*. *Classical Literary Criticism*. Ed. Russell and Winterbottom. 143–87.
Lucan. *Civil War*. Trans. Susan H. Braund. Oxford World's Classics. Oxford: Oxford UP, 1992.
——. *Lucan: 'The Civil War'*. Trans. J.D. Duff. Loeb Classical Library. 2 vols. Cambridge, MA: Harvard UP; London: Heinemann, 1928.
Lucretius. *'De Rerum Natura'*. 3rd edn. Trans. W.H.D. Rouse; rev. Martin Ferguson Smith. Loeb Classical Library. Cambridge, MA: Harvard UP; London: Heinemann, 1975.
Lupton, Julia Reinhard. *Citizen-Saints: Shakespeare and Political Theology*. Chicago: U of Chicago P, 2005.
——. *'The Jew of Malta'*. Cheney, ed. *Cambridge Companion to Marlowe*. 144–57.
Machiavelli, Niccolò. *Discourses on Livy*. Trans. Julia Conway Bondanella and Peter Bondanella. Oxford World's Classics. Oxford: Oxford UP, 1997.
——. *Niccolò Machiavelli: 'The Prince'*. 2nd edn. Trans. Robert M. Adams. New York: Norton, 1992.
Macksey, Richard. 'Longinus'. *The Johns Hopkins Guide to Literary Theory & Criticism*. Ed. Michael Groden, Martin Kreiswirth, and Imre Szeman. Baltimore: Johns Hopkins UP, 2005.
MacLean, Gerald M. 'The Debate over Lucan's *Pharsalia*'. *Time's Witness: Historical Representation in English Poetry, 1603–1660*. Madison: U of Wisconsin P, 1990. 26–44.
MacLure, Millar, ed. *Marlowe: The Critical Heritage 1588–1896*. London: Routledge and Kegan Paul, 1979.
——, ed. *The Poems: Christopher Marlowe*. Revels Plays. London: Methuen, 1968.
Maguire, Laurie E. 'Marlovian Texts and Authorship'. Cheney, ed. *Cambridge Companion to Marlowe*. 41–54.
——. *Shakespearean Suspect Texts: The 'Bad' Quartos and Their Contexts*. Cambridge: Cambridge UP, 1996.
Mahood, M.A. *Poetry and Humanism*. London: Jonathan Cape, 1950.
Marcus, Leah S. *The Politics of Mirth: Jonson, Herrick, Milton, Marvel, and the Defense of Old Holiday Pastimes*. Chicago: U of Chicago P, 1986.
——. 'Textual Indeterminacy and Ideological Difference: The Case of *Dr. Faustus*'. *Renaissance Drama* 20 (1989): 1–29.
——. 'Textual Instability and Ideological Difference: The Case of *Doctor Faustus*'. *Unediting the Renaissance: Shakespeare, Marlowe, Milton*. London: Routledge, 1996. 38–67.
Martin, L.C., ed. *Marlowe's Poems*. New York: Dial P, 1931.
Martin, Richard A. 'Fate, Seneca, and Marlowe's *Dido, Queen of Carthage*'. *Renaissance Drama* ns 11 (1980): 45–66.
Martindale, Charles. 'The Epic of Ideas: Lucan's *De Bello Civili* and *Paradise Lost*'. *Comparative Criticism* 3 (1981): 133–56.

Martindale, Charles. *Latin Poetry and the Judgement of Taste: An Essay in Aesthetics*. Oxford: Oxford UP, 2005.

——. *Redeeming the Text: Latin Poetry and the Hermeneutics of Reception*. Cambridge: Cambridge UP, 1993.

——, ed. *Ovid Renewed: Ovidian Influences on Literature and Art from the Middle Ages to the Twentieth Century*. Cambridge: Cambridge UP, 1988.

Martz, Louis L., ed. *'Hero and Leander' by Christopher Marlowe: A Facsimile of the First Edition, London 1598*. New York: Johnson Reprint, 1972.

Masten, Jeffrey. 'Playwrighting: Authorship and Collaboration'. *A New History of Early English Drama*. Ed. John D. Cox and David Scott Kastan. New York: Columbia UP, 1997. 357–82.

——. *Textual Intercourse: Collaboration, Authorship, and Sexualities in Renaissance Drama*. Cambridge: Cambridge UP, 1997.

Masters, Jamie. *Poetry and Civil War in Lucan's 'Bellum Civile'*. Cambridge: Cambridge UP, 1992.

Maus, Katharine Eisaman. 'Introduction'. *The Alchemist*. Bevington, ed. *English Renaissance Drama*. 861–7.

McAdam, Ian. *The Irony of Identity: Self and Imagination in the Drama of Christopher Marlowe*. Newark: U of Delaware P; London: Associated UP, 1999.

McCabe, Richard A. 'Elizabethan Satire and the Bishops' Ban of 1599'. *Yearbook of English Studies* 11 (1981): 188–93.

McDiarmid, John F. *The Monarchical Republic of Early Modern England: Essays in Response to Patrick Collinson*. Aldershote, Hampshire: Ashgate P, 2007.

McDonald, Russ. 'Marlowe and Style'. Cheney, ed. *Cambridge Companion to Marlowe*. 55–69.

McKerrow, Ronald B., ed. *The Works of Thomas Nashe*. Rev. F.P. Wilson. 5 vols. Oxford: Basil Blackwell, 1958.

McLaren, Anne. 'Rethinking Republicanism: *Vindiciae, Contra, Tyrannos* in Context'. *Historical Journal* 49 (2006): 23–52.

Mebane, John S. *Renaissance Magic and the Return of the Golden Age*. Lincoln: U of Nebraska P, 1989.

Merchant, W. Moelwyn, ed. *Edward the Second*. New Mermaids. London: Black; New York: Norton, 1967.

Meres, Francis. *Palladis Tamia*. Smith, G.G., ed., *Elizabethan Critical Essays*. 2: 308–24.

Miller, David L. 'The Death of the Modern: Gender and Desire in Marlowe's *Hero and Leander*'. *South Atlantic Quarterly* 88 (1989): 757–87.

Minshull, Catherine. 'The Dissident Subtext of Marlowe's "Doctor Faustus"'. *English* 39 (1990): 193–207.

——. 'Marlowe's "Sound Machevill"'. *Renaissance Drama* 13 (1982): 35–53.

Montrose, Louis Adrian. ' "The perfecte paterne of a Poete": The Poetics of Courtship in *The Shepheardes Calender*'. *Texas Studies in Literature and Language* 21 (1979): 34–67.

——. *The Subject of Elizabeth: Authority, Gender, and Representation*. Chicago: U of Chicago P, 2006.

Moore, Hale. 'Gabriel Harvey's References to Marlowe'. *Studies in Philology* 23 (1926): 337–57.

Moulton, Ian Frederick. '"Printed Abroad and Uncastrated": Marlowe's *Elegies* and Davies' *Epigrams*'. *Marlowe, History, and Sexuality: New Critical Essays on Christopher Marlowe*. Ed. Paul Whitfield White. New York: AMS P, 1998. 77–90.

Mullaney, Steven. *The Place of the Stage: License, Play, and Power in Renaissance England*. Chicago: U of Chicago P, 1988.

Mulryne, J.R., and Takashi Kozuka, eds. *Shakespeare, Marlowe, Jonson: New Directions in Biography*. Aldershot, Hampshire: Ashgate P, 2006.
Neuse, Richard. 'Atheism and Some Functions of Myth in Marlowe's *Hero and Leander*'. *Modern Language Quarterly* 31 (1970): 424–39.
Nicholl, Charles. ' "By my onely meanes sett downe": The Texts of Marlowe's Atheism'. Mulryne and Kozuka, eds. *Shakespeare, Marlowe, Jonson*. 153–66.
——. 'Marlowe, Christopher (*bap*. 1564, *d*. 1593)'. *Oxford Dictionary of National Biography*. Oxford UP, 2006. http://www.oxforddnb.com/view/article/18079.
——. *The Reckoning: The Murder of Christopher Marlowe*. New York: Harcourt Brace, 1992.
Nicolson, Marjorie Hope. *Mountain Gloom and Mountain Glory: The Development of the Aesthetics of the Infinite*. 1959; Seattle: U of Washington P, 1997.
Norbrook, David. *Writing the English Republic: Poetry, Rhetoric, and Politics, 1627–1660*. Cambridge: Cambridge UP, 1999.
Oliver, H.J., ed. *'Dido Queen of Carthage' and 'The Massacre at Paris': Christopher Marlowe*. Revels Plays. Cambridge, MA: Harvard UP, 1968.
Orgel, Stephen. 'Tobacco and Boys: How Queer Was Marlowe?' *GLQ: A Journal of Lesbian and Gay Studies* 6 (2000): 555–76.
——, ed. *Christopher Marlowe: The Complete Poems and Translations*. Harmondsworth: Penguin, 1971.
Otis, Brooks. *Ovid as an Epic Poet*. 2nd edn. Cambridge: Cambridge UP, 1970.
Ovid. *Ovid*. 2nd edn. Trans. Frank Justus Miller; rev. G.P. Goold. Loeb Classical Library. 6 vols. Cambridge, MA: Harvard UP; London: Heinemann, 1984.
Oxford Classical Dictionary. Ed. Simon Hornblower and Antony Spawforth. 3rd edn. Oxford: Oxford UP, 2003.
Parker, John. *The Aesthetics of Antichrist: From Christian Drama to Christopher Marlowe*. Ithaca: Cornell UP, 2007.
Parker, Matthew. 'To the Reader'. *The Whole Psalter*. London, 1567.
Patterson, Annabel. *Censorship and Interpretation: The Conditions of Writing and Reading in Early Modern England*. Madison: U of Wisconsin P, 1984.
——. *Reading Holinshed's Chronicles*. Chicago: U of Chicago P, 1994.
Peltonen, Markku. 'Citizenship and Republicanism in Elizabethan England'. Van Gelderen and Skinner, eds. *Republicanism*. 1: 85–106.
——. *Classical Humanism and Republicanism in English Political Thought, 1570–1640*. Cambridge: Cambridge UP, 1995.
Perry, Curtis. *Literature and Favoritism in Early Modern England*. Cambridge: Cambridge UP, 2006.
——. 'The Uneasy Republicanism of Thomas Kyd's *Cornelia*'. *Criticism* 48 (2006): forthcoming.
Plato. *The Collected Dialogues of Plato*. Ed. Edith Hamilton and Huntington Cairns. Princeton: Princeton UP, 1961.
Pocock, J.G.A. *The Machiavellian Moment: Florentine Political Thought and the Atlantic Republican Tradition*. Princeton: Princeton UP, 1975.
Polybius. *The Rise of the Roman Empire*. Trans. Ian Scott-Kilvert. Harmondsworth: Penguin, 1979.
Poole, Kristen. 'The Devil's in the Archive: *Doctor Faustus* and Ovidian Physics'. *Renaissance Drama* 35 (2006): 191–219.
——. '*Dr. Faustus* and Reformation Theology'. Sullivan, Cheney, and Hadfield, eds. *Early Modern English Poetry*. 96–107.
——. 'Garbled Martyrdom in Christopher Marlowe's *The Massacre at Paris*'. *Comparative Drama* 32 (1998): 1–25.

Potter, David. 'Marlowe's Massacre at Paris and the Reputation of Henri III of France'. Grantley and Roberts, eds. *Christopher Marlowe*. 70–95.
Potter, Lois. 'Marlowe in the Civil War and Commonwealth: Some Allusions and Parodies'. Friedenreich, Gill, and Kuriyama, eds. *A Poet and a Filthy Play-Maker*. 73–82.
——. 'Marlowe in Theatre and Film'. Cheney, ed. *Cambridge Companion to Marlowe*. 262–81.
Praz, Mario. 'Machiavelli and the Elizabethans'. *Proceedings of the British Academy* 14 (1928): 49–97.
Proser, Matthew N. *The Gift of Fire: Aggression and the Plays of Christopher Marlowe*. Renaissance and Baroque Studies and Texts 12. New York: Peter Lang, 1995.
Riddell, James A. 'Ben Jonson and "Marlowes Mighty Line"'. Friedenreich, Gill, and Kuriyama, eds. *A Poet and a Filthy Play-Maker*. 37–48.
Riggs, David. 'The Killing of Christopher Marlowe'. *Stanford Humanities Review* 8 (2000): 239–51.
——. 'Marlowe's Life'. Cheney, ed. *Cambridge Companion to Marlowe*. 24–40.
——. 'The Poet in the Play: Life and Art in *Tamburlaine* and *The Jew of Malta*'. Mulryne and Kozuka, eds. *Shakespeare, Marlowe, Jonson*. 205–26.
——. *The World of Christopher Marlowe*. London: Faber, 2004.
Roberts, Gareth. 'Necromantic Books: Christopher Marlowe, *Doctor Faustus* and Agrippa of Nettesheim'. Grantley and Roberts, eds. *Christopher Marlowe*. 148–71.
Roberts, Penny. 'Marlowe's *The Massacre at Paris*: A Historical Perspective'. *Renaissance Studies* 9 (1995): 430–41.
Romany, Frank, and Robert Lindsey, eds. *Christopher Marlowe: The Complete Plays*. London: Penguin, 2003.
Ronan, Clifford J. '*Pharsalia* 1.373–378: Roman Parricide and Marlowe's Editors'. *Classical and Modern Literature* 6 (1986): 305–09.
Rosner-Siegel, Judith A. 'The Oak and the Lightning: Lucan, *Bellum Civile* 1.135–157'. *Athenaeum* 61 (1983): 165–77.
Rowland, Richard, ed. '*Edward II*'. Oxford: Clarendon, 1994. Vol. 3 of Gill, ed., *Works*.
Rudd, Niall. 'Daedalus and Icarus (i) From Rome to the End of the Middle Ages'. Martindale, ed. *Ovid Renewed*. 21–35.
——. 'Daedalus and Icarus (ii) From the Renaissance to the Present Day'. Martindale, ed. *Ovid Renewed*. 37–53.
Russell, D.A., and Michael Winterbottom. *Classical Literary Criticism*. Oxford World's Classics. Oxford: Oxford UP, 1972.
Sales, Roger. *Christopher Marlowe*. New York: St. Martin's P, 1991.
Sallust. *Jurgurthine War and Conspiracy of Catiline*. Trans. S.A. Handford. Harmondsworth: Penguin, 1963.
——. *Sallust*. Trans. J.C. Rolfe. Loeb Classical Library. Cambridge, MA: Harvard UP; London: Heinemann, 1931.
Salmon, J.H.M. 'Stoicism and Roman Example: Seneca and Tacitus in Jacobean England'. *Journal of the History of Ideas* 50 (1989): 199–225.
Sanders, Julie. *Ben Jonson's Theatrical Republics*. New York: St. Martin's P, 1998.
Sanders, Wilbur. *The Dramatist and the Received Idea: Studies in the Plays of Marlowe and Shakespeare*. Cambridge: Cambridge UP, 1968.
Savile, Henry, trans. *The ende of Nero and beginning of Galba Fower bookes of the Histories of Cornelius Tacitus. The life of Agricola*. Oxford, 1591.

Schellhase, Kenneth C. *Tacitus in Renaissance Political Thought*. Chicago: U of Chicago P, 1976.
Scott, Jonathan. 'Classical Republicanism in Seventeenth-Century England and the Netherlands'. Van Gelderen and Skinner, eds. *Republicanism*. 1: 61–84.
——. *Commonwealth Principles: Republican Writing of the English Revolution*. Cambridge: Cambridge UP, 2004.
Scott, Margaret. 'Machiavelli and the Machiavel'. *Renaissance Drama* 15 (1984): 147–74.
Sedinger, Tracey. 'Sidney's *New Arcadia* and the Decay of Protestant Republicanism'. *Studies in English Literature 1500–1900* 47 (2007): 57–77.
Sedley, David L. *Sublimity and Skepticism in Montaigne and Milton*. Ann Arbor: U of Michigan P, 2005.
Segal, Charles. *Orpheus: The Myth of the Poet*. Baltimore: Johns Hopkins UP, 1989.
Shakespeare, William. *The Riverside Shakespeare*. Ed. G. Blakemore Evans. 2nd edn. Boston: Houghton, 1997.
Shannon, Laurie. *Sovereign Amity: Figures of Friendship in Shakespearean Contexts*. Chicago: U of Chicago P, 2002.
Shapiro, James. '"Metre meete to furnish Lucans style": Reconsidering Marlowe's *Lucan*'. Friedenreich, Gill, and Kuriyama, eds. *A Poet and a Filthy Play-Maker*. 315–25.
Sharpe, Kevin, and Peter Lake, eds. *Culture and Politics in Early Stuart England*. Stanford: Stanford UP, 1993.
Shaw, Philip. *The Sublime*. New Critical Idiom. London: Routledge, 2006.
Shawcross, John T. 'Signs of the Times: Christopher Marlowe's Decline in the Seventeenth Century'. Friedenreich, Gill, and Kuriyama, eds. *A Poet and a Filthy Play-Maker*. 63–71.
Shepard, Alan. *Marlowe's Soldiers: Rhetorics of Masculinity in the Age of the Armada*. Aldershot, Hampshire: Ashgate P, 2002.
Shepherd, Simon. 'A Bit of Ruff: Criticism, Fantasy, Marlowe'. Downie and Parnell, eds. *Constructing Christopher Marlowe*. 102–15.
——. *Marlowe and the Politics of Elizabethan Theatre*. New York: St. Martin's P, 1986.
Shuger, Debora. *Censorship and Cultural Sensibility: The Regulation of Language in Tudor-Stuart England*. Philadelphia: U of Pennsylvania P, 2006.
——. *Sacred Rhetoric: The Christian Grand Style in the English Renaissance*. Princeton: Princeton UP, 1988.
Sidney, Sir Philip. *The Poems of Sir Philip Sidney*. Ed. William A. Ringler, Jr. Oxford: Clarendon, 1962.
Sinfield, Alan. *Faultlines: Cultural Materialism and the Politics of Dissident Reading*. Berkeley: U of California P, 1992.
——. 'Marlowe's Erotic Verse'. *Early Modern English Poetry: A Critical Companion*. Ed. Patrick Cheney, Andrew Hadfield, and Garrett A. Sullivan, Jr. New York: Oxford UP, 2007. 125–35.
Skinner, Quentin. 'Classical Liberty and the Coming of the English Civil War'. Van Gelderen and Skinner, eds. *Republicanism*. 2: 9–28.
——. 'Classical Liberty, Renaissance Translation and the English Civil War'. *Visions of Politics, Volume 2: Renaissance Virtues*. Cambridge: Cambridge UP, 2002. 308–43.
——. *The Foundations of Modern Political Thought*. 2 vols. Cambridge: Cambridge UP, 1978.
——. *Liberty before Liberalism*. Cambridge: Cambridge UP, 1998.

Skinner, Quentin. 'The Republican Ideal of Political Liberty'. *Machiavelli and Republicanism*. Ed. Gisela Bock, Quentin Skinner, and Maurizio Viroli. Cambridge: Cambridge UP, 1990. 293–309.
Smith, G. Gregory, ed. *Elizabethan Critical Essays*. 2 vols. London: Oxford UP, 1904.
Smith, Nigel. *Literature and Revolution in England 1640–1660*. New Haven: Yale UP, 1994.
Smith, Sir Thomas. *De Republica Anglorum*. Ed. Mary Dewar. Cambridge: Cambridge UP, 1982.
Smuts, Malcolm. 'Court-Centered Politics and the Uses of Roman Historians, c.1590–1630'. Sharpe and Lake, eds. *Culture and Politics in Early Stuart England*. 21–43.
———. *Culture and Power in England 1585–1685*. New York: St. Martin's P, 1999.
Spenser, Edmund. *The Poetical Works of Edmund Spenser*. Ed. J.C. Smith and Ernest de Sèlincourt. 3 vols. Oxford: Clarendon, 1909–10.
Stapleton, M.L. *Harmful Eloquence: Ovid's 'Amores' from Antiquity to Shakespeare*. Ann Arbor: U of Michigan P, 1996.
Steane, J.B. *Marlowe: A Critical Study*. Cambridge: Cambridge UP, 1964.
Stewart, Alan. 'Edward II and Male Same-Sex Desire'. Sullivan, Cheney, and Hadfield, eds. *Early Modern English Drama*. 82–95.
———. *Philip Sidney: A Double Life*. New York: St. Martin's P, 2000.
Sullivan, Garrett A., Jr., Patrick Cheney, and Andrew Hadfield, eds. *Early Modern English Drama: A Critical Companion*. New York: Oxford UP, 2006.
Tacitus. *The Annals of Imperial Rome*. Trans. Alfred John Church and William Jackson Brodribb. New York: Barnes & Noble, 2007.
———. *The Histories*. Trans. W.H. Fyfe. Ed. D.S. Levene. Oxford World's Classics. Oxford: Oxford UP, 1997.
Teskey, Gordon. *Delirious Milton: The Fate of the Poet in Modernity*. Cambridge, MA: Harvard UP, 2006.
Thomas, Vivien, and William Tydeman, eds. *Christopher Marlowe: The Plays and Their Sources*. London: Routledge, 1994.
Tilmans, Karin. 'Republican Citizenship and Civic Humanism in the Burgundian-Habsburg Netherlands (1477–1566)'. Van Gelderen and Skinner, eds. *Republicanism*. 1: 107–126.
Tromly, Fred B. *Playing with Desire: Tantalization in the Works of Christopher Marlowe*. Toronto: U of Toronto P, 1998.
Tuck, Richard. *Philosophy and Government, 1572–1651*. Cambridge: Cambridge UP, 1993.
Turner, Myron. 'Pastoral and Hermaphrodite: A Study in the Naturalism of Marlowe's *Hero and Leander*'. *Texas Studies in Language and Literature* 17 (1975): 397–414.
Van Gelderen, Martin. 'Aristotelians, Monarchomachs and Republicans: Sovereignty and *respublica mixta* in Dutch and German Political Thought, 1580–1650'. Van Gelderen and Skinner, eds. *Republicanism*. 1: 195–218.
———, and Quentin Skinner. 'Introduction.' Van Gelderen and Skinner, eds. *Republicanism*. 1: 1–6.
———, and Quentin Skinner, eds. *Republicanism: A Shared European Heritage*. 2 vols. Cambridge: Cambridge UP, 2002.
Velema, Wyger R.E. '"That a Republic Is Better Than a Monarchy": Anti-Monarchism in Early Modern Dutch Political Thought'. Van Gelderen and Skinner, eds. *Republicanism*. 1: 9–26.
Vickers, Brian, ed. *English Renaissance Literary Criticism*. Oxford: Oxford UP, 1999.

Vindiciae, Contra Tyrannos or, Concerning the Legitimate Power of a Prince over the People, and of the People over a Prince. Trans. George Garnett. Cambridge: Cambridge UP, 1994.

Virgil. *Virgil*. Trans. H. Rushton Fairclough. Loeb Classical Library. 2 vols. Cambridge, MA: Harvard UP; London: Heinemann, 1935.

Voegelin, Eric. 'Machiavelli's Prince: Background and Formation'. *Review of Politics* 13 (1951): 142–68.

Walker, Greg. *Writing under Tyranny: English Literature and the Henrician Reformation*. Oxford: Oxford UP, 2005.

Wall, Wendy. 'Authorship and the Material Conditions of Writing'. *Cambridge Companion to English Literature 1500–1600*. Ed. Arthur F. Kinney. Cambridge: Cambridge UP, 2000. 64–89.

——. 'Dramatic Authorship and Print'. Sullivan, Cheney, and Hadfield, eds. *Early Modern English Drama*. 1–11.

——. *The Imprint of Gender: Authorship and Publication in the English Renaissance*. Ithaca: Cornell UP, 1993.

Watson, Robert N. *The Rest is Silence: Death as Annihilation in the English Renaissance*. Berkeley: U of California P, 1994.

Weil, Judith. *Christopher Marlowe: Merlin's Prophet*. Cambridge: Cambridge UP, 1977.

Weinberg, Bernard. 'Translations and Commentaries of Longinus, "On the Sublime", to 1600: A Bibliography'. *Modern Philology* 47 (1950): 145–51.

Weiskel, Thomas. *The Romantic Sublime: Studies in the Structure and Psychology of Transcendence*. Baltimore: Johns Hopkins UP, 1976.

Wheeler, Stephen. 'Lucan's Reception of Ovid's *Metamorphoses*'. *Arethusa* 35 (2002): 361–80.

White, Paul Whitfield. 'Marlowe and the Politics of Religion'. Cheney, ed. *Cambridge Companion to Marlowe*. 70–89.

Wiggins, Martin, and Robert Lindsey, eds. *Edward the Second*. London: A & C Black, 1997.

Wilson, Richard. 'Tragedy, Patronage, and Power'. Cheney, ed. *Cambridge Companion to Marlowe*. 207–30.

——. ' "Writ in Blood": Marlowe and the New Historicists'. Downie and Parnell, eds. *Constructing Christopher Marlowe*. 116–32.

Wilson-Okamura, David Scott. 'Republicanism, Nostalgia, and the Crowd'. *Spenser Studies* 17 (2003): 253–73.

Winch, Donald. 'Commercial Realities, Republican Principles.' Van Gelderen and Skinner, eds. *Republicanism*. 2: 293–310.

Wise, Valerie Merriam. 'Flight Myths in Ovid's *Metamorphoses*: An Interpretation of Phaethon and Daedalus'. *Ramus* 6 (1977): 44–59.

Womersley, David. 'Sir Henry Savile's Translation of *Tacitus* and the Political Interpretation of Elizabethan Texts'. *Review of English Studies* 42 (1991): 313–42.

Woodhouse, A.S.P, and Douglas Bush, eds. *A Variorum Commentary: The Poems of John Milton: The Minor English Poems*. 3 vols. New York: Columbia UP, 1975.

Woods, Susanne. 'Freedom and Tyranny in Sidney's *Arcadia*'. *Sir Philip Sidney's Achievements*. Ed. M.J.B. Allen, Dominic Baker-Smith, Arthur F. Kinney, with Margeret M. Sullivan. New York: AMS P, 1990. 165–75.

Worden, Blair. 'Ben Jonson among the Historians'. Sharpe and Lake, eds. *Culture and Politics in Early Stuart England*. 67–89.

Worden, Blair. 'English Republicanism'. *Cambridge History of Political Thought 1450–1700*. Ed. J.H. Burns and Mark Goldie. Cambridge: Cambridge UP, 1991. 443–75.

——. 'Republicanism, Regicide and Republic: The English Experience'. Van Gelderen and Skinner, eds. *Republicanism*. 1: 307–28.

——. *The Sound of Virtue: Philip Sidney's Arcadia and Elizabethan Politics*. New Haven: Yale UP, 1996.

Wright, Johnson Kent. 'The Idea of a Republican Constitution in Old Régime France'. Van Gelderen and Skinner, eds. *Republicanism*. 1: 289–306.

Žižek, Slavoj. *The Sublime Object of Ideology*. London: Verso, 1989.

Zunder, William. *Elizabethan Marlowe: Writing and Culture in the English Renaissance*. Cotingham, Hull: Unity, 1994.

Index

Ahl, Frederick, 43
Altman, Joel, 185
Amphion, 75–6, 176
aristocracy, 32, 100, 121, 161, 162
Aristotle, 26, 27, 32, 96, 153, 161, 176
Armitage, David, 78–81
Ascham, Roger, 39
Augustus Caesar, 51, 54, 55–6, 58, 152
'author', use of, 90–1
authorship, 1–3, 6, 9, 14–15, 18, 21, 50–77, 80, 82, 91–5, 111, 118–19, 137, 169, 172, 174, 176, 188
  genealogy of, 192, *see also* republicanism, and authorship

Bacon, Francis, 152, 166, 167
Baines, Richard, 31
Bancroft, Richard, 24
Bartels, Emily, 81–2
Barthes, Roland, 1
Bartholomew Day's Massacre, St, 29, 140, 142, 144
Bawcutt, N.W., 126–7, 128–31, 135
Beacon, Richard, 3, 33, 78, 80, 96, 122
Beard, Thomas, 31
Benston, Kimberly, 20
Beza, Theodore, 144
Blissett, William, 9, 105, 145–7, 157
Bloom, Harold, 20, 124, 131
Boadicea, 154
Bodin, Jean, 27, 129
Bolinbroke, Henry, 78
Boralevi, Lea Campos, 135
Breefe Discourse, Delcaring…Laudable Customs of London, 125
Briggs, Julia, 140
Brutus, Lucius Junius, 33, 35, 156
Brutus, Stephanus Junius, the Celt, 33
Buchanan, George, 30, 166
Burke, Edmund, 12, 13, 47, 106, 186, 189
Burke, Peter, 149–50
Burnett, Mark Thornton, 91, 94

Caesar, Julius, 9, 10, 34–5, 44–5, 47–8, 69, 70–1, 72–3, 79–80, 83, 85, 86, 94, 95, 104–5, 115, 126–7, 128, 129, 130, 131, 136, 145–7, 157, 158, 170, 174–5, 188
Camillus, 103, 143
Campbell, Thomas, 17–18
Cartelli, Thomas, 163
Catholicism, 21, 28–9, 122, 140–5, 170
Catiline, 153–4
Chapman, George, 31, 34, 38, 69, 77
Cicero, 10, 12, 25, 39, 46, 62–3, 75, 95, 142, 149, 152, 153, 166, 167, 169, 188
  De officiis (*On Obligations*), 26, 35, 124
  Republic, The, 32
citizen, 10, 21, 28, 57–8, 63, 73, 102–3, 114, 125–6, 154, 164
civil war, 9, 121–64
  Roman, 146, 154
Clifton Shakespere Society, 18
Coiro, Ann Baynes, 64
Coleridge, Samuel Taylor, 185, 186
Collinson, Patrick, 3, 22, 32–3, 105, 122, 170
colonization, 81
comedy, republican, 136–8
commerce, 123–7, 131, 136–8, 179
  and policy, 132–3
  and republicanism, 134
commonwealth, 4, 10, 30, 32, 34, 36, 37, 65, 75, 101, 124–5, 131, 143, 189, *see also* Jewish Commonwealth
consent, 36, 62, 88, 96, 99–100, 143, 154, 160
consuls, 41, 79, 98–100, 114, 170
Cornelia, *see* Kyd
Corpus Christi College, Oxford, 25
'country's good', use of, 141
Cranmer, Thomas, 24
Cuffe, Henry, 151
Cunningham, J.S., 104
Cutts, John P., 175

243

Davies, Sir John, 59
Day, Angel, 38–9
Day, Henry, 17, 41, 47–8
Deats, Sara Munson, 86
democracy, 14, 16–17, 32, 54, 100, 121, 129, 137, 161, 180
De Republica Anglorum, *see* Smith, Sir Thomas
Devereaux, Robert, *see* Essex, earl of
Dido, Queen of Carthage, 2, 20, 78, 80, 81, 82–96, 115, 118, 163, 175, 179
Doctor Faustus, 2, 20, 36, 135, 158, 164, 165, 168–87, 189
Dollimore, Jonathan, 11
Dowden, Edward, 18
Draco, 129
Drayton, Michael, 76–7

Edward II, 36, 37, 121, 122, 139, 146, 148–64, 175, 179, 187, 189
election, 33, 36, 37, 79, 143, 161
Eliot, T.S., 61, 122
Elizabeth I, 50, 58, 140, 151
Elyot, Thomas, 39
empire, 7, 10, 17, 22, 25, 58, 80, 187
  language of, 112
  and liberty, 21, 78–120, 121, 124
Empire, Roman, 9, 17, 35, 51, 57, 63, 71, 146, 150–1, 154
'empire', use of, 81, 112
Empiricus, Sextus, 165, 176
English Faust Book, *see Faust Book*
Erasmus, Desiderius, 25
Erne, Lukas, 34–5
Essex, earl of, 151, 152, 170
eternity, 60, 164, 182, 184, 189, *see also* fame; immortality

fame, 10, 12, 15, 53, 69, 108, 111, 133, 174, 189, *see also* eternity; immortality
Faust Book, English, 168, 172
Forker, Charles R., 149, 153
Forsyth, Neil, 191
Foucault, Michel, 1
'free', use of, 97, 140–1, 160, 173
free state, 22, 62–3, 66, 75, 124–5, 137
freedom, 10–12, 16–19, 20, 22, 29, 35–7, 46, 49, 50–77, 78–120, 123–7, 131, 138, 148, 154, 160, 166, 173, 187, 191–2, *see also* liberty
'freedom', use of, 123
'friends', use of, 98
friendship, 98–102, 107, 112–13, 119, 128, 143, 156, 163, 179
Fuller, David, 104, 115–16, 118

Garnier, Robert, 34–5, 73, 159
Gentillet, Innocent, 138
Gill, Roma, 53, 84, 127, 135
Godshalk, W.L., 157
Goldberg, Jonathan, 163
Gorges, Arthur, 5, 8, 42–3
Gosson, Stephen, 51
government, three kinds of, 121–2
Greenblatt, Stephen, 2, 11, 81
Greene, Robert, 2, 39–40, 124
Greneway, Richard, 26
Greville, Fulke, 40–1
Grimalde, Nicholas, 26
Grotius, Hugo, 169–70
Guy, John, 32

Hadfield, Andrew, 3–4, 6, 8, 28, 30, 33, 34, 36, 37, 118–19, 140
Hall, John, 17, 38, 49
Hamlin, William, 165, 167, 168
Hannibal, 95–6, 175–6
Hardie, Philip, 95–6, 176
Hardison, O.B., Jr., 7
Harrington, James, 8, 63, 78
Hattaway, Michael, 151, 152
Hazlitt, William, 18
Helgerson, Richard, 1
hereditary succession, 25, 33, 36, 109, 113, 119, 120, 129, 140, 141, 143, 161
Hero and Leander, 7, 9, 31, 38, 50, 68–75, 77, 158
Herrick, Robert, 64, 65, 68
Heywood, Thomas, 26
Hobbes, Thomas, 17, 20
Holinshed, Raphael, 32, 149, 152, 154
Holland, Philemon, 26
Homer, 56, 71, 107, 118, 183
  Iliad, 13, 38, 41, 56
  Odyssey, 38
Honan, Park, 25, 27, 152

Hotman, François, 26, 29, 30, 144–6, 150, 188
House of Commons, 32
Hughes, Merritt Y., 67
Huguenots, 21, 29, 122, 140–8

immortality, 15, 56–7, 82, 88, 99, 133, 168–9, 176–8, 180, *see also* eternity; fame
imperialism, 82, 86
Italicus, Silius, 95

James, Heather, 51
James I (and VI), 29, 40
Jewish Commonwealth, 134–6, *see also* commonwealth; *Respublica Hebraeorum*
Jew of Malta, The, 9, 21, 36, 37, 83, 121, 122–39, 160, 179
Job, 127
Johnson, W.R., 10
Jonson, Ben, 1, 3, 5, 22, 34, 39, 55, 66, 68, 132, 149, 151, 188, 190
  Alchemist, The, 61–4, 132
  Poetaster, 2

Kant, Immanuel, 12, 13, 106–7, 184–5, 189
Keefer, Michael, 170, 175–6
King's School, Canterbury, 24
Kocher, Paul, 114, 144, 145
Kyd, Thomas, 9, 29, 30–1, 73, 153, 159, 190
  Cornelia, 34–6

Lake, Peter, 139
Le Roy, Louis, 26
Lesser, Zachery, 138–9
Levin, Harry, 20, 44–5, 63
Lewis, C.S., 7
'liberal', use of, 123, 160
liberty, 9–12, 36, 58, 65, 68, 75, 78, 79, 80, 97, 100, 101, 140–1, 142, 152, 166, 169, 173, *see also* freedom
  classical, 192
  of conscience, 191
  and empire, *see* empire, and liberty
  of language, 112
  'liberty', use of, 81, 112, 123, 160
  and the sublime, 188

Livy, 26, 31, 62, 95, 98, 99, 102, 103, 114, 152, 169, 175, 188
Lodge, Thomas, 51, 159, 160
Longinus, Dionysius, 12–18, 20, 38–9, 42, 47, 49, 52, 56, 61, 74, 77, 87, 106–8, 147, 164, 181, 184, 189
Lucan, 2–3, 17, 21, 69–75, 80, 82–6, 104–5, 114, 116–17, 119, 125–9, 131, 133, 136, 139, 143–4, 145–6, 147, 155, 157–9, 169, 181, 183, 188, 189
  and landscape, 69–70
  and Ovid, 51, 71, 74
  reception, 42–3
  and tragedy, 35
Lucan's First Book, 19, 24–49, 69, 82, 84, 104, 114–15, 118, 123, 124, 125–9, 135, 140, 170, 189
Lucretius, 76, 172
Lyly, William, 25

Machiavelli, Niccolò, 27–8, 32, 62–3, 78, 79, 95, 102–3, 105, 111–12, 121, 136, 138, 142–3, 144, 166
  Art of War, 130
  Discourses on Livy, 27, 32, 33, 79, 102–3, 121–2, 124–31, 133
  Prince, The, 27, 32, 122, 127, 130, 134, 138, 150, 151
  and Tacitus, *see* Tacitus, and Machiavelli
Maclean, Gerald M., 42–3
Manwood, Sir Roger, 50
Marcus, Leah, 65, 170
Marlowe, Christopher, for individual works, *see under specific titles*
  assassination, 31
  atheism, 31
  biography, 24–32
  classical education, 25–7
  and counterfeiting, 30–1
  epic phase of, 69
  and France, 29
  and the Netherlands, 29
  Ovidian poetics, 50–77
  and Scotland, 29–30
  and Shakespeare, 149
  and tragedy, 86
Martin, L.C., 85
Martindale, Charles, 7, 17
Mary, Queen of Scots, 30

Massacre at Paris, 29, 36, 121, 122, 129, 139–48, 160
Masters, Jamie, 104–5
May, Thomas, 5, 8, 42–3
McDonald, Russ, 39
Meres, Francis, 3, 41
Merton College, Oxford, 151
Milton, John, 1, 27, 30, 63, 73, 168, 190–2
  Areopagitica, 31
  Il Penseroso, 66–8
  L'Allegro, 66–8
  Paradise Lost, 190–2
mixed government, 32, 37, 100, 134, 136
monarchical republic, 32–42, 100, 112, 122, 142, 160, 170, 179, see also monarchy; republic
monarchy, 8, 11, 21, 22, 27, 28, 31, 32, 33, 36, 50, 75, 97, 98, 99, 100, 121, 122, 123, 128, 129, 131, 134, 140, 141, 142, 145, 148, 150, 161, 162, 178, 180
Montaigne, Michel de, 42, 167, 168
Mornay, Philippe du Plessis, 33, 101, 142, 156
Musaeus, 75

Nashe, Thomas, vi, 31, 189–90
nationhood, 1, 6, 28, 57–8, 64, 79, 96, 133–5, 154, 170, 179, 184, 192
Neoplatonism, 108, 110, 184–5, see also Plato
the Netherlands, 29–30, 131, 135, 149, 170
Nicholl, Charles, 28
Nietzsche, Friedrich Wilhelm, 41–2
nobility, 28
Norbrook, David, 3–8, 17, 33, 174, 184, 188

Orgel, Stephen, 45, 66
Orpheus, 75–6, 93
Ovid, 2–3, 25, 50–75, 117, 120, 187, 189
  and authorship, 53
  Amores, 2, 9, 22, 50, 53, 58, 103, see also Ovid's Elegies
  Ars amatoria, 57
  counter-Augustine politics, 54–7
  counter-Virgilian career, 57
  and democracy of desire, 53–4
  Heroides, 50, 53, 70, 82
  Medea, 2–3, 57
  Metamorphoses, 2, 57, 170
  Ovid's Elegies, 36, 50, 53–9, 123, 187, see also Ovid, Amores

Parker, Matthew, 25, 41
Parliament, English, 100
'parliament', use of, 160
Parnassus plays (Cambridge University), 41
'passion', use of, 63
'Passionate Shepherd to His Love, The', 2, 7, 50, 59–68, 82, 87, 91, 93, 96, 107–8, 117, 118, 119, 136–7, 146, 147, 158, 163, 179, 188
patriotism, 8, 22, 28, 35, 97
'patriot king', 78–80
Patterson, Annabel, 154–5
Paulin, J., 65–6
Peltonen, Markku, 3–4, 22, 33, 37, 80, 125
Petowe, Henry, 9
Phalaris, 130
Philip II of Spain, 29, 180
Plato, 12, 15, 31, 56, 75, 153, 166, 180, 182, 183, see also Neoplatonism
'plays of policy', 121, 122, see also policy
Pocock, J.A., 5
poet-playwright, 2, 18, 21, 41, 51, 63
policy, 121, 122–4, 133, 136, 138, 166, see also 'plays of policy'
'policy', use of, 37
'politics of mirth', 68
Polybius, 26, 31, 32, 95, 152, 161, 176, 188
popular sovereignty, 96–7
primeval poet, 75–7
Prince of Parma, 29, 135, 179–80
Priscus, Helvidius, 98
Privy Council, 28
Puttenham, George, 76

Ralegh, Sir Walter, 43, 59, 93, 149
rapture, 50–77
representation, 3, 8, 22, 24–49
  political, 6, 43
republic, 142, 162
  erotic, 73
  and monarchy, 145
  Protestant, 28

republicanism, 4–5, 102, 112–13, 120, 132, 145, 148, 168, 169, 179
  and authorship, 81, 123, 148, 158, 182, 187
  characteristics of, 36
  classical, 26
  and fictions, pre-Marlovian, 34
  and freedom, 22
  Huguenot, 33–4
  kingship, 100–1
  language, 96
  marriage, 72
  and the sublime, 62, 80
  tyrant, 105
  values, 138
  and women, 73
Respublica Hebraeorum, 122–39, see also Jewish Commonwealth
rhetoric, 38, 73–4, 92
  sacred, 41
  three styles of, 38
Riggs, David, 25, 26–7, 31
rights, 36
'rights', use of, 141
Roman Empire, see Empire, Roman
Rowland, Richard, 152

Sallust, 26, 62, 78–80, 102, 121, 152, 153–4, 169
Samnites, 127
Sanders, Wilbur, 139–40
Sappho, 16, 52–3
Savile, Henry, 26, 150–2, 154, 167
Scott, Jonathan, 30
Sedley, David, 42, 167–8
'senate', use of, 123–4, 141–2
Shakespeare, William, 3, 4, 5, 7, 22, 28, 34, 66, 68, 149, 188
Shaw, Philip, 12–14, 185
Shuger, Debora, 31–2, 39, 40, 148–9, 155
Sidney, Algernon, 8, 78
Sidney, Sir Philip, 3, 5, 22, 30, 33–4, 76, 142, 188
Sidney, Sir Robert, 29, 135
skeptical sublime, 165–87
skepticism, 165–7
Skinner, Quentin, 3, 9–10, 21, 22, 26, 27, 28, 29, 46, 62–3, 80, 95, 96, 97, 124, 134, 144

Smith, Sir Thomas, 32–3, 100, 161
Spenser, Edmund, 1, 3–4, 22, 27, 44, 50, 58, 82, 96, 158–9, 166, 172, 183, 188, 192
'state of war', 46
Steane, J.B., 7
sublime, the, 12–21, 37–8, 39–42, 49, 56, 86–94, 97, 105–6, 111, 118, 128, 132, 137, 147–8, 152, 163–4, 169, 174, 183, 184, 186, 189–92, see also skeptical sublime
  author-based aesthetic, 189
  authorship, 92
  classical, 189
  of divine ambition, 105, 109–10, 119
  of divine beauty, 105, 107, 110–11, 119
  empiricist, 13
  erotic, 93
  Faustian, 93
  freedom, 86
  and gender, 16
  history of, 13–14
  and infinity, 132, 136
  intertextual, 15, 189
  Kantian, 107, 184–5
  and language, 13, 77, 86, 88, 106
  Lucanian, 61, 117, 118
  and madness, 31–2
  and masculinity, 119
  naturalist, 13
  poetics of, 110
  postmodern, 13
  rationalist, 13
  and republicanism, 96, 186, 190–1
  Sapphic, 52–3
  scene of, 86, 87
  and sodomy, 163–4
  subject-based aesthetic, 189
  and tragedy, 41–2
Swinburne, Algernon Charles, 18–19, 39, 77, 188

Tacitism, 122, 148–64, 166–7
  red and black, 150
Tacitus, 26, 37, 95, 98, 102, 130, 135, 152, 153–4, 167, 169, 170, 188
  and Machiavelli, 150, 151
Tamburlaine, Part One, 36–7, 44, 60–1, 78, 80, 96–112, 160
Tamburlaine, Part Two, 78, 80, 112–20

Tamburlaine plays, 2, 11, 18–19, 20, 28, 36, 139, 152, 160, 163, 164, 175, 179
Terentianus, 16–17
Thomas, Vivien, 144, 172
Toffanin, Giuseppe, 150
Tuck, Richard, 166–7, 168, 169
tyranny, 10–11, 20, 35, 37, 40–1, 51, 73, 88, 96, 101, 126–7, 131, 136, 141, 143, 150–1, 154, 158, 187, 191–2
'tyrant', use of, 101–2, 112–13

Uz, men of, 127

van Gelderen, Martin, 134
Vavasour, Nicholas, 139

Vindiciae, Contra Tyrannos, or, concerning the legitimate power of a prince over the people, and of the people over a prince, 33, 34, 101, 142–4, 151, 152, 156, 160, 161, 163
Virgil, 25, 44, 53, 74, 158
virginity, 74–5, 102
virtù, 10, 28, 63, 95, 112
virtue, 28, 63, 95, 111, 123

Wall, Wendy, 1, 2
Walsingham, Sir Francis, 27, 152
Walsingham, Thomas, 152
Warton, Christopher, 26
Weinberg, Bernard, 38
Williams, Raymond, 41
Worden, Blair, 8, 34